Journal of the Early Book Society
for the study of manuscripts and printing history

Edited by Martha W. Driver
Volume 14, 2011

Copyright © 2011
Pace University Press
41 Park Row, Rm. 1510
New York, NY 10038

All rights reserved
Printed in the United States of America

ISBN: 978-1-935625-06-3
ISSN: 1525-6790

Member

Council of Editors of Learned Journals

✸ ™ The paper used in this publication meets the minimum requirements of American National Standard for information Sciences—Permanence of Paper for printed Library Materials,
ANSI Z39.48—1984.

The *Journal of the Early Book Society* is published annually. *JEBS* invites longer articles on manuscripts and/or printed books produced between 1350 and 1550. Special consideration will be given to essays exploring the period of transition from manuscript to print. Articles should not exceed 8000 words or thirty typed pages. Authors are asked to follow *The Chicago Manual of Style*. A Works Cited list at the end of the text should include city, publisher, and date. Manuscripts are to be sent, in triplicate, along with an abstract of up to 150 words, to Martha Driver, Early Book Society, Department of English, Pace University, 41 Park Row, New York, New York 10038. Only materials accompanied by a self-addressed, stamped envelope (or international reply coupon) will be returned. Members of the Early Book Society who are recent authors may send review books for consideration to Susan Powell, Reviews Editor, School of English, Sociology, Politics and Contemporary History (ESPaCH), University of Salford, Salford M5 4WT UK. Brief notes on recent discoveries, highlighting little-known or recently uncovered texts and/or images, may be sent to Linne R. Mooney, Centre for Medieval Studies, King's Manor, University of York, York YO1 2EP UK. Subscription information may be obtained from Martha Driver or from Pace University Press.

Those interested in joining the Early Book Society or with editorial inquiries may contact Martha Driver by post or e-mail (MDriver@Pace.edu). Information may also be found at <www.nyu.edu/projects/EBS>. For ordering information, call Pace University Press at 212-346-1405 or visit http://www.pace.edu/press. Institutions and libraries may purchase copies directly from Ingram Library Services (1-800-937-5300).

The editor wishes to thank Gill Kent, Russell Spangler, Noah Efroym, and Mark Hussey, Chair, Editorial Committee, Pace University Press, for their help and advice on this issue.

Journal of the Early Book Society
for the study of manuscripts and printing history

Editor:
Martha W. Driver, *Pace University*

Associate Editors:
Linne R. Mooney, *University of York*
Susan Powell, *University of Salford*

Editorial Board:
Matthew Balensuela, *DePauw University*
Julia Boffey, *Queen Mary, University of London*
Cynthia J. Brown, *University of California, Santa Barbara*
Richard F. M. Byrn, *University of Leeds*
James Carley, *York University*
Joyce Coleman, *University of Oklahoma*
Margaret Connolly, *University of St Andrews*
Susanna Fein, *Kent State University*
Alexandra Gillespie, *University of Toronto*
Vincent Gillespie, *Lady Margaret Hall, Oxford University*
Stanley S. Hussey, *Lancaster University*
Ann M. Hutchison, *Pontifical Institute of Mediaeval Studies and York University*
Michael Kuczynski, *Tulane University*
William Marx, *University of Wales, Lampeter*
Carol M. Meale, *Bristol University*
Charlotte C. Morse, *Virginia Commonwealth University*
Daniel W. Mosser, *Virginia Polytechnic Institute and State University*
Ann Eljenholm Nichols, *Winona State University*
Judy Oliver, *Colgate University*
Michael Orr, *Lawrence University*
Steven Partridge, *University of British Columbia*
Derek Pearsall, *Harvard University*
Pamela Sheingorn, *Baruch College and The City University of New York Graduate School and University Center*
Alison Smith, *Wagner College*
Toshiyuki Takamiya, *Keio University*
Andrew Taylor, *University of Ottawa*
John Thompson, *Queen's University, Belfast*
Ronald Waldron, *King's College, University of London*
Edward Wheatley, *Loyola University*
Mary Beth Winn, *SUNY Albany*

Contents

Articles

Compilation and Contemplation: Beholding Thomas Hoccleve's *Series* in Oxford, Bodleian Library, MS Selden supra 53   1
    DAVID WATT

Julian of Norwich in the Fifteenth Century: The Material Record, Maternal Devotion, and London, Westminster Cathedral Treasury MS 4   41
    VICKIE LARSEN

Caxton's Exemplar for *The Chronicles of England*?   75
    DANIEL WAKELIN

Printing for Purgatory: Indulgences and Related Documents in England, 1476 to 1536   115
    R. N. SWANSON

Writing Fame: Epitaph Transcriptions in Renaissance Chaucer Editions and the Construction of Chaucer's Poetic Reputation   145
    ARNOLD SANDERS

Nota Bene: Brief Notes on Manuscripts and Early Printed Books Highlighting Little-Known or Recently Uncovered Items or Related Issues

Pre-Fifteenth-Century Scribes Copying Middle English in More than One Manuscript   179
    RALPH HANNA

Documents and Books: A Case Study of Luket Nantron and Geoffrey Spirleng as Fifteenth-Century Administrators and Textwriters   195
    DEBORAH THORPE

The Middle English Cooking Recipes in New York Public Library 217
Whitney MS 1
   PAUL ACKER

A Record Identifying Thomas Hoccleve's Father 233
   ESTELLE STUBBS and LINNE MOONEY

Lord Rivers and Oxford, Bodleian Library, MS Bodley 264: 239
A *Speculum* for the Prince of Wales?
   OMAR KHALAF

Manuscripts of "A Prince out of the North" 251
   NICOLE CLIFTON

Descriptive Reviews

Alexandra Barratt 261
Anne Bulkeley and her Book: Fashioning Female Piety in Early Tudor England. A study of London, British Library, MS Harley 494
   J. T. RHODES

James P. Carley, ed. 264
John Leland: De uiris illustribus: On Famous Men
   SUSAN POWELL

Margaret Connolly 268
The Index of Middle English Prose. Handlist XIX: Manuscripts in the University Library, Cambridge (Dd-Oo)
   SUSAN POWELL

Joseph A. Dane 270
Abstractions of Evidence in the Study of Manuscripts and Early Printed Books
   CARL JAMES GRINDLEY

Orietta Da Rold and Elaine Treharne, eds. 272
Textual Cultures: Cultural Texts
   MARGARET CONNOLLY

A. C. De La Mare and Laura Nuvoloni 275
Bartolomeo Sanvito: The Life and Work of a Renaissance Scribe
   PAMELA ROBINSON

A. S. G. Edwards, ed. 280
Tudor Manuscripts, 1485-1603
   OLIVER PICKERING

John Block Friedman 283
Brueghel's Heavy Dancers: Transgressive Clothing, Class, and Culture in the Late Middle Ages
   MARTHA DANA RUST

Ralph Hanna 286
The English Manuscripts of Richard Rolle: A Descriptive Catalogue
   MARGARET CONNOLLY

E. A. Jones and Alexandra Walsham, eds. 289
Syon Abbey and its Books: Reading, Writing and Religion c. 1400–1700

Claes Gejrot, Sara Risberg, and Mia Åkestam, eds.
Saint Birgitta, Syon and Vadstena. Papers from a Symposium in Stockholm 4–6 October 2007
   VERONICA O'MARA

John N. King, ed. 293
Tudor Books and Readers: Materiality and the Construction of Meaning
   DANIEL WAKELIN

Anne Lawrence-Mathers and Philippa Hardman, eds. 296
Women and Writing, c.1340-c.1650. The Domestication of Print Culture
   BRENDA M. HOSINGTON

Susan Powell, ed. 300
John Mirk's *Festival edited from British Library MS Cotton Claudius A.II*
   JOSEPH J. GWARA

Raluca L. Radulescu and Cory James Rushton, eds. 304
A Companion to Medieval Popular Romance
   MICHAEL JOHNSTON

Nigel Ramsay and James M. W. Willoughby, eds. 308
Hospitals, Towns, and the Professions
   PAMELA ROBINSON

Kari Anne Rand 311
The Index of Middle English Prose. Handlist XX: Manuscripts in the Library of Corpus Christi College, Cambridge
   VERONICA O'MARA

Jayne Ringrose 314
Summary Catalogue of the Additional Medieval Manuscripts in Cambridge University Library acquired before 1940
   SUE POWELL

Nila Vázquez 317
The Tale of Gamelyn *of the* Canterbury Tales: *An Annotated Edition*
   ESTELLE STUBBS

Christiania Whitehead, Denis Renevey, and Anne Mouron, eds. 320
The Doctrine of the Hert: A Critical Edition with Introduction and Commentary

Denis Renevey and Christiania Whitehead, eds.
A Companion to the Doctrine of the Hert: The Middle English Translation and its Latin and European Contexts
  MARGARET CONNOLLY

About the Authors   325

Compilation and Contemplation: Beholding Thomas Hoccleve's *Series* in Oxford, Bodleian Library, MS Selden Supra 53

DAVID WATT

Thomas Hoccleve's *Series* is a sophisticated compilation of texts linked by its narrator's account of making the book that preserves them.[1] The narrator's account of literally making his book is so important to the structure of the *Series* that John Burrow has suggested it might better be known as the "Book of Thomas Hoccleve."[2] Given the narrator's claim that his book is meant "forth to goo / Among þe peple," it seems reasonable to ask what others might have made of it.[3] In an attempt to answer this question, the article that follows engages in a close reading of what Jerome McGann would call the "linguistic code" of the *Series*.[4] This close reading focuses on the form and content of two stanzas in "Learn to Die"—the first part of the *Series* that the narrator claims to have set out to make—and their relationship to the book as a whole.[5]

It may seem as though this article will take a formalist approach. It will. However, my definition of the book as a whole expands the unit of analysis to include what McGann would describe as its "bibliographic code."[6] My close reading of the *Series* attempts to consider text and language alongside what Stephen Nichols calls "the important supplements that were part and parcel of medieval text production: visual images and annotation of various forms (rubrics, 'captions,' glosses, and interpolations)."[7] As Roger Chartier writes, and as Hoccleve knew from experience, "readers . . . never confront abstract, idealized texts detached from any materiality. They hold in their hands or perceive objects and forms whose structures and modalities govern their reading or hearing, and consequently the possible comprehension of the text read or heard."[8] The premise for the argument that follows is that the best way to understand what people might have made of Thomas Hoccleve's book is to examine how it was literally made.

The way that Oxford, Bodleian Library, MS Selden Supra 53 was made provides evidence that its makers and readers perceived Hoccleve's *Series* as a textual mirror—a compilation designed to encourage contemplation. As Sister Ritamary Bradley and subsequent critics have argued, medieval writers used the term *speculum* (mirror) to describe many different kinds of books, from scripture to story collections, from confessional manuals to advice for princes.[9] What connects the generically diverse texts known as mirrors is the kind of self-reflexive contemplation they either encourage or allow. For example, Hugh of St. Victor justifies calling one of his books a mirror because it is designed to help readers behold themselves critically: "and it is rightly called a mirror; for we can see in it as a mirror in what state we are, whether beautiful or deformed, just or unjust."[10] The narrator in the *Series* attempts to undertake this kind of self-reflection as he stands in front of a literal mirror in the "Complaint." When he fails to identify any immediately obvious faults, he concludes that "Men in her owne cas bene blinde alday."[11] As the *Series* progresses, he turns his attention from his literal mirror to various textual mirrors: moral treatises, exemplary stories, and "Learn to Die," his translation of the first part of Heinrich Suso's *Horologium Sapientiae*.

This article focuses on two stanzas in "Learn to Die" because their appearance in MS Selden Supra 53—the most authoritative scribal copy of the *Series*—invites readers to see the book as a textual mirror and to engage in the kind of self-reflexive contemplation modeled in the compilation as a whole. The first two sections explore the form and content of these stanzas in two manuscripts made by Hoccleve himself between 1422 and 1426.[12] The third and fourth sections examine the appearance of these stanzas in MS Selden Supra 53. The fifth section considers the possible reception of the *Series* in the Selden manuscript in light of other textual mirrors written by its main scribe. The final section asserts that additions to the Selden manuscript made by other hands reveal that its early readers made this book out to be a compilation designed for contemplation and that they, in turn, contributed to its making.

"Learn to Die" in San Marino, Huntington Library MS HM 744

Although most readers today know "Learn to Die" as part of the *Series*, the text also appears as a discrete (albeit incomplete) item in San Marino, Huntington Library, MS HM 744, an autograph collection of poems later bound with other didactic texts. "Learn to Die" is a dialogue in which Sapientia (wisdom) instructs a young disciple to prepare himself for death. In the first of the two stanzas under consideration in this article, Sapientia instructs the disciple to prepare for death through inward contemplation:

> Beholde inward the liknesse and figure
> Of a man dyynge / and talkynge with thee
> ¶ The disciple of þat speeche took good cure
> And in his conceit bisyly soghte he
> And ther withal / considere he gan and see
> In him self put the figure and liknesse
> Of a yong man of excellent fairnesse[13]

The linguistic and bibliographic codes governing the possible comprehension of this stanza in MS HM 744 encourage the reader to draw a clear distinction between death and life, wisdom and folly. The transposition of the words "liknesse and figure" in the first line and "figure and liknesse" in the penultimate line suggests that the stanza has a chiastic structure—that the final line will offer a mirroring effect or reversal of some kind. This initially seems to be the case: while Sapientia instructs the disciple to behold the image "Of a man dying and talkynge with thee" in the first two lines, the disciple instead begins his meditation by imagining the figure "Of a yong man of excellent fairnesse." The rhyme royal stanza form contributes to this apparently chiastic structure by encouraging readers to comprehend these seven lines as a unit of meaning. The manuscript's layout reinforces this reading. Hoccleve divides the stanzas by means of spacing and a decorative device. The literary form of the stanza and its layout on the page seem to preclude the need for any further punctuation, and Hoccleve rarely provides any at the end of a line or stanza.[14] Read as a self-contained unit, the stanza encourages readers to juxtapose the young man of excellent fairness that the disciple seems to start contemplating with the image of the dying man whom Sapientia has instructed him to imagine. The stanza invites readers to juxtapose the wisdom of contemplating death with the folly of ignoring it.

The next stanza obliges the reader to modify this interpretation radically. It begins with a relative clause in the objective case, compelling the reader to look either back or forward for the main clause:

> Whom deeth so ny / ransakid hadde and soght
> That he withynne a whyle sholde die
> And for his soules helthe / had he right noght
> Disposid / al vnreedy / hens to hie
> Was he / and therfore he bygan to crie
> With lamentable vois / in this maneere
> That sorwe and pitee greet / was it to heere[15]

Grammatically, this stanza cannot be read in isolation. Its reader must recognize that the relative clause with which it begins modifies the "figure and liknesse / Of a yong man" that the disciple sees at the end of the first. Thus the reader must modify his or her comprehension of the previous stanza as a whole.

The enjambment between these two stanzas has a sobering effect.[16] It introduces, then modifies, the reader's apprehension of death. The syntax of the grammatical unit that carries across the stanza division articulates the importance of the dying man's age. The fact that it is a young man of apparent vitality who is "ransakid . . . and soght" by death is surprising. It reminds readers that death is always near and that everyone needs to prepare for it. The relationship between the initial impression made by the disciple and its subsequent modification contributes to this idea as well. While the disciple initially seems to be foolish, ignoring Sapientia's advice, he turns out to be exemplary, making death immediate by imagining the way it might afflict a young man who is the mirror image of himself. He engages in the contemplation that precedes wisdom, and he helps the reader prepare for the subsequent account of this mental process.

The enjambment that takes place across this stanza break insists on the importance of contemplation on the part of the reader as well. Together these stanzas induce rumination: just as a ruminant animal draws cud back into its mouth to chew it further before digesting it, so too the reader must draw the first stanza back into his or her mind before fully digesting the meaning of both. Having done so, the reader recognizes the moral irony underlying this scene: the apparently healthy young man is actually dying, and the apparently foolish disciple is actually wise. The mirroring structure introduced by the figure of chiasmus does not apply to the first stanza alone: it applies to both. Together, these stanzas compel the reader to engage in the kind of contemplation that the disciple models.

The present state of MS HM 744 implies that its owners may have valued this passage for this very reason. Almost all of the poems that Hoccleve has compiled in this manuscript are religious in tone, though "Learn to Die" provides the clearest link with the other didactic material bound with it within twenty years of its initial production, possibly by a member of the Fyler family.[17] The nonautograph section of MS HM 744 contains ten items, depending on how one counts them, including a table for determining Easter day (1387–1527), a copy of Isidore of Seville's *Consilia*, and a version of "Erthe upon Erthe" written as prose.[18] The title of one item, Augustine's *De contemptu mundi*, might serve for the whole compilation, which invites readers to see worldly things—bodies in particular—as if their primary function is to provide the opportunity for spiritual contemplation. Even the potentially unorthodox texts included in this book focus on contempt for worldly things, especially *The Seven Works of Mercy Bodily* and "The Eight Ghostly Dwelling Places." The texts in MS HM 744 all encourage the contemplative practice that the disciple models in "Learn to Die." As a compilation made in part by its owners, MS HM 744 reveals their interest in this kind of contemplation.

"Learn to Die" in Durham, University Library, MS Cosin V.iii.9

The other autograph copy of "Learn to Die" likewise engages its reader in the kind of contemplation that the disciple models. "Learn to Die" is one of the texts that comprises the *Series* in Durham, University Library, MS Cosin V.iii.9. As the text that the narrator initially sets out to translate, it is of central thematic importance in the *Series*, and a sophisticated textual frame governs its possible comprehension in this book.

The *Series* opens with a "Complaint": those who see the narrator refuse to acknowledge that he has recovered from "the wilde infirmite" with which he was once afflicted.[19] Just as the narrator ends his "Complaint," a friend arrives at his door. Their conversation constitutes the second part of the book, a "Dialogue" in which the narrator makes it clear that he intends to circulate the "Complaint" and also plans to translate another text into English:

> In Latyn haue I seen a smal tretice,
> Wiche Lerne for to Die callid is . . .
> And that haue I purposid to translate.[20]

The narrator reveals that this translation will form part of a book that he owes to Humphrey, Duke of Gloucester. The friend eventually acknowledges that this is a reasonable endeavor, but he insists that the narrator also needs to assuage women offended by his earlier translation of Christine de Pisan's *Epistre de Cupid*. The narrator dutifully complies, and the next part of his book consists of his translation of the "Fabula de quadam imperatrice Romana" ["The Story of a Certain Roman Empress"] from the *Gesta Romanorum*. When the friend returns, this time "a wike or two" after "this tale endid was," he discovers that the narrator's exemplar lacks a moralization to the tale.[21] He helpfully provides one, which the narrator also copies into his book. "Learn to Die" finally appears at this point. Somewhat anticlimactically, the narrator brings his translation to an end after completing just one of the four parts he initially promises, claiming that "The othir iii partes which in this book / Of the tretice of deeth expressid be, / Touche Y nat dar."[22] In place of the missing parts he copies a short prose text on the "Joys of heaven," the ninth lesson read on "A[ll] halwen day."[23]

Although he intends "This book thus to han endid," the friend returns once more to ask that he translate another tale from the *Gesta Romanorum* for the benefit of his son, this time the "Fabula de quadam muliere mala" ["The Story of a Certain Wicked Woman"].[24] This time the narrator's exemplar includes a moralization; its completion brings the narrative to an end. MS Cosin V.iii.9 closes by dedicating this copy to Joan Beaufort, the Countess of Westmoreland. Like "Learn to Die," most of the component texts in the *Series* can be read on their own or as part of the book as a whole.

The one substantive textual variant between the two autograph versions of the two stanzas of "Learn to Die" under consideration here may reflect its place in the Series as a whole. Where MS HM 744 reads "Beholde *inward* the liknesse and figure," MS Cosin V.iii.9 reads *now* (fig. 1). "Learn to Die" suggests that amendment is an urgent matter: later in the text, the image of the dying man laments, "Whan tyme was, fynde kowde Y no tyme / Me to correcte of myn offense and cryme."[25] However, the word *now* in MS Cosin V.iii.9 seems even more apt in the *Series*, where the narrator's sense of urgency is an important theme. In the "Dialogue" he tells his friend that he wants to translate "Learn to Die" because it will help others to recognize the danger of putting off self-reflection and amendment:

> Man may in þis tretiis / hereaftirward,
> If þat him like rede and biholde,
> Considre and see wel þat it is ful hard
> Delaie acountis til liif bigynne colde.
> Shorte tyme is þanne of hise offensis oolde
> To make a iust / and trewe reckenynge;
> Sharpnesse of peine / is therto greet hinderinge.[26]

The narrator in the *Series* is acutely aware of the danger of putting things off, since he is already fifty-three years of age and believes that "Ripenesse of deeth faste vppon me now hastiþ."[27] The use of *now* in the *Series* both stresses the narrator's urgent need to amend and invites the reader to engage in self-reflexive contemplation at this moment in the text.[28]

The narrator's urgency is palpable from the very beginning of the *Series*. While its first part, the "Complaint," ends with the narrator thanking God for his old age and illness, which have provided him the opportunity to "amende my sinful gouernaunce,"[29] most of the text up to this point focuses on the narrator's sense that the body he inhabits betrays him. It is at this point that he devotes considerable time to examining his body in a mirror in order to understand why others refuse to acknowledge his recovery:

> And in my chaumbre at home whanne þat I was
> Mysilfe alloone I in þis wise wrouȝte.
> I streite vnto my mirrour and my glas,
> To loke howe þat me of my chere þouȝt,
> If any othir were it than it ouȝt,
> For fain wolde I, if it not had bene riȝt,
> Amendid it to my kunnynge and myȝt.[30]

Despite the narrator's willingness to examine himself and amend, however, he finds that no signs of his illness are visible. The urgency of his attempt to amend is palpable, and he returns to his mirror repeatedly in order to see why others still think he suffers the effects of his illness:

> Many a saute made I to this mirrour,
> Thinking, "If þat I looke in þis manere
> Amonge folke as I nowe do, noon errour
> Of suspecte look may in my face appere.
> This countinaunce, I am sure, and þis chere,
> If I it forthe vse, is nothing repreuable
> To hem þat han conceitis resonable."[31]

Though he examines himself carefully, he cannot find anything to amend. He ultimately admits that he does not know what to do next: "How shal I do? Wiche is the beste way / My troublid spirit for to bringe in rest?"[32]

The narrator concludes his reflection by confirming his commitment to do everything in his power to remedy his situation: "If I wiste howe, fain wolde I do the best."[33] At the end of the "Complaint" he finds a book of advice in which Reason gives words of consolation to a "wooful man."[34] By reading this book and applying Reason's words to his own plight, he learns to set less store "By the peoples ymaginacioun, / Talkinge this and þat of my siknesse."[35] He concludes by offering to God "Thanke of myn elde and of my seeknesse."[36] By urgently seeking his own amendment, the narrator seems to anticipate Sapientia's instructions to the disciple at the end of "Learn to Die":

> Lifte vp thyn yen. Looke aboute and see
> Diligently, how many folkes blynde
> In hir conceites nowadayes be.
> They close and shitte the yen of hir mynde.
> They nat keepe in hir conceit serche and fynde
> Vnto what ende needes they shuln drawe,
> And al for lak of dreede of God and awe.[37]

Although the narrator feels blind in his attempt to examine himself in front of his mirror, his inclusion of "Learn to Die" in the compilation provides evidence that he has opened his mind's eye and that he is determined to "serche and fynde" what is necessary to achieve spiritual change. And the narrator undertakes his compilation precisely because he feels dread and awe for God.

Like the mirror scene in the "Complaint," the two stanzas in "Learn to Die" under consideration in this article present a scene of self-reflexive contemplation that engages the reader's sense of morality through irony. It is ironic that the narrator, who is over fifty years of age, fails to see any signs of affliction when he looks at himself in an actual mirror in the "Complaint." It is more understandable that the disciple in "Learn to Die," who is relatively young, would fail in this way. It is therefore ironic that the young disciple turns out to be far more successful than the older narrator in his ability to imagine death's approach. This moral irony is resolved through the compilation that the narrator makes, which ultimately demonstrates that he is capable of selecting appropriate texts for contemplation. In the end, the older narrator learns to imitate his younger counterpart, modeling his own process of self-reflection on the disciple's. The change from *inward* in MS HM 744 to *now* in MS Cosin V.iii.9 suggests that the narrator sees "Learn to Die" as a mirror in which he can behold himself and amend immediately, which is exactly what he says he will do when he literally examines himself in his mirror in the "Complaint." The word *now* also invites other readers to join him in reflection at this precise moment in the text.

"Learn to Die" in MS Selden Supra 53

The appearance of these two stanzas of "Learn to Die" in MS Selden Supra 53 extends this invitation in a dramatic manner. A miniature that appears on folio 118r separates them more emphatically than the stanza divisions that appear in the autograph manuscripts (fig. 2).[38] The miniature's location initially reinforces the misreading that the first stanza's form and content suggest, and its appearance seems to confirm that these two stanzas should be read separately. As the reader's eyes move from the textual depiction of "a yonge man / of excellent fairnesse" in last line of the first stanza, they must cross over the image of a young man positioned centrally in the miniature before the reader passes to the second stanza. He stands beside the bed of a dying man who is menaced by a skeleton with a rod in his hand. It is tempting to see this miniature as evidence of the kind of "negligence and rape" of which Chaucer accuses his scribe Adam.[39] However, by initially reinforcing the misreading that the first stanza suggests, the miniature makes the second stanza's reversal even more profound.[40]

By both visually reinforcing the potential misapprehension of the first stanza and representing the modification introduced by the second, the miniature helps the reader to understand even more fully the implications of the transition between them. As I argue above, the second stanza modifies the first by obliging the reader to recognize that death may be closer than it seems. The miniature initially seems to distance death by focalizing death's presence through the eyes of the disciple. At the end of the first stanza, readers are left with the impression that the miniature provides the disciple's view: he is imagining a young man who is near a dying man in bed. The second stanza eliminates one step, and a second look at the miniature reveals what the reader should see: the disciple imagining a dying man. By contemplating the miniature while reading and rereading this passage, the reader of this manuscript therefore takes the first step in preparing for death by recognizing that it is nearer than it first appears.

The miniature in MS Selden Supra 53 ensures that this book provides the means for readers to undertake the kind of reflection modeled by the disciple: it supplies the reader with an image to behold in the mind as the account of the disciple's contemplation proceeds. The miniature's location and content heighten the sense of moral irony conveyed by this passage. Whoever was responsible for its inclusion in this particular book had clearly read the *Series* carefully and was determined to help others see it in a particular way.

COMPILATION AND CONTEMPLATION 11

This miniature's representation of the dying man's body reveals the care taken in producing MS Selden Supra 53 as a means to promote contemplation. A reader of the Selden manuscript would almost certainly return to this particular image of the dying man by leafing back in the book itself or recalling it to his or her mind's eye when reaching the dying man's self-depiction later in the text:

> See how my face wexith pale now,
> And my look ful dym and heuy as leed.
> Myn yen synke eek deepe into myn heed,
> And torne vpsodoun, and myn hondes two
> Wexen al stif and starke and may nat do.[41]

The imperative construction in this passage is directed towards the disciple yet it seems to bypass him and invite the reader to gaze directly at the dying man. Something similar occurs when the image tells the disciple to "Let me be your ensaumple and your mirour, / Lest yee slippe into my plyt miserable."[42] This imperative is directed towards the disciple, yet readers might respond to it directly, and they might look back to the miniature while doing so. In order to turn back to the miniature, readers would need to grasp the parchment, a material reminder of mortality, between their fingers as they hold the book in their hands.

While examining or reexamining the miniature, readers might note a marginal gloss supplied by the scribe in red ink on the same leaf:

> ¶ Vide ergo nunc similitudinem
> hominis morientis 7 tecum
> per*iter loquentis.
> [See therefore now the likeness of the man dying
> and speaking with you from experience.][43]

This gloss appears beside lines 85 and 86, which are an English translation of the Latin. The note's employment of the word *nunc* may explain Hoccleve's preference for *now* in place of *inward* in the *Series*: this English translation is closer to Suso's Latin. But readers might also respond to the immediacy of its imperative to imagine the dying man in both the text and the miniature at this particular moment. While the gloss simply echoes the imperative that Sapientia directs towards the disciples, readers might recognize that they, too, should contemplate the dying man.

Readers ruminating on the text, gloss, and miniature might be tempted to focus on the connotations of the word *similitudinem*, which can also mean resemblance or sameness. In this sense, the word invites readers to examine the similarities between the disciple and the dying man, particularly given the way that they are visually depicted in this manuscript. A reader who spends much time contemplating the two figures in the miniature will surely be struck by their similitude. The miniature represents both with the same hair, no doubt because they were in clerical orders. This, combined with the similarity in their faces, suggests that the image of the dying man is the disciple's projection of himself having endured adversity. By contemplating the similarity between the disciple and the dying man, the reader can see that the disciple's wisdom lies in his recognition of the need for amendment and his ability to imagine such an effective mirror in order to examine himself. By imagining such an effective mirror, the disciple becomes exemplary.

MS Selden Supra 53 is made the way it is in order to provide the material needed for the kind of contemplation undertaken by the disciple. The image of the dying man in "Learn to Die" may be experienced directly by readers, yet it is focalized through the eyes of the disciple in the text, gloss, and miniature. In other words, the linguistic and bibliographic codes governing the possible comprehension of "Learn to Die" in this manuscript remind readers to follow the disciple's example as they respond to the imperatives themselves. This is perhaps most obvious when one recognizes that the disciple is the central figure in the miniature. This visual reminder of focalization has an important consequence in the *Series*, where the narrator reads and responds to "Learn to Die" in turn as he makes it part of the *Series*. His compilation of this text follows the model of the disciple's exemplary contemplation. Like the disciple in "Learn to Die," the narrator in the *Series* becomes a model for the kind of contemplation that leads to self-examination and amendment. The book he compiles provides the means.

MS Selden Supra 53 as a Compilation for Contemplation

MS Selden Supra 53 as a whole is also a compilation designed for contemplation. Its size provides one indication that it was designed for individual devotional use. It is relatively small, 250 millimeters by 185, the kind of object that Margaret Aston would call a lap book.[44] More important is that its contents—both those provided by the main scribe as well as those added later—point to its use as a compilation encouraging the kind of self-examination and amendment considered so far. This section explores the relationship between the three texts written by the main scribe in the manuscript: Hoccleve's *Regiment of Princes*, which begins imperfectly and runs from folio 1r to folio 76r; the *Series*, which runs from folio 76r to folio 148r; and Lydgate's *Danse Macabre* (Text A), which runs from folio 148r to folio 158v.

MS Selden Supra 53 seems initially to have been designed to preserve these three texts. The other three texts it preserves were all added to the manuscript at some stage after its initial production. The *Regiment of Princes* begins imperfectly, and it is possible that another text preceded it, though this is doubtful for two reasons. First, the missing text makes up exactly two quires of eight, and the remainder of the book is made up of quires of eight. There are some lost leaves throughout the text. All of these losses result in textual loss except in the case of the last quire, which was initially a quire of eight but has had the final two leaves removed without the loss of text. Second, all other surviving manuscripts of the *Series* as a whole, apart from Hoccleve's autograph, preserve these texts together, and the only one to include additional texts, Coventry City Record Office MS Acc. 325/1, begins with Hoccleve's *Regiment* and adds material at the end of the book.

The continuous foliation of the three texts copied by the main scribe has several implications. It means that MS Selden Supra 53 preserves the whole of the *Series*. This represents a decision made on the part of the compiler: while the *Series* generally survives intact, there are several instances of its component parts circulating separately. It also reveals that all three texts were conceived as one bibliographic unit. This book does not employ booklet production: the *Series* begins on the same leaf on which the *Regiment of Princes* ends, and the *Danse Macabre* begins on the same leaf on which the *Series* ends. The relationship between these texts in the book is the result of a conscious decision on the part of its compiler. It was not an isolated decision, though. Every nonautograph compilation that includes the *Series* as a whole also includes the *Regiment* and the *Danse Macabre*.

In his discussion of the presence of these three poems in Yale, Beinecke MS 493, David Lorenzo Boyd writes, "In such a context, the compilation of the *Series* and the *Dance of Death* with the *Regiment* is significant, for it strongly suggests that all three poems were approached by some readers/compilers in similar ways."[45] I believe the same holds true of MS Selden Supra 53, and it is worth pursuing a separate study of this book because it provides insight into how the earliest compiler of the *Series* approached it. MS Selden Supra 53 indicates that its compiler, whether the main scribe himself or someone responsible for his work, saw the *Series* as a whole and a connection between it, the *Regiment*, and the *Danse Macabre*.

It is fairly easy to see why the compiler of MS Selden Supra 53 might have seen a connection between the ostensibly autobiographical narrators in the *Series* and in the *Regiment* or between the focus on death in the *Series* and in the *Danse Macabre*. It is perhaps less obvious, though no less important, that the *Regiment* and *Danse Macabre* both have something in common with each other: they both explicitly draw attention to themselves as mirrors.

The prologue to the *Regiment* identifies its sources as three mirrors for princes: Aristotle's *Secretum Secretorum*, Jacobus de Cessolis's *Book of Chess*, and Giles of Rome's *Regiment of Princes*.[46] The narrator claims that he is compiling exemplary material from these books for Prince Henry so that he can "beholde heer and rede / That in hem thre is scatered fer in brede."[47] One of Hoccleve's innovations in the *Regiment* is its ostensibly autobiographical frame. Two thousand of the poem's five and a half thousand lines are devoted to the narrator's dialogue with an old man; his process of self-reflection serves as an exemplar for the prince as much as the translation that follows. D. C. Greetham, Judith Ferster, Antony Hasler, and Anna Torti all point out the way in which the prologue and main text mirror each other.[48] The narrator reflects upon his life as a young man in order to establish himself as a suitable mirror for the prince. The old man insists that the narrator must turn away from his "childish misreuled conceit," which has led him to do himself "harm and deceit."[49] The narrator learns by paying close attention to the example provided to him by the old man, who can also be seen as a reflection of the narrator.

Lydgate's text does not employ anything like the ostensibly autobiographical frame of the *Regiment*, yet its prologue does seem to provide information about its translator's intentions. He aims to provide a plain English translation of a textual mirror in which others might behold and amend themselves:

> That prowde folkes whiche that ben stoute & bolde
> As in a myrrowre to for yn her reasoun
> Her owgly fyne there clearely may beholde.
>
> By ensample that thei yn her ententis
> A-mende her life in eueri maner age.[50]

Just before the individual figures are introduced and addressed, the text again reminds readers that it is a mirror of universal applicability: "In this myrrowre eueri wight mai fynde / That hym behoueth to gone vpon this daunce."[51] This is a mirror, then, in which readers are invited to consider the common fate of all as well as to look for the figure most similar to themselves in order to reflect upon their own mortality.

The part of "Learn to Die" that appears in MS Selden Supra 53 as part of the *Series* expresses the same aim. Sapientia instructs the disciple to learn the wisdom that begins with "the dreede of God."[52] The first stage is to learn to die, to recognize "þat man is mortel," and to prepare for the possibility that death may come without any notice: "to han ay / Bothe herte and soule redy hens to go."[53] The disciple imagines a dying man who exhorts him as follows:

> Let me be your ensaumple and your mirour,
> Lest yee slippe into my plyt miserable.
> With God, depsende of your youthe the flour.
> If yee me folwe, into peril semblable
> Yee entre shuln. To god yee yow enable.
> In holy wirkes your tyme occupie,
> And, whyle it tyme is, vices mortifie.[54]

The narrator in the *Series* believes that the process of translating "Learn to Die" will enable him to purge his own sins by occupying his time in holy works. Like the translator in Lydgate's prologue, he believes that it might help others:

> For I not oonly but, as that I hope,
> Many another wiʒt eke therby shal
> His conscience tenderly grope,
> And wiþ himsilfe acounte and recken of al
> That he hath in this liif wrouʒt, greet or small,
> While he tyme hath, and freissh witt and vigour,
> And not abide vnto his deeþis hour.⁵⁵

Both the text itself and the account of its place in the *Series* suggest that the narrator imagines that "Learn to Die" provides an example and a mirror that other readers can use to behold their own mortality and follow the disciple's example, amending before it is too late. Texts made to provide readers with this kind of textual mirror were well known in the early fifteenth century. The *Myror of Sinners*—variously and mistakenly ascribed to St. Augustine, St. Bernard, and Richard Rolle—commonly employs the idea of contemplating death as an appropriate way of avoiding sin. It argues that anyone who "sauouredyn and vnderstoden, and purueieden for the laste thynges" would amend immediately.⁵⁶ Lydgate's *Danse Macabre* and "Learn to Die" certainly seem to be based on this premise, though other parts of the *Series* and MS Selden Supra 53 provide different models for amendment as well.

The order of MS Selden Supra 53 suggests that the *Series* provides a transition between two different types of mirrors. The *Regiment* presents a narrator who learns from his dialogue with an old man and subsequently compiles exemplary material drawn from three mirrors for princes for Prince Henry. The *Series* presents a slightly older version of this narrator who wants to compile a different kind of mirror for Henry's brother, Humphrey; he eventually settles on "Learn to Die," but he copies it only after he has compiled another exemplary tale to assuage his sins against women. The *Danse Macabre* presents a mirror text very much like "Learn to Die," one that exhorts its readers to consider their own personal end. The inclusion of Lydgate's *Danse Macabre* alongside Hoccleve's "Learn to Die" is not surprising. It would likely have been profitable financially for the compiler because it met needs of readers looking for such a text. It might also have led to another kind of profit: it might benefit the soul of the compiler as well as that of the reader. The major difference between the compiler of MS Selden Supra 53 and the compiler of the *Series* is this: whereas Hoccleve's narrator explicitly says this is why he is busy making a compilation with a translation of "Learn to Die" at its heart, the scribe's intentions must be inferred from the books he has made.

Books Made by the Selden Scribe

MS Selden Supra 53 does not provide evidence about the specific reader or readers for whom it was made. However, a great deal can be inferred about the kind of audience for whom it might have been made based on the main hand in the manuscript, which Burrow describes as writing "a good anglicana formata" dateable to "early in the second quarter of the fifteenth century."[57] The same hand appears in at least three other manuscripts: Bristol, Public Library, MS 8 (Lydgate, *Troy Book*; fig. 3); Manchester, John Rylands University Library, MS Eng. 98 (Nicholas Love, *Mirror of the Blessed Life of Christ*; fig. 4); and Oxford, Bodleian Library, MS Digby 230 (Lydgate, *Troy Book, Siege of Thebes*, and the *Siege of Jerusalem*).[58] Linne Mooney has identified the copyist responsible for this hand as the Selden scribe.[59] It is possible that the same scribe was also responsible for Cambridge, Queens' College Library, MS 24 (12), a copy of Hoccleve's *Regiment*, and Oxford, Bodleian Library, MS Rawlinson C.446, another copy of Lydgate's *Troy Book*.[60] The decorative borders and initials in these manuscripts, at times supplemented by the use of gold leaf, locate their production in London and Westminster.[61] The quality of the scribe's hand, the decoration, and even the size of the books suggest that the books made by the Selden scribe would have been reasonably costly.

The books made by the Selden scribe were made for readers who had substantial means but they were not made for the royal dedicatees named in them. None of the books made by the Selden scribe are presentation copies. MS Selden Supra 53 was not made for Humphrey, Duke of Gloucester, the person for whom the narrator in the *Series* ostensibly makes his book; nor was it was made for Henry V, though Hoccleve's narrator describes making a copy of the *Regiment* for Henry while he was still Prince of Wales. The Bristol copy of Lydgate's *Troy Book* was not made for Henry V either, though its prologue also describes the book as having been started for Henry when he was Prince of Wales:

> For to obeie withoute variaunce
> My lordes byddyng fully and plesaunce,
> Whiche hath desire, sothly for to seyn,
> Of verray knyghthod to remembre ageyn
> The worthynes, yif I schal nat lye,
> And the prowesse of olde chivalrie
> By cause he hath joye and gret deynté
> To rede in bokys of antiquité,
> To fyn only vertu for to swe
> Be example of hem and also for to eschewe
> The cursyd vice of slouthe and ydelnesse.[62]

Lydgate's prologue figures Prince Henry's desire to remember the deeds of chivalry as the means by which he might follow their example and avoid the vices of sloth and idleness. Lydgate goes on to describe how this type of reading is particularly suitable for the prince, whose manliness is beyond the poet's ability to describe:

> So he enjoyeth in vertuous besynesse
> In al that longeth to manhood, dar I seyn;
> He besyeth evere, and therto is so fayn
> To hawnte his body in pleies marcyal
> Thorugh excersice t'exclude slouthe at al,
> After the doctrine of Vygecius:
> Thus is he bothe manful and vertuous,
> More passyngly than I can of hym write.
> I wante connyng his highe renoun t'endite,
> So moche of manhood men may in hym sen.[63]

Lydgate's allusion to Vegetius in a passage recounting his inability to express Henry's manliness calls to mind a passage in Hoccleve's *Series* where the narrator recounts his inability to express Humphrey's manliness.[64] The narrator reveals in the "Dialogue" that he considered making a copy of Vegetius's *Art of Chivalry* for Humphrey before opting for "Learn to Die." He claims that the duke has already demonstrated his mastery of knighthood on the field and would rather have a devotional text.⁶⁵ Hoccleve implies that other readers might benefit from behaving like Humphrey, aspiring to imitate his manly deeds, and reading the same exemplary texts. If such readers could not own books as lavish as Humphrey's or Henry's, they could own books copied from the same exemplars.

Hoccleve's discussion of Humphrey's manliness and desire for exemplary texts provides one reason readers might have aspired to be like him. The narrator in the *Series* is preoccupied by the possibility readers might avoid heresy if they were to act more like men and read books about manly men doing manly things. Hoccleve reveals a similar preoccupation in his invective against Oldcastle:

> Bewar Oldcastel / & for Crystes sake
> Clymbe no more / in holy writ so hie!
> Rede the storie of Lancelot de lake,
> Or Vegece of the aart of Chiualrie,
> The seege of Troie / or Thebes / thee applie
> To thyng þat may to thordre of knyght longe!
> To thy correccioun / now haaste and hie,
> For thow haast been out of ioynt al to longe.⁶⁶

Hoccleve suggests that Oldcastle might have avoided heresy if he had acquired a copy of a book about the Siege of Troy or Thebes; Lydgate completed versions of both texts within a decade of the Oldcastle rising; the Selden scribe copied both books. This scribe, or whoever was responsible for his work, anticipated that readers would want books not only that were copied from the same exemplars as those directed towards noble readers but that would enable them to follow the example of these noble readers—if not in their military exploits, then at least in their reading habits.

It is notable in this regard that the texts copied by the Selden scribe were all written after 1409. Hoccleve's *Regiment* was complete by the end of 1411; Lydgate's *Troy Book* was underway from 1412 to 1420 and his *Siege of Thebes* from 1420 to 1421. The Selden manuscript is even more up-to-date, containing as it does the *Regiment* along with the *Series*, which Hoccleve wrote from 1419 to 1421, and Lydgate's *Danse Macabre*, which was complete in the 1430s—the same decade as the book itself. The readers for whom the Selden scribe was making books wanted material that was as up-to-date as possible. The connection between the up-to-date quality of this material and orthodoxy can be seen most clearly in the Selden scribe's production of a copy of Nicholas Love's *Mirror of the Blessed Life of Christ* in Manchester, John Rylands University Library, MS Eng. 98. Love's text, which was completed around 1410, establishes Archbishop Arundel's *Constitutions* (1409) as an important context for its circulation.[67]

A Latin memorandum that circulated with copies of Love's text explicitly describes how the author diligently followed the prescriptions laid down by the *Constitutions* and presented the text to Arundel, who examined it and commended it in the hope that it would benefit the faithful and refute the Lollards:

> Memorandum quod circa annum domini Millesimum quadrigentesimum decimum, originalis copia huius libri, scilicet Speculi vite Christi in Anglicis.' Presentabatur Londoniis per compilatorem eiusdem .N. Reuerendissimo in Christo patri & domino, Domino Thome Arundell, Cantuarie Archiepiscopo, ad inspiciendum & debite examinandum antequam fuerat libere communicata. Qui post inspeccionem eiusdem per dies aliquot.' retradens ipsum librum memorato eiusdem auctori.' Proprie vocis oraculo ipsum in singulis commendauit & approbauit, necnon & auctoritate sua metropolitica, vt pote catholicum, puplice communicandum fore decreuit & manduit, ad fidelium edificacionem, & hereticorum siue lollardorum confutacionem. Amen. (7)

> [Memorandum: that around the year 1410, the original copy of this book, that is, *The Mirror of the Life of Christ* in English, was presented in London by its compiler, N, to the Most

> Reverend Father and Lord in Christ, Lord Thomas Arundel, Archbishop of Canterbury, for inspection and due examination before it was freely communicated. Who after examining it for several days, returning it to the above-mentioned author, commended and approved it personally, and further decreed and commanded by his metropolitan authority that it rather be published universally for the edification of the faithful and the confutation of heretics or lollards.][68]

Arundel's commendation of this text recognizes that many readers desired material that would enable them to examine themselves and amend their manner of living. The reforms undertaken by the Fourth Lateran Council of 1215, calling for the laity to be prepared for annual communion, were still in place. According to St. Paul, one can prepare oneself for the Eucharist only through judicious self-assessment:

> Examine yourselves, and only then eat of the bread and drink of the cup. For all who eat and drink without discerning the body, eat and drink judgment against themselves. For this reason many of you are weak and ill, and some have died. But if we judged ourselves, we would not be judged. But when we are judged by the Lord, we are disciplined so that we may not be condemned along with the world. (1 Cor. 11:28–32)

In the Augustinian tradition, scripture provided the mirror for such self-reflection. This tradition was still popular in the late fourteenth century, when the author of the *Cloud of Unknowing* wrote that "Goddes worde, ouþer wretyn or spokyn, is licnid to a mirour."[69] Other textual mirrors designed to supplement scripture were also popular. Jean Delumeau argues that Canon 21 of the Lateran Council of 1215 led to the creation of an influential genre of confessional manuals with titles like *Specchio della vera penitenza*, *Specchio della confessione*, and *Miroir de l'ame*.[70] Love's *Mirror* combines scripture and manual, encouraging readers to examine themselves in a controlled way.

Love's *Mirror* is designed to edify the faithful by encouraging the kind of self-examination that would allow them to take communion and ultimately to achieve salvation. Its prologue begins by noting the two things necessary for salvation: "pacience in herte & ensaumple of vertues & gude liuyng of holy men writen in bokes."[71] Love asserts the central importance of books because it is through them that readers can "byholdeth inwardly" the words and deeds of Christ, the most exemplary of men. His book thus contains "diuerse ymaginacions of cristes life"[72] in order to enable the reader to engage in "deuoute meditaticion."[73] Ultimately, the most necessary and profitable reward of meditation is "perfite despysing of þe worlde, in pacience, suffryng of aduersitees, & in encrese & getyng of vertues.'[74] *The Mirror of the Blessed Life of Christ* aims to enable its readers to reach this aim through their contemplation of "þe lord of vertues, whose lif is þe mirrour of temperance & alle oþer vertues."[75]

The *Mirror*'s presentation of a vernacular text that reinforces orthodox doctrine rather than encouraging individual interpretation is likely what led Arundel to commend it for confuting heretics or Lollards. The potential risks associated with the production or consumption of scripture after 1409 led to a demand for other kinds of texts designed to enable readers to engage in the kind of self-examination deemed necessary for their salvation. Love's text successfully met the needs of an audience looking for orthodox reading material in the vernacular designed for contemplative purposes; according to Sargent, "Love's *Mirror* survives in 64 manuscripts, of which 60 were originally complete."[76] The surviving manuscripts suggest that Love's text was important, though it was merely one of several popular early fifteenth-century texts designed to meet the needs of readers looking for exemplary material.

Indeed, given Hoccleve's description of the potentially ameliorative effects of stories about the Siege of Troy or Thebes, Love's *Mirror* was merely one of several texts copied in the hand of the Selden scribe that met the needs of an audience who wanted to read exemplary material. Readers aspiring to avoid looking like the out-of-favor Oldcastle might have used Lydgate's versions of these stories in Bristol, Public Library, MS 8 and Oxford, Bodleian Library, MS Digby 230 for their own edification. It seems reasonable to think that MS Selden Supra 53 was made to meet the aspirations of such readers as well.

Did MS Selden Supra 53 Meet the Aspirations of Its Readers?

The present state of MS Selden Supra 53 suggests that this book did move some of its readers to read and respond to the *Series* as a textual mirror. These readers seem to have used it to examine themselves through contemplation in order to amend anything they might find to be amiss, just as Hoccleve's narrator tries to amend when he beholds his body in front of his mirror or just as the disciple tries to amend as he beholds the image of the dying man. And these readers contributed to the compilation themselves. The margins of folio 118r—the leaf on which the miniature appears—are filled with responses, frequently repeating phrases found in the passage about the need to keep death's proximity in mind. They are in several different hands and interspersed with the marginal glosses provided by the scribe. What is notable about these responses is that they appear at this point in the text. There are almost no interventions in the margins manuscript up to this point, yet this leaf is full of commentary. This kind of response continues in the rest of the manuscript but it is at its most intense on folio 118r.

Several of the comments are notable because they supplement the kind of contemplation that the miniature encourages. They reveal how readers have been moved by the miniature to engage with the manuscript and provide some indication as to how they undertook this engagement. At the very top of the leaf, one reader has written, "Vos modo viuentes et mundi vana tenentes prestis qui fragiles este mei memores" [You fragile creatures who stand out now for being alive and clinging onto the empty things of the world, be mindful of me].[77] This note draws attention to the inward focus of contemplation as well as its immediate relevance. It would fit equally well with both of the textual variants Hoccleve uses in this passage. On the one hand, the imperative it enunciates, *este mei memores*, addresses the kind of reflection stressed by Hoccleve's use of *inward* in MS HM 744. On the other hand, its use of *modo* clearly aligns it with Hoccleve's use of *now* in MS Cosin V.iii.9. From either perspective, it underlines the fact that contemplation of death (or the dying man) is imperative and urgent.

The disciple has already recognized this and is contemplating death inwardly; the imperative in this note, therefore, seems addressed to the reader, commanding him or her to follow the disciple's example—and thus to avoid the dying man's anxiety. Readers might contemplate the pronoun *mei* [me] further as well: it may be read as referring to death, to the dying man, to the disciple, or even to the narrator. If *mei* is read as referring to the first two, it reinforces the scene's insistence that death be contemplated. If *mei* refers to the latter two, it also suggests that readers should remember the model for contemplation. Because it can be read in all of these ways, the pronoun helps readers to contemplate death while also considering others who have done the same, either with success (the disciple) or without (the dying man).

The imperative voice is repeated in another note on the page, one that appears again on folio 127v. This note makes a slightly different point about the present, warning readers against the limitations associated with simply seeing oneself in one's current state.

> Iudicii me*m*or esto mei viue*n*s
> homo lavte. Na*m*que meu*m*
> nu*n*c cras q*ue* tuu*m* forsan
> erit arte—
> [Be mindful of my judgment, man living sumptuously. For what is mine today will perhaps be yours tomorrow by some means.][78]

On the one hand, contemplation is clearly necessary insofar as one must constantly be mindful of the future in order to live a meaningful life. On the other hand, the note stresses the urgency of contemplation by using both the word *nunc* (i.e., *now, today*) and *cras* (i.e., *tomorrow, in the future*). The need to account for more than one's immediate state is emphasized throughout the notes: *cras* is repeated six times in the notes on this leaf. The image of the young man who lies dying on the page—in both the text and the miniature—underscores the urgency that the variant *now* that appears in this passage in the *Series* seems to convey that tomorrow may arrive sooner than one expects. The imperative voice stresses the need for the reader to engage in contemplation at this moment; this note goes beyond the textual gloss provided by the scribe, which repeats instructions made in the imperative to the disciple. This note is an imperative addressed directly to the reader; it exhorts the reader to engage in the contemplation modeled in the text. The number of other notes that appear on this leaf suggests that at least some readers responded to this imperative. They then added annotations in an attempt to enhance its contemplative value for themselves or others.

This marginal notation suggests that MS Selden Supra 53 succeeded in employing aspects of its bibliographic code to encourage readers to behold the narrator's book and body in a particular way. However, the marginal notation in MS Cosin V.iii.9 suggests that the effect achieved by MS Selden Supra 53 could be achieved through the linguistic code of the text itself. In other words, the makers of MS Selden Supra 53 did not fundamentally alter the way that readers engaged with these two stanzas of the text, though they may have aimed to enhance this engagement. The following couplet appears in the margin of MS Cosin V.iii.9 in a later hand (fig. 1):

> Before thou pretend any evil in thyn harte
> Remember the end when thow shalt departe.[79]

Like several others in the manuscript, the couplet is bracketed by the tag "quod Carter." The tag makes the note extend through all three stanzas on this leaf, but the couplet itself is perpendicular to the main text and bridges the stanzas on either side of the miniature in MS Selden Supra 53. Like the miniature and the notes in the Selden manuscript, the couplet reveals that this particular reader had read the stanzas carefully and understood their relationship to one another. It indicates that whoever was responsible for it had internalized the sense of the lines and provided a supplement to enhance their own contemplation of the text. The choice of this particular couplet seems to justify the choice of miniature in the Selden manuscript, since it also focuses on the importance of recognizing death's proximity even—perhaps especially—when one is very young.

The couplet's imperative voice is also significant. It does not simply repeat the text word for word: hence the imperative form addresses the reader directly, modifying the lesson to make it immediately relevant to the reader. By supplementing the text in this manner, this reader has effectively modeled his or her behavior after that of the narrator, who copies exemplars he deems to be relevant and applicable to his own circumstances as well as the well-being of others. The couplet is certainly relevant to the text presented on the leaf and it seems to present a common response to this passage. The proliferation of notes on this leaf suggests that readers of MS Selden Supra 53 were encouraged to engage more directly with this scene than were the readers of MS Cosin V.iii.9.

MS Selden Supra 53 provides another kind of provocative evidence of a common response to "Learn to Die," evidence that reinforces the view that the narrator's behavior was seen as exemplary by early readers. In its present condition it includes three additional texts in hands other than that of the Selden Scribe. Lines 65 to 80 of Lydgate's *Danse Macabre* (Text B) appear on folio 158v, following the conclusion of Text A; the remaining space on that leaf is filled by four rhyming French lines. Another hand altogether has copied a verse form of "Earth upon Earth" at the end of the manuscript on folio 159v.[80] This final text has clearly been conceived of separately from the rest of the manuscript. It was likely bound into the manuscript at a later date. As I note above, a prose version of this text appears in MS HM 744, where it was likewise conceived of separately. The readers or owners of MS HM 744 and MS Selden Supra 53 seem to have made a connection between "Learn to Die" and "Erthe Upon Erthe." By adding the latter text to their own compilations, these readers provide evidence that they read their books carefully and that the model for compilation and contemplation set forth by the narrator in the *Series* was particularly relevant.

University of Manitoba

NOTES

1. The most accessible printed edition of the *Series* as a whole is Thomas Hoccleve, *"My Compleinte" and Other Poems*, ed. Roger Ellis (Exeter, UK: Exeter University Press, 2001). For ease of reference, I cite the *Series* by referring to its item number in the edition (VII), indicating the component part cited (each is numbered from 1 to 5), and providing the line number(s). Where relevant, I have consulted Thomas Hoccleve, *Thomas Hoccleve's Complaint and Dialogue*, ed. John Burrow, EETS o.s. 313 (Oxford: Oxford University Press, 1999).

2. John Burrow, "The Poet and the Book," in *Genres, Themes, and Images in English Literature from the Fourteenth to the Fifteenth Century*, ed. Piero Boitani and Anna Torti, Tübinger Beiträge zur Anglistik 11 (Tübingen,

Germany: Gunter Narr Verlag, 1988), 238. See also Burrow, "Hoccleve's *Series*: Experience and Books," in *Fifteenth-Century Studies: Recent Essays*, ed. Robert F. Yeager (Hamden, CT: Archon Books, 1984), 259–274.

3. Ellis, VII:2, ll. 85–90.

4. Jerome McGann, *The Textual Condition* (Princeton, NJ: Princeton University Press, 1991), 77.

5. For studies of "Learn to Die," see Christina von Nolcken, "'O, Why Ne Had Y Lerned for to Die?': *Lerne for to Dye* and the Author's Death in Thomas Hoccleve's *Series*," *Essays in Medieval Studies* 10 (1993): 27–51; and Steven Rozenski, Jr. "'Your Ensaumple and Your Mirour': Hoccleve's Amplification of the Imagery and Intimacy of Henry Suso's *Ars Moriendi*," *Parergon* 25.2 (2008): 1–16.

6. McGann, *Textual Condition*, 77.

7. Stephen G. Nichols, "Introduction: Philology in a Manuscript Culture," *Speculum* 65.1 (1990): 7. In this sense, my approach falls under the rubric of New Philology, though Nichols himself stresses the fact that the approach is more a *renovatio* of an older way of reading.

8. Robert Chartier, "Labourers and Voyagers: From the Text to the Reader," *Diacritics* 2.2 (1992): 50.

9. Sister Ritamary Bradley, "Backgrounds of the Title *Speculum* in Mediaeval Literature," *Speculum* 29.1 (1954): 100–115. I cite other critics who consider the idea of the mirror in Hoccleve's writing (D. C. Greetham, Judith Ferster, Antony Hasler, and Anna Torti) below.

10. Hugh of St. Victor, *Expositio in Regulam Beati Augustini* (Patrilogia Latina, clxxvi, 923D–924A). Translation cited in Bradley, "Backgrounds," 111.

11. Ellis, VII:1, l. 170.

12. For the textual significance of these two autograph copies, see John Bowers, "Hoccleve's Two Copies of 'Lerne to Dye': Implications for Textual Critics," *Papers of the Bibliographical Society of America* 83.4 (1989): 437–472.

13. MS HM 744, fol. 56r. Cf. Ellis, VII:4, ll. 85–90. For the sake of clarity, the transcriptions of these two stanzas expand contractions and abbreviations.

14. Burrow and Doyle assert in *Thomas Hoccleve: A Facsimile of the Autograph Verse Manuscripts*, ed. J. A. Burrow and A. I. Doyle, EETS s.s. 19 (Oxford: Oxford University Press, 2002), xxxix, that it is very rare for Hoccleve to provide punctuation in such instances.

15. MS HM 744, fol. 56r; Ellis, VII:4, ll. 91–98.
16. Hoccleve frequently employs this kind of stanzaic enjambment, though its effects merit further attention.
17. For a full discussion of the relationship between the parts of the manuscript, see David Watt, "'I This Book Shal Make': Thomas Hoccleve's Self-Publication and Book Production," *Leeds Studies in English* 34 (2003): 133–160.
18. For the full catalogue description, see C. W. Dutschke, *Guide to Medieval and Renaissance Manuscripts in the Huntington Library*, 2 vols. (San Marino, CA: Huntington Library, 1989), 1:247–251.
19. Ellis, VII:1, l. 40.
20. Ellis, VII:2, ll. 205–206; 211.
21. Ellis, VII:3, ll. 953–954.
22. Ellis, VII:4, ll. 918–920.
23. Ellis, VII:4, l. 926.
24. Ellis, VII:5, l. 1.
25. Ellis, VII:4, ll. 412–413.
26. Ellis, VII:2, ll. 225–231.
27. Ellis, VII:2, ll. 247.
28. For an alternative account of this scene and the potentially autobiographical elements in these scenes, see Penelope Doob, *Nebuchadnezzar's Children: Conventions of Madness in Middle English Literature* (New Haven, CT: Yale University Press, 1974); Burrow responds to some of Doob's arguments in J. A. Burrow, "Autobiographical Poetry in the Middle Ages: The Case of Thomas Hoccleve," *Proceedings of the British Academy* 68 (1982): 389–412; and Burrow, *Thomas Hoccleve*, Authors of the Middle Ages 4 (Aldershot, UK: Variorum, 1994). See also Stephan Kohl, "More than Virtues and Vices: Self-Analysis in Hoccleve's 'Autobiographies,'" *Fifteenth-Century Studies* 14 (1988): 115–127; George MacLennan, *Lucid Interval: Subjective Writing and Madness in History* (Rutherford, NJ: Fairleigh Dickinson University Press, 1992); and Stephen Medcalf, "Inner and Outer," in *The Later Middle Ages*, The Context of English Literature (London: Methuen, 1981), 107–171.
29. Ellis, VII:4, l. 406.
30. Ellis, VII:1, l. 155–161.

31. Ellis, VII:1, ll. 163–165.
32. Ellis, VII:1, ll. 173–174.
33. Ellis, VII:1, l. 175.
34. Ellis, VII:1, l. 310.
35. Ellis, VII:1, ll. 380–381.
36. Ellis, VII:1, l. 410.
37. Ellis, VII:4, ll. 869–875.
38. The *punctus* at the end of line 90 may seem to indicate a pause as well, though this scribe regularly places a *punctus* at the end of a line of verse.
39. Chaucer, "Chaucers Wordes unto Adam, His Owne Scriveyn," in *The Riverside Chaucer*, ed. Larry D. Benson (Boston: Houghton Mifflin, 1987), 650, l. 7.
40. On the thematic significance of misreading in the *Series*, see Karen Smyth, "Reading Misreadings in Thomas Hoccleve's *Series*," *English Studies* 87.1 (2006): 3–22.
41. Ellis, VII:4, ll. 654–658.
42. Ellis, VII:4, ll. 295–296.
43. MS Selden Supra 53, fol. 118r.
44. Margaret Aston, "Lap Books and Lectern Books: The Revelatory Book in the Reformation," in *The Church and the Book*, ed. R. N. Swanson (Woodridge, UK: Boydell and Brewer, 2004), 163–189.
45. David Lorenzo Boyd, "Reading Through the *Regiment of Princes*, Hoccleve's *Series* and Lydgate's *Dance of Death* in Yale Beinecke MS 493," *Fifteenth-Century Studies* 20 (1993): 17.
46. For a more detailed study of the text and its sources, see Nicholas Perkins, *Hoccleve's* Regiment of Princes: *Counsel and Constraint* (Cambridge, UK: Cambridge University Press, 2001).
47. Thomas Hoccleve, *Thomas Hoccleve: The Regiment of Princes*, ed. Charles R. Blyth, TEAMS (Kalamazoo, MI: Medieval Institute Publications, 1999), ll. 2135.
48. D. C. Greetham, "Self-Referential Artifacts: Hoccleve's Persona as Literary Device," *Modern Philology* 86.3 (1989): 242–251; Judith Ferster, *Fictions of Advice: The Literature and Politics of Counsel in Late Medieval England* (Philadelphia: University of Pennsylvania Press, 1996); Antony Hasler, "Hoccleve's Unregimented Body," *Paragraph* 13 (1990): 164–183; Anna

Torti, *The Glass of Form: Mirroring Structures from Chaucer to Skelton* (Cambridge, UK: Brewer, 1991).

49. Hoccleve, *Regiment,* ll. 195–196.

50. John Lydgate, *The Dance of Death, Edited from MSS. Ellesmere 26/A.13 and B.M. Lansdowne 699, Collated with the Other Extant MSS,* ed. Florence Warren, intro. and notes by Beatrice White, EETS o.s. 181 (London: Oxford University Press, 1931), ll. 31–34.

51. Ibid., ll. 49–50.

52. Ellis, VII:4, l. 20.

53. Ellis, VII:4, ll. 43; 50–51.3.

54. Ellis, VII:4, ll. 295–301.

55. Ellis, VII:2, ll. 218–224.

56. "The Myror of Synneres," in *Yorkshire Writers: Richard Rolle of Hampole and His Followers,* 2 vols., ed. C. Horstman (London: Swan Sonnenschein, 1895–1896), 2:436.

57. Burrow in Hoccleve, *Complaint and Dialogue,* xii.

58. I would like to acknowledge the debt I owe to Dr. Ryan Perry, who helped me to recognize the connection between these manuscripts through his presentation to the Early Books Society sessions at Kalamazoo in 2009 and our subsequent conversations.

59. Linne Mooney's role in identifying the manuscripts in which the Selden scribe has been found is given in Perkins, *Hoccleve's* Regiment, 169–170 n.72.

60. Further work remains to be done to identify more certainly the development of this scribe's hand and its relationship to that of other contemporary scribes.

61. For a description of the features of MS Selden Supra 53, see Kathleen Scott, *Later Gothic Manuscripts 1390–1490,* A Survey of Manuscripts Illuminated in the British Isles 6 (London: Harvey Miller, 1996).

62. John Lydgate, *Lydgate's Troy Book,* 3 vols., ed. Henry Bergen, EETS e.s. 97, 103, 106 (London: Kegan Paul, Trench, Trübner, 1906–1910), ll. 73–83.

63. Ibid., ll. 84–93.

64. For an alternative reading of manliness in this scene, see Andrew Lynch, "'Manly Cowardyse': Thomas Hoccleve's Peace Strategy," *Medium Aevum* 73.2 (2004): 306–323.

65. Ellis, VII:2, ll. 561–567.

66. MS HM 111, fol. 10r; cf. Thomas Hoccleve, *Hoccleve's Works: The Minor Poems*, ed. F. J. Furnivall et al, EETS e.s. 61 and 73 (London: Oxford University Press, 1970), 2:193–200.
67. Nicholas Watson, "Censorship and Cultural Change in Late-Medieval England: Vernacular Theology, the Oxford Translation Debate, and Arundel's Constitutions of 1409," *Speculum* 70.4 (1995): 822–864.
68. Nicholas Love, *The Mirror of the Blessed Life of Christ: The Reading Text*, ed. Michael Sargent (Exeter, UK: Exeter University Press, 2004), 7; trans. Michael Sargent, xv.
69. *The Cloud of Unknowing and the Book of Privy Counselling*, ed. Phyllis Hodgson, EETS o.s. 218. (London: Oxford University Press, 1944), 72.
70. On the first, see *Le speculum laicorum*, ed. J. Th. Welther (Paris, 1914), iii; on the second, see Jean Delumeau, *Sin and Fear: the Emergence of a Western Guilt Culture, 13th–18th Centuries*, trans. Eric Nicholson (New York: St. Martin's Press, 1990), 198–201. See also L. E. Boyle, "The Fourth Lateran Council and Manuals of Popular Theology," in *The Popular Literature of Medieval England*, ed. T. J. Heffernan (Knoxville: University of Tennessee Press, 1985), 30–43.
71. Love, *Mirror*, 9:12–13. Several other Nicholas Love manuscripts may be by the same scribe or someone closely related to him. For examples of the possible connections, see A. I. Doyle, "The Study of Love's *Mirror*, Retrospect and Prospect," in *Nicholas Love at Waseda*, ed. Shoichi Oguro, Michael Sargent, and Richard Beadle (Cambridge, UK: Brewer, 1997), 163–174.
72. Love, *Mirror*, 11:10–11.
73. Ibid., 11:9.
74. Ibid., 11:34–36.
75. Ibid., 12:36–37.
76. Ibid., ix n.1.
77. MS Selden Supra 53, fol. 118r.
78. Ibid., fol. 118r.
79. MS Cosin V.iii.9, fol. 54v.
80. *Erthe Upon Erthe, Printed from Twenty-Two Manuscripts*, ed. Hilda M. R. Murray, EETS o.s. 141 (London: Kegan Paul, Trench, Trubner, 1911), 7.

WORKS CITED

Manuscripts

Bristol, Public Library, MS 8.
Coventry, City Record Office, MS 325.
Durham, University Library, MS Selden Supra 53.
Manchester, John Rylands University Library, MS Eng. 98.
Oxford, Bodleian Library, MS Digby 230.
Oxford, Bodleian Library, MS Rawlinson C. 446.
Oxford, Bodleian Library, MS Selden Supra 53.
San Marino, California, Huntington Library, MS HM 744.
New Haven, CT, Yale University, Beinecke Library, MS 493.

Primary Sources

Chaucer, Geoffrey, "Chaucers Wordes unto Adam, His Owne Scriveyn." In *The Riverside Chaucer*, ed. Larry D. Benson. Boston: Houghton Mifflin, 1987, 650.

The Cloud of Unknowing and the Book of Privy Counselling. Edited by Phyllis Hodgson. EETS o.s. 218. London: Oxford University Press, 1944.

Erthe Upon Erthe, Printed from Twenty-Two Manuscripts. Edited by Hilda M. R. Murray. EETS o.s. 141. London: Kegan Paul, Trench, Trubner, 1911.

Hoccleve, Thomas. *Hoccleve's Works: The Minor Poems*. Edited by F. J. Furnivall et al. EETS e.s. 61 and 73. London: Oxford University Press, 1970.

——. *Thomas Hoccleve's Complaint and Dialogue*. Edited by John Burrow. EETS o.s. 313. Oxford: Oxford University Press, 1999.

——. *Thomas Hoccleve: The Regiment of Princes*. Edited by Charles R. Blyth. TEAMS. Kalamazoo, MI: Medieval Institute Publications, 1999.

——. *"My Compleinte" and Other Poems*. Edited by Roger Ellis. Exeter, UK: Exeter University Press, 2001.

——. *Thomas Hoccleve: A Facsimile of the Autograph Verse Manuscripts*. Edited by J. A. Burrow and A. I. Doyle. EETS s.s. 19. Oxford: Oxford University Press, 2002.

Love, Nicholas. *The Mirror of the Blessed Life of Christ: The Reading Text*. Edited by Michael Sargent. Exeter, UK: Exeter University Press, 2004.

Lydgate, John. *Lydgate's Troy Book.* Edited by Henry Bergen. EETS e.s. 97, 103, 106, 3 vols. London: Kegan Paul, Trench, Trübner, 1906–1910.

———. *The Dance of Death, Edited from MSS. Ellesmere 26/A.13 and B.M. Lansdowne 699, Collated with the Other Extant MSS.* Edited by Florence Warren; introduction and notes by Beatrice White. EETS o.s. 181. London: Oxford University Press, 1931.

"The Myror of Synneres." In *Yorkshire Writers: Richard Rolle of Hampole and His Followers,* ed. C. Horstman, 2 vols. London: Swan Sonnenschein, 1895–1896, 2:436–440.

Le speculum laicorum. Edited by J. Th. Welther. Paris, 1914.

Secondary Sources

Aston, Margaret. "Lap Books and Lectern Books: The Revelatory Book in the Reformation." In *The Church and the Book,* ed. R. N. Swanson. Woodridge, UK: Boydell and Brewer, 2004, 163–189.

Bowers, John. "Hoccleve's Two Copies of 'Lerne to Dye': Implications for Textual Critics." *Papers of the Bibliographical Society of America* 83.4 (1989): 437–472.

Boyd, David Lorenzo. "Reading Through the *Regiment of Princes*: Hoccleve's *Series* and Lydgate's *Dance of Death* in Yale Beinecke MS 493." *Fifteenth-Century Studies* 20 (1993): 15–34.

Boyle, L. E. "The Fourth Lateran Council and Manuals of Popular Theology." In *The Popular Literature of Medieval England,* ed. T. J. Heffernan. Knoxville: University of Tennessee Press, 1985, 30–43.

Bradley, Sister Ritamary. "Backgrounds of the Title *Speculum* in Mediaeval Literature." *Speculum* 29.1 (1954): 100–115.

Burrow, J. A. "Autobiographical Poetry in the Middle Ages: The Case of Thomas Hoccleve," *Proceedings of the British Academy* 68 (1982): 389–412.

———. "Hoccleve's *Series*: Experience and Books." In *Fifteenth-Century Studies: Recent Essays,* ed. Robert F. Yeager. Hamden, CT: Archon Books, 1984, 259–274.

———. "The Poet and the Book." In *Genres, Themes, and Images in English Literature from the Fourteenth to the Fifteenth Century,* ed. Piero Boitani and Anna Torti. Tübinger Beiträge zur Anglistik 11. Tübingen, Germany: Gunter Narr Verlag, 1988, 230–245.

———. *Thomas Hoccleve*. Authors of the Middle Ages 4. Aldershot, UK: Variorum, 1994.

Chartier, Roger. "Labourers and Voyagers: From the Text to the Reader." *Diacritics* 2.2 (1992): 49–61.

Delumeau, Jean. *Sin and Fear: the Emergence of a Western Guilt Culture, 13th–18th Centuries*. Translated by Eric Nicholson. New York: St. Martin's Press, 1990.

Doob, Penelope. *Nebuchadnezzar's Children: Conventions of Madness in Middle English Literature*. New Haven, CT: Yale University Press, 1974.

Doyle, A. I. "The Study of Love's *Mirror*, Retrospect and Prospect." In *Nicholas Love at Waseda*, ed. Shoichi Oguro, Michael Sargent, and Richard Beadle. Cambridge, UK: Brewer, 1997, 163–174.

Dutschke, C. W. *Guide to Medieval and Renaissance Manuscripts in the Huntington Library*, 2 vols. San Marino, CA: Huntington Library, 1989.

Ferster, Judith. *Fictions of Advice: The Literature and Politics of Counsel in Late Medieval England*. Philadelphia: University of Pennsylvania Press, 1996.

Greetham, D. C. "Self-Referential Artifacts: Hoccleve's Persona as a Literary Device." *Modern Philology* 86.3 (1989): 242–251.

Hasler, Antony. "Hoccleve's Unregimented Body." *Paragraph* 13 (1990): 164–183.

Lynch, Andrew. "'Manly Cowardyse': Thomas Hoccleve's Peace Strategy." *Medium Aevum* 73.2 (2004): 306–323.

Kohl, Stephan. "More than Virtues and Vices: Self-Analysis in Hoccleve's 'Autobiographies.'" *Fifteenth-Century Studies* 14 (1988): 115–127.

MacLennan, George. *Lucid Interval: Subjective Writing and Madness in History*. Rutherford, NJ: Fairleigh Dickinson University Press, 1992.

McGann, Jerome. *The Textual Condition.* Princeton, NJ: Princeton University Press, 1991.

Medcalf, Stephen. "Inner and Outer." In *The Later Middle Ages*. The Context of English Literature. London: Methuen, 1981, 107–171.

Nichols, Stephen G. "Introduction: Philology in a Manuscript Culture." *Speculum* 65.1 (1990): 1–10.

Perkins, Nicholas. *Hoccleve's* Regiment of Princes: *Counsel and Constraint*. Cambridge, UK: Cambridge University Press, 2001.

Rozenski, Steven, Jr. "'Your Ensaumple and Your Mirour': Hoccleve's

Amplification of the Imagery and Intimacy of Henry Suso's *Ars Moriendi*." *Parergon* 25.2 (2008): 1–16.

Scott, Kathleen. *Later Gothic Manuscripts 1390–1490*. A Survey of Manuscripts Illuminated in the British Isles 6. London: Harvey Miller, 1996.

Smyth, Karen. "Reading Misreadings in Thomas Hoccleve's *Series*." *English Studies* 87.1 (2006): 3–22.

Torti, Anna. *The Glass of Form: Mirroring Structures from Chaucer to Skelton*. Cambridge, UK: Brewer, 1991.

von Nolcken, Christina. "'O, Why Ne Had Y Lerned for to Die?': *Lerne for to Dye* and the Author's Death in Thomas Hoccleve's *Series*." *Essays in Medieval Studies* 10 (1993): 27–51.

Watson, Nicholas. "Censorship and Cultural Change in Late-Medieval England: Vernacular Theology, the Oxford Translation Debate, and Arundel's Constitutions of 1409." *Speculum* 70.4 (1995): 822–864.

Watt, David. "'I This Book Shal Make': Thomas Hoccleve's Self-Publication and Book Production." *Leeds Studies in English* 34 (2003): 133–160.

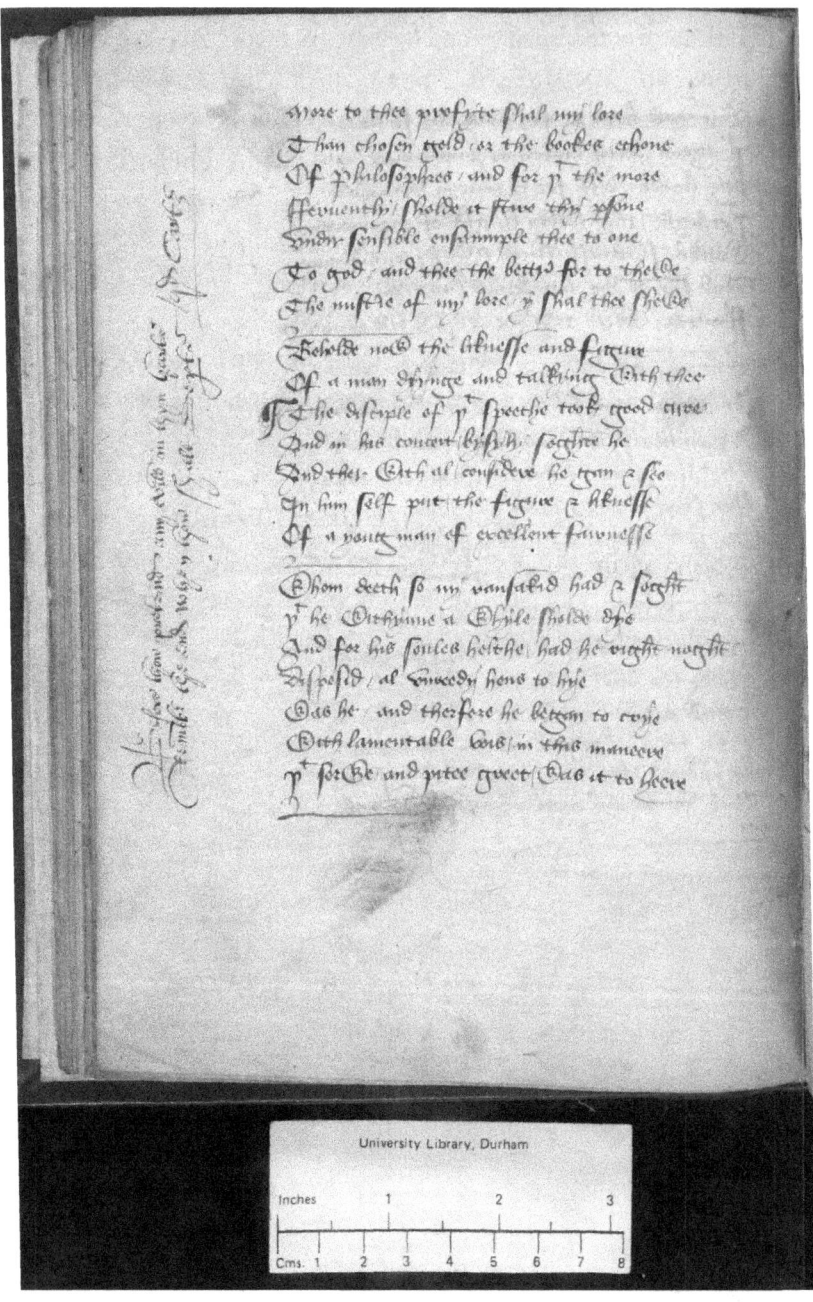

Figure 1. Durham, University Library, MS Cosin V.iii.9, f. 54v; reproduced by permission of Durham University Library.

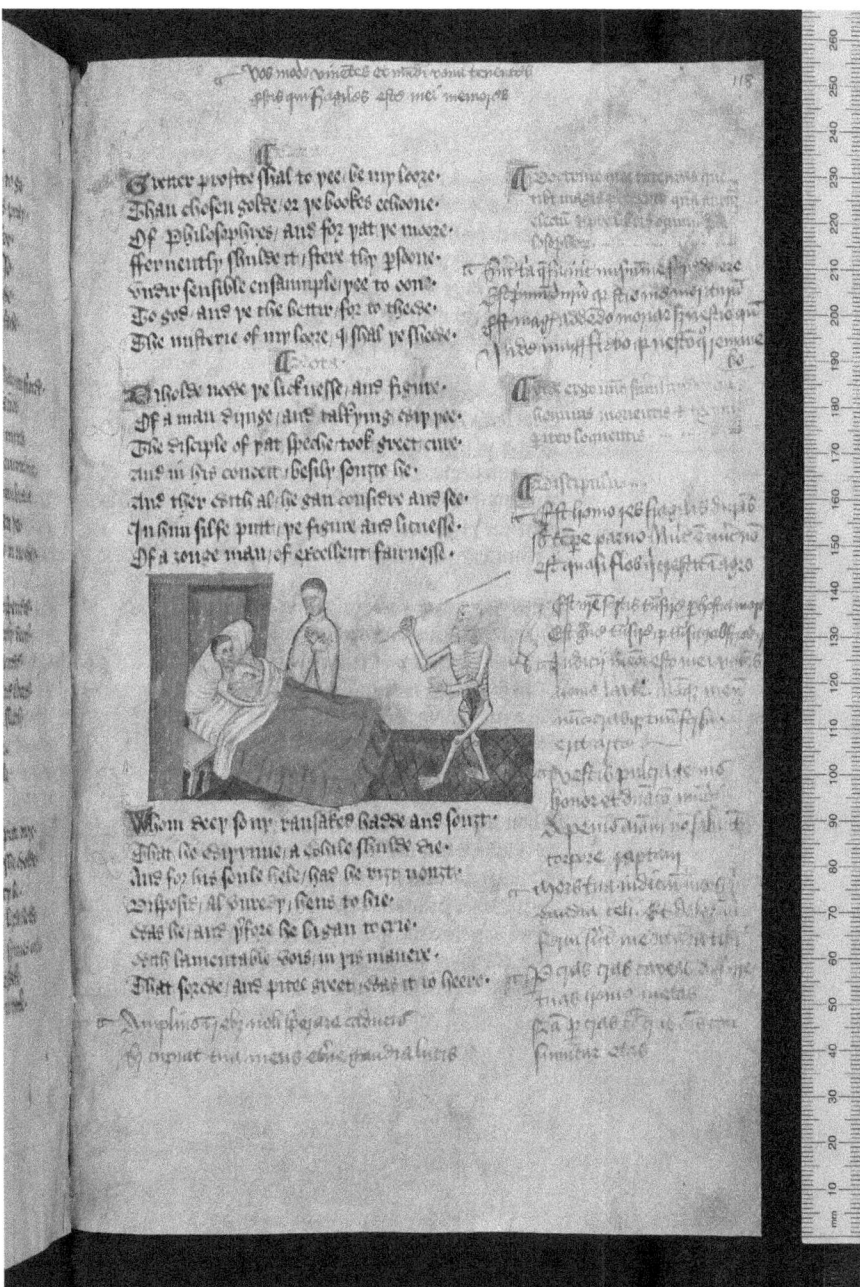

Figure 2. Oxford, Bodleian Library, MS Selden Supra 53, f. 118r; reproduced by permission of the Bodleian Library, University of Oxford.

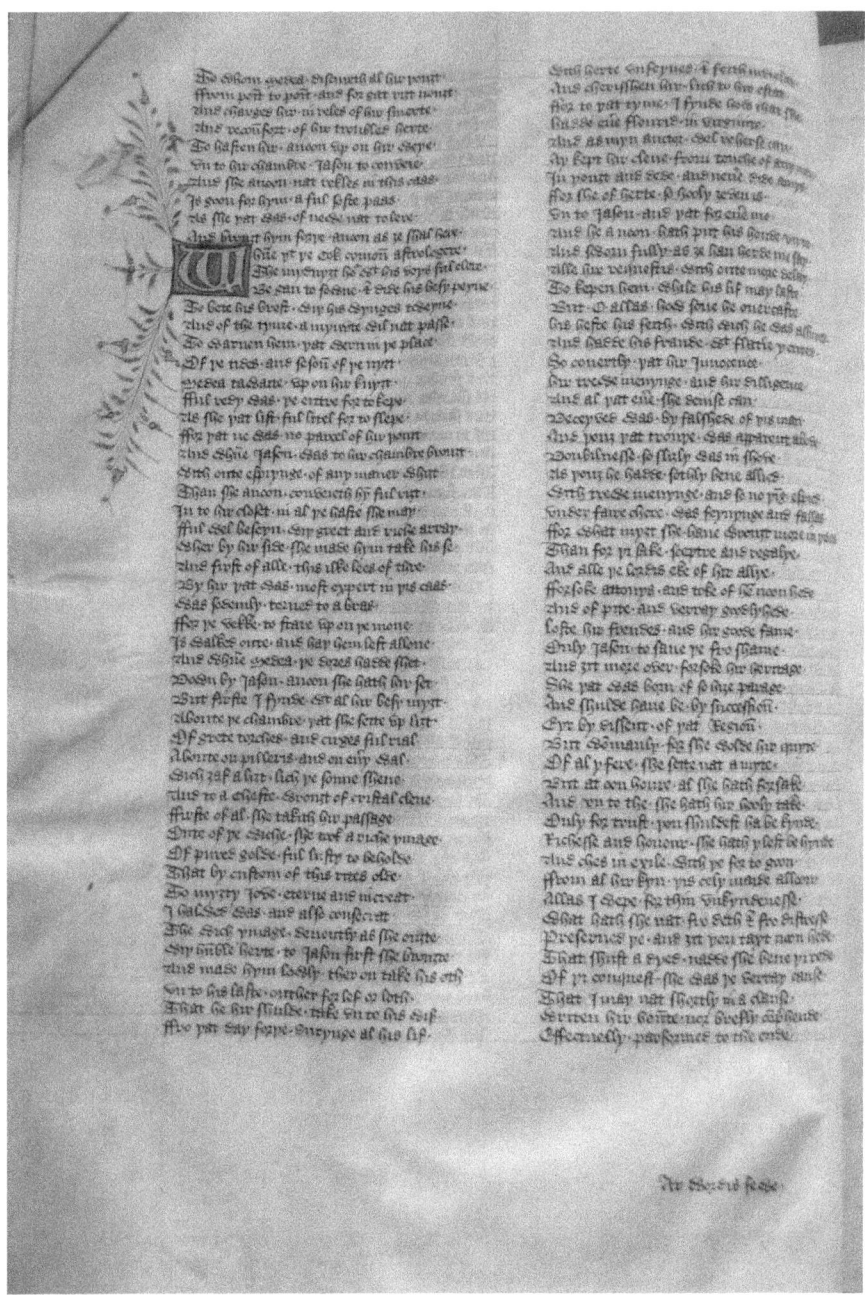

Figure 3. Bristol, Reference Library, MS 8, f. 8v; reproduced by permission of the Bristol Reference Library.

Figure 4. Manchester, John Rylands University Library, MS Eng. 98, f. 56r; reproduced by courtesy of the University Librarian and Director, The John Rylands University Library, The University of Manchester.

Julian of Norwich in the Fifteenth Century: The Material Record, Maternal Devotion, and London, Westminster Cathedral Treasury MS 4

VICKIE LARSEN

The relationship between reader and book has long shaped Western culture's imagination of what it means to be a "self." In a literate society, how we read—*why* we read—and what we think we are doing to ourselves in the process informs our notions of an "I" that is itself a kind of text, itself both object and subject of our reading and reflection.[1]

Jennifer Bryan compels us here to observe reading as a complex cognitive, emotional, and political practice, an event that is both personal and cultural.[2] She places the "relationship" between a reader and a book at the origins of Western humanism in that human beings define themselves as individuals, selves (as opposed to collectives, other types of beings, or objects), through their relationships with books. The artifacts of medieval reading that the Early Book Society examines, in conversations, conference panels, and here in *JEBS*, testify to the specific acts of reading through which those reading selves were formed or reformed. Our materially grounded work relies upon a notion of reading as a historically and culturally situated technology, a thick product of "taste," and a deeply personal act; and we discover again and again that all readers—the literary, the professional, the uncritical, the romantic, the aroused—have their pieties, those desires through which the self comes to be and know itself. The readers imagined by the manuscript I examine here read to improve themselves, to redirect their attention, to rearrange their desires, and to reshape themselves in relation to a divine being they took quite seriously, not just as a creative force in its own right, but as a locus for personal transformation and self-knowledge. They use this book, Westminster Cathedral Treasury MS 4, within a network of relationships between readers, ideas, emotions, biological experiences, and objects to reorganize their "selves," a product they clearly see as malleable and intensely connected to their embodied life experiences.

By all accounts, pious readers propped up the book trades in both manuscript and print during the fifteenth and sixteenth centuries, and their spiritual ambitions reshaped some of the products of the fourteenth-century literary "renaissance."[3] Here I focus on one of those products: the only medieval manuscript of Julian of Norwich's long text, *A Revelation of Love*, an extremely abridged fifteenth-century version of her book describing a series of visions she experienced during a serious illness in 1373. The text in Westminster Cathedral Treasury MS 4 has probably never been read in a medieval-literature classroom, and most scholars of Julian disregard it as an incomplete variant.[4] Nonetheless, within the history of reading, the Westminster text bears witness to the methodology some of Julian's readers used, the cognitive and emotional exercises their devotional reading facilitated, and *A Revelation*'s role in the formation of the late-medieval literate subject.

The Westminster version of Julian's text implicates gender in these late-medieval devotional readers' efforts to organize their interior selves. This version of Julian's text was compiled for readers who were compelled to read as women, either because they *were* women, or because reading *as a woman* was in itself a rewarding devotional practice. While I am not prepared here to posit a medieval theory of gendered interiority or even gendered spiritual ambition, I do claim maternity as the central hermeneutic that allows the Westminster version of Julian's text to harness gendered experiences and attachments and redirect them toward devotional ends. While the experience offered to the reader by Julian's full text is complex and nuanced, and the female body certainly abounds in the text, the Westminster variant places this body at its very center and suggests that medieval readers, like recent psychoanalytic critics of Julian's text, saw the reproductive female body as a space wherein psychodevotional work could reorganize the self.

Westminster Cathedral Treasury MS 4 offers little hard evidence of its provenance. It is a late fifteenth- or early sixteenth-century pocket-sized florilegium, a collection of abridged texts, in a mid-fifteenth-century east Midlands dialect.[5] A single professional scribe working in the London area wrote out its four texts.[6] The book opens with two Psalm commentaries frequently attributed to Walter Hilton, *Qui habitat* and *Bonum est* (Psalms 90/91 and 91/92), followed by selections from Hilton's *Scale of Perfection* and the selections from the long version of Julian's *Revelation* (occupying folios 72v–112r).[7] Edmund Colledge and James Walsh take the fifty-year span between the dialect of the texts in the Westminster manuscript and its scribal hand as an indication that all four abridged texts were composed earlier and further north and were subsequently transcribed into this manuscript, which implies that this variant of the *Revelation* circulated in at least two manuscripts in at least two geographical regions. Hugh Kempster has argued convincingly for the textual independence of the Westminster variant within Julian's larger manuscript tradition, lending substance to the notion that this variant calls for analysis as a coherent vehicle for Julian's text.[8] The compiler is certainly a medieval reader at work, selecting passages from various chapters and weaving them together into a new text, and I focus primarily on this reader, despite the presence of other, later readers in the margins. The marginalia testify to a small group of seventeenth-century readers who do not share the compiler's agenda (or Julian's) and use their commentary to reconnect this text to ecclesiastical sacramental practices.[9]

What project did this compiler take on? Marleen Cré rightly encourages us to consider the entire Westminster manuscript as a unified collection that is concentrated on a single theme: contemplation.[10] As Cré reads it, the manuscript's texts converse with one another on the subject of "contemplation defined in terms of enclosure and ascent played out in the metaphors of Psalms 90.2, 90.3 and 90.9, as well as in sensory terms (seeing, being shown, feeling.)"[11] In order to participate in this conversation, the compiler excises most of Julian's text and narrows its sweeping scope. The compiler omits nearly all of Julian's autobiographical references, the specific content of most of her visions, and the interior narrative that links the visions to her analysis.

The resulting text is largely a theological meditation, barely recognizable as the narrative of Julian's experience. Julian's inclination to return to the subjects of sin and suffering are all but gone in the Westminster variant in which her text becomes a 707-line treatise that examines just two interdependent subjects: seeing oneself in relation to a divine creator and contemplating the nature of maternity.

Maternal and contemplative ambitions come together in this text to reinforce and extend one another. The Westminster treatise establishes a relationship between mothering and contemplative prayer such that the experiences of the maternal body (gestation, birth, breast-feeding), the physical acts of mothers' work (bodily caregiving), and the set of relationships offered by it (reciprocal love relationships based upon trust and communication) become mechanisms for a form of contemplative piety useful to readers for whom maternity could function as a spiritual heuristic device. It is unclear whether the Westminster adaptation of Julian's text was produced or used by women who had maternal experiences, or if it simply implies its relevance to such readers by reclaiming and redirecting maternal experiences to shape a literate devotional self.

Liz Herbert McAvoy argued in 1998 that: "far from being simply an aspect of Julian's theology or a theoretical idea used as an analogy to explicate theological insight, Julian's perception of motherhood becomes the matrix out of which develops a means of access to the divine."[12] In her more recent work, McAvoy uses the critical discourse of psychoanalysis to map that matrix onto the "pre-symbolic site of unity which underpins all human existence."[13] Quoting Julia Kristeva, McAvoy claims that maternity in Julian's short and long texts offers a:

> 'realm which does not reduce the subject to one of understanding, but instead opens up within the subject this other scene of pre-symbolic functions.' It is, therefore, a specifically female space since it draws upon the (unremembered but always latent) lost union with the mother and (again recalling the there-and-not-there of Julian's encounter), 'is no more than the place where the subject is both generated and negated.'[14]

For McAvoy, Julian structures her entire long and short texts around this embedded maternal body, a heuristic device that allows Julian to use a body to convey meaning where language would fail. McAvoy reads Julian's long and short texts as discourses that occur within the Kristevan semiotic *chora*, that prediscursive space of primary unity with the mother.[15]

The compiler of the Westminster version emphasizes the effect McAvoy examines and allows other material to drop away so that what remains is organized by the maternal in its logic, its structure, and its language. Importantly, the Westminster version omits Julian's expansive and detailed opening vision of the Passion and begins with a description of a newly pregnant Mary, moments after the Annunciation, exuding the "wisdom," "trewthe," and humility that her new condition has taught her (ll. 1–75).[16] The compiler then turns quickly to the subject of prayer, pulling excerpts from twelve chapters of Julian's long version to urge readers to become less guarded in their communication with their God and to engage in affective devotion (ll. 76–531). This section is filled with the language and imagery of pregnancy and birth, and asserts that shame and spiritual doubt cripple the efforts of humans (figured as children) to communicate with their creator (figured as a mother). The final section (ll. 532–707) returns to the subjects of shame and doubt to develop and resolve the difficulties they pose by using Julian's treatment of Christ as a mother.

Throughout all three sections, the physical work and emotional attachments of motherhood are used to figure a complex array of relationships: of God and creation, of Christ within the Trinity, and of the church and its members. This focus on motherhood comes, of course, from Julian's original, as McAvoy and others have noted, but the Westminster compiler gives it a more precise meaning by changing Julian's original text into a much shorter treatise on prayer, suggesting that maternity contains a kind of legible knowledge that can be called upon to meet contemplative goals, to approach and communicate with God.[17]

The nexus of motherhood and prayer is immediately visible in the opening passage of the Westminster version of *A Revelation*, in which the compiler, mirroring the popular Hours of the Virgin in Books of Hours, begins with a description of the Annunciation. Here, however, we have a description of Mary's soul rather than the visual image of her body that typically opens matins, the first of the Little Hours.[18] The compiler, seemingly uninterested in Julian as an author, or in her special experience and status, or in her Christocentric devotional practices, passes over the opening she uses in the long version of the *Revelation*, "This is a revelation of love that Jhesu Christ our endles blisse, made in sixteen shewinges," and begins instead with the claim that "Oure gracious and goode lorde God shewed me in party the wisdom and the trewthe of the soule of oure blessed Lady, Saynt Mary"[19] (see fig. 1). While the original opening foregrounds the centrality of the Passion in the source text, the opening of the Westminster version, which introduces the incompletely elided narrator "me," implies that the subject of the showings was not Christ at all, but Mary, in particular the qualities of "wisdom and trewthe" that characterize her from the initial moments of her pregnancy. Within the first seven lines, this version twice declares that "her maker . . . wolde be borne of her," emphasizing the paradox produced by the primary unity between Christ and Mary—both are creator and created.[20]

Implicating Mary's body in this paradox and describing it through abstract qualities releases the reader from constrained social definitions of the body and its relation with the divine. The opening in the Westminster text encourages an allegorical reading of the gestating body and integrates the body of the pregnant self with its interiority and with the divine. A pregnant Mary engaged in the work of gestating the Christian narrative appears to the unnamed speaker not in the form of a physical body but as the embodiment of "wisdom" and "trewthe" that define Mary's pregnancy and control Westminster's opening image.

The compiler, always a careful reader of the source text, jumps in line 11 from the fourth chapter of Julian's long version to the seventh, pursuing these two qualities: "This wysedom and trewth made her to beholde her God so gret, so hygh, so mighty, and so good, that the gretenes and the nobilte and beholdyng of God fulfylled her of reverent dred."[21] The qualities associated with her pregnancy allow her to "beholde her God" and produce in her an affective response that Julian calls "reverent dred." Passing over so much of Julian's original opening chapters allows the compiler to offer this image of pregnancy as a protocol for reading the remainder of the text. The compiler returns to the qualities of "wisdom and trewthe" again four hundred lines later, at a point where Julian assigns them to "mannys soule" as a "creature in God," saying that "Trewthe seeth God, and wysedom beholdith God, and of thees two commyth the thyrd, and that is marveylous holi delyte in God, which is love."[22] In other words, the maternal body of Mary and "mannys soule," described as wise and true, will engender a third quality—the knowledge of love.

In the case of Mary, "delyte in God" is glossed as the "reverent dred" that emerges when she enters into a relationship with a deity by way of her pregnancy. The compiler pursues this "reverent dred" or "knowledge of love" to its endpoint in Julian's text, including her statement that "clerenes and clennes of trowth and wysedom makith hym to se and to be knowen that he us made for love, in which love God endelesly kepith hym."[23] The wisdom and truth offered by entering into a relationship with the deity will make available knowledge of what humans are "made for" and how their creator relates to them as creations. Here in the opening, as elsewhere, we find the Westminster compiler stringing together passages from the long version to depict maternal experiences as a form of self-awareness through which the body can not only learn of itself as a created being but also internalize the desires of its creator and be reshaped, re-created, by the knowledge of its own purpose in a larger narrative.

In itself, opening with a Marian image is not especially surprising, given the concentration on Mary in late-medieval devotion, but the specific nature of this invocation sets it apart from other available Marian images. Mary is described in the Westminster version's opening as an essentially maternal figure, but she resembles neither the "simple maiden and a meeke, yong of age, a little waxen above a child," from Julian's fourth chapter, nor the traditional *mater dolorosa* or *stabat juxta Christi crucem* from the hymns that focus on Mary's purity and suffering.[24] That weeping mother portrayed in late-medieval paintings, manuscripts, and sculptures identifies so completely with her son that her suffering becomes a portal for believers seeking a heightened emotional response to the Passion, one that is characterized by grief at the maternal loss of the child. As a model of motherhood, the *mater dolorosa* is a site of self-denial, sacrifice, and suffering. Her child suffers and she is powerless, unable to intervene or control her own role as witness to his drama. Middle English Marian lyrics employ this image, in this case, in conversation with her son:

[Mary] Sune, wat sal me to rede?
Thi pine pined me to dede:
Let me deyn thee biforen.

[Jesus] Moder, mitarst this mith leren
Wat pine tholen that children beren,
Wat sorwe haven that child forgon.

[Mary] Sune, y wot y kan thee tellen
Bute it be the pine of helle
More sorwe ne woth y non.[25]

[Mary] Son, what shall I do?
Your pain pains me to death:
Let me die before you.

[Jesus] Mother, first you must learn
What pain suffer those who children bear,
And what sorrow they have who children lose.

[Mary] Son, I know I can tell you
Unless it is the pain from hell,
More sorrow have I never known.

Here Christ extends the role of suffering to encompass all mothers, asserting that suffering is the *sine qua non* of motherhood ("Wat pine tholen that children beren"), an assertion that Mary then endorses when she says, "Sune, y wot y kan thee tellen." In this woman, motherhood and pain are aesthetically combined to create an image of beautiful and desirable suffering. Readers can affiliate with Mary and engage in a form of empathetic suffering grounded in a real knowledge of the nature of maternal love and loss and a desire to translate that emotional power into religious devotion. The Westminster version of Julian's text replaces this suffering mother with one who is primarily wise, true, and humble but also fundamentally happy, and thus offers a competing notion of religiously inscribed motherhood for its readers. This vision of Mary offers readers an alternative emotional hook; rather than viewing motherhood as an impediment to contemplation and rather than allying themselves with the mother who witnesses her child's gruesome execution, readers are invited to ally themselves with her as she discovers her pregnancy, filled with awe at the unity between herself and her creator and with humility at the role her body will play. This vision of the body and its physical and social functions as acceptable and lovable to the divine and as a structure that could be a *tool* rather than an *impediment* to the reader's development of a contemplative self preoccupies the Westminster version of Julian's text, as we see below.

Bryan, in her recent book-length treatment of devotional reading, argues that late-medieval devotional readers used their texts as mirrors to see themselves and to perform intentional work on their interior realms, to perform individual self-help by seeing themselves in and against their devotional objects, "first as a habit of reading and then as a habit of mind."[26] Bryan's work illustrates the history of devotional reading as a specialized technology through which readers were able to "map the boundaries of the heart and script the affective life of the soul, amplifying and reorienting desire through the passionate rhetoric of devotional meditation."[27] She devotes a full chapter to the cognitive and emotional experience offered to readers of Julian's long text. The first half of Julian's full text places the reader in direct contact with ghastly images of the destruction of Christ's body, bleeding, drying up, crusting over, crumbling. Bryan argues that Julian's juxtaposition of very vivid images of Christ's Passion with treatments of sin and motherhood, particularly with the scene of Mary at the Annunciation, shows Julian, our model reader, trying to unravel "the problem of the Passion ... that is of the soul's core understanding of itself."[28] For Bryan, the experience of reading Julian is one that forces the reader to weigh the option of coming to "understand itself in relation to a 'seeing' of the Passion, how it is disciplined and developed through pain and loss, how it understands its own separateness and individuality," against the self-envisioning available in the rich image of the pregnant Mary, containing within herself so much more than she is and seeing herself humbled in the sight of her creator and her creation.[29] Bryan demonstrates that Julian takes up a deep conflict within the available methods of self-envisioning in late-medieval devotional reading and thought.

Bryan focuses on Julian as a devotional reader and writer more so than the experience her text offers its readers. For Bryan, Julian's long text testifies to the psychodevotional work of its own creation and presumably to the experience it makes available for its readers. However, only two medieval manuscripts of Julian's text have survived, and neither of them offers readers the experience Bryan describes. British Library Additional MS 37790 contains an earlier, shorter version of her text, and the Westminster manuscript contains this severely abridged version. Julian's full text is available only in seventeenth-century manuscripts produced by English Catholic women who left England to pursue the religious life in a Benedictine convent in Cambrai, Flanders (now in France).[30] The emergence of two distinct seventeenth-century manuscripts of Julian's full text from the English continental foundations implies the existence of at least two exemplars, but scholars have no medieval manuscript to which we can link the readers Bryan imagines for Julian.[31] It should be clear that my purpose is not to undermine Bryan's examination of the complex experience available to readers of the full text but to amplify her analysis by contrasting it to an alternate experience we find in the material record. The actual readers whose book we can examine have neither the experience that Bryan describes nor that which Julian created.

The critical distinction between reading Julian's full text and reading the Westminster version is the absence of the Passion entirely. If it is true, as Bryan claims, that Julian ultimately rejects the type of self-formation that occurs through Passion suffering, it is as if the Westminster compiler obliges Julian by eliminating it, along with the bulk of Julian's treatments of sin, guilt, and salvation.[32] A process of organizing the self through trauma, abandonment, and desire for return is unavailable in the Westminster version of *A Revelation*; the experience on offer instead is one of envisioning the self as always enclosed within, served by, or united with, a loving maternal creator.

The Westminster text appropriates the work of the maternal body by assigning to the physiological aspect of mothering a typological relationship to the work of God, mapping the function of God onto the female body. For instance, in a vivid passage taken from chapter 24 of the long version, Julian is invited to enter Christ's womb through his side wound:

> Also with glad chere oure lord loked into his syde and behelde, enjoyenge. And with his swete lokynge he ledde furthe the understondyng of his creaturys by the same wounde into his side, withyn. And there he shewed a feyre, delectable place, and large inow for all mankynde that shall be sauf to reste in pees and love. And therwith he brought to mynde his dereworthy blod and his precious water whiche he lett poure all oute for love.[33]

Here Christ's habitable body is a place where one is "sauf to reste in pees and love" and where blood and water pour out "for love." These associations differ markedly from medieval maternal discourses in which the body in birth is abject or unruly, such as those Wendy Harding discusses from Margery Kempe's *Book*, in which birth is a process so violent that at times mothers were put in restraints, or those Gail Gibson finds in medieval dramas in which birth is an "obscene" event that can only take place offstage and without its messy blood and water.[34] While birth was surrounded by rituals of abjection, including a period of postpartum confinement during which mothers remained in seclusion for forty days (forty-six if they gave birth to a girl) and were not permitted to enter a church until their purification or "churching" ceremony at the end of that period, the Westminster variant, following Julian's original but intensifying the effect through compaction, portrays birth as a cleansing process.[35] Some four hundred lines after this passage, the compiler returns to the blood and water of birth to depict them as purifying and salvific, declaring Christ's "derewothy blode and preciouse water it is plenteous to make us feyre and clene."[36]

The maternal body, mapped onto Christ, is described in Westminster's selections as a willing agent in a peaceful birthing, a notion that the compiler continues to develop in the closing with several additional images of the deity engaged in the physiological aspects of mothering: the Trinity enclosing mankind; the concentric wombs of Christ, humans, and God; and Christ birthing and breast-feeding.[37] These physiological images call attention to the visible aspects of birth that were commonly shielded from view, advertising the uterus as a "feyre, delectable place" and the blood and water of birth as an expression of love. The rejection of cultural prohibitions regarding the birthing body allows this text to validate maternal physiology and experience and convert them into mechanisms of devotion. For the devotional reader, Westminster reconciles the inner self, the outer self, and the larger social role of women within the family and the community. Because "the world" and pious interiority were often depicted as opposing forces, Westminster's validation of mothering (a biological, social, and cultural practice) relieves the tension between the life of devotion and a life in the world.

The Westminster version of Julian's *Revelation* offers readers the interrelated terms *lykenesse* and *kynde* to ground their devotional practices. Julian uses these terms to compare the physical and social effects of reproduction and creation, a relationship that is particularly useful to the Westminster compiler. Julian maps creation onto birth through the deeply theological notion of a God who created humans in his own likeness, who has reproduced himself in kind. The compiler includes passages in which God's relationship with his creations emerges from their likeness to him, and thus he attends to humans "for love of the soule that he hath made to hys owne lyknes."[38] This creation contract is based upon the obligations related to reproduction: the creation of another in one's likeness, the production of kind or kin, initiates a unique set of commitments. The Westminster version depicts the relationship established by birth as the beginning of a continuous reciprocal relationship in which mothering is what Julian calls "service":

> We be brought ayen, by the moderhed of mercy and grace, into oure kyndely stede, where that we were made by the moderhed of kynde love, whiche kynde love that never levith us. Oure kynde moder, oure gracious moder, for he wolde all wholly become our moder in all thing, he toke the grounde of his werke full lowe and full myldely in the maydens wombe, takyng fleshe of her, redy in our pore fleshe, hymselfe to do the servyce and the office of moderhed in all thyng. The moders servyce is nereste, redieste and sureste.[39]

Playing upon the dual and related uses of "kind" in Middle English as both "kin" and that behavior which pertains to kin—"kindness"—Julian sets forth the nature of the maternal contract. Within Mary's pregnant body, Christ finds his lifework as divine mother to all creatures. He is born as a mother by a mother, and that process takes place through physical reproduction. The line in which a maternal Christ is united to his mother in kind ("takying fleshe of her") is unique to the Westminster version and extends the metaphorical act of taking the "grounde of his werke ... in the meydens wombe" by adding a physical aspect to his production. "The moders servyce" points to the social obligations incurred within relationships of "lykenesse" and "kynde" as distinct from but extending the physiological function that initiates them. By playing out the fullness of these two words, the Westminster text invites readers to envision familial contracts as a way of gaining perspective into divine contracts so that contemplation could use family life for spiritual ends.

In the Westminster version, the gendered work of tending to children, like the physiological work of bearing them, allows motherhood to offer an understanding of God's relationship with humans, but Westminster also positions mothers as mediators within that relationship. In one of Julian's more complex and innovative theological assertions, and one that this version pursues eagerly, she claims that God's relationship with humans is not only similar to mothering but occurs by means of it, since "It is he that dothe it in the creature by whom that it is done."[40] Mothers facilitate and sustain the relationship that is mandated by "lykenesse" on behalf of themselves and on behalf of God. The validation of motherhood redefines the maternal body and reassigns the labor associated with mothering by positioning it both as a metaphor for the creator and as creation's primary physiological and social mechanism. In psychoanalytic terms, for Julian, the primary unity with the mother is a primary unity with the divine Other and is therefore the site to which all mystical experiences return.

After establishing a typological relationship between motherhood and creation, Julian pursues that relationship through the most intimate of human interactions, a parent's attention to a child's basic bodily functions. Julian and the Westminster compiler map God's response to the most basic needs of his creatures, articulated as the "simplest office that longith to our body," onto a parent's response to the bodily needs of her child.[41] Julian uses the motherly work of physical caregiving as a rhetorical tool to explain to her readers how God views the bodies of his creations. Quite early in the text, the compiler selects an uncomfortably intimate physical passage from chapter 6 of the long version (one that even the Sloane 2499 manuscript of the "complete" text omits):

> A man goeth upryght, and the soule [food] of his bodi is sperd [closed] as a purse ful feyre. And when it is tyme of his necessary, it is opened and sperd ayen well honestely. And that is he that doth this; he shewyth that he seeth, he commyth downe to us, to the lowest party of our nede, for he hath no dispyte of that that he hath made, nether he hath no disdeyne to serve us at the symplest office that longith to our body in kynde, for love of the soule that he hath made to hys owne lykenes.[42]

The *Middle English Dictionary* indicates that "his necessary" and "our nede" are late-medieval euphemisms for the evacuation of the bowels or bladder. If "soule" is read literally as "food" here, as Colledge and Walsh as well as Watson and Jenkins convincingly posit, this line becomes much clearer: a man walks upright and his food is hidden as in a beautiful purse; when the time comes for him to relieve himself of it, the purse is opened and then closed again quite efficiently.[43] Julian's point here is that God is invested in the human body and is interested even in the events of the toilet precisely because of his role as *artifex* in relation to human bodies ("for love of the soule that he hath made to hys owne lykene").

In the discussion above, I omit the quotation marks that Watson and Jenkins insert around the phrase "He commyth downe to us, to the lowest party of our need" because they create an editorial distinction regarding the meaning of the word "seeth" that the Westminster manuscript does not justify. The quotation marks force a reading in which God *says* that he "commyth downe to us," a reading in which "seeth" is a form of the Middle English verb "seien," which is "to say." While the seventeenth-century Sloane manuscript omits the entire passage, and the phrasing in the Paris manuscript supports Watson and Jenkins' reading of "seeth" as "says," the Westminster manuscript uses the construction "he shewyth that he seeth, he commyth downe to us," which offers a reading in which God *sees* when he "commyth downe to us."⁴⁴ This phrasing invokes the Middle English verb "sen," or "to see," and suggests that God watches people on the toilet. The Westminster version points to the absence of privacy around toiletry that characterizes parenting, suggesting that God's interest in human bodies resembles that of a mother changing diapers and presiding over potty time. The discomfort caused by this intimate bodily surveillance offers the reader a space within which he or she can contemplatively cross over the notion of the body as an obstacle to spiritual ambition.

The hurdle associated with being seen "in one's necessary" is, of course, shame. Bodily shame, emerging from human frailty and need, is potentially silencing, preventing the contemplative prayer Julian advocates. In the Westminster version, the toilet, watched over by a compassionate and helpful mother, is the site where that shame is overcome. Grounded in the knowledge that the maker has "no dispyte of that that he hath made" and moreover feels no "disdeyne to serve us at the symplest office that longith to our body in kynde," the reader is invited to enter *intact* into a relationship with his or her maker. The body, even in the presence of its own abject feces, is not available as an agent of separation from the deity but binds the self to its maker in a primal unity. Coming to terms with the body and its functions and frailties is a devotional process of accepting one's humanity in the presence of a deity, a knowledge analogous to that which Mary gains when, through the metaphysical event immediately preceding the opening of this text, she realizes her stature in relation to her deity. The Westminster version endorses and facilitates this contemplative project by incorporating Julian's most fundamental quotation from a maternal God, "I am grounde of thi besekyng," in which God claims responsibility for human need by claiming to have created it, replacing shame in his presence with humility.⁴⁵ The compiler returns to the topic of abjection five hundred lines later, in a passage in which a child, in the midst of its shame, runs to its mother:

> For when it is diseasid or adred, than yt rennynth hastily to the moder. And yf may do no more, it cryeth on the modir for helpe with all the myghtis. So wyll our lorde that we do as a meke chylde, sayeng thus: "My kind moder, my gracious modyr, my dereworthy moder, have mercy on

me. I have made myselfe foule and unlyke to the, and I ne
may ne can amende yt, but with thyne helpe and grace."[46]

This passage compares the praying subject to a "fouled" child who appears at the foot of her mother because she, as Julian goes on to say, "trustith to the love of the moder in well and in wo."[47] It is not the reproductive body of the mother that Julian and the Westminster compiler use to encourage the reader to give voice to human frailty and need, but its extension, the service work of mothering, the "swete gracious handis of our modyr" that "be redy and dilygent about us."[48] The attentive work of the mother's hands about the body of the child both is and imagines the position of God in relation to his creatures. The fouled child voices an automatic and unscripted plea ("it cryeth on the modir for helpe") by which she fulfills her role in reciprocal relationship with both her mother and God, using a form of prayer that is organized by those relationships. Her honest description of her abjection, figured as the loss of likeness, "unlyke to the," and her request for help reinforces her mother's commitment to her and completes the circle of reciprocity. Speaking of and through human need redefines bodily functions and even bodily abjection as devotional opportunities through which the reader is reminded that the view one has of the self as "foule" is not shared by the mother/creator and should not impede devotional progress but rather should produce communication.

Because of its focus on prayer, the Westminster version emphasizes the communicative aspect of the relationship between God and his creatures and, by extension, mothers and their children. But it does not foreground speaking or even piety as essential maternal skills, but rather listening. The Westminster version asserts that the maternal qualities of God make him an approachable and inviting listener, a figure with whom a relationship built on honest communication is both automatic and desirable, saying, "Ful glad and mery is our lord God of our prayer; he lokith theraftir and he wolde have it. For with his grace it makith us lyke to hymselfe in condicion as we be in kynde."[49] The relationship between God and humans, initially based upon their "lyke[ness]" to him in "kynde," is extended through reciprocal communicative acts: prayer and response. The compiler includes a short passage from chapter 41 of the long version that affirms the importance of listening in reciprocal relationships: "But yet ofte tymis our truste is not full, for we be not sure that God heryth us, as we thynke, for oure unworthynes and for that we fele nothing. For we be as bareyne and as drye often tymes aftir oure prayer as we were before."[50] Julian employs the similes "bareyne" and "drye" to describe the experience of speaking in the absence of an attentive listener, an impediment to which the Westminster text offers the image of a fertile God who not only listens to prayer but claims responsibility for the needs it expresses. Julian quotes God as saying, "I make the to wyll yt," which she explains as "our lord God is grounde hymselfe of whom our prayers spryngthith." Julian attributes to God a maternal ear and interest in the prayer of his creations. The version in the Westminster manuscript establishes this attentive, nonjudgmental, and maternal God to encourage readers to speak freely in order to complete the relationship between themselves and God that begins with creation and continues with the daily service that God performs. In so doing, this text offers an alternative to negative attitudes toward women's speech. For example, the *Book to a Mother*, a late fourteenth-century text for lay readers, disparages women's speech along with their sexual desire and avarice, saying, "ne se vanitiees, ne telle ne here idel tales, ne to speke veine words, ne to have lusting and likinges and worldi worshupes."[51] While the *Book to a Mother* seeks to silence female readers, the Westminster Julian redeems female speech by validating the language that emerges within relationships in which "prayer and . . . truste be both alyke large."[52] The logic of this version's argument is that reading and contemplating as a woman will allow readers to establish rewarding relationships between themselves and God as a result of their ability to conceptualize God as a mother who attentively listens to her offspring and also to call up the affective attachments that underlie those services. This "familiar" relationship is present in the long version of Julian's text, but is complicated by her concentration on other issues such as sin, suffering, and redemption and does not emerge as a singular argument in the way that it does in the Westminster version. The compiler of Westminster, in contrast, condenses this source material using motherhood as a way of imagining mystical union.

Bryan suspects that "Julian feels that the interiorizing abjection fostered by private devotional models of the Passion is dangerous and excessive, threatening to cut the beholder off from the very mercy he seeks."[53] The

Westminster version does not allow the reader to consider this form of devotion, but advocates and supports a kinder, gentler form of contemplative prayer for readers who can access both maternal and spiritual ambition. Neither does it suggest the use of intermediaries such as saints or confessors or physical rituals like fasting; instead, it instructs its readers in direct communication with a deity who is depicted as "the fyrste resceyver" of prayer, which he accepts "right thankefully and hyghly enjoyeth."[54] The form of prayer encouraged here is frequent, original, and honest; it voices gratitude, praise, and desire. But perhaps most important, the prayer advanced by the Westminster version has contemplative goals: "And this by his swete grace shall we in oure owne meke contynuyng prayer, [come] unto hym now in this lyf by many prevey touchynges of swete gostly sytis and felying, mesured to us as our symplenes may beer it."[55] Through "contynuyng prayer," "we," the author and reader, aspire to encounter the deity "in this lyf" through sensations and sightings. This version is quite clear in the contemplative (or mystical) nature of its methods, declaring that "it is God's wil that we seke into the beholdyng of hym, for by that shall he shewe us hymselfe of his speciall grace when he wyll."[56] It comes as no surprise, given the Westminster compiler's stated intentions, that Colledge and Walsh take it as an instruction manual for professional contemplatives and that Kempster sees it as a text for those living the "mixed life," a pseudo-monastic lifestyle observed within the homes of laity.[57] The contemplative speaker, Julian herself, and her personal visionary experience may have been conspicuously elided by the Westminster compiler, but Julian continues to instruct her readers in contemplative prayer and to direct them toward it by way of the maternal body and the work of mothering.

Despite frequently positioning the reader in the role of a child in relation to God, the rhetorical success of the Westminster version relies upon the reader's understanding, not of childhood, but of motherhood. The closing section takes from Julian's long version the bulk of the passages in which Julian figures God and the Church as mothers. The text positions the reader as the child in his or her relationship to God and to the Church, but it describes the dynamic of that relationship from the perspective of the mother: "In oure goostly furthbryngyng . . . [Christ] kendelyth oure undirstondyng, he addith oure weyes, he esyth oure consciens, he comfortith oure soule, he lyghtith our hart and yevyth us, in party, knowing and louyng in his blessed godhed."⁵⁸ A birthing Christ ("furthbryngyng") adopts the maternal responsibilities of teaching, guiding, easing, comforting, gladdening, and loving and, as in much of the text, the reader is positioned as the child who receives such parenting. Nonetheless, in a rhetorically complex maneuver, the reader's perspective on the parenting relationship is assumed to be that of the mother; as an inventory of maternal nurturing behaviors, this list of Christ's services is a litany of a mother's ideals rather than a child's. The stable and uninterrupted good mothering that features in this passage and throughout the Westminster text is not an ideal that has any real force for children, who always hope their mothers are good ones but do not have access to the detailed inventory of what that entails. Perceiving motherhood as a stable and continuously nurturing function is neither a certainty nor an ambition for the child. The Westminster version proposes that if the contract of "kinde" organizes the interaction between mother and child, the "kyndely chylde despeyryth not of the moders love, and kyndely the childe presumyth not of itself, kyndly the chylde lovyth the moder and each of them both the other."⁵⁹ Children do not conceive of themselves as presumptuous ("presumyth . . . of itself") when they "despeyryth" of their mothers love by refusing to return it. This is a mother's perspective on mothering, a conceptualization of the parenting relationship in which mothers are bound by a commitment to serve while children may or may not reciprocate. In this closing passage, the Westminster version elevates the maternal contract and allows it to function as a typologically rich site for conceiving of God as sharing in a similar contract with the reader. It remains unclear who the intended or actual readers of the Westminster manuscript were. Kempster argues that the Westminster variant is a sterilized abridgement censored by a male compiler for an audience of female laity living the mixed life, and Cré speculates that Westminster's readers might have been enclosed monks or nuns.⁶⁰ The popularity of devotional reading during the fifteenth century motivated writers, compilers, and translators to produce and adapt religious texts for an increasingly diverse audience. Anne Dutton, Felicity Riddy, Nicole Rice, and others have found evidence of a circuit wherein vernacular religious texts were produced, consumed, and circulated by way of familial and spiritual relationships between enclosed professional religious and pious laity.⁶¹ As scholars study these relationships and the books they produced, it has become counterproductive to create distinctions between the reading practices of the professional religious and those of the laity. As Bryan notes, "some of these readers were inside the cloister and some of them were outside, but their devotional reading blurred traditional boundaries between the active and contemplative lives."⁶² Like Bryan, I am compelled to turn away from what kind of people these readers were to what has become a more compelling set of questions regarding reading at the close of the Middle Ages: What were the cognitive and emotional procedures that governed all of this pious reading? If the final decades of the Middle Ages were ones when popular reading took a pious turn, where were its hooks and rewards?

The near absence of fathers, husbands, and clergy (the last of whom figure at least fleetingly in Julian's long and short texts, and the first of whom appear throughout in images of God the Father) in this version frees it to construct an image of a powerful female body engaged in the work of reproduction and service, not under kinship and lineage mandates or within a paternalist church but as an autonomous figure. Medieval narratives are prone to feature mothers who are compelled to prove their fidelity and produce heirs. Consider Griselda in Chaucer's "Clerk's Tale," who is married to Walter solely to provide him with an heir. He then takes her children from her, claiming to have killed them in order to test her allegiance to him. Like Griselda, the mother in the romance *Lay le Freine*, who must abandon one of her twin daughters in order to protect her sexual fidelity, is bound by the paternal codes that structure her role in the family. Even parish priests involved themselves in mothering decisions. A handbook for parish priests in the Bodleian Library instructs priests to warn their parishioners against allowing their children in their beds, swaddling them, or leaving them unattended.⁶³ In these and other medieval discourses, procreation and parenting take place under the intense pressure and constant surveillance of husbands who view wives and children as property to be managed and clergy who view mothers as impure, unskilled, and careless. The Westminster version of Julian's text, however, is one in which mothers are depicted as operating without those patriarchal controls. Permission to speak, in prayer or otherwise, is not granted by husbands or earned through suffering but emerges from knowledge of compassionate listening, physical labor, and their centrality to reciprocal relationships.

McAvoy uses Amy Hollywood's psychoanalytic language to describe the power of this deified maternal force to "render it possible that 'endless, ceaseless, illimitable desire might be thought and lived outside of the phallic law of [female] impotence.'"[64] The Westminster variation of Julian's text seems to isolate the conflation of subjects that McAvoy describes, a conflation that, for her, "points towards the unity of a mystical encounter with God in which the subject is endlessly generated, defined, relinquished and negated, in which all and nothing is possible."[65] McAvoy uses Julian's full text to reject the misogynist fetishization of the phallus that characterizes the psychoanalytic mode. The rich symbolism of the mother and maternity—in Julian's full text more generally and in the Westminster variant more specifically—generates, defines, relinquishes, and negates the reading self. The absence of the phallus opens up a space for what McAvoy calls an "extra-Symbolic expression of fully embodied female practices."[66] In other words, the power of the procreative body dominates Julian's text, and in particular the Westminster version, such that no space remains for lack and there is no need for masculinized configurations of power.

As a result of its specialized methodology, the Westminster version of Julian's *Revelation* does not contain the fullness of what Bryan describes as Julian's "paradigms of reflection—of divine surveillance and human beholding, of self-scrutiny and discipline—in order to test their limits, running them through various permutations to see whether they cannot be transformed into redeeming and connective rather than isolating and potentially despairing configurations."[67] This manuscript's readers do not see the complex acts of considering and rejecting, transforming or accepting that make up Julian's devotional self-formation, but they see their results. The manuscript sets forth a model of devotion that is wholly "connective" in that it connects the reader to the divine and shapes a devotional self by way of the biological and social roles of the body and the expenditure of time and energy in "fully embodied" familial roles and community pursuits. The Westminster compiler may rob his or her readers of the opportunity to consider deeply the discipline available in devotion to the Passion, but in exchange he or she reclaims the maternal body and mothers' work as symbolically powerful agents of life-giving and life-sustaining biological and social practices and employs them to both describe and be contemplative experiences that lay or enclosed practitioners with maternal experiences or ambitions could use in the formation and reformation of their reading selves.

The Westminster manuscript was owned in the late sixteenth century by Frances Lowe, who inscribed the final page with the message, "My selfe wif be once and forever of all bene." This declaration defining herself as a wife first is followed by a series of signatures in the same hand, first, presumably, her husband's, "Thomas Lowe," four times, and then her own twice, using alternate spellings, "Frances" and "Frauncis." Perhaps the type of devotional practice this book offers, shared by the professional religious and pious laity during the fifteenth century, also appealed to the as-yet-unknown Mrs. Lowe after the Reformation. We might hope that she found this variant of Julian's *A Revelation of Love* a useful guide to making the daily work of mothering a source of "connective" spiritual knowledge and contemplative practice and a mirror through which she could refine her notion of who "Frances" or "Frauncis" was.

University of Michigan-Flint

Acknowledgments

My warmest thanks to Dr. Tony Trowels and Westminster Abbey for generously assisting me in examining and procuring images of Westminster Cathedral Treasury, MS 4; Canon Christopher Tuckwell at Westminster Cathedral for allowing an image from the manuscript to be published here; and the T. Anne Cleary International Dissertation Research Fellowship at the University of Iowa for partly funding my archival work for this project.

NOTES

1. Jennifer Bryan, *Looking Inward: Devotional Reading and the Private Self in Late Medieval England* (Philadelphia: University of Pennsylvania Press, 2008), 4.
2. The notion of reading as a social and political technology is rooted in the treatment of reading by practitioners of cultural studies such as Michel de

Certeau, "Reading as Poaching," in *The Practice of Everyday Life*, trans. Steven Randall (Berkeley: University of California Press, 1984); Janice A. Radway, *Reading the Romance: Women, Patriarchy, and Popular Literature* (Chapel Hill: University of North Carolina Press, 1984); and Radway, *A Feeling for Books: The Book-of-the-Month Club, Literary Taste and Middle Class Desire* (Chapel Hill: University of North Carolina Press, 1997). Bryan's inclination to examine devotional reading as a psychological procedure does not negate or undermine social theories of reception but attempts to unpack the internal process of subject formation that those methods rely upon.

3. See, e.g., Kate Harris, "Patrons, Buyers and Owners: The Evidence for Ownership and the Role of Book Owners in Book Production and the Book Trade," in *Book Production and Publishing in Britain 1375–1475*, ed. Jeremy Griffiths and Derek Pearsall (Cambridge, UK: Cambridge University Press, 1989), 163–199.

4. Exceptions include Marleen Cré and Hugh Kempster, whose work I address later in this article.

5. Julian of Norwich, *Of the Knowledge of Ourselves and of God: A Fifteenth Century Spiritual Florilegium*, ed. and trans. James Walsh and Edmund Colledge (London: Mowbray, 1961), v–vii.

6. N. R. Ker, *Medieval Manuscripts in British Libraries, 1: London* (Oxford: Clarendon, 1969), 418–419; Edmund Colledge and James Walsh, "Introduction," in Julian of Norwich, *A Book of Showings to the Anchoress Julian of Norwich* (Toronto: Pontifical Institute of Mediaeval Studies, 1978), 9.

7. After being first printed in translation by B. Foucard in 1956 and by Edmund Colledge and James Walsh in 1961, the Westminster manuscript was published in its original Middle English by Hugh Kempster in 1997 and by Nicholas Watson and Jacqueline Jenkins in 2006. B. Foucard, "A Cathedral Manuscript," *Westminster Cathedral Chronicle* 50 (1956): 41–43, 59–60, 74–75, 89–90, 108–110; Julian, *Of the Knowledge*, 417–431; Hugh Kempster, "Julian of Norwich: The Westminster Text of a Revelation of Love," *Mystics Quarterly* 23.4 (1997): 177–245; Julian of Norwich, *The Writings of Julian of Norwich*, ed. Nicholas Watson and Jacqueline Jenkins, Brepols Medieval Women's Series (University Park: Pennsylvania State University Press, 2006), 417–431.

8. Kempster, "Julian of Norwich," 185.

9. None of the seventeenth-century readers who left readers' marks in the margins of this manuscript seem to have responded explicitly to the compiler's appeal to maternal ambition. For instance, on fol. 105v, as Julian compares breast-feeding to communion, the reader writes "Eucharistia" in the margin. We might have preferred for this reader to draw attention to the remarkable comparison, but he or she draws us to the sacramental and thus communal and public ritualization of it.

10. Marleen Cré, "'This Blessed Beholding': Reading the Fragments from Julian of Norwich's *A Revelation of Love* in London, Westminster Cathedral Treasury, MS 4," in *A Companion to Julian of Norwich*, ed. Liz Herbert McAvoy (Cambridge, UK: D.S. Brewer, 2008), 117.

11. Ibid., 119.

12. Liz Herbert McAvoy, "'The Moders Service': Motherhood as Matrix in Julian of Norwich," *Mystics Quarterly* 24.4 (1998): 194.

13. Liz Herbert McAvoy, "'For We Be Doubel of God's Making': Writing, Gender and the Body in Julian of Norwich," in *A Companion to Julian of Norwich*, ed. Liz Herbert McAvoy (Cambridge, UK: D.S. Brewer, 2008), 173.

14. Ibid. McAvoy quotes from Julia Kristeva, "Revolution in Poetic Language," in *A Kristeva Reader*, ed. Toril Moi (Oxford, Blackwell, 1986), 95.

15. Ibid., 173n. McAvoy explains Kristeva's use of Plato's term *chora* and refers readers to Kristeva, "Revolution in Poetic Language," 93–98.

16. I refer here to manuscript line numbers, available in Kempster, "Julian of Norwich."

17. The function of maternity in the long version has been taken up by a number of scholars. See especially Alexandra Barratt, "'In the Lowest Part of Our Need': Julian and Medieval Gynecological Writing," in *Julian of Norwich: A Book of Essays*, ed. Sandra J. McEntire, Garland Medieval Casebooks 21 (New York: Garland, 1998), 239–256; Catherine Innes-Parker, "Subversion and Conformity in Julian's Revelation: Authority, Visions and the Motherhood of God," *Mystics Quarterly* 23.2 (1997): 7–35; Claire Sisco King, "The Poetics and Praxis of Enclosure: Julian of Norwich, Motherhood, and Rituals of Childbirth," *Comitatus: A Journal of Medieval and Renaissance Studies* 35 (2004) 71–82; Maud Burnett McInerney, "'In the Meydens Womb': Julian of Norwich and the Poetics of Enclosure," in *Medieval Mothering*, ed. John Carmi Parsons and Bonnie Wheeler, vol. 3 of *The New*

Middle Ages (New York: Garland, 1996), 157–182; and Andrew Sprung, "The Inverted Metaphor: Earthly Mothering as Figura of Divine Love in Julian of Norwich's *Book of Showings*," in *Medieval Mothering*, ed. John Carmi Parsons and Bonnie Wheeler, vol. 3 of T*he New Middle Ages* (New York: Garland, 1996), 183–199.

18. Janet Backhouse and the British Library, *Books of Hours* (London: British Library, 1985), 16.
19. Julian, Writings, 418.
20. Ibid.
21. Ibid., 419.
22. Ibid., 426.
23. Ibid., 427.
24. Ibid., 137.
25. Karen Saupe, ed., "33," *Middle English Marian Lyrics*, TEAMS (Kalamazoo, MI: Medieval Institute Publications, 1998), 88–89. Translation mine.
26. Bryan, *Looking Inward*, 3.
27. Ibid.
28. Ibid., 155.
29. Ibid., 147.
30. See Watson and Jenkins's introduction in Julian, *Writings*; and Elisabeth Dutton, "The Seventeenth-Century Manuscript Tradition and the Influence of Augustine Baker," in *A Companion to Julian of Norwich*, ed. Liz Herbert McAvoy (Cambridge, UK: D.S. Brewer, 2008), 127–138.
31. Both Paris, Bibliothèque Nationale MS Fonds Anglais 40 and London, British Library MS Sloane 2499 are associated with these English foundations. For additional information on the foundation movement, see Claire Walker, *Gender and Politics in Early Modern Europe: English Convents in France and the Low Countries* (Houndmills, UK: Palgrave Macmillan, 2003).
32. Bryan, *Looking Inward*, 156.
33. Julian, *Writings*, 423.
34. Gail McMurray Gibson, "Scene and Obscene: Seeing and Performing Late Medieval Childbirth," *Journal of Medieval and Early Modern Studies* 29.1 (1999): 16; and Wendy Harding, "Medieval Women's Unwritten Discourse on Motherhood: A Reading of Two Fifteenth-Century Texts," *Women's Studies* 21 (1992): 205.

35. A description and text of the "churching" ceremony is available in Adolf Franz, ed., *Die kirchlichen Benediktionen im Mittelalter*, 2 vols. (Graz, Austria: Akademische Druck- u. Verlagsanstalt, 1960), available in translation in John Raymond Shinners, *Medieval Popular Religion, 1000–1500: A Reader*, Readings in Medieval Civilizations and Cultures (Peterborough, UK: Broadview, 1997), 260.
36. Julian, *Writings*, 431.
37. Ibid., 427 and 429.
38. Ibid., 420.
39. Ibid., 428–429.
40. Ibid., 429.
41. Ibid., 420.
42. Ibid.
43. Julian of Norwich, *A Book of Showings to the Anchoress Julian of Norwich*, ed. Edmund Colledge and James Walsh, 2 vols. (Toronto: Pontifical Institute of Mediaeval Studies, 1978), 306, n35; Julian, *Writings*, 142 (note on ll. 29–31).
44. The Paris, Bibliothèque Nationale MS Fonds Anglais 40 manuscript reads (with editorial quotation marks) "And that it is he that doeth this, it is shewed ther wher he seith: 'He cometh downe to us.'" Julian, *Writings*, 143. London, British Library MS Sloane 2499 omits the passage.
45. Julian, *Writings*, 424.
46. Ibid., 430.
47. Ibid.
48. Ibid., 431.
49. Ibid., 424.
50. Ibid.
51. Adrian James McCarthy, ed., *Book to a Mother: An Edition with Commentary*, Salzburg Studies in English Literature, Elizabethan & Renaissance Studies 92 (Salzburg, Austria: Institut für Anglistik und Amerikanistik, Universität Salzburg, 1981), 124.
52. Julian, *Writings*, 425.
53. Bryan, *Looking Inward*, 163.
54. Julian, *Writings*, 424.
55. Ibid., 426.

56. Ibid., 421.
57. Julian, *Of the Knowledge*, 417.
58. Julian, *Writings*, 430.
59. Ibid.
60. Cré, "'This Blessed Beholding,'" 122; Hugh Kempster, "A Question of Audience: The Westminster Text and Fifteenth-Century Reception of Julian of Norwich," in *Julian of Norwich: A Book of Essays*, ed. Sandra J McEntire, Garland Medieval Casebooks 21 (New York: Garland, 1998), 257–289.
61. Anne M. Dutton, "Passing the Book: Testamentary Transmission of Religious Literature to and by Women in England 1350–1500," in *Women, the Book and the Godly: Selected Proceedings of the St. Hilda's Conference, 1993*, ed. Lesley Smith and Jane H. M. Taylor (Cambridge, UK: D.S. Brewer, 1995), 41–51; Valerie Edden, "The Devotional Life of the Laity in the Late Middle Ages," in *Approaching Medieval English Anchoritic and Mystical Texts*, ed. Dee Dyas, Valerie Edden, and Roger Ellis. Christianity and Culture (Cambridge, UK: D.S. Brewer, 2005), 35–49; Nicole Randolph Rice, "Spiritual Ambition and the Mixed Life: Middle English Devotional Rules and the Shaping of Lay Piety," PhD diss., Columbia University, 2002; Felicity Riddy, "'Women Talking about the Things of God': A Late Medieval Sub-Culture," in *Women and Literature in Britain, 1150–1500*, ed. Carol Meale (Cambridge, UK: Cambridge University Press, 1993), 104–125. On Carthusian textual dissemination among laity, see Robert A. Horsfield, "The Pomander of Prayer: Aspects of Late Medieval English Carthusian Spirituality and Its Lay Audience," in *De cella in seculum*, ed. Michael Sargent (Cambridge, UK: D.S. Brewer, 1989), 205–213. On Middle English texts circulating within and around Syon Abbey and a description of specific high-status laywomen readers, see Ann M. Hutchison, "Devotional Reading in the Monastery and in the Late Medieval Household," in *De cella in seculum*, ed. Michael Sargent (Cambridge, UK: D.S. Brewer, 1989), 215–227. For a thorough discussion of the larger cultural response to visionary literatures in fifteenth-century England, see Kathryn Kerby-Fulton, *Books under Suspicion: Censorship and Tolerance of Revelatory Writing in Late Medieval England* (Notre Dame, IN: University of Notre Dame Press, 2007).
62. Bryan, *Looking Inward*, 2.

63. Shinners, *Medieval Popular Religion*, 17.
64. McAvoy, "'For We Be Doubel,'" 178–179. McAvoy quotes from Amy Hollywood, *Sensible Ecstasy: Mysticism, Sexual Difference, and the Demands of History* (Chicago: University of Chicago Press, 2002), 278.
65. McAvoy, "'For We Be Doubel,'" 179.
66. Ibid., 178.
67. Bryan, *Looking Inward*, 163.

WORKS CITED

Manuscripts

London, British Library MS Sloane 2499.
London, Westminster Cathedral Treasury MS 4.
Paris, Bibliothèque Nationale MS Fonds Anglais 40.

Primary Sources

Foucard, B. "A Cathedral Manuscript." *Westminster Cathedral Chronicle* 50 (1956): 41–43, 59–60, 74–75, 89–90, 108–110.
Franz, Adolf, ed. *Die kirchlichen Benediktionen im Mittelalter*, 2 vols. Graz, Austria: Akademische Druck- u. Verlagsanstalt, 1960.
Julian of Norwich. *A Book of Showings to the Anchoress Julian of Norwich*. Edited by Edmund Colledge and James Walsh. Toronto: Pontifical Institute of Mediaeval Studies, 1978.
———. *Of the Knowledge of Ourselves and of God: A Fifteenth Century Spiritual Florilegium*. Edited and translated by James Walsh and Edmund Colledge. London: Mowbray, 1961.
———. *The Writings of Julian of Norwich*. Edited by Nicholas Watson and Jacqueline Jenkins. Brepols Medieval Women Series. University Park: Pennsylvania State University Press, 2006.
Kempster, Hugh. "Julian of Norwich: The Westminster Text of a Revelation of Love." *Mystics Quarterly* 23.4 (1997): 177–245.
McCarthy, Adrian James, ed. *Book to a Mother: An Edition with Commentary*. Salzburg Studies in English Literature. Elizabethan & Renaissance Studies 92. Salzburg, Austria: Institut für Anglistik und Amerikanistik, Universität Salzburg, 1981.

Saupe, Karen, ed. "33." In *Middle English Marian Lyrics*. TEAMS. Kalamazoo, MI: Medieval Institute Publications, 1998, 88–89.

Shinners, John Raymond. *Medieval Popular Religion, 1000–1500: A Reader*. Readings in Medieval Civilizations and Cultures. Peterborough, UK: Broadview, 1997.

Secondary Sources

Backhouse, Janet, and the British Library. *Books of Hours*. London: British Library, 1985.

Barratt, Alexandra. "'In the Lowest Part of Our Need': Julian and Medieval Gynecological Writing." In *Julian of Norwich: A Book of Essays*, ed. Sandra J. McEntire. Garland Medieval Casebooks 21. New York: Garland, 1998, 239–256.

Beaven, Alfred B. and Corporation of London Court of Common Council Library Committee. *The Aldermen of the City of London Temp. Henry III.–1908. With Notes on the Parliamentary Representation of the City, the Aldermen and the Livery Companies, the Aldermanic Veto, Aldermanic Baronets and Knights, Etc*. London: E. Fisher & Co., 1908.

Bryan, Jennifer. *Looking Inward: Devotional Reading and the Private Self in Late Medieval England*. Philadelphia: University of Pennsylvania Press, 2008.

Certeau, Michel de. "Reading as Poaching." In *The Practice of Everyday Life*, trans. Steven Randall. Berkeley: University of California Press, 1984.

Colledge, Edmund, and James Walsh. "Introduction." In Julian of Norwich, *A Book of Showings to the Anchoress Julian of Norwich*. Edited by Edmund Colledge and James Walsh. Toronto: Pontifical Institute of Mediaeval Studies, 1978, 9.

Cré, Marleen. "'This Blessed Beholding': Reading the Fragments from Julian of Norwich's *A Revelation of Love* in London, Westminster Cathedral Treasury, MS 4." In *A Companion to Julian of Norwich*, ed. Liz Herbert McAvoy. Cambridge, UK: D.S. Brewer, 2008, 116–126.

Dutton, Anne M. "Passing the Book: Testamentary Transmission of Religious Literature to and by Women in England 1350–1500." In *Women, the Book and the Godly: Selected Proceedings of the St. Hilda's Conference, 1993*, ed. Lesley Smith and Jane H. M. Taylor. Cambridge, UK: D.S. Brewer, 1995, 41–54.

Dutton, Elisabeth. "The Seventeenth-Century Manuscript Tradition and the Influence of Augustine Baker." In *A Companion to Julian of Norwich*, ed. Liz Herbert McAvoy. Cambridge, UK: D.S. Brewer, 2008, 127–138.

Edden, Valerie. "The Devotional Life of the Laity in the Late Middle Ages." In *Approaching Medieval English Anchoritic and Mystical Texts*, ed. Dee Dyas, Valerie Edden, and Roger Ellis. Christianity and Culture. Cambridge, UK: D.S. Brewer, 2005, 35–49.

Gibson, Gail McMurray. "Scene and Obscene: Seeing and Performing Late Medieval Childbirth." *Journal of Medieval and Early Modern Studies* 29.1 (1999): 7–24.

Gillespie, Vincent. "Syon and the English Market for Continental Printed Books: The Incunable Phase." *Religion and Literature* 37.2 (2005): 27–49.

Harding, Wendy. "Medieval Women's Unwritten Discourse on Motherhood: A Reading of Two Fifteenth-Century Texts." *Women's Studies* 21 (1992): 197–209.

Harris, Kate. "Patrons, Buyers and Owners: The Evidence for Ownership and the Role of Book Owners in Book Production and the Book Trade." In *Book Production and Publishing in Britain 1375–1475*, ed. Jeremy Griffiths and Derek Pearsall. Cambridge, UK: Cambridge University Press, 1989, 163–199.

Hollywood, Amy. *Sensible Ecstasy: Mysticism, Sexual Difference, and the Demands of History*. Chicago: University of Chicago Press, 2002.

Horsfield, Robert A. "The Pomander of Prayer: Aspects of Late Medieval English Carthusian Spirituality and Its Lay Audience." In *De cella in seculum*, ed. Michael Sargent. Cambridge, UK: D.S. Brewer, 1989, 205–213.

Hutchison, Ann M. "Devotional Reading in the Monastery and in the Late Medieval Household." In *De cella in seculum*, ed. Michael Sargent. Cambridge, UK: D.S. Brewer, 1989, 215–227.

Innes-Parker, Catherine. "Subversion and Conformity in Julian's Revelation: Authority, Visions and the Motherhood of God." *Mystics Quarterly* 23.2 (1997): 7–35.

Kempster, Hugh. "A Question of Audience: The Westminster Text and Fifteenth-Century Reception of Julian of Norwich." In *Julian of Norwich:*

A Book of Essays, ed. Sandra J. McEntire. Garland Medieval Casebooks 21. New York: Garland, 1998, 257–289.

Ker, N. R. *Medieval Manuscripts in British Libraries*, 1: London. Oxford: Clarendon Press, 1969.

Kerby-Fulton, Kathryn. *Books under Suspicion: Censorship and Tolerance of Revelatory Writing in Late Medieval England*. Notre Dame, IN: University of Notre Dame, 2007.

King, Claire Sisco. "The Poetics and Praxis of Enclosure: Julian of Norwich, Motherhood, and Rituals of Childbirth." *Comitatus: A Journal of Medieval and Renaissance Studies* 35 (2004): 71–82.

Kristeva, Julia. "Revolution in Poetic Language." In *A Kristeva Reader*, ed. Toril Moi. Oxford: Blackwell, 1986.

McAvoy, Liz Herbert. "'The Moders Service': Motherhood as Matrix in Julian of Norwich." *Mystics Quarterly* 24.4 (1998): 181–197.

———. "'For We Be Doubel of God's Making': Writing, Gender, and the Body in Julian of Norwich." In *A Companion to Julian of Norwich*, ed. Liz Herbert McAvoy. Cambridge, UK: D.S. Brewer, 2008, 166–180.

McInerney, Maud Burnett. "'In the Meydens Womb': Julian of Norwich and the Poetics of Enclosure." In *Medieval Mothering*, ed. John Carmi Parsons and Bonnie Wheeler. Vol. 3 of The New Middle Ages. New York: Garland, 1996, 157–182.

Meale, Carol, ed. *Women and Literature in Britain, 1150–1500*. Cambridge, UK: Cambridge University Press, 1993.

Radway, Janice A. *A Feeling for Books: The Book-of-the-Month Club, Literary Taste and Middle Class Desire*. Chapel Hill: University of North Carolina Press, 1997.

———. *Reading the Romance: Women, Patriarchy, and Popular Literature*. Chapel Hill: University of North Carolina Press, 1984.

Rice, Nicole Randolph. "Spiritual Ambition and the Mixed Life: Middle English Devotional Rules and the Shaping of Lay Piety." PhD dissertation, Columbia University, 2002.

Riddy, Felicity. "'Women Talking about the Things of God': A Late Medieval Sub-Culture." In *Women and Literature in Britain, 1150–1500*, ed. Carol Meale. Cambridge, UK: Cambridge University Press, 1993, 104–125.

Sprung, Andrew. "The Inverted Metaphor: Earthly Mothering as Figura of Divine Love in Julian of Norwich's *Book of Showings*." In *Medieval Mothering*, ed. John Carmi Parsons and Bonnie Wheeler. Vol. 3 of *The New Middle Ages*. New York: Garland, 1996, 183–199.

Walker, Claire. *Gender and Politics in Early Modern Europe: English Convents in France and the Low Countries*. Houndmills, UK: Palgrave Macmillan, 2003.

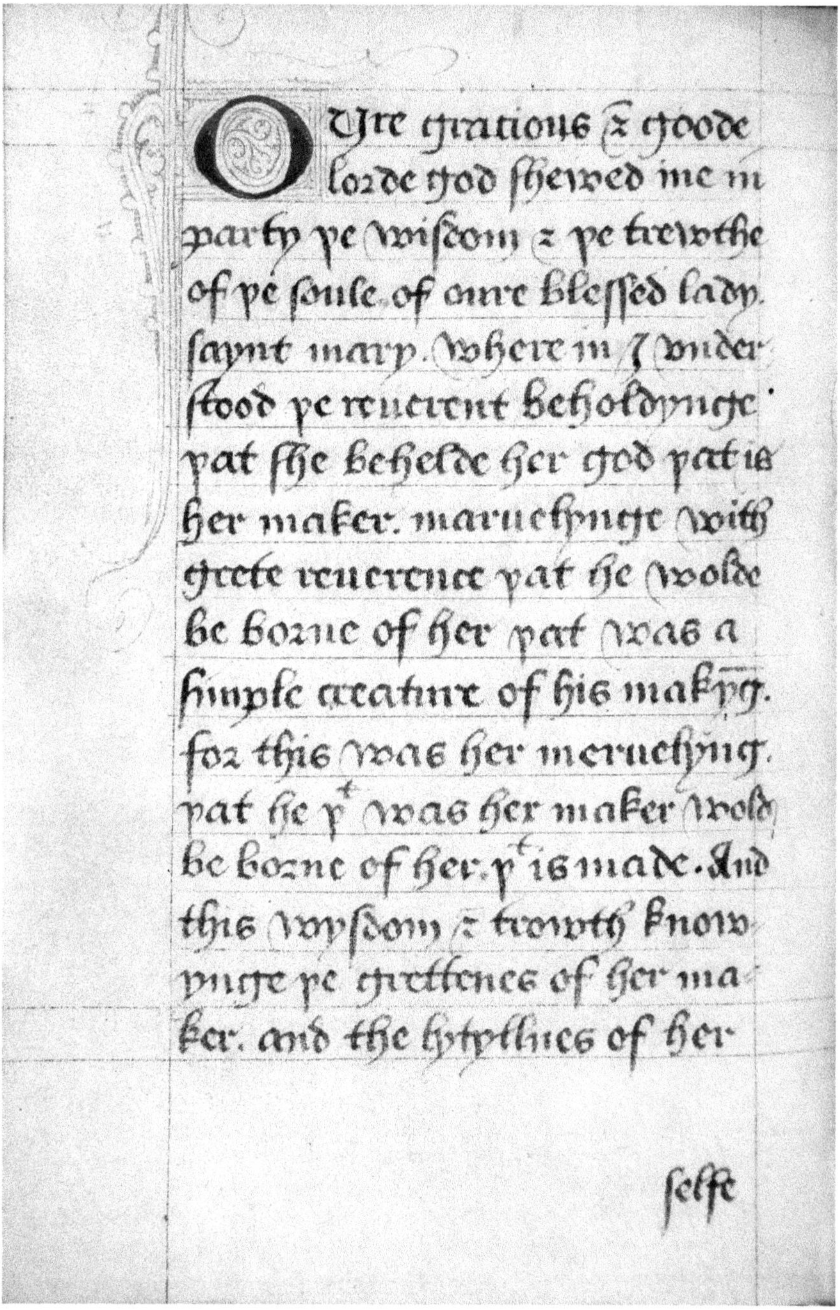

Oure graciouse & goode
lorde god shewed me in
party ye wisdom & ye trewthe
of ye soule of oure blessed lady.
saynt mary. where in I under
stood ye reuerent beholdynge
yat she behelde her god yat is
her maker. maruelynge with
grete reuerence yat he wolde
be borne of her yat was a
simple creature of his makyng.
for this was her meruelyng.
yat he yt was her maker wold
be borne of her yt is made. And
this wysdom & trewth know
ynge ye gretnes of her ma
ker. and the lytylnes of her
selfe

Figure 1. London, Westminster Cathedral Treasury MS 4, fol 72v. The opening lines of the Westminster version of Julian of Norwich's *A Revelation of Love*. Copyright Westminster Cathedral

Caxton's Exemplar for *The Chronicles of England*?

DANIEL WAKELIN

The direct exemplars used by early printers show us much about the printers' working practices—whether and how they "cast off" copy; how they handled space and layout—and about their responses to Middle English literature in the years around 1500—how far it seemed to need updating; how closely it deserved to be transmitted. So, happily for the history of printing, literature, and language, there are several exemplars recognized from the presses of the second generation of English printers, Wynkyn de Worde and Richard Pynson.[1] But from the first generation, such as William Caxton or the printers in Oxford and St. Albans, fewer exemplars are known. From Caxton's press, we know only the exemplar for Lorenzo Traversagni's *Nova rhetorica* (1478), and from the Oxford press of "the printer of Rufinus," who came there from Cologne, only that for Rufinus's *Symbola apostolorum* (1478).[2]

Besides these Latin texts, only one English manuscript has been firmly recognized as even spending time in Caxton's workshop—the "Winchester" manuscript of Malory's Arthurian writings—and this was seemingly not the exemplar for Caxton's 1485 edition.[3] It has also been suggested but ultimately doubted that Oxford, Magdalen College, MS 213 was a collateral source for Caxton's 1483 edition of Gower's *Confessio Amantis*, for checking against rather than printing from;[4] and it has been hypothesized but admitted unprovable that London, British Library, MS Harley 1900, was copied into a separate manuscript, now lost, in which the text was updated and rewritten to serve as Caxton's exemplar for Trevisa's English *Polychronicon*.[5] As yet no direct exemplar is known for one of Caxton's editions in English for which he is most famous.

It might, though, be possible to identify the exemplar for Caxton's first edition of the Middle English prose *Brut*, which he calls, more descriptively, *The Chronicles of England* (*STC* 9991).[6] This edition was printed in 1480 and was innovative in several respects: it was the first chronicle printed in English; it involved technical innovations in the use of justification and signatures; and it was the first dated use of Caxton's Type 4. It includes a blank leaf, a prologue, and a table of contents by Caxton in a first unnumbered quire of eight leaves (most likely added later). The rest of the book is in quires of eight leaves, a to y, apart from the final quire y, which has only six. Quire a begins with another blank leaf, and then the prose *Brut*, extending to the year 1419, runs through signatures a2r to u3v. This ends at the foot of signature u3v with the words "in rewle and in gouernaunce," but Caxton's edition then adds seamlessly to it from the top of signature u4r to signature y6v a continuation of the chronicle to 1461 found only in manuscripts descending from Caxton's edition (as is noted below).[7] Lister M. Matheson argues convincingly that Caxton composed the continuation himself.[8]

But where did Caxton get the prose *Brut* from? In a brilliant tracing of the textual tradition, Matheson deduces that Caxton got the prose *Brut* from a manuscript of the textual tradition that Matheson calls "CV-1419(r&g): B, subgroup (c)," that is, the Common Version, Group B, subgroup (c), extending to the year 1419, ending with the words "in rewle and in gouernaunce" and en route including or excluding various elements.[9] Matheson's exhaustive search allows him to note that this textual tradition is "represented" by only "a single manuscript," namely manuscript HM 136 in the Henry E. Huntington Library, San Marino, California. This manuscript is "important" for studying the textual tradition because "a text of this type formed the basis for William Caxton's."[10]

One might wonder whether manuscript HM 136 was in fact copied from Caxton's edition of *The Chronicles of England*. After all, there are six other manuscripts of which that is true,[11] and there are extant far more manuscripts copied from printed books than there are manuscript exemplars for such books.[12] (Indeed, it is noted below that a further short excerpt from Caxton's continuation has been added to the end of HM 136.) However, it is argued here that the likeness between this manuscript and the printed book is even closer than has hitherto been suggested but that the relationship runs in the other direction: it is argued that beyond those few folios of continuation, HM 136 was not a copy from Caxton's edition but rather was the exemplar for the edition of *The Chronicles of England* printed in 1480.

The Marks in Manuscript HM 136

Manuscript HM 136 in the Huntington Library is a parchment manuscript of the mid-fifteenth century, certainly after 1419, the date of the last events in the Common Version of *Brut* in this copy. The main scribe uses a hand modeled on the secretary script typical of the mid- to late fifteenth century. The handwriting is in some places fairly current, with minims run together and *e* "reversed," but in other places there is some slow care, with horns and broken strokes adorning several letters. The layout includes a certain amount of decoration: the first folio has a painted border; most of the chapter titles run on from the end of the preceding chapter but are in red; and the chapters themselves begin with blue lombards with red tracery and are punctuated with blue paraphs. The frame is ruled but the lines are not, and for the main text there are between thirty-nine and forty-two lines of text on each page.[13] The manuscript is in quires of eight leaves, and the Common Version of the prose *Brut* to 1419 ends with the words "in rewle and in goue*r*naunce" a little way down the verso of the fourth leaf of quire 20. (The short addition to the remainder of this quire is discussed below.)

The manuscript has been annotated heavily by several people. There are several Latin prophecies and scholarly annotations in late fifteenth-century and early sixteenth-century hands. There are the names of several owners or readers, such as one Dorothy Helbarton, who wrote her name umpteen times (slightly obsessively) and John Leche, who wrote his *ex libris* inscription on a rear flyleaf. Similar *ex libris* inscriptions link this owner to other English and Latin manuscripts and to the distinguished Cheshire branch of the Leche family. (It should, though, be noted that many current comments on the manuscript's early owners and annotations will be clarified and corrected by research forthcoming from Anthony Bale, Julia Boffey, and Masako Takagi.)[14]

It is another set of marks added to HM 136 that offers the most important evidence that this was Caxton's exemplar. These marks have not been discussed in previous studies of the manuscript nor of *The Chronicles of England* but they deserve to be, because they seem to be marks by somebody using the manuscript for printing from it.[15] They occur throughout the 311 pages of the prose *Brut* to 1419. With a few exceptions, they consist of one, two, or three of the following components.

The first component occurs in the left-hand margin beside a line of text. It is a small circle about two millimeters in diameter, drawn in dark ink. The circle is usually at the extreme fore-edge of verso pages or in the gutter of rectos and is therefore sometimes trimmed or buried so that it is difficult to see (especially on the microfilm).

The second component occurs level with the circle but much closer to the left-hand edge of the text-block. It is a pair of virgules drawn in dark ink like this: //. The scribes of fifteenth-century manuscripts often used a pair of virgules to guide the rubricator to add a paraph mark (¶) at the point thus noted.[16] However, in HM 136 a paraph would almost never be customary at these points, as there is seldom a clear break in the prose there.

Then, in the middle of many lines marked with two virgules and/or a circle, there occurs the third component. It is ^, like an upturned letter *v*, drawn in perhaps slightly paler brown ink than the the virgules and circles. It looks most like the caret mark used by fifteenth-century scribes to insert text interlineally when correcting; it is placed between words at a low level, almost below the line of text.[17] It slightly suggests a more upright version of the mark that Malcolm Parkes calls the *simplex ductus*, which was "placed within a verse to separate matters erroneously run together," and here it does indeed separate things (as is noted below).[18] On no occasion does this seeming caret occur where text seems to be missing in HM 136. Manuscript HM 136 does also contain twenty-four other interlinear insertions, many of them with a real caret,[19] but those caret marks for interlineation seem to be by the scribe, whereas the seeming carets that accompany circles and/or virgules differ in ink color, size, and style.

There are 307 sets of these marks. Most sets have the marginal circle; most also have the double virgules next to the text. Some fifty-four sets have, in addition, the seeming caret in the middle of the line.[20] There are some exceptions: fourteen times the circle and seeming caret occur without the virgules;[21] nine times the circles, virgules, and seeming caret straddle two subsequent lines rather than marking just one;[22] and a few other glitches occur, such as the duplication of the marks or the separation of their components by a line or two.[23] But three fifths of the sets are uniform in having a circle and virgules, and a further fifth in having a circle, virgules, and a seeming caret, too, so the marks are very regular in their appearance.

Moreover, they are regular in their position, for they recur at intervals of between thirty-nine and forty-two lines of the manuscript's text and most often after forty or forty-one lines. Only seldom do they recur after smaller or larger intervals, just once after only thirty-seven lines and once after forty-five.[24] As the manuscript most often has only forty lines of text or fewer per page, albeit with much variation, the marks appear successively further down each page, until just a few times the arithmetic makes them skip a page entirely and then occur twice on the following one.

The placing of these marks becomes even more regular just under halfway through. On folio 65r, the circle and virgules occur next to the first line of the page, after a count of forty-three lines of text;[25] and thereafter on 172 of the remaining 182 pages of the manuscript the marks appear on this top line on each page. The exceptions are five pages where they appear on the first line but are duplicated on the last line of the preceding page,[26] three pages where they appear on the first line but are duplicated on the second or third line,[27] and two other oddities.[28]

Oddities aside, it is the overwhelming regularity of their spacing that suggests the significance of these marks. For the pair of virgules in the margin almost always falls at the precise point in the text where a page break falls in Caxton's edition of *The Chronicles of England* in 1480, unless there is a seeming caret. Where there is a seeming caret, then that always falls where a page break does in the edition. That is, when Caxton's page break occurs at a line break in this manuscript, the line is marked with virgules; when his page break occurs at a point in the middle of a line in this manuscript, it is marked with the seeming caret. This coincidence occurs precisely with 293 of the 307 sets of marks in HM 136. There are only fourteen of the 307 sets of marks in HM 136 in which none of the components coincides with Caxton's page break precisely, and even with those fourteen, Caxton's page break does usually fall just a few lines, words, or even letters away (as explained below). The most likely explanation of this methodical annotation and its coincidence with Caxton's page breaks is that these markings were made by somebody in Caxton's workshop using HM 136 as the exemplar for *The Chronicles of England* in 1480.

Of course, circles, virgules, and seeming carets are tricky to date paleographically, so it is worth checking whether they were not prompts to Caxton's edition but were the work of somebody collating manuscript HM 136 against Caxton's edition at a later date. Amazingly, somebody has written the name "Caxton" on a flyleaf in an eighteenth- or nineteenth-century hand; but "Caxton" could be a shorthand title for the prose *Brut*, given Caxton's printing of it, so it need not imply any close study of the manuscript.[29]

But could somebody have marked up the printed book's page breaks in this manuscript out of some curious bibliographical fervor? Eighteenth-century scholars did study other copies carefully on occasion.[30] Yet probabilities make this explanation unlikely. If a bibliographer had marked up the manuscript, he would have struck lucky: the text he would have chosen to collate was the only surviving example of the textual tradition that Caxton followed, and followed in meticulous verbal detail, too (as is shown below); and he would have found his task lightened by the coincidence that 171 of the manuscript's page breaks occur exactly where Caxton's do, and 82 more occur at the manuscript's line breaks. This coincidence would be more difficult for a scribe to achieve in transferring prose to an unruled page than for a printer. And for such a manuscript then to be used by a bibliographer interested in comparing the two books' page breaks would be a fluky coincidence that, while possible, is less likely than that these marks were made in preparing Caxton's edition from this manuscript.

Casting Off with These Marks

How, though, did these marks assist in preparing Caxton's edition? There are broadly three ways in which they could serve: to allow the printer to calculate how many pages and quires the manuscript would become in the printed edition, perhaps for setting text *seriatim*, or in textual order; to allow him to "cast off" his copy so that he could print it out of textual sequence or "by forme"; and to record where page breaks fell so that a corrector could more easily proofread the copy against the manuscript.[31] Which would the marks in HM 136 best serve?

Minimal marks like the mere circles, virgules, and dashes in HM 136 might suggest some simpler process of setting copy: merely calculating the number of pages required and keeping track of where one page ended as one went along to avoid error in the next page in sequence and to ease correcting. The use of a small circle near the fore-edge and of a pair of virgules in the near margin is also found in the exemplar for an edition of Werner Rolewinck's *Paradisus conscientiae* printed by Arnold ther Hoernen in Cologne in 1475. Other evidence suggests that this Cologne edition was set not by forme but *seriatim*, in textual sequence.[32] The similarity of the marks and notably the lack of any numbering or quire or leaf signatures in HM 136 might suggest that Caxton's first edition of *The Chronicles of England* was also set *seriatim*.[33]

Setting by forme required calculation in advance of the place at which the pages set nonsequentially would begin and end, so that whichever forme was set first, the compositor could begin (for example, in the outer forme) both signature 1r and signature 8v, which were cognate and on one side of a sheet (in a folio edition), and so on, before later printing the reverse pages in similar pairs (in such a case, in the inner forme).[34] To keep track of this process, some other exemplars for English incunables have numbers or letters specifying exactly where each page in a quire begins; such specificity occurs, for example, in the only previously identified exemplar for one of Caxton's editions, that for Traversagni's *Nova rhetorica* (1478), and in the exemplars for three English editions printed by Wynkyn de Worde and Richard Pynson between 1493 and 1495.[35]

In HM 136 there are no numbers or letters to identify pages or quires, so it is interesting to ask how the manuscript could really have been used for casting off. However, Lotte Hellinga suggests that casting off might unfold in two "rounds," one to calculate the page breaks, another to specify the structure of quires.[36] If one purpose in casting off was to calculate which quire structure would best suit the manuscript, then specifying quire signatures in the first round might indeed be premature and the marks in HM 136 could be merely the first round of casting off. Yet that might not be the case either: Hellinga also notes that in some exemplars for incunables, including the Oxford edition of Rufinus's *Symbola apostolorum* in 1478, some of the marks were very discreet—just "small strokes," crosses, "squiggles," "little dashes between lines" or mere sets of "three or four small dots at the beginning of the marked-off page."[37] If the copy was to be returned to its owner, then the printer could not make too great a mess.[38] So the tininess of the marks in HM 136 does not preclude their use for setting the text by forme.

The process of setting the text by forme became more important as printers in England began to use a two-pull press on full sheets, which seems to have begun in Oxford about 1479 and in Caxton's workshop around 1480, the time of printing *The Chronicles of England*.[39] Therefore the question of whether the marks in HM 136 do reflect setting by forme in 1480 is of considerable interest for the history of Caxton's press. This matter requires further inquiry, but from preliminary inquiry I hypothesize that the edition was set by forme.

Some evidence that supports this hypothesis comes from the places where the printed page break does not follow a manuscript line break marked neatly by virgules, which was the usual tendency in this edition and in other incunables for which an exemplar has been found. While people casting off editions in the 1470s had tended to propose a printed page break at a line break in the manuscript, they sometimes shifted the printed page break to the middle of a manuscript line and sometimes marked that shift in the exemplar; such shifts are known as "free" page breaks, as opposed to "fixed" ones tacked to manuscript line breaks.[40] Such "free" page breaks occur in HM 136 in places where the seeming carets in HM 136 shift the proposed page break from the pair of virgules at the start of a manuscript line to some other point in the line and in four more places where the seeming carets shift the proposed page break to a point late in the preceding line just before the pair of virgules.[41]

These seeming carets, then, look like frequent attempts to correct some miscalculation of how much text would fit or be desirable to print before the end of the page by shifting the end just a few words later (or, much less often, earlier). Though it is impossible to be sure at which stages each of the different marks were added to HM 136, it is tempting to hypothesize that the seeming carets were added after the initial casting off with circles and virgules, as problems emerged. (As noted above, the ink of the seeming carets is slightly paler than that of the circles and virgules.) Of the forty-one pages on which the compositor was able to shift the place where the page would end to a "free" position, some thirty-four fell in the outer forme.[42] This suggests that the outer forme might have been printed first, because it was here that the compositor could shift the place where the page would end, presumably because he had not yet set the following page. By contrast, only seven "free" page breaks fell in the inner forme, which suggests that there was less chance to move the page end in the inner forme and that its pages were more often set after those that would follow them in textual order but that had been previously printed as part of the outer forme.

Moreover, in all seven places where a page in the inner forme was able to end with a "free" page break marked with a seeming caret, that seeming caret shifts the page end to the end of a word, rather than splitting it over the page break, or to the end of a sentence, paragraph, or chapter, rather than interrupting sense or creating "widows."[43] (Widows are tiny sections of text stranded at the top of a page before a large textual division, unpopular with early printers.)[44] Rather than reflecting a decision to end this page in the inner forme, such "free" page breaks could reflect a decision instead to *start the subsequent page in the outer forme* in such a place that would have its own logic (for example, to avoid starting a page mid-word or with a "widow"); that could be the prerogative of the person setting the outer forme: to shift where he started as well as where he ended. So it seems that the compositor was able to move his printed page end away from a manuscript line break more often in the outer forme, which suggests that these pages might have been printed first. This is a little surprising. It is said that there was a tendency for English printers to print the inner forme first, but that may not be the case here.[45]

There is further corroborating evidence that the pages were set by forme, and the outer forme first, out of textual sequence, in the twenty-eight places where something goes askew. Things go askew because there is no seeming caret to mark a "free" page break away from a manuscript line ending; because the circles, pairs of virgules, or carets were entered twice on different but nearby lines, and only one set fits the printed page breaks; or because the markings in HM 136 diverge from the page break in Caxton's edition by as little as a few letters to as much as a couple of lines.

Of these twenty-eight places, where no markings in HM 136 fit Caxton's page break exactly or where there are two sets of marks, ten fell at the end of pages in the outer forme. Nine of these ten page ends do have markings in the manuscript but just oddly placed or duplicated. This possibility of "free" page ends, and helpful marking of those page ends for future reference, suggests that these pages in the outer forme were set before the subsequent page in the inner forme.[46] The next set of anomalous page ends, thirteen of the twenty-eight, occurred in the inner forme, but all at the foot of the fourth verso, which, in these folio quires of eight, would be set at the same time as the fifth recto facing it on a full sheet. In this part of the inner forme, one could ignore the casting-off marks quite safely, as the two pages in textual order, signatures 4v and 5r of the quire, were done together; there was no chance to forget any oddities in the page breaks. Nor were any further casting-off marks added to these pages, and nor would they need to be, as the two facing pages in sequence were both set at the same time.[47] By contrast, only five places where the planned page ending was ignored or adjusted occurred elsewhere in the inner forme.[48]

So there were sixty-nine occasions when pages ended not at a manuscript line break marked with a circle and pair of virgules but instead with a "free" page break at a seeming caret in the middle of the manuscript line (41 occasions) or with some other glitch (28 occasions), of which sixty-nine only twelve would be awkward to achieve if setting by forme and setting the outer forme first.

This newly identified exemplar requires fuller investigation for the light it might throw on the order of printing at Caxton's press, and each of the glitches deserves further investigation in particular. But as well as hypothesizing that Caxton's compositor did indeed set by forme and set the outer forme first, from this exemplar it is also possible to generalize from the seeming caret more about the compositor's preferences.

First, his avoidance of splitting words over page breaks is evident. Some five times when the break between manuscript lines, marked with a circles and/or virgules, splits a word in two, the seeming caret prevents this split over the break between pages in print:

CAXTON'S EXEMPLAR 85

HM 136:	°	called Bellyngesgate aftir his owne name and when this Be lyn ^ had regned nobely xj yer and iiij monthes he deid and lith
Chronicles:	[b4r] [b4v]	that is called Belyngesgate after his owne name and when this belin had regned nobely xj. yere he died and lieth atte newe Troie
HM 136:	°//	meny men had grete wonder ¶ The goodman that had dre med ^ this dreme / had tolde it to a kny3t that tho was moste priue with the kyng of all men / and the knyght me called Ha
Chronicles:	[h2r] [h2v]	meny men had grete wonder The goodman that had dremed this dreme had told it to a knyght that tho was most priue with the kyng of all men / and the knyght was called Hamundes sone[49]

Again, even in the second half of the manuscript, when the compositor was following the manuscript's own page breaks, he shifted the break to avoid splitting the word:

HM 136:		of hem that sey it ther come oute blode of the tombe of Tho
	//	mas ^ some tyme Erle of lancastre / as fressh as fressh as that day þat
Chronicles:	[q3r]	of hem that saw it ther come oute blode of the tombe of Thomas
	[q3v]	some tyme Erle of lancastre as fressh as that day that he was do to[50]

As well as these shifts, on one occasion the compositor drew the circle and virgules in the left-hand margin at the top of a page but then seems to have realized that the manuscript's own page break split the word "assembled": Jack Straw's mob "assem | bled hem vp on the blak heth" (*assembled themselves at Blackheath*).[51] But rather than put a seeming caret before "assem" on the bottom of the previous page, he instead wrote "assem" in the margin of the next page before "bled hem vp on the blak heth," with a caret in the same style as the seeming carets to mark the insertion; and sure enough, Caxton's page begins with "assembled" united. By contrast, it should be noted that the compositor twice followed the manuscript in splitting a word over a page break ("knygh= | tes," "Esche= | ker") and twice moved the page break to the middle of the manuscript line with a seeming caret and thus split words.[52] But one split word was the compound "wherfor" (*wherefore*) split after "wher" (*where*), which could be interpreted by a compositor as a separate word, and these four anomalies are outnumbered by the nine times he removed word splits at manuscript line breaks when they became printed page breaks.

The same concern to avoid splitting words thus is evident in the work of other compositors of the 1470s, including the compositor of Traversagni's *Nova rhetorica* at Caxton's press in 1478.[53] This exemplar, then, confirms that contemporary dislike of page breaks that interrupt words.

The seeming carets in this exemplar also suggest a dislike for widows. In manuscript HM 136, headings for new chapters do not often begin on new lines but follow the preceding chapter continuously on the same line, but distinguished by red ink. Caxton instead sets chapter headings on a new line, a procedure that risks creating more widows. So on six occasions the seeming caret put the printed page break not at the manuscript line break but at some nearby chapter title:

HM 136:		forne hym and he regned xv^e yere and died and lith at newe
	○	Troie ^ How Kymor regned after Seisil his fadre and he be
		gat Howan that regned after Ca*pitulo* xxvij°
Chronicles:	[b4v]	done beforne hym and he regned xv. yere and died and lith
		at newe Troie
	[b5r]	How kymor regned after seisell his fadre and he begate howan
		that regned after Ca. xxvij
HM 136:	°//	Edward howe Robert the Brus had dryve hem out of the land
		and disherited hem ^ Howe kyng Edward dubbed at westmynstre
		xiiij^e score knyghtes Ca*pitulo* C° iiij^{xx} ~ ~ ~
Chronicles:	[l1r]	playned vn to kyng Edward how Robert the Brus had driue
		hem oute of the land and disherited hem .
	[l1v]	How kyng Edward dubbed at westmynster xxiiij. score kny=
		ghtes Ca*pitulo* C . lxxx[54]

Even when printed page breaks follow the manuscript page breaks, the compositor thrice more interrupts that alignment to avoid widows before new chapters.[55]

This avoidance of widows is also evident on another occasion, when the circle and virgules proposed a page break at the top of a manuscript page that had the last three lines of a chapter as a widow. Caxton's edition avoids the widow by ignoring the circle and virgules and trimming the text slightly:

HM 136:	° //	maner So that he bigate on me this childe ¶ But neuer myght I wit of him what he was ne whens he come / ne what was his name Of the ansuere of Merlyn wherfor the kyng axed why his werk myȝt not stond that he had bigonne ner proue Capitulo lxij°
Chronicles:	[c8r]	ner so that he begate this child / but neuer myȝt I wit what he was
	[c8v]	Of the ansuerd of Merlyn wherfor the kyng axed why his werk myȝt not stond that he had bigonne ner proue Capitulo .lxij.[56]

This is uncharacteristic inaccuracy for *The Chronicles of England*'s handling of its exemplar, but the need to avoid widows could explain why the compositor altered the text and ignored the casting off marks, especially if he had set signature c8v in the outer forme first, daring to start where a new chapter title starts—not seeing that he would then have trouble fitting the end of the preceding chapter onto the previous page when he printed it later in the inner forme.

Finally, the person casting off decided to ease the work of calculating where to begin pages out of sequence by deciding that the printed edition would follow the exemplar's own page breaks closely, from HM 136 folio 65r, or the end of printed quire h (as noted above). This could have eased his calculations of page breaks if setting by forme. But he did not ease the process as much as he might have, for although both the manuscript and the printed book are quired in eights, by the time the page breaks become coterminous, the manuscript is starting quire 9 (fol. 65r) but the printed book is still on the last page of its eighth quire (sig. h8v), so quires of the exemplar could not have been divided among different compositors or tracked quire by quire with any ease.[57] Yet at this point the compositor decided to follow the exemplar very closely indeed, even in its page breaks.

The Textual Relationship

It is the closeness of the manuscript and printed book in this and other respects that finally confirms that Caxton's edition was set from this manuscript. In general, the manuscript is the sole witness to the branch of the textual tradition that Caxton follows (as noted above, following Matheson's study). In particular, the collation of a sample from the edition with the manuscript shows that Caxton's edition is copied from the manuscript—and that their close relationship could not have arisen conversely, by the scribe copying from Caxton's print.

The collated sample (9,754 words on 21 pages) was not randomly selected but consisted of pages which had unusual markings at their page ends and other pages chosen to ensure a sample from throughout the text.[58] Yet the collation does suggest some tentative hypotheses. First, it confirms Matheson's observation about the general affiliation and shows that HM 136 and Caxton's edition are identical in more than 98.22% of 9,754 words, in the substantives (that is, in lexis and grammar but not in orthography or punctuation). This percentage is remarkably close to that found by comparing a sample of the edition of Lydgate's *The Fall of Princes* printed by Richard Pynson (1494) with its long-recognized manuscript exemplar, in which some 98.26% of words were identical in the substantives (1,303 of 1,326 words).[59]

The close similarity between Caxton's first edition of *The Chronicles of England* and HM 136 is accordant, then, with that of another English incunable and its exemplar. Of course, print and manuscript often diverge in accidentals—in the variable spelling, punctuation, and abbreviation common in Middle English—but even in those respects *The Chronicles of England* diverges less often and more systematically than one might expect.[60] Most noticeable is the punctuation: when HM 136 has a blue paraph, Caxton's edition almost always leaves a blank space for a handwritten one.

When HM 136 and Caxton's edition *do* diverge, in two thirds of these divergences (66.67% of 174 divergent words) the manuscript preserves the main textual tradition reproduced by the modern editor (Brie) from other manuscripts, and it is Caxton's edition that is the odd one out. Often these divergences can be readily explained as slips by the compositor: for example, the compositor misreads "howe he pursued" as "howe be pursued," either mistaking the hooked *h* of the scribe's hand modeled on secretary for a *b* or muddling these similar letters in his type case.⁶¹ Once he omits the adverb "nowe," and he might conceivably miss it because it is the last word before the end of a line in HM 136.⁶² A concern such as that for "widows" might prompt two divergences, cutting the words "more openly" and even cutting "our lord Ihesu crist" down to "our lord" to let a chapter finish on one line rather than straggling onto the next line, which would then be left predominantly blank before the next chapter title.⁶³

Such omissions in Caxton's edition suggest that his is the later text that introduces divergences from the earlier. Moreover, in the few divergences (13.22%, or 23 of 174 divergent words) in which Caxton produces the text preferred by Brie and HM 136 diverges from it, two things occur. For eight of these divergent words, HM 136 differs from Brie's text but does reproduce the text of one or both of the manuscripts he collates in his *apparatus criticus* (MSS D and O), so HM 136 is not outlandish.⁶⁴ On the other occasions, he corrects obviously ungrammatical or nonsensical text in HM 136—the gibberish "righ" to "right"⁶⁵—or he updates the language in few tiny details (noted below). So even when Caxton's divergence from HM 136 converges with the mainstream textual tradition, such convergence could come from the simple processes of correction that compositors, like scribes, made as they reproduced words.

By contrast, when HM 136 follows the mainstream textual tradition but Caxton diverges, HM 136 could not have restored the mainstream textual tradition, if it were copied from Caxton's edition, by simple guesswork. For example, there are divergences that seem to stem from eyeskip: the compositor for Caxton's edition on one occasion omitted just two words, shortening "from þe toure of london þurgh london vn to *seint* Giles" into "from the toure of london vn to seint Giles,"⁶⁶ and on two occasions jumped from the middle of one line to the middle of the next, as for example here:

HM 136: othe / that arose ayens his liege lorde the noble kyng Edward
and falsely made hym kynge of Scotland / as is said bifore
and his sone sholde be kyng of Scotland that was of age
of v yere ¶ And so thurgh this cursed counceill Dauid

> *Chronicles:* forswore ayens his othe that arose ayens his liege lord the noble kyng Edward and falsely made hym kyng of Scotland that was of age of v. yere And so thurgh this cursed counceil[67]

It would be less easy for somebody to copy HM 136 from Caxton's edition and work out what to restore in such lines than it would for a compositor setting *The Chronicles of England* from the manuscript to err by means of eyeskip. A few smaller words are also dropped in ways that suggest Caxton's edition was copied from the manuscript and not vice versa. For example, at the end of original prose *Brut* in the manuscript, the text lists some fees paid by Rouen to Henry V: "all man*er* customes and fee fermes and kateremes <gap> | <gap> marce"; then one more sentence completes the text to 1419. The gap is unfilled in most manuscripts and was likely intended for the exact number of marks paid. In HM 136 the gap straddles a page break and "marce" begins a page after an odd space on the first line; then the next sentence begins: "And þan þe kyng entred in to þe toune." Given the odd gap and the stranded word "marce," it would be easy for somebody setting copy from HM 136 to overlook "marce" or decide to omit it. And sure enough, Caxton's edition omits the unit of currency ("marce") as well as the number, leaving a gap not much bigger than that usually left to add a paraph: "alle maner customes and fee fermes and kateremes <gap> And than the kyng entred in to the toune." If instead this manuscript had been copied from the printed book, then it would be harder to guess which unit of currency was omitted and to reinsert it; indeed, the manuscripts that are known to be copied from Caxton's edition omit "marce," too.[68] Overall, then, Caxton's edition looks like a close and accurate copy of manuscript HM 136.

Caxton's Deliberate Divergences

There are, though, a few divergences odder than simple errors—but still explicable. They are intriguing for what they suggest about Caxton's processes of "editing," and they confirm processes of updating and of historical curiosity found in his printing of Malory's works and other histories such as Trevisa's English *Polychronicon*.

The first set of such divergences occurs when Caxton or his colleague updates the Middle English of the prose *Brut*. Such updating of archaic forms or removal of dialectally striking forms has been noted in other texts that Caxton claims to have revised by updating the language, such as Trevisa's English *Polychronicon*.[69] The same thing happens in the sample of *The Chronicles of England*. Once Caxton updates the archaic verb "wyten" into "knoweth."[70] The other efforts to update vocabulary and grammar occur more regularly, almost systematically, albeit never in every possible instance. Some six times in the 9,754 collated words, the edition updates "greek" as the name of the country to "Grece."[71] Some eight times it replaces the verb *nim*, which was becoming archaic during the fifteenth century, with forms of the verb *take*. (Often the modern printed edition by Brie has *take*, but again HM 136 follows MSS D and/or O in Brie's *apparatus criticus*, which do have *nim*.)[72] And most commonly, some ten times in the collated pages it alters the phrase "that me called Diane" or similar for different characters. This phrase uses the impersonal pronoun *me*, equivalent to modern English *one*, and can be translated as *whom people called Diane*; but the impersonal pronoun *me* was becoming archaic, and that is likely why Caxton's edition changes these phrases to the passive construction "that was called Diane" and so on.[73] The regularity of these divergences between the manuscript and print throws fascinating light on the work of Caxton's press and on linguistic attitudes in the late fifteenth century. Further study might yield other evidence of Caxton's handling of English works.

The second and third sets of divergences are less regular, yet while they might seem to make the printed book look less close to HM 136, both sets of divergences continue to reflect the manuscript closely—and conversely, also leave their mark on the manuscript. The second set includes larger structural changes. As in Malory's works, which Caxton seems to unite into a larger whole while simultaneously rendering the text into smaller chapters, so in *The Chronicles of England*, Caxton takes care to articulate the structure of the text.[74] First, he adds onto *The Chronicles of England* his continuation, seamlessly joined, and he also seems to have intended his 1480 edition of a geographical work, *The Description of Britain*, to be sold alongside *The Chronicles of England* for binding with it, as the two texts do indeed survive together in many extant copies.[75] These elements he adds to what he found in HM 136. But the manuscript was already subdivided into chapters, most with separate titles and consecutive numbers, so Caxton added in his edition a table of contents, helping readers to negotiate the chapters. He also, curiously, modified two chapter titles in the collated sample of text:

HM 136:	Here may a man here that England was furst called Albion and thurgh whom it had the name
Chronicles:	How the lande of Englonde was fyrst namd Albyon And by what encheson it was so namd
HM 136:	Amen And aftir this kyng henry þe iiij^e regned kyng henry his sone kyng of Englond Capitulo CC xliiij^{to} ~
Chronicles:	Of kyng Henry the v. that was kyng henries sone Capitulo ducentesimo xliiij.[76]

Whereas these chapter titles are anomalously chatty and narrative in the manuscript (and the second is confusing), Caxton standardizes their phrasing with *How* or *Of* for the printed edition—the phrasing used for all but nine of 263 chapter titles.[77] Moreover, beyond the collated sample, Caxton's edition lacks a title for chapter 179 in the text, though it nevertheless appears in his table of contents ("How sir Robert the Brus was crouned c*apitulo* c. lxxix"); and in HM 136 this chapter title was omitted by the original scribe too—no doubt the reason for Caxton's omission—but was then added to the manuscript in a different ink and different fifteenth-century hand in wording similar to Caxton's ("How Robrt [*sic*] the bruys was crowned in *sain*t Iohns toun ca*pitul*o Clxxix^o").[78] While the table of contents and these few different chapter titles do diverge between the manuscript and the printed book, the divergences seem explicable given Caxton's known care for such paratexts. And the chapter title added later to HM 136, echoing the printed table of contents, may suggest further the proximity between Caxton's book and this manuscript—albeit a complex proximity with two directions of influence.

Similarly, the third and final set of divergences is regular and explicable. On five occasions in the collated sample, *The Chronicles of England* adds a few words not found in the main textual tradition of the prose *Brut* nor in

HM 136. Yet these additions could reflect a regular process of editing, for they all clarify the identities of people by expanding their names or connections in some way:

HM 136		Caxton
The kynges messagiers	>	The messagiers of the kyng Vortiger
the messagiers	>	the kynges messagiers
þe Erle	>	the Erle of Fiffe
the kyng	>	kyng Edward
Erle of Arundell	>	Erle of Arundell as his fadre had bene[79]

Considered as clarifications of people's identities, these alterations are as regular and helpful as updated archaisms; they are handy in a chronicle of the English and Scottish aristocracies, with their tendencies to shared names, competing affinities, and knotty genealogies. These few altered words (in a sample of 9,754) suggest something about the intellectual engagement of Caxton or his compositor and in particular about their historical passions— passions suggested by Caxton's long-standing commitment to printing histories and his modifications of the history in Malory's Arthurian romance, drawing on this very chronicle.[80] They also confirm the sense from the textual tradition of Trevisa's English *Polychronicon*, where the manuscripts closest to Caxton's—one of them perhaps being the exemplar of his exemplar— include a few comments glossing people and places, comments that Caxton incorporates into his text.[81]

Manuscript HM 136 has almost no written markings in it telling the compositor to add the modernizations of vocabulary or added identifications of people which appear in the first printed edition of *The Chronicles of England*. As has been noted of the "Winchester" manuscript of Malory's works, Caxton presumably did not want to deface a loaned exemplar and so added "running corrections" during typesetting.[82] However, there are four added identifications that appear in Caxton's edition and not otherwise in the textual tradition but that have been interlineated into HM 136 by a second scribe:

HM 136 (with interlineations in markings ⌐ and ¬)		Caxton
his wyfe ⌐^Emme¬	>	his wife Emme
his moder ⌐/Em¬	>	his moder Emme
þe kyng ⌐his fadir¬	>	þᵉ kyng his fadre
kyng Edwardes sone ⌐^called	>	kyng Edwardes sone called
Edward with the long schank*es*¬		edward with long scha*n*kes[83]

Beyond the pages collated fully, there are three other added identifications of people's identities interlineated into HM 136 and printed in full in Caxton's edition.[84]

On the one hand, the identifications *lacking* in HM 136 confirm that HM 136 was not originally copied from Caxton's printed edition—for a scribe would be unlikely to omit in a systematic way only those phrases identifying people (of which the prose *Brut* naturally has many anyway) unique to Caxton's edition—but rather that Caxton's copy must be a descendant of HM 136. Other signs of eyeskips by Caxton's compositor (noted above) confirm this direction of textual affiliation.

The identifications then *interlineated* into HM 136 seem to confirm the close proximity between HM 136 and Caxton's edition. Yet, on the other hand, these interlineations into HM 136 beg questions. Might they be signs of somebody tinkering with the text before or while Caxton's compositor set the pages, as though beginning to envisage the editing process? It is teasing that the handwriting of these interlineations is similar to that which added some running headings of kings' names in the manuscript, as far as one can tell,[85] and similar to the hand which added "assem" when *assembled* straddled a page break; the carets used for some of these interlineations are similar to the seeming carets that mark the page breaks. But it is difficult to make confident judgments about such tiny pieces of writing, and the precise meaning of these marks is unclear.

Further Links between Manuscript and Print

Might these interlineations instead be signs of somebody checking Caxton's edition against the manuscript? This is feasible, given that she or he interlineated into and so maybe checked only a few pages. They suggest that the influence between manuscript and printed book could flow in both directions.

After all, finally, at some stage somebody did copy into HM 136 a short excerpt of Caxton's edition: an excerpt of the continuation of the prose *Brut* from 1419.[86] As noted above, the manuscript is in quires of eight leaves, and the Common Version of the prose *Brut* to 1419 ends with the words "in rewle and in gouernaunce" three lines down the verso of the fourth leaf of quire 20. But then somebody added to the rest of this verso and to the next folio and recto after that (that is, up to the recto of leaf 6 of quire 20) a short excerpt from the start of Caxton's continuation beyond 1419.[87] (The following verso was left blank and the final two leaves of quire 20 were removed at some point.)

The individual graphs used by the scribe of this excerpt of the continuation are often very similar to those of the main scribe of the rest of the manuscript, although the general aspect of the handwriting differs to some extent. The layout differs, too, as the scribe of the excerpt of the continuation uses more and longer lines on each page, leaves large gaps between chapters, and leaves spaces for painted initials, clearly following Caxton's use of spacing before new chapters.

Moreover, the text of this added continuation follows Caxton's text closely: of 2,115 words, only six diverge from Caxton's text in substantives.[88] The manuscript excerpt of the continuation even repeats an erroneous dittography in Caxton's edition ("distroyeng of of heretikes") and has an odd word division in the name of the feast day "whit sontyd" (*Whitsuntide*) where Caxton's edition has a mid-word line break ("whit | sontyd").[89] Moreover, it is possible that the handwriting and orthography of this continuation in HM 136 were influenced by Caxton's book: majuscules in the manuscript excerpt of the continuation, especially in some Latin verses, closely resemble the uppercase letters in Caxton's edition; and whereas the earlier scribe of HM 136 uses thorn (þ) a lot, which Caxton often removed, the scribe of the continuation from 1419 uses only one thorn, and at the end of a line where he might have felt that he was running out of room.[90]

Finally and crucially, this continuation from 1419 to 1461 is known otherwise only in Caxton's edition and in manuscripts copied from it entirely or in this part.[91] And it seems that here, too, this final part of manuscript

HM 136, which is set out differently from the rest—and without any of the casting-off marks either—was not the source for Caxton's edition but was copied from it.

Yet this copy is visibly an afterthought and is soon abandoned: it stops at the foot of a recto just two lines into chapter 247, having left space for the heading of this chapter, and leaving the verso overleaf unused.[92] This addition from Caxton's text, along with its interruption, thus raises puzzling questions about which scribe or owner of HM 136 could both provide this book to Caxton as an exemplar and then copy into it or have copied into it only an incomplete excerpt of Caxton's edition. Such questions need answering by further research into the manuscript's provenance. Further research is also needed in order to confirm or deny the hypotheses offered here about Caxton's printing from this exemplar by forme and by the outer forme first rather than *seriatim*; about his or his compositor's interest in avoiding word splits and widows; about the interest in updating Middle English; and about the interest in expanding historical details. However, the combination of the casting-off marks with a collation of 9,754 words does suggest strongly that manuscript HM 136 is Caxton's exemplar. With that exemplar identified, all manner of questions about Caxton's processes of editing and printing English can be asked and perhaps answered afresh.

University of Cambridge

Acknowledgments

I must thank two anonymous readers as well as Anthony Bale, Richard Beadle, Julia Boffey, Alexandra Gillespie, Hope Johnston, Mary Robinson, Toshiyuki Takamiya, Satoko Tokunaga, and especially Masako Takagi for helpful feedback on this piece. None of them is responsible for any errors in the article. This research was made possible by a generous grant from the Huntington Library to spend time at the library as a Foundation Fellow from January to March 2009.

NOTES

1. For lists of examples before 1500, see N. F. Blake, "Manuscript to Print," in *Book Production and Publishing in Britain 1375–1475*, ed. Jeremy Griffiths

and Derek Pearsall (Cambridge, UK: Cambridge University Press, 1989), 403–432 (426–429, nos. 1, 6, 7, 8, 10, 12); and Margaret Lane Ford, "Author's Autograph and Printer's Copy: Werner Rolewinck's *Paradisus conscientiae*," in *Incunabula: Studies in Fifteenth-Century Printed Books Presented to Lotte Hellinga*, ed. Martin Davies (London: British Library, 1999), 109–128 (119–125); and for English examples 1500–1640, see J. K. Moore, *Primary Materials Relating to Copy and Print in English Books of the Sixteenth and Seventeenth Centuries*, Oxford Bibliographical Society Occasional Publications 24 (Oxford: Oxford Bibliographical Society, 1992), 11–18.

2. José Ruysschaert, "Les manuscrits autographes de deux œuvres de Lorenzo Guglielmo Traversagni imprimées chez Caxton," *Bulletin of the John Rylands Library* 36 (1953): 191–197; A. C. de la Mare and Lotte Hellinga, "The First Book Printed in Oxford: The *Expositio symboli* of Rufinus," *Transactions of the Cambridge Bibliographical Society* 7 (1978): 184–244; Blake, "Manuscript to Print," 423 (no. 17), omits the latter from the relevant list on 426–429, although he mentions it earlier in his chapter (405–406).

3. Takako Kato, *Caxton's Morte D'Arthur: The Printing Process and the Authenticity of the Text*, Medium Ævum Monographs ns 22 (Oxford: Society for the Study of Medieval Languages and Literature, 2002), 14–16, 21.

4. Contrast Gavin Bone, "Extant Manuscripts Printed from by W. de Worde, with Notes on the Owner, Roger Thorney," *The Library* 4th ser., 12 (1932): 284–306 (285); with N. F. Blake, "Caxton's Copy-Text of Gower's *Confessio Amantis*," in N. F. Blake, *William Caxton and English Literary Culture* (London: Hambledon Press, 1991), 187–198 (190–191).

5. Ronald Waldron, "Caxton and the *Polychronicon*," in *Chaucer in Perspective: Middle English Essays in Honour of Norman Blake*, ed. Geoffrey Lester (Sheffield, UK: Sheffield Academic Press, 1999), 375–394 (380–381). Ronald Waldron, ed., *John Trevisa's Translation of the* Polychronicon *of Ranulph Higden, Book VI*, Middle English Texts 35 (Heidelberg, Germany: Winter, 2004), xxviii–xxxi, does not discuss the hypothesis further.

6. Quotations from Caxton's edition are hereafter cited as "*Chronicles*" with signatures and line numbers thus: "sig. a4r:30." There is a facsimile entitled *Chronicles of England, Westmynstre, 1480*, The English Experience: Its Record in Early Printed Books Published in Facsimile 508 (Amsterdam: Theatrum Orbis Terrarum, 1973). The modern edition by Friedrich W. D. Brie, ed.,

The Brut or The Chronicles, EETS os 131, 136, 2 vols. (London: Kegan Paul, Trench, Trübner, 1906–1908), is hereafter cited as "Brie" with page and line numbers thus: "35:2."

7. *Catalogue of Books Printed in the XVth Century now in the British Library: Part XI: England*, ed. Lotte Hellinga ('t Goy-Houten, Holland: Hes and De Graaf, 2007), 11:116–118 (hereafter cited as "*BMC*, XI"); Nicolas Barker, "Caxton's Typography," *Journal of the Printing Historical Society* 11 (1976): 114–133 (123); William Blades, *The Biography and Typography of William Caxton, England's First Printer*, ed. James Moran (1877; London: Muller, 1971), 117, 123, 245–246.

8. Lister M. Matheson, *The Prose* Brut: *The Development of a Middle English Chronicle* (Tempe, AZ: Medieval and Renaissance Texts and Studies, 1998), 123–124, 157, 164.

9. Ibid., 123–124; Lister M. Matheson, "Printer and Scribe: Caxton, the *Polychronicon* and the *Brut*," *Speculum* 60 (1985): 593–614 (594–595, 598–599).

10. Matheson, *Prose* Brut, 118, 157, 339.

11. Matheson, "Printer and Scribe," 595–596; Blake, "Manuscript to Print," 420 (no. 4).

12. Lotte Hellinga, "Manuscripts in the Hands of Printers," in *Manuscripts in the Fifty Years after the Invention of Printing*, ed. J. B. Trapp (London: Warburg Institute, 1983), 3–11 (4); see also Blake, "Manuscript to Print," 419–425.

13. San Marino, CA, Henry E. Huntington Library, MS HM 136, hereafter cited as "HM 136" with folio and line numbers thus: "fol. 77v:4." For descriptions, see C. W. Dutschke, *Guide to Medieval and Renaissance Manuscripts in the Huntington Library*, 2 vols. (San Marino, CA: Huntington Library, 1989), 1:181–183; Friedrich W. D. Brie, *Geschichte und Quellen der mittelenglische Proschronik* The Brute of England *oder* The Chronicles of England (Marburg: N. G. Elwert'sche, 1905), 63, 110–111, where it is listed as "Cheltenham 8858"; and John Thompson, ed., "Huntington MS. HM 136," in *The Imagining History Portal*, last modified July 2, 2006, http://www.qub.ac.uk/imagining-history/resources/wiki/index.php/Huntington_MS._HM_136.

14. HM 136, fol. vii^r, the first recto after quire 22 (8 leaves, lacking 7–8). See an almost identical *ex libris* in Oxford, Trinity College, MS 13, fol. 104r; MS 14, fol. 69r; MS 16 (part A); MS 49, fol. 295v. The signatures in London, British Library, MS Additional 41321, fols. 33v, 72v, and 11v are different.

For previous discussion, see Jeremy Griffiths, "The Manuscripts," in *Lollard Sermons*, ed. Gloria Cigman, EETS os 294 (Oxford: Oxford University Press, 1989), xi–xxx (xv, n. 1); R. W. Pfaff, *New Liturgical Feasts in Late Medieval England* (Oxford: Oxford University Press, 1970), 50–51; John M. Manly, Edith Rickert, et al., ed., *The Text of the "Canterbury Tales," Studied on the Basis of All Known Manuscripts*, 8 vols. (Chicago: University of Chicago Press, 1940), 1:540–544; and in the information file kept at the Huntington Library.

15. Masako Takagi, "Research Note—1/4: Study on the Prose *Brut* MSS in relation to William Caxton's *Chronicles of England* (1480)," *Kyorin University Review* 22 (2010): 101–114 (107), mentions these marks in the light of my discussion of them with her on April 2, 2009.

16. M. B. Parkes, *Pause and Effect, An Introduction to the History of Punctuation in the West* (Aldershot: Scolar, 1992), 305 s.v. paraph, 307 s.v. virgula suspensiva, illustrated in pl. 28, by chance from another fifteenth-century manuscript of the Middle English prose *Brut*.

17. Charles Johnson and Hilary Jenkinson, *English Court Hand, A.D. 1066 to 1500: Illustrated Chiefly from the Public Records*, 2 vols. (Oxford: Clarendon Press, 1915), 1:78, illustrates five variant forms of the caret. Some fifteenth-century scribes form a caret more like two short virgules //, but this seems to be a more casual caret in which its two strokes fail to converge.

18. Parkes, *Pause and Effect*, 307 s.v. simplex ductus, 12, 118–119 (n. 54).

19. But not all interlinear insertions had a caret mark: see, e.g., "in thraldome and bondage ⌐of⌐ The kyng Pandras of greek," without any caret mark (fol. 3r:19; cf. *Chronicles*, sig. a4r:12; Brie, 6:20). One of the interlineations without a caret mark was accompanied by crossing out "the truage that was woned to be paied [at]⌐to⌐ Rome" (fol. 16v:1; *Chronicles*, sig. b8v:40; Brie, 39:18). Including these 24 interlinear insertions, there are 57 corrections in the manuscript.

20. Eleven sets lack the circle, though it seems likely to have been trimmed off the fore-edge by binders: HM 136, fols. 2v:6, 10v:16, 24v:7, 54v:19, 56v:17, 57v:18, 60v:14, 84v:1, 89v:1, 90v:1, 102v:1.

21. HM 136, fols. 2r:5, 8v:12, 9v:13, 11v:21, 12r:23, 16v:42, 20r:39, 33v:35, 38v:26, 40v:34, 41r:35, 49v:22, 105v:1, and 106v:44 with 107r:1 (straddling a page break). In 9 of these 14 instances, virgules at the line end would have

separated off the last few words of a chapter or sentence or would have split a word in two; by contrast, the seeming caret appears at a clear break in sentence, chapter, or word.

22. HM 136, fols. 7v:8 with 7v:12, 10v:15–16, 43r:38 with 43r:40, 58r:15–16, 59r:16–17, 82r:1–2, as well as on subsequent lines of text straddling a page break in the manuscript on fols. 17v:40 and 18r:1; 92v:43 and 93r:1; 124v:45 and 125r:1.

23. The glitches are discussed below as important clues to the significance of the marks.

24. HM 136, fols. 7r:7 and 8r:10.

25. The previous set of marks was on the last line of fol. 64r:42 The person marking the text counted 43 lines, which led him or her to the top of fol. 65r:1, skipping fol. 64v entirely. *Chronicles* follows the manuscript's page breaks from sig. h8v onwards.

26. HM 136, fols. 83r:1 (and also 82v:42), 93r:1 (and also 92v:44), 107r:1 (and also 106v:44), 125r:1 (and also 124v:45), 144r:1 (and also 143v:42).

27. HM 136, fols. 91r:1 and 91r:2, 104v:1 and 104v:3 and 112v:1 and 112v:2.

28. HM 136, fol. 106r, where they appear only on line 2, and fol. 101v, where they appear on lines 1 and 41 but not on fol. 102r.

29. HM 136, fol. iii^r. I owe this suggestion to Alexandra Gillespie.

30. For example, a copy of a later edition of *The Chronicles of England* (London: William de Machlinia, [ca. 1486]; *STC* 9993), now in London, British Library, shelfmark IB.55463, contains notes in red ink comparing its omissions and inclusions with the prose *Brut* in London, British Library, MS Egerton 650, which has corresponding notes in pencil in the same hand (e.g., printed sig. F8v and MS fol. 2r; printed sig. V3r and MS fol. 74v; printed sig. aa8r and MS fol. 108v; printed sig. bb4r and MS fol. 111r). This annotator calls MS Egerton 650 "my MS. C" and also compares his two other manuscripts of the text, which he calls "A" and "B," although the notes about "A" and "B" do not fit the details of HM 136.

31. Ford, "Author's Autograph," 111; and Philip Gaskell, *A New Introduction to Bibliography* (Oxford: Clarendon Press, 1972), 41, 50, note the various procedures that such marks can reveal.

32. Ford, "Author's Autograph," 112–113.

33. It is interesting to recall here that Caxton learned to print in Cologne

and that Arnold ther Hoernen of Cologne had close connections with the press in Oxford; see Lotte Hellinga, *William Caxton and Early Printing in England* (London: British Library, 2010), 26–32, 78–79.

34. On these processes, see Gaskell, *New Introduction*, 81–82; Lotte Hellinga, "Press and Text in the First Decades of Printing," in *Libri, tipografi e biblioteche: Ricerche storiche dedicate a Luigi Balsamo*, ed. Instituto di Biblioteconomia e Paleografia Università degli Studi, Parma, 2 vols. (Florence, Italy: Olschki, 1997), 1:1–23 (4–5); Lotte Hellinga, "Introduction," in *Catalogue of Books Printed in the XVth Century now in the British Library: Part XI: England*, ed. Lotte Hellinga ('t Goy-Houten, Holland: Hes and De Graaf, 2007), 11:1–84 (21–22); and for recent thinking, G. Thomas Tanselle, *Bibliographical Analysis: A Historical Introduction* (Cambridge, UK: Cambridge University Press, 2009), 39–41.

35. See, respectively, Ruysschaert, "Manuscrits autographes," 194–195; Robert W. Mitchner, "Wynkyn de Worde's Use of the Plimpton Manuscript of *De proprietatibus rerum*," *The Library* 5th ser., 6 (1951): 7–18 (8); Margery M. Morgan, "Pynson's Manuscript of *Dives and Pauper*," *The Library* 5th ser., 8 (1953): 217–228 (217); Margery M. Morgan, "A Specimen of Early Printer's Copy: Rylands English MS. 2," *Bulletin of the John Rylands Library* 33 (1950–1): 194–196; with further observations by Daniel Wakelin, "Writing the Words," in *The Production of Books in England c. 1350–c. 1500*, ed. Alexandra Gillespie and Daniel Wakelin (Cambridge, UK: Cambridge University Press, 2011), 34–58 (56–58).

36. Hellinga, "Introduction," 22.

37. See both Hellinga, "Introduction," 21; and de la Mare and Hellinga, "First Book," 198. For minimal marks used to cast off copy-text, see Moore, *Primary Materials*, pl. 1, with a dash between lines 16 and 17 reflecting the page break shown in pl. 2; and Wytze Gs. Hellinga, *Copy and Print in the Netherlands: An Atlas of Historical Bibliography* (Amsterdam: North-Holland Publishing, 1962), 95 and pl. 13, with a mere scratch.

38. Percy Simpson, *Proof-Reading in the Sixteenth, Seventeenth and Eighteenth Centuries*, with an introduction by Harry Carter (1935; Oxford: Oxford University Press, 1970), 57; Blake, "Caxton's Copy-Text," 196–197.

39. Hellinga, "Press and Text," 4; Hellinga, "Introduction," 23–24. The Oxford edition of Rufinus's *Symbola apostolorum* was printed nonsequential-

ly but on half-sheets (Hellinga, "Introduction," 23–24; and *BMC*, XI, 234).
40. Ruysschaert, "Manuscrits autographes," 196; de la Mare and Hellinga, "First Book," 201; Ford, "Author's Autograph," 114.
41. For the latter, see HM 136, fols. 10v:15–16 (*Chronicles*, sig. b3v; Brie, 24:24), 17v:42 with virgules on 18r:1 (*Chronicles*, sig. c2v; Brie, 43:11), 58r:15–16 (*Chronicles*, sig. h1v; Brie, 137:9), 124v:45 with virgules on 125r:1 (*Chronicles*, sig. q4v; Brie, 311:34). I have also counted them as "free" page breaks.
42. *Chronicles*, sigs. a2r (HM 136, fol. 1v:2), a4r (fol. 3v:8), b1r (fol. 8v:12), b2r (9v:13), b3r (fol. 10v:15), b4r (fol. 11v:21), b8v (fol. 16v:2), c1r (fol. 16v:42), c2r (fol. 17v:40), c5v (fol. 21v:1), d6v (fol. 30v:29), d7v (fol. 31v:30), e4r (fol. 36v:17), e5v (fol. 38r:23), e7v (fol. 40r:31), e8v (fol. 41r:35), f5v (fol. 46v:14), f8v (fol. 49v:22), g4r (fol. 53r:23), g6v (fol. 55v:17), h1r (fol. 58r:15), h3r (fol. 60r:14), h6v (fol. 63r:40), i3r (fol. 68r:1), n8v (fol. 105v:1), p2r (fol. 115r:1), q3r (fol. 124r:1), q4r (fol. 124v:45), q6v (fol. 127v:1), r1r (fol. 130r:1), s2r (fol. 139r:1), s3r (fol. 140r:1), s7v (fol. 144v:1), t5v (fol. 150v:1). Ten of these seeming carets shift the end of the pages so that they fall at breaks between words, sentences, or chapters.
43. *Chronicles*, sigs. a2v (HM 136, fol. 2r:5), b4v (fol. 12r:23), e1v (fol. 33v:35), e6r (fol. 38v:26), e8r (fol. 40v:35), f3v (fol. 44v:4), h2v (fol. 59v:14). By contrast, in the preceding list of 34 "free" page ends in the first-printed outer forme, only 10 shifts followed sense in these ways (namely, from the previous note, the page ends of *Chronicles*, sigs. b2r, b4r, c1r, c5v, d6v, e8v, f8v, g4r, h6v, q3r), while by contrast, some break up syntactical units (such as "kyng Arthur" in HM 136, fol. 36v:17, to "kyng | Arthur" in *Chronicles*, sig. e4r–v) which might be thought less desirable.
44. On the dislike of widows, see Hellinga, *Copy and Print*, 113–114.
45. Hellinga, "Introduction," 22.
46. In *Chronicles*, sig. h2r ends with a seeming caret at HM 136, fol. 59r:17 (Brie, 139:24), not with the virgules at fol. 59r:16; sig. l1r ends with a seeming caret at fol. 82r:2 (Brie, 200:4), not with the virgules at fol. 82r:1; sig. l2r ends with a seeming caret at 82v:41 (Brie, 202:26), not with the alternative set of virgules at fol. 83r:1; sig. m2r ends with a seeming caret at fol. 91r:2 (Brie, 223:18), not with the alternative set of virgules at fol. 91r:1; sig. m4r ends with a seeming caret at fol. 92v:43 (Brie, 228:19), not with the virgules

at fol. 93r:1; sig. n7v ends with a seeming caret at fol. 104v:3 (Brie, 256:21), not with the virgules at fol. 104v:1; sig. o2r ends with a seeming caret at fol. 106v:44 (Brie, 262:29), not at the alternative seeming caret at fol. 107r:1; sig. o7v ends at fol. 112v:2 (Brie, 277:2), not with the alternative set of virgules at fol. 112v:1; sig. r5v ends at fol. 134v:1 (Brie, 336:12) with a seeming caret and an unusual marking, on which see n. 51 below. Among these ten page ends in the other forme, only the page end for sig. l7v is wholly unmarked at fol. 88v:1 (Brie, 217:6); it is only one word into the line, away from the virgules at the line break, and falls at a new chapter title, an obvious place to break even without a seeming caret.

47. In *Chronicles*, sig. a4v ends unmarked at HM 136, fol. 4r:11 (Brie, 8:20), not with the virgules at fol. 4r:8; sig. c4v ends unmarked at fol. 20v:3 (Brie, 49:6), not at the circle and seeming caret at fol. 20r:39; sig. f4v ends unmarked at fol. 45v:9 (Brie, 104:22), not with the virgules at fol. 45v:8; sig. g4v ends unmarked at fol. 53v:20 (Brie, 125:27), not with the virgules at fol. 53v:22; sig. i4v ends unmarked at fol. 69r:41 (Brie, 166:19), not with the virgules on fol. 69v:1; sig. k4v ends unmarked at fol. 77r:43 (Brie, 187:21), not with the virgules at fol. 77v:1; sig. l4v ends unmarked at fol. 85v:3 (Brie, 209:11), not with the virgules at fol. 85v:1; sig. m4v ends unmarked at fol. 93v:1, two words into the line (Brie, 229:33), not with the virgules at the line break; sig. n4v ends unmarked at fol. 101r:41 (Brie, 249:3), not with the virgules at fol. 101v:1; sig. o4v ends unmarked at fol. 109r:43 (Brie, 269:7), not with the virgules at fol. 109v:1; sig. p4v ends unmarked at fol. 117v:3 (294:14), not with the virgules at fol. 117v:1; sig. s4v ends unmarked at fol. 141v:1, four words into the line (Brie, 354:6), not with the virgules at the line break; sig. t4v ends unmarked at fol. 149r:42 (Brie, 374:2), not with the virgules at fol. 149v:1.

48. In *Chronicles*, sig. a6r ends at HM 136, fol. 5v:3 (Brie, 11:27); sig. a8r ends at fol. 7v:8 (Brie, 16:16), not fol. 7v:12; sig. c8r ends at fol. 24r:1 (Brie, 57:18); sig. f2v, ends at fol. 43r:37 (in the section on Cadwallader, printed in Matheson, *Prose* Brut, 59); sig. s7r ends at fol. 143v:42 (Brie, 360:6).

49. Respectively, HM 136, fol. 11v:20–21, and *Chronicles*, sig. b4r:39 and b4v:1 (Brie, 27:9); HM 136, fol. 59r:16–17, and *Chronicles*, sig. h2r:40 and h2v:1–2 (Brie, 139:24). See also HM 136, fol. 16v:41–42, and *Chronicles*, sig. c1v:1 (Brie, 40:25); HM 136, fol. 33v:34–35, and *Chronicles*, sig. e2r:1

(Brie, 80:23); HM 136, fol. 40v:34–35, and *Chronicles*, sig. e8v:1 (Brie, 97:17); HM 136, fol. 43r:37–38, and *Chronicles*, sigs. f2v:38 and f3r:1 (in the section on Cadwallader, printed in Matheson, *Prose* Brut, 59); HM 136, fol. 49v:21–22, and *Chronicles*, sig. g1r:1 (Brie, 115:13).

50. HM 136, fols. 123v:43 and 124r:1, and *Chronicles*, sig. q3r:40 and q3v:1 (Brie, 309:17).

51. HM 136, fol. 134r–v, reproduced in *Chronicles*, sig. r6r:1 (Brie, 336:12). As far as one can tell with so few letters, "assem" seems to be in the same ink, and the use of the slanting long *s* would fit a dating to the fifteenth century.

52. Respectively, HM 136, fol. 123r–v (using yogh: "knyȝ | tes"), and *Chronicles*, sigs. q2v–23r (Brie, 308:11); HM 136, fol. 138r–v, and *Chronicles*, sigs. s1v–s2r (Brie, 346:26); HM 136, fol. 53v:20, "har | deknoght" split across *Chronicles*, sigs. g4v–g5r (Brie, 125:27); HM 136, fol. 130r:1, "wher | for" split over *Chronicles*, sig. r1r–v (Brie, 323:32).

53. Ford, "Author's Autograph," 114–115; N. F. Blake, *Caxton: England's First Publisher* (London: Osprey, 1976), 85–86. The second edition of *The Chronicles of England* in 1482 removes a few more word splits at page breaks (*BMC*, XI, 130). Masako Takagi informs me that all the quires of the second edition of *Chronicles* have some differences in page breaks from the first edition (except for quires p and t) but that only one page break diverges from that of the first edition of *Chronicles* (sig. m5r) and thereby restores that of HM 136 (fol. 93r–v).

54. HM 136, fol. 12r:22–24, and *Chronicles*, sigs. b4v–b5r (Brie, 28:20–21); HM 136, fol. 82r:1–3; *Chronicles*, sig. l1r–v (Brie, 200:3–4). See also HM 136, fol. 9v:13, and *Chronicles*, sig. b2v (Brie, 22:1); HM 136, fol. 38v:26, and *Chronicles*, sig. e6v (Brie, 92:13); HM 136, fol. 53r:23, and *Chronicles*, sig. g4v (Brie, 124:20); HM 136, fol. 63r:40, and *Chronicles*, sig. h7r (Brie, 150:26). Despite a seeming caret preceding the chapter title on HM 136, fol. 20r:39, and *Chronicles*, sig. c4v (Brie, 49:4–7), that chapter title ends up in fact on the previous page, and the chapter number is printed as though a separate heading on sig. c5r.

55. HM 136, fol. 21v:1, and *Chronicles*, sig. c6r (Brie, 51:23); HM 136, fol. 88v:1, and *Chronicles*, sig. l8r (Brie, 217:6); HM 136, fols. 101v:41, and 102r:1, and *Chronicles*, sig. n5v (Brie, 250:8).

56. HM 136, fol. 24r:1–3; *Chronicles*, sig. c8r–v (Brie, 57:15–18).

57. Therefore the alphabetical quire signatures in the manuscript are out of kilter with the quire signatures in the printed book by one page; e.g., the signature "vj" appears at the foot of fol. 153r, marking the manuscript's quire structure—though accidentally looking like a herald for the printed "v1r" which begins its text overleaf at the top of fol. 153v.

58. *Chronicles*, sigs. a2r, a3v, a4r, a4v, a8r, b4v, c7v, c8r, d1r, f2v, f4v, g4v, h2r, l4v, n4v, n7v, o7v, p4v, s7r, t4v, and the hypothesized antecedents, HM 136, fols. 3v–4r, 7r–v, 58v–59r, 85r–v, 101r, 104r–v, 112r–v, 117r–v, 143v, 149r; and also *Chronicles*, sig. d1r, and the hypothesized antecedent, HM 136, fols. 24v–25r, which is reproduced online at "HM 136," in *Guide to Medieval and Renaissance Manuscripts in the Huntington Library*, http://sunsite3.berkeley.edu/hehweb/HM136.html.

59. That is, Manchester, John Rylands Library, MS Eng. 2, identified in Morgan, "Specimen," 194–196. Wakelin, "Writing the Words," 56–58, mentions this sample, taken from Manchester, John Rylands Library, MS Eng. 2, fol. 29r–v, and John Lydgate, *The Fall of Princes* (London: Richard Pynson, 1494; STC 3175), sigs. e1r–e2v.

60. For the term *substantive*, see Gaskell, *New Introduction*, 339–342. However, I did count as substantive any divergent spellings of proper nouns or grammatical inflections that could obscure the information conveyed; e.g., "Greneschall" in HM 136, fol. 7r:15, changed to "Grenescheld" in *Chronicles*, sig. a8r:8–9, over the line break (Brie, 15:16); "ye knowyth" in HM 136, fol. 112r:24, which could at a push be a polite imperative in context, changed to the declarative "ye knowe" in *Chronicles*, sig. o7v:24 (Brie, 276:18).

61. HM 136, fol. 24v:30; *Chronicles*, sig. d1r:23 (Brie, 59:18).

62. HM 136, fol. 7r:11; *Chronicles*, sig. a8r:5 (Brie, 15:12).

63. HM 136, fol. 101r:27, and *Chronicles*, sig. n4v:24 (Brie, 248:21); HM 136, fol. 149r:3, and *Chronicles*, sig. t4v:3 (Brie, 372:32).

64. Brie's MS D is Dublin, Trinity College, MS 490, which Matheson, *Prose Brut*, 118–119, puts in group CV-1419(r&g): B, subgroup (a), close to HM 136; MS O is Oxford, Bodleian Library, MS Douce 323, which Matheson, *Prose Brut*, 80, puts in group CV-1333. In another 8 divergences, neither HM 136 nor Caxton's edition preserves Brie's text, but HM 136 does again preserve readings from MSS D, O, or both D and O in Brie's *apparatus criticus*.

65. HM 136, fol. 104r:7 and *Chronicles*, sig. n.7v:7 (Brie, 255:21). Some-

times *Chronicles* corrects errors in ways that cause its text to diverge from the mainstream textual tradition (Brie) even more: e.g., Brie, 208:29, has "þere was in Engeland a rybaude"; HM 136, fol. 85r:29–20, has the ungrammatical "the was in Englond a ribaud"; *Chronicles*, sig. 14v:25, corrects it into the grammatical but unauthoritative "tho was in englond a ribaude," reading the nonsensical "the" in HM 136 as the Middle English adverb *tho* (*"then"*).
66. HM 136, fol. 149r:40, and *Chronicles*, sig. t4v:36 (Brie, 374:1).
67. HM 136, fol. 104r:20–22, and *Chronicles*, sig. n7v:19–21 (Brie, 256:1–2). See also HM 136, fol. 23r:28–29, and *Chronicles*, sig. c7v:26, though *Chronicles* here also adds the words "*and* wist not" (Brie, 55:30–31).
68. HM 136, fol. 156r:42–156v:1; *Chronicles*, sig. u3v:38 (Brie, 391:14). Compare the lack of "marce" in, for example, London, British Library, MS Cotton Claudius A.viii, fol. 15v:10–11, on which see Matheson, *Prose* Brut, 162; and n. 92 below; or Cambridge, Peterhouse, MS 190, fol. 197r:7, on which see Lister M. Matheson, ed., *Death and Dissent: Two Fifteenth-Century Chronicles* (Woodbridge, UK: Boydell, 1999), 74–76.
69. Waldron, "Caxton and the *Polychronicon*," 388–390.
70. HM 136, fol. 23v:14, and *Chronicles*, sig. c8r:14 (Brie, 56:22).
71. HM 136, fol. 2v:14, and *Chronicles*, sig. a3v:9 (Brie, 5:8); HM 136, fol. 3r:10, 3r:15, 3r:19, and *Chronicles*, sig. a4r:4, a4r:9, a4r:13 (Brie, 6:11, 6:17, 6:21); HM 136, fol. 3v:23, 3v:33, and *Chronicles*, sig. a4v:14, a4v:22–23 (Brie, 7:30, 8:4).
72. HM 136, fol. 3v:32, and *Chronicles*, sig. a4v:22 (Brie, 8:3, reading from MS D); HM 136, fol. 45r:16, 45r:38, and *Chronicles*, sig. f4v:11, f4v:32 (Brie, 103:23, 104:14); HM 136, fol. 45v:6, and *Chronicles*, sig. f4v:38 (Brie, 104:20); HM 136, fol. 85r:26, and *Chronicles*, sig. l4v:23 (Brie, 208:27, reading from MS O); HM 136, fol. 101r:14, and *Chronicles*, sig. n4v:13 (Brie, 248:9, reading from MSS D and O); HM 136, fol. 112r:16, and *Chronicles*, sig. o7v:15 (Brie, 276:11, reading from MS D). And see also HM 136, fol. 1r:25, and *Chronicles*, sig. a2r:24, where Brie, 2:4, does have "no*m*me." *BMC*, XI, 130, notes a further replacement of "nome" with "toke" in the second edition of *Chronicles* in 1482. On *nim*, see *OED*, *nim*, v., which dates few of its quotations after ca. 1450.
73. HM 136, fol. 2v:17, and *Chronicles*, sig. a3v:12 (Brie, 5:10); HM 136, fol. 3v:13–14, 3v:34–35, 3v:39–40, and *Chronicles*, sig. a4v:5–6, a4v:24–

25, a4v:29 (Brie, 7:22, 8:5, 8:9–10); HM 136, fol. 12r:9, and *Chronicles*, sig. b4v:25 (Brie, 28:5); HM 136, fol. 23v:7, 23v:19, and *Chronicles*, sig. c8r:7, c8r:19 (Brie, 56:14, 56:26); HM 136, fol. 45r:6, and *Chronicles*, sig. f4v:2 (Brie, 124:22); HM 136, fol. 53v:18, and *Chronicles*, sig. g4v:36 (Brie, 125:24); HM 136, fol. 85r:29, and *Chronicles*, sig. l4v:25 (Brie, 208:30). And interestingly, in two uses of "that me called" near the start of HM 136 (fol. 2v:17, 2v:30), somebody using a different, darker ink added a macron to *e* to signal an abbreviated *n*, giving "me*n*," as though uneasy with "me"; Caxton did not print "me" or "me*n*" here but again "that was called" (*Chronicles*, sig. a3v:11, a3v:24; Brie, 5:10, 5:27). On *me*, see *OED*, *me*, pron. 2, which records no uses after ca. 1525; and Tauno F. Mustanoja, *A Middle English Syntax: Part I: Parts of Speech* (Helsinki, Finland: Société Neophilologique, 1960), 219–222.

74. On Caxton's editing of Malory thus, see Kato, *Caxton's Morte D'Arthur*, 34, 37–39, 41–42.

75. *BMC*, XI, 117; Paul Needham, *The Printer and the Pardoner* (Washington, DC: Library of Congress, 1986), 66–67.

76. Respectively HM 136, fol. 1r:1–2, and *Chronicles*, sig. a2r:1–2 (Brie, 1:1–4, which has a completely different first heading again); HM 136, fol. 149r:4–5, and *Chronicles*, sig. t4v:4–5 (Brie, 373:1–2, which is closer to HM 136, but still not identical).

77. In the text and table for *Chronicles*, the only anomalous chapter titles are the initial unnumbered prologue (again, sig. iir, but with *How* on sig. a2r, as noted above); the first numbered chapter (sigs. iir, a3v); two chapters called "The prophecie of Merlyn" (chap. 160, on sigs. vi^r, i8v–k1r; and chap. 211, on sigs. vii^r, n2v), and chaps. 68 (sigs. iii^v, d2v), 206 (sig. m7r, but with *How* on sig. vii^r), 224 (sigs. vii^r, p2v), and 240 (sig. r5v, not separately listed on sig. vii^v). The chapter title is omitted, apart from the numbering, for chap. 249, on sig. u8v, but it begins with *Of* on sig. viii^r.

78. HM 136, fol. 81v:31–32; *Chronicles*, sigs. vi^r:36 and l1r:30 (Brie, 199:23–24, slightly different).

79. HM 136, fol. 23v:15, 23v:20, and *Chronicles*, sig. c8r:15, c8r:20–21 (Brie, 56:22–23, 56:27); HM 136, fol. 112r:19–20, and *Chronicles*, sig. o7v:19 (Brie, 276:13); HM 136, fol. 117r:34–35, and *Chronicles*, sig. p4v:33 (Brie, 294:7); HM 136, fol. 143v:40, and *Chronicles*, sig. s7r:35–36 (Brie, 360:5). It

should be noted that once Caxton cuts such detail, "Sir Aliʒaundre of Seton the sone" becomes "Sir Aliʒaundre of Seton" (HM 136, fol. 112r:7; *Chronicles*, sig. o7v:6; Brie, 276:2, reading from MSS D and O with "þe sone").

80. As traced in Masako Takagi, "Arthurian Geography: King Arthur's Roman War Episode in Malory (1485) and in the *Chronicles of England* (1480)," *Kyorin University Review* 21 (2009): 127–135; Masako Takagi, "William Caxton's Alteration of Text: The Case of Belyn and Brenne from 1480 to 1485," *Kyorin University Review* 19 (2007): 121–130; Masako Takagi and Toshiyuki Takamiya, "Caxton Edits the Roman War Episode: The *Chronicles of England* and Caxton's Book V," in *The Malory Debate: Essays on the Texts of 'Le Morte Darthur,'* ed. Bonnie Wheeler, Robert L. Kendrick, and Michael N. Salda, Arthurian Studies 47 (Cambridge, UK: Brewer, 2000), 169–190. Kathleen Tonry, "Reading History in Caxton's *Polychronicon*," *Journal of English and Germanic Philology* (forthcoming), traces Caxton's work and repute as a historian.

81. Waldron, "Caxton and the *Polychronicon*," 380, esp. n. 6, lists three glosses on people and places and a few other clarificatory corrections.

82. N. F. Blake, "Caxton Prepares His Edition of the Morte Darthur," in N. F. Blake, *William Caxton and English Literary Culture* (London: Hambledon Press, 1991), 199–211 (202).

83. Brie does not record these words in his modern edition of the main textual tradition. HM 136, fol. 53r:25, 53r:31, and *Chronicles*, sig. g4v:3, g4v:9 (cf. Brie, 124:22, 124:27); HM 136, fol. 101r:32–33, 101r:40–41, and *Chronicles*, sig. n4v:30–31, n4v:37–38 (cf. Brie, 248:27, and 249:2).

84. HM 136, fol. 48v:24–25: "And after this Eldred Edwyne ⌜^sone of Edmond⌝ his broþer regned"; *Chronicles*, sig. f8r:5–6: "And after this Eldred Edwyne sone of Edmond his brother regned" (not in Brie, 113:1); HM 136, fol. 51r:1: "spake to the duke ⌜^Richard⌝ that the duke yafe him his suster ⌜^Emma⌝ to wyfe"; *Chronicles*, sig. g2r:18–19: "spake to the duke richard that the duke yaf hym his sustre Emma to wyfe" (not in Brie, 118:17).

85. On interlinear "Ric*hard*" (fol. 51r:1), majuscule *R* and the curl of abbreviation after *c* resemble the running headings "Ric*hard* ij" on some folios (fols. 136r, 137r); on interlinear "Edward" (fol. 101r), the majuscule *E*, loops on *w* and *d*, and the general aspect resemble the running heading "Edward

iij" (fol. 129r). It is not possible, though, to be sure about such small samples of handwriting.

86. Noted in Matheson, *Prose Brut*, 163–165.

87. HM 136, fols. 156v:4–158r:39; *Chronicles*, sigs. u4r:3–u6r:25 (Brie, 491:1–497:6), noted in Matheson, "Printer and Scribe," 595–596. In *Chronicles* the full continuation covers sigs. u4r–y6r (Brie, 491–497).

88. In HM 136, "of" is added, "as" is omitted, "lasse masse" is mangled as "last mast," echoing "first" a few words earlier, "pray" becomes more correctly "prayde," and "regnyng" becomes less satisfactorily "regned."

89. HM 136, fol. 157v:6, and *Chronicles*, sig. u5r:20, spelling it as "destroyng" (Brie, 494:15); HM 136, fol. 156v:34, and *Chronicles*, sig. u4r:36 (Brie, 492:11).

90. HM 136, fol. 157v:29. HM 136 does omit the chapter titles but leaves room for them, as though intending to add them in a different ink that unfortunately did not materialize.

91. Matheson, *Prose Brut*, 164–165; Matheson, "Printer and Scribe," 594–601, 610–613.

92. HM 136, fol. 158r. The appearance suggests some unexpected interruption, although the excerpt of the continuation does thus end by completing a grammatical unit and completing the life of Henry V. A copy from Caxton's edition in London, British Library, MS Cotton Claudius A.viii, fols. 7r–18r, excerpts only the last part of the Common Version to 1419 and the first part of the continuation from 1419 to 1422 on the life of Henry, but it stops more neatly at the end of a chapter. See Matheson, *Prose Brut*, 162.

WORKS CITED

Manuscripts

Cambridge, Peterhouse, MS 190.
Dublin, Trinity College, MS 490.
London, British Library, MS Additional 41321.
London, British Library, MS Cotton Claudius A.viii.
London, British Library, MS Egerton 650.
Manchester, John Rylands Library, MS Eng. 2.
Oxford, Bodleian Library, MS Douce 323.

Oxford, Trinity College, MS 13.
Oxford, Trinity College, MS 14.
Oxford, Trinity College, MS 16.
Oxford, Trinity College, MS 49.
San Marino, CA, Henry E. Huntington Library, MS HM 136.

Primary Sources

Brie, Friedrich W. D., ed. *The Brut or The Chronicles*, EETS os 131, 136, 2 vols. London: Kegan Paul, Trench, Trübner, 1906–1908.

The Chronicles of England. Westminster: William Caxton, 1480; *STC* 9991.

The Chronicles of England. London: William de Machlinia, ca. 1486; *STC* 9993. London, British Library, shelfmark IB.55463.

Chronicles of England, Westmynstre, 1480. The English Experience: Its Record in Early Printed Books Published in Facsimile 508. Amsterdam: Theatrum Orbis Terrarum, 1973.

Lydgate, John. *The Fall of Princes*. London: Richard Pynson, 1494; *STC* 3175.

Matheson, Lister M., ed. *Death and Dissent: Two Fifteenth-Century Chronicles*. Woodbridge, UK: Boydell, 1999.

Waldron, Ronald, ed. *John Trevisa's Translation of the* Polychronicon *of Ranulph Higden, Book VI*. Middle English Texts 35. Heidelberg, Germany: Winter, 2004.

Secondary Sources

Barker, Nicolas. "Caxton's Typography." *Journal of the Printing Historical Society* 11 (1976): 114–133.

Blades, William. *The Biography and Typography of William Caxton, England's First Printer*. Edited by James Moran. 1877; London: Muller, 1971.

Blake, N. F. *Caxton: England's First Publisher*. London: Osprey, 1976.

———. "Caxton Prepares His Edition of the Morte Darthur." In N. F. Blake, *William Caxton and English Literary Culture*. London: Hambledon Press, 1991, 199–211.

———. "Caxton's Copy-Text of Gower's *Confessio Amantis*." In N. F. Blake, *William Caxton and English Literary Culture*. London: Hambledon Press, 1991, 187–198.

———. "Manuscript to Print." In *Book Production and Publishing in Britain 1375–1475*, ed. Jeremy Griffiths and Derek Pearsall. Cambridge, UK: Cambridge University Press, 1989, 403–432.

Bone, Gavin. "Extant Manuscripts Printed from by W. de Worde, with Notes on the Owner, Roger Thorney." *The Library* 4th ser., 12 (1932): 284–306.

Brie, Friedrich W. D. *Geschichte und Quellen der mittelenglische Proschronik* The Brute of England *oder* The Chronicles of England. Marburg, Germany: N. G. Elwert'sche, 1905.

Catalogue of Books Printed in the XVth Century now in the British Library: Part XI: England. Edited by Lotte Hellinga. 't Goy-Houten, Holland: Hes & De Graaf, 2007.

de la Mare, A. C., and Lotte Hellinga. "The First Book Printed in Oxford: The *Expositio symboli* of Rufinus." *Transactions of the Cambridge Bibliographical Society* 7 (1978): 184–244.

Dutschke, C. W. *Guide to Medieval and Renaissance Manuscripts in the Huntington Library*, 2 vols. San Marino, CA: Huntington Library, 1989.

Ford, Margaret Lane. "Author's Autograph and Printer's Copy: Werner Rolewinck's *Paradisus conscientiae*." In *Incunabula: Studies in Fifteenth-Century Printed Books Presented to Lotte Hellinga*, ed. Martin Davies. London: British Library, 1999, 109–128.

Gaskell, Philip. *A New Introduction to Bibliography*. Oxford: Clarendon Press, 1972.

Griffiths, Jeremy. "The Manuscripts." In *Lollard Sermons*, ed. Gloria Cigman, EETS os 294. Oxford: Oxford University Press, 1989, xi–xxx.

Hellinga, Lotte. "Introduction." In *Catalogue of Books Printed in the XVth Century now in the British Library: Part XI: England*, ed. Lotte Hellinga. 't Goy-Houten: Hes and De Graaf, 2007.

———. "Manuscripts in the Hands of Printers." In *Manuscripts in the Fifty Years after the Invention of Printing*, ed. J. B. Trapp. London: Warburg Institute, 1983, 3–11.

———. "Press and Text in the First Decades of Printing." In *Libri, tipografi e biblioteche: Ricerche storiche dedicate a Luigi Balsamo*, ed. Instituto di Biblioteconomia e Paleografia Università degli Studi, Parma, 2 vols. Florence, Italy: Olschki, 1997, 1:1–23.

———. *William Caxton and Early Printing in England*. London: British Library, 2010.

Hellinga, Wytze Gs. *Copy and Print in the Netherlands: An Atlas of Historical Bibliography*. Amsterdam: North-Holland Publishing, 1962.

Johnson, Charles, and Hilary Jenkinson. *English Court Hand, A.D. 1066 to 1500: Illustrated Chiefly from the Public Records*, 2 vols. Oxford: Clarendon Press, 1915.

Kato, Takako. *Caxton's Morte D'Arthur: The Printing Process and the Authenticity of the Text*. Medium Ævum Monographs ns 22. Oxford: Society for the Study of Medieval Languages and Literature, 2002.

Manly, John M., Edith Rickert, et al., eds. *The Text of the "Canterbury Tales," Studied on the Basis of All Known Manuscripts*, 8 vols. Chicago: University of Chicago Press, 1940.

Matheson, Lister M. "Printer and Scribe: Caxton, the *Polychronicon* and the *Brut*." *Speculum* 60 (1985): 593–614.

———. *The Prose* Brut: *The Development of a Middle English Chronicle*. Tempe, AZ: Medieval and Renaissance Texts and Studies, 1998.

Mitchner, Robert W. "Wynkyn de Worde's Use of the Plimpton Manuscript of *De proprietatibus rerum*." *The Library* 5th ser., 6 (1951): 7–18.

Moore, J. K. *Primary Materials Relating to Copy and Print in English Books of the Sixteenth and Seventeenth Centuries*. Oxford Bibliographical Society Occasional Publications 24. Oxford: Oxford Bibliographical Society, 1992.

Morgan, Margery M. "Pynson's Manuscript of *Dives and Pauper*." *The Library* 5th ser., 8 (1953): 217–228.

———. "A Specimen of Early Printer's Copy: Rylands English MS. 2." *Bulletin of the John Rylands Library* 33 (1950–1951): 194–196.

Mustanoja, Tauno F. *A Middle English Syntax: Part I: Parts of Speech*. Helsinki, Finland: Société Neophilologique, 1960.

Needham, Paul. *The Printer and the Pardoner*. Washington, DC: Library of Congress, 1986.

Parkes, M. B. *Pause and Effect, An Introduction to the History of Punctuation in the West*. Aldershot, UK: Scolar, 1992.

Pfaff, R. W. *New Liturgical Feasts in Late Medieval England*. Oxford: Oxford University Press, 1970.

Ruysschaert, José. "Les manuscrits autographes de deux œuvres de Lorenzo Guglielmo Traversagni imprimées chez Caxton." *Bulletin of the John Rylands Library* 36 (1953): 191–197.
Simpson, Percy. *Proof-Reading in the Sixteenth, Seventeenth and Eighteenth Centuries.* With an introduction by Harry Carter. 1935; Oxford: Oxford University Press, 1970.
Takagi, Masako. "Arthurian Geography: King Arthur's Roman War Episode in Malory (1485) and in the *Chronicles of England* (1480)." *Kyorin University Review* 21 (2009): 127–135.
———. "Research Note—1/4: Study on the Prose Brut MSS in relation to William Caxton's *Chronicles of England* (1480)." *Kyorin University Review* 22 (2010): 101–114.
———. "William Caxton's Alteration of Text: The Case of Belyn and Brenne from 1480 to 1485." *Kyorin University Review* 19 (2007): 121–130.
Takagi, Masako, and Toshiyuki Takamiya. "Caxton Edits the Roman War Episode: The *Chronicles of England* and Caxton's Book V." In *The Malory Debate: Essays on the Texts of 'Le Morte Darthur,'* ed. Bonnie Wheeler, Robert L. Kendrick, and Michael N. Salda. Arthurian Studies 47. Cambridge, UK: Brewer, 2000, 169–190.
Tanselle, G. Thomas. *Bibliographical Analysis: A Historical Introduction.* Cambridge, UK: Cambridge University Press, 2009.
Thompson, John, ed. "Huntington MS. HM 136." In *The Imagining History Portal.* Last modified July 2, 2006. http://www.qub.ac.uk/imagining-history/resources/wiki/index.php/Huntington_MS._HM_136.
Tonry, Kathleen. "Reading History in Caxton's *Polychronicon.*" *Journal of English and Germanic Philology* (forthcoming).
Wakelin, Daniel. "Writing the Words." In *The Production of Books in England c.1350–c. 1500*, ed. Alexandra Gillespie and Daniel Wakelin. Cambridge, UK: Cambridge University Press, 2011, 34–58.
Waldron, Ronald. "Caxton and the Polychronicon." In *Chaucer in Perspective: Middle English Essays in Honour of Norman Blake*, ed. Geoffrey Lester. Sheffield, UK: Sheffield Academic Press, 1999, 375–394.

Printing for Purgatory: Indulgences and Related Documents in England, 1476 to 1536[1]

R. N. SWANSON

As Peter Stallybrass has recently insisted in no uncertain terms, printers do not print books, they print sheets. What happens to those sheets after they have been printed is none of their concern, unless the printer is also the publisher. Books naturally attract the attention of bibliographers, but printed sheets do not have to be turned into books. This is potentially important for historians of print and print culture, for in the early days of the new technology (as, indeed, even now) many sheets were single-sided products, speedily produced and distributed. Even if books, they did not have to be large: small pamphlets and other material could also be run off relatively speedily. Such minor printing, often intentionally produced as ephemeral, has rightly been identified as one of the foundations of a successful printing house.[2] In the market, such products might be considered as "cheap print," although there was no automatic correlation between such printing and market price: in some circumstances, the products might be inexpensive to produce yet still be sold dearly if the distributor could command the market.

Large quantities of single-sheet printed material were produced in England between 1476 and 1536, a good deal of it being linked to the advertising, marketing, and distribution of the various spiritual privileges which fall under the generic heading of "indulgences."[3] The terminal dates are themselves watersheds in English printing history: an indulgence-related document, a confessional letter issued in 1476 for the collection to fund warfare against the Turks, was among Caxton's first products at Westminster,[4] while 1536 effectively marks the Henrician Reformation's elimination of indulgences from English religion,[5] ending a printing tradition which arguably had played a vital part in the shift to the new technology over the preceding sixty years as an important—but neglected—chapter in the history of early English printing.[6] As a category of "cheap print," these documents certainly merit consideration but raise their own specific issues. Three points particularly call for attention: the relationship between print and manuscript "cultures" as print became increasingly accepted in England; the significance of such printing tasks for the printers themselves and for the establishment of print; and finally, issues of textual control and validation in the new technology.

Some preliminary comment is needed on the actual documents. They can be separated into four classes, although separation and allocation are not always easy or straightforward.[7] Moreover, boundaries become fluid as the emphasis moves away from indulgences (sometimes in conjunction with other aspects of devotion) and towards other types of devotional printing. Four categories are identified here, but subsequent discussion will focus almost exclusively on the first two.

The most important documents were the "confessional letters" or "letters of confraternity."[8] These were in effect sold, the printed sheets being equivalent to receipts for the purchases.[9] Such letters generally gave their holders the power to choose a confessor to confer plenary absolution at the point of death and usually also offered promises of remission of the sufferings which might be imposed by God in Purgatory after death as satisfaction for sins incompletely expunged whilst alive. The letters were usually in Latin but were occasionally printed in English;[10] and were almost always printed on parchment or vellum (probably because they had to be robust as portable documents with an uncertain but potentially long aftersales life).[11] They were printed as form documents, with gaps left at appropriate points to allow the purchaser's name and the date and place of purchase to be inserted by hand. (As printing became more sophisticated, some letters also left spaces to allow Latin word endings to be adjusted for the gender and number of purchasers for each form, as in printed forms issued on behalf of the Roman hospital of Santo Spirito from around 1515 to 1520.)[12]

The most important characteristic of such letters—and the distinctive feature which required them to be produced for retention—was the conferral of the power to choose a confessor. The chosen confessor often acquired thereby a delegation of papal absolutionary authority to absolve sins, an authority which would otherwise be reserved to episcopal and papal jurisdiction (although exclusions sometimes remained, depending on the precise terms of the indulgence grant). By remitting the *culpa*, the guilt, of the sins by means of that papally delegated absolution, the confessor also conferred the indulgence and remitted the consequent *pena*, the satisfaction for sins due to God which would otherwise be purged in Purgatory after death.[13]

The second and third categories may be seen as species of the same genus. Both are effectively publicity material. One, which is fairly common among the surviving documents, consists of printed announcements in English (and on paper) of the spiritual privileges offered by an institution or its agents. These range in size from small postcard-sized fliers to large densely printed sheets like those listing the privileges of the hospital of Santo Spirito in Rome, which were in effect posters.[14] The other class, likewise in English and on paper, comprises leaflets advertising where a specific indulgence could be obtained from specially appointed confessors. So far only one example is known, advertising the indulgence of the Roman hospital of Santo Spirito as being available from confessors at the Franciscan house in Ipswich.[15]

The final, fourth, category is miscellaneous. Its function is specifically devotional—to encourage prayers by offering rewards (or incentives) for the recitation. One subgroup comprises woodcuts depicting scenes such as Christ as the Man of Sorrows or the Pieta, often surrounded by the Arma Christi, promising indulgence in return for devotion.[16] The origins of these woodcuts are unknown, but they were presumably printed specifically for sale, as unofficial ventures aimed deliberately at a market. These were prints of manageable size, which could be inserted into devotional texts by their owners or used in other contexts.[17] With them can perhaps be combined other devotional printing such as the sheet recording a devotion supposedly located at "Newton in Suffolk," which one scholar has condemned as a forgery.[18] Such single-sided products exemplify market-oriented speculative printing, merging into a broader category of petty amuletic and devotional printing which was, of necessity, also cheap and ephemeral.[19]

The boundary between the indulgenced woodcuts and broader categories of devotional printing is made even more porous by the use of almost identical depictions (although in these instances lacking the pardon statement) to illustrate other printed texts and by the distribution of such woodcuts as prints in their own right. Indeed, boundaries are breached with one woodblock, produced for members of the guild of St. Anne at Lincoln and perhaps linked with an indulgence, which is now known only because it was used among the illustrations in a printed book of hours.[20]

Another subgroup is represented by a single surviving badly damaged example detailing pardons offered in return for prayers for the health and state of King Henry VIII, his queen (Catherine of Aragon), and their daughter Princess Mary.[21] Who issued this is unknown, but its size suggests that it was meant for public display (as a wall poster or on a handheld board). It was at least a "semiofficial" publication, maybe distributed by church hierarchs. Other small documents that might be included here were also printed, including slips certifying completion of the confessional process (and sometimes also affirming participation in the benefits of an indulgence), but these are almost impossible to integrate effectively into any argument.[22] At some point the single-sided devotional prints merge into other types of devotional "cheap print," the surviving small pamphlets which also recorded prayers and offered indulgences;[23] but the sheet requesting prayers for the royal family remains generically distinct. Cheap print outlining devotional exercises continued after 1536, but the material printed specifically to encourage acquisition of indulgences, especially from pardoners, had no future.

Indulgences catered for and to a mass market, and were indeed cheaply printed.[24] Their selling price, however, was not dictated by their production costs; as confessional letters were often distributed in fraternity membership drives and handed over as subscription receipts, individual letters were "sold" for anything from one penny to thirteen shillings and four pence, a range from one penny to twelve pence being most common, and four pence seemingly being the general level.[25] Such letters might almost be considered a spiritual form of paper currency, in that their face value (or selling price) bore no necessary relation to their intrinsic value (as promissory notes to buy off the pains of Purgatory) or to their costs of production. Alongside the cheaply printed confessional letters, the low costs of reproducing the other two indulgence-related formats is important, because that outlay was not recouped; as advertising, these documents were produced to be distributed with no return.

The survival record for this material is dire. Many texts survive only in unique and mutilated copies, often rescued from book bindings. Some are so fragmentary that they are almost useless.[26] At least one has been lost within living memory without being fully recorded.[27] There is at least one other case in which no known original copy survives, but a transcript from a lost copy was included in a nineteenth-century volume.[28] The original documents that have survived outside bookbindings have incomplete provenances and so lack full historical contexts. However, future research may increase the number of known survivors. In recent years, closer examination of bookbindings has added to the list,[29] and the tally will probably grow as the search for early printed material expands to local record offices and private archives; even major library collections may yet hold unnoticed additional texts and copies.[30]

These documents were rarely meant to have a long life, but some were not totally ephemeral. Publicity material and confessional letters might be needed only for one specific fund-raising campaign, but where there were regular and repeated collections all types of material would need to be produced for the long term. If old documents were not simply reused, or material not produced in sufficient quantities to last for the whole anticipated life span of the collection (production on that scale being inherently unlikely), then the long-term needs of the collection would require intermittent—sometimes frequent—reprinting to maintain stocks. This might be done without changing the text, even when some updating might be expected. Confessional letters for York's guild of St. Christopher and St. George in 1529—and presumably in earlier years of the decade—still referred to Leo X as the current pope even though he had died in 1521.[31]

The regularity of reprinting varied. In some cases, confessional letters were printed in sufficient numbers to last several years,[32] but others carried the precise year of production, which would limit their sell-by date.[33] Purchasers were expected to retain their letters until the confessional privilege was invoked, which might be some years after purchase. In the 1550s John Hooper, bishop of Worcester and Gloucester, inquired whether any of his subjects were still being buried with their confessional letters—letters which had not been distributed in England for some fifteen years.[34]

Hooper's inquiry points to another aspect of the longevity of confessional letters, whether handwritten or printed: that many were kept not until death but beyond it; they were grave goods. Large numbers of pardons were apparently disturbed when churchyards were grubbed out during the building of Somerset House in Edward VI's reign.[35]

The printed material, especially when distributed through pardoners and similar agents, fits into a generic context that had been established in the fourteenth century and had remained stable over the intervening years. Its production was in continuity with mass-produced handwritten documents, both confessional letters and publicity leaflets.[36] By the early 1400s, there was probably already a linguistic distinction between the vernacular of many (but not all) publicity documents and the Latin of confessional letters.[37] Pardoners probably carried around not just the statements of privileges, intended as scripts for oral delivery,[38] but also the batches of letters they were to sell. (Only confessional letters were sold as documents; because the pardons they offered and the confessors' delegated absolutional powers remained latent until the point of death, both needed formal advance documentary validation.) With the shift to print, the pardoners and agents presumably still carried the letters, but some of the publicity may have been tackled differently, especially in large towns. The vernacular schedules could be glued to church doors, as attested to for the Rounceval Guild at Charing Cross, London, and the Guild of Our Lady in Boston, Lincolnshire, so becoming available for public perusal without the pardoners as oral intermediaries.[39] Such publicity was firmly ephemeral in function, unlike some early handwritten schedules of privileges, which were apparently returned to "base," possibly for later reuse.[40]

How the production and distribution of this printed material should be interpreted remains uncertain, partly because the basis for interpretation is largely conjectural. How the various pieces of the puzzle might fit together is also elusive—assuming that the available pieces, which certainly do not fit together, are indeed fragments of a single picture. For instance, a unique copy of a printed but undated publicity leaflet survives for the Guild of the Name of Jesus in St. Paul's Cathedral, London.[41] The listed spiritual privileges exclude the massive temporal indulgence which Humphrey Newton, of Pownall in Cheshire, noted in his list of pardon acquisitions, and which he clearly thought that he had obtained from the guild.[42] That discrepancy cannot be explained. The printed sheet is very much a flier: it is eye-catching and a straightforward statement. It survives wrapped around an almanac dating from 1522, effectively providing a paperback binding for the pamphlet. The almanac itself seems typical of the products distributed by chapmen and peddlers; scattered evidence indicates that pardoners combined indulgence distribution with such petty trading.[43] Can it be assumed that the St. Paul's leaflet was distributed in this way, or is that an improper reading of uncertain evidence?[44]

Similar difficulties arise with another sheet (again a unique copy) printed for St. Roche's Hospital, Exeter.[45] The hospital was small; its collecting activities have left few traces.[46] Yet it was active in York diocese in 1523, when its agent had a collecting license valid within the jurisdiction of the dean and chapter of York Minster.[47] Similar licenses were presumably granted for areas of the diocese under the archbishop's jurisdiction, possibly also for the archdeaconry of Richmond, but no record survives. A problem here is to bridge the gap between Exeter and York and unite the two records, especially when nothing in the York records indicates the nature and scale of the privileges and indulgences being offered by the hospital's agents within the diocese in return for donations. The printed leaflet promises no more than that "ye daye that they do say a pater noster an Ave and a Crede it is graunted to them that they schal never in fecte nor greved w^t the stroke of ye pestylence." Was this all that was offered in Yorkshire in 1523, being nevertheless expected to attract sufficient donations to cover the costs of operating so far from base?

A final example of the difficulty of integrating a printed indulgence document with a collecting structure comes from the palmers' guild in Ludlow, Shropshire. This major association had a complex collecting system with agents who toured central and southern England to gather installments towards the total subscription.⁴⁸ The guild's surviving archives⁴⁹ give no hint that it issued confessional letters, and offer no sign that it commissioned printed indulgence-related documents. Yet a single, undated, printed confessional letter supposedly issued by the guild survives, offering appropriate spiritual privileges.⁵⁰ The document names Leo X as pope, but the above-cited case of York's St. Christopher and St. George Guild shows that the Ludlow document need not have actually dated from his pontificate.⁵¹ How does this document fit into the picture of the guild's collecting arrangements suggested by its surviving archives? Was it distributed to aspiring members by the guild's agents on their tours? Or is it evidence of an entirely different collecting structure, a statement of additional privileges offered only to those who had fully paid their dues—even if possibly distributed by the same circulating agents?⁵²

Unanswerable questions can only be left unanswered. Other issues allow concrete consideration. One concerns the expansion of print within the indulgence trade. This was a slow process: there was no immediate full switch from manuscript to print.⁵³ Handwritten and printed documents used in the indulgence business existed in parallel throughout the period, although print's role gradually increased. This expansion cannot be traced in detail or in total, but the factors that affected it can be discussed.

Print had obvious advantages over manuscript production for indulgence distributions. The need for extensive publicity and multiple copies of confessional letters generated an effective system of mass production even before print. In the fourteenth and fifteenth centuries it was not uncommon for several hundred copies of specific texts to be regularly produced to publicize collecting campaigns, especially for collections linked to cathedral fabric funds.⁵⁴ Handwritten confessional letters were as sophisticated as their printed successors, being likewise produced as forms with gaps being left to insert names and dates as appropriate.⁵⁵ In this regard, print marked a technological breakthrough but not a conceptual change for its products. How print broke into this market needs further examination. It seems a straightforward assumption that organizers of indulgence campaigns immediately saw the benefits and enthusiastically adopted the new process. Reality appears more complex.

Here the continuity of manuscript production alongside print is important. The well-attested dualism of manuscript literary volumes alongside printed texts was to some extent a matter of choice, especially where a manuscript was copied from a printed text.[56] For indulgence-related documents, different considerations may apply. This, after all, was material for which cost mattered, especially if there was to be no return. Overall cheapness, however, was not determined merely by comparing simple production estimates for printed and manuscript documents. Other considerations had to be factored in, including the accessibility of a printer and the costs of travel and transport when dealing with him. In terms of basic cost-effectiveness, and taking all of the costs into account, for the sponsors of an indulgence distribution who were located far from a printing center it may still have been cheaper to continue with manuscript production than to undertake the time-consuming and costly process of arranging print at a distance. This might be a consideration throughout the period, but the imperatives in individual cases are rarely apparent.

One uncertainty here—and a complicating factor—is that many of the printed texts float in a kind of limbo. They may have been issued *for* a particular body; but that need not mean that they were issued *by* it as official commissions. In very few cases can links between institutions and printers be directly established, chiefly from accounts. Like the original purchasers or readers of such documents, scholars assume—and unless there is reasonable evidence to the contrary, can only assume—that the texts were authorized products and the collections did benefit the named causes. Yet modern scholars are often no better placed to make that assumption than those original purchasers or readers of the documents; the documents' claims must be taken on trust, much as the buyer of a document printed at York in the 1520s accepted the promises supposedly made on behalf of the monastery of massive indulgences in exchange for financial support of Langley in Kent.[57] He was conned—the monastery did not exist.

Who actually commissioned and paid for the printing of these early indulgence documents? There are good grounds for arguing that in the early days of English printing, this was done not by the people running the institutions or causes intended to benefit from the sales but by lesser distributors—the regional agents. Several collections of the 1470s and 1480s are represented by both printed confessional letters and manuscript letters using the same texts, indicating insufficient administrative centralization of the collections to ensure standardization in production of the pardon documents. It would, frankly, be bizarre for any central administration to have used both production methods in tandem. What perhaps happened is that regional agents—or even the more local pardoners below them—received a master text of the confessional letter and organized reproduction as they saw fit.[58] It was the regional agents, or those in closest proximity to the London printshops, who commissioned the printed copies and either then took them out on their own rounds or supplied them to subsidiary pardoners (how that was managed is unknown).

On this model, the permeation of print through the indulgence trade would, initially, have been highly regionalized in southeastern and central-southern England (occasionally extending at least as far north as Oxford).[59] Coverage was probably inconsistent, varying from campaign to campaign. However, the possibility still existed of wider penetration or at least of awareness of the new technology, because not every purchaser of a letter would be from this limited area, and the documents would be carried elsewhere.

How long this agent-centered model persisted cannot be determined. The benefit of centralized distribution of printed letters for a national collection was certainly recognized in instructions for the distribution of a crusade indulgence in 1489. Yet the difficulties of access to a printer mean that continuation of manuscript production alongside print can be suggested for major collections even into the sixteenth century—for collections with small catchment areas, the benefits of adopting print may have been outweighed by the real costs throughout the period. If the sole evidence for documentary production linked to an indulgence distribution is a single printed document of unknown provenance, it does not follow that all other relevant confessional letters or publicity documents were printed. Nor, conversely, does it follow that collections leaving no printed evidence relied exclusively on handwritten texts.

The problem of access to a printer (which reflects the problem of the economics of printing and the scale of investment needed to establish a printshop) was persistent. Beyond Westminster and London, printed indulgence-related documents are known only from York and Cambridge. York produced them intermittently after 1510, while production at Cambridge is known only briefly in the 1520s—so briefly that comment is almost impossible.[60] The evidence from York is as patchy and elusive as the broader evidence of printing in the city, suggesting, at worst, repeated attempts to establish a printshop there or at best unappreciated continuity.[61] In most places, one determinant of the recourse to print would therefore be ease of access to London and the relative cost benefits of using a London printer against local manuscript production. Print clearly radiated out from London (initially from Westminster), and the geographical distribution of institutions which used documents printed in London for their indulgence distributions increased accordingly: Boston, Ludlow, Salisbury, Exeter, and Beverley all join the list.[62] Some nationwide collections, such as those for the Carmelite order, also used print;[63] while some private projects—for instance, collections for individuals seeking to pay off ransoms to the Turks—presumably began in London and then grew into national collections, carrying their printed documents with them for wider distribution.

Not every collection exploited print; but to seek fully to explain this failure is to argue from silence. As suggested, even as late as the late 1520s it may not have been automatically worthwhile to leap into print; cheap print was still not cheap enough once all the factors were taken into account.

If ease of access to a printer was an important consideration for the potential customer when deciding whether to use the new technology or not, then for the printer the availability of customers was no less significant. To establish a printshop was a major investment. It required considerable amounts of capital for the press, for the type, and for other costs. Technological limitations, especially the need for economy when using limited amounts of type, made production of a large volume—maybe anything bigger than a single gathering—a time-consuming process. The early English printers did produce big books, but they also needed short-term contracts to give immediate cash flow; they had to be jobbing printers to some extent.[64]

This is where printing for the indulgence trade enters into the equations, for it was exactly that kind of short-term contract printing. Numerous short campaigns, with numerous short print runs providing numerous small payments, might suffice to keep a printshop ticking over, covering basic costs as larger projects matured.[65] The cheap print of the indulgence trade could usually be produced quickly; one-sided, perhaps with multiple settings on a sheet, it needed little investment of time or labor yet provided income. Printing on parchment was technologically more demanding and took longer but was still not particularly time-consuming.

Evidence of print runs for this material is limited and often relates to documents which no longer survive, making a full sense of the scale of the work undertaken elusive. Yet indulgence-related printing could offer a series of small bread-and-butter jobs much like those of modern print shops—whatever the historic stature of the likes of Wynkyn de Worde and Richard Pynson, the early printers were also an early version of Prontaprint or Kinkos. In 1502 to 1503, for instance, the dean and chapter of St. George's Chapel, Windsor, paid Pynson ten shillings for seven hundred copies of a papal bull tied to their recent acquisition of a pardon.[66] In the 1520s, accounts of the Rounceval Guild of Charing Cross mention batches of "briefs"—publicity documents—purchased from Wynkyn de Worde at eight pence per hundred, and later indulgence letters from Richard Copeland at eighteen pence per hundred.[67] In 1533 to 1534, York's Corpus Christi Guild paid for three hundred printed letters, which were presumably linked to its own indulgences or to those of the hospital of St. Thomas, which was overseen by the guild. The payment—three shillings and eight pence—also covered purchase of an image of St. Thomas.[68] A few years earlier, York City Council had obtained a thousand printed briefs for ten shillings.[69]

This was indeed cheap print (although York's city council splashed out an additional three shillings for a woodcut of Wolsey's arms to embellish the briefs, paying for it directly rather than via the printer).[70] It was also, of course, erratic print, and if it consisted wholly of one-off commissions it would be unreliable as a source of income for the printer. What was really needed was a consistent run of such tasks—a series of repetitive contracts. Richard Pynson's career shows that such contracts were available, examples being his printing for Santo Spirito Hospital in Rome between 1515 and 1520 and for the Boston Guild of Our Lady from the 1510s until his death in 1530.[71]

Only the latter case provides evidence beyond the surviving documents, in the accounts of Boston's guild of Our Lady, which record print runs and costs for a few years in the early 1520s.[72] Pynson printed annually for the guild: confessional letters, publicity documents (sometimes seemingly in two different classes, as great and small briefs), and "jubilees" (what those were is unclear as no known copy survives, but the price suggests they were relatively small documents). The letters were priced at fifty-three shillings and fourpence per thousand, the briefs at thirty shillings per thousand, and the jubilees at just five shillings per thousand. As Pynson is not always named as the printer, some of these products may have been printed by someone else; but what impresses is the total scale of the activity. If Pynson did print everything, then in 1524 to 1525 he would have produced seven thousand each of parchment letters and great briefs, and five thousand jubilees, receiving just over twenty-six pounds sterling.[73]

Annual figures obviously fluctuated, but in the mid-1520s the guild officials seemingly assumed an annual demand for around four thousand letters; the demand for the other documents is not clear. Pynson's profit on the contracts is incalculable—some of the price differentials must reflect varying input costs, such as the price of parchment for producing the letters (and possibly greater wastage) against the paper for the briefs and jubilees.[74] Nevertheless, even if profit was minimal, what mattered was that the business's basic running costs were met, providing leeway not just for investment in larger projects being slowly brought to fruition but also to keep things going during slack periods.

Jobbing printing may have been particularly vital in the early days of a printshop, giving the initial cash flow to ensure its continuity. That London absorbed so much of this work between 1476 and 1536 may itself be significant for the geography of English printing: without sustained regional demand for material like that needed for indulgence collections, there would not be the revenue to sustain an incipient printshop, and it would go under. Much is made of how Caxton and his successors played to the market, particularly the market in liturgical and devotional works; they had to, if they were to survive. But liturgical works were themselves big investments. They guaranteed returns, but only after they had been printed, and that took time. Cheap print such as indulgence-related documents also guaranteed returns—smaller but enough to provide the lifeblood. However, only sustained continuity in the contracts would ensure that the printshop kept going: interrupted flow would make the difference between profit and loss, between continuity and collapse.

The third issue to be considered here, control and validation, redirects attention to the customers, and perhaps to their own overseers. Print—cheap or not—had real benefits. One, in the context of indulgence distribution, was that print allowed greater control and centralization as the agent-centered model of commissioning documents gave way to one where the collection's lead organizers took over. This is evident early on in regulations for a crusade collection in 1489 which used printed confessional letters.[75] The instructions describe the printed forms;[76] they also insist that local agents obtain the forms from the central administrator as needed. Here there is control over the text, over the activities of the local collectors, and potentially over numbers, and therewith a mechanism to check receipts.

How things actually worked out is unknown—only the instructions and a few confessional letters survive—but centralization and control extended to other collections over the next decades. Again, details are elusive, but that the Rounceval Guild of Charing Cross commissioned documents from a printer and seemingly organised their nationwide distribution suggests control and centralization.[77] In the 1520s, the Boston guild's regular annual commissioning of material from Richard Pynson suggests something similar—with additional control in the fact that the confessional letters often bore the precise year of printing, imposing a clear sell-by date.

Where there were no pardons, just publicity leaflets, control and centralization might still be imposed. At York in 1527 to 1528, the city council organized the publicity for an indulgence campaign to fund repair of the city bridges and supervised production of the briefs. These were duly passed on—actually, sold on at cost price—to the agents who toured the country. Controlling the publicity allowed the city council to ensure that the agents all delivered the same message.[78] In theory, with the printed publicity being widely displayed, there would be less opportunity for the misrepresentations that critics (including church hierarchs) had often complained about as characteristic of a pardoner's spiel.[79] Whether that really worked cannot be tested.

A different but related issue generated by the mass production of print centered on the reliability of the texts, but this need not have been a bigger problem than with manuscript production. As with the handwritten material, mass production in print did not mean flawless production; the scribal errors of manuscripts became the typographical errors of the press, although the character of the errors may have changed during the transition. Whereas the manuscript scribes can be presumed—justifiably or not—to have possessed some degree of latinity, and their errors were often visual as eyes slipped or abbreviations were misread, the compositors of printed texts may have been illiterate in Latin and based their work on a copytext, usually handwritten. (Such a text was perhaps being provided when York City Council paid eight pence for a handwritten copy of a brief for its bridge collection in 1527).[80]

Poor latinity is not uncommon in the confessional letters (the English publicity documents are noticeably "cleaner"), as letters are misread, words run together, and abbreviations ignored. Some errors may be due to the basic technological difficulties of manipulating text—errors of composition rather than of comprehension—but the two together doubled the failings. The erroneous and erratic texts continued to circulate; proofreading did not detect the mistakes. Indeed, that there was proofreading may be doubted, especially when documents were reissued. In these cases, earlier issues probably supplied the base text, subject to any obviously needed amendment. Unthinking and ignorant reproduction could introduce anachronisms and new mistakes.

The case of York's Guild of St. Christopher and St. George at York can again be cited here, but now in more detail. The guild acquired further spiritual privileges from Pope Leo X in the final years of his reign and presumably printed confessional letters immediately afterwards.[81] What can be presumed to be similar letters were still being printed in 1529. Evidently, however, no one had thought to check on the need for revisions to the base text: Leo X was still being described as "now pope" almost ten years after his death.[82] Failure to correct the error may explain why the guild's collection in Exeter diocese was suspended by the diocesan vicar-general two years later, the collectors' letters being decried as false and deceitful.[83] Inspection of the documents at that point may at last have exposed the anachronism—but that it had evaded detection for so long (if it indeed had) is also noteworthy.

That disciplinary action in Exeter diocese is of a piece with similar oversight of indulgence distributions in the manuscript age.[84] Where the shift to print did see a significant change in authorizing processes was in the introduction of a kind of censorship. Several early-sixteenth-century confessional letters identify not only the printer but one or more church officials who had inspected the pardon and effectively thereby attested that the printed text did not misrepresent the spiritual privileges. This suggests real anxiety to oversee the indulgence trade and to assure buyers of the veracity and validity of the privileges. It is matched by signs of similar concern on some publicity schedules, but there the emphasis is on validating the texts as epitomes of papal bulls, so the authorities' role is slightly different.[85] When this practice began is uncertain—for publicity schedules it may have started during the manuscript period in authorization of pardoner's "scripts."[86]

The notations on the printed documents complement contemporary signs of developing concern to check printed books,[87] and are matched by other evidence of anxiety about the control and validation of indulgence-related activity. Particularly striking is the document issued to a group for whom John Mortymer secured indulgences and privileges at Rome in 1506. This is a printed form, in which names were to be inserted by hand. Given its limited application, only a few copies were needed. The extant example bears a manuscript notarial attestation declaring its conformity with the original grant.[88] A decade later, a printed publicity leaflet declaring the benefits offered by two merchants for contributions towards their ransom was clearly a private enterprise. To warrant its authenticity it reproduces (in Latin) the grant of the collecting license issued by Archbishop Warham of Canterbury.[89] Such certifications indicate awareness of the weaknesses inherent in print, but these were dangers that the authorities had long appreciated. They fit into a much older pattern of concern about control and validation of pardons and (especially) pardoners and of recognition of the threat to souls (and, indeed, to the Church's own authority) posed by unauthorized charlatans who exploited the system.

In his play of *The Pardoner and the Friar*, the sixteenth-century playwright John Heywood has a pardoner proclaim his wares in a parish church.[90] Although exaggerated and satirical, his declamation is probably a fairly reliable depiction of what actually happened. While the pardoner is not obviously using a printed publicity schedule (but he may be, for all we know), he is plying a trade. He urges his audience to come up to buy "letters" and "images";[91] these could easily be printed confessional letters and woodblock prints. He is, perhaps, a kind of chapman or peddler and may be selling other printed goods as well, the other (relatively) cheap print of the chapman's trade, extending even up to full books of hours.[92]

This potential combining of indulgence-related material and other printed products merely reinforces the argument that cheaply printed documents produced for the English indulgence trade between 1476 and 1536 cannot be divorced from other contemporary printing, religious and secular. However, they do form a distinct category, which poses its own questions about the impact and integration of print into English culture at the time. It could be argued that indulgence-related material, at least in the fifteenth century, provided many people in England with their first contact with the products of the new technology as documents which they could acquire for themselves or which would be available for public display and use. That so little material survives, and that that little can rarely be fully contextualized, is a real challenge to scholars seeking to place and assess this material in context. There are major issues about production, distribution, and reception; about the choices made when deciding whether to adopt the new technology or maintain a manuscript tradition. Linguistic distinctions, the development of flyposting, and the mobility of the documents, all feed into discussions of the development and nature of literacy and of how far and how quickly print penetrated England's culture. The guillotine which came down on the printing of indulgence-related documents in 1536 did not end the use of cheap print in religious contexts, but it did end a specific strand in the history of print in England.

University of Birmingham

NOTES

1. The first version of this article was completed in 2005 to 2006, while holding a British Academy/Leverhulme Trust Senior Research Fellowship, and with much of the work being done during my tenure of the Agnes Gund and Daniel Shapiro Membership at the Institute for Advanced Study, Princeton. I am grateful to the School of Historical Studies at Birmingham Univer-

sity for additional funding for the time spent at Princeton. The article was originally intended as a contribution to a volume of essays which will not now appear, and has been amended for publication here. Much of the final revision was completed while I held the John E. Sawyer Fellowship at the National Humanities Center in North Carolina in 2010. The article draws on and complements research for my book, R. N. Swanson, *Indulgences in Late Medieval England: Passports to Paradise?* (Cambridge, UK: Cambridge University Press, 2007); unreferenced generalizations receive fuller substantiation in that volume.

2. P. Stallybrass, "'Little Jobs': Broadsides and the Printing Revolution," in S. A. Baron, E. N. Lindquist, and E. F. Shevlin, eds., *Agent of Change: Print Culture Studies after Elizabeth L. Eisenstein* (Amherst, MA: University of Massachusetts Press, 2007), 315–341; see esp. comments at 315, 323, 340.

3. A summary listing is in A. W. Pollard and G. R. Redgrave, *A Short-Title Catalogue of Books Printed in England, Scotland, and Ireland, and of English Books Printed Abroad, 1475–1640*, 3 vols., 2nd ed., rev. W. A. Jackson, F. S. Ferguson, and K. F. Pantzer (London: Bibliographical Society, 1976–1991), 2:2–9; 3:279. (Hereafter "*STC*"; unless otherwise necessary, only *STC* numbers are cited in notes).

4. *STC* 14077c. 106. P. Needham, *The Printer and the Pardoner: An Unrecorded Indulgence Printed by William Caxton for the Hospital of St. Mary Rounceval, Charing Cross* (Washington, DC: Library of Congress, 1986), 32, 84.

5. The death knell is generally held to have sounded in a proclamation issued in December 1535/January 1536: see P. L. Hughes and J. F. Larkin, eds., *Tudor Royal Proclamations*, 3 vols. (New Haven, CT, and London: Yale University Press, 1964–1969), 1:236–237. See also Swanson, *Indulgences*, 491 n. 96.

6. Indulgences have received attention as individual documents and occasionally as a genre, but their overall historical contribution to the early history of English printing has not been considered in detail. Several relevant documents are reproduced in K. W. Cameron, *The Pardoner and His Pardons: Indulgences Circulating in England on the Eve of the Reformation, with a Historical Introduction* (Hartford, CT: Transcendental Books, [1965]). Texts of most known indulgences printed before 1500 are in E. G. Duff and Lotte Hellinga, *Printing in England in the Fifteenth Century: E. Gordon Duff's Bibliography with Supplementary Descriptions, Chronologies and a Census of Copies by Lotte*

Hellinga (London: British Library with the Bibliographical Society, 2009), nos. 204–220, suppls. 13–23.

7. It is, for instance, unclear where *STC* 14077c. 23A should fit; it may be the kind of "image" alluded to by the pardoner in John Heywood's play *The Pardoner and the Friar*; see R. Axton and P. Happé, eds., *The Plays of John Heywood* (Cambridge, UK: D.S. Brewer, 1991), 100.

8. R. N. Swanson, "Letters of Confraternity and Indulgence in Late-Medieval England," *Archives*, 25 (2000): 40–57.

9. As is bluntly recognised in a Mercedarian document of 1532: *STC* 14077c. 123.

10. *STC* 14077c. 51, of 1491, for the Crutched Friars of London (see photograph in H. Thomas, "An Indulgence Printed by Pynson, 1491," *British Museum Quarterly*, 9 [1934]: pl. X) and the Mercedarian letter mentioned in note 9 are both in English.

11. For printing on parchment, see L. Hellinga, "Printing," in L. Hellinga and J. B. Trapp, eds., *The Cambridge History of the Book in Britain, vol. III, 1400–1557* (Cambridge, UK: Cambridge University Press, 1999), 93–94.

12. *STC* 14077c. 90–97.

13. Swanson, *Indulgences*, 118.

14. E.g., *STC* 14077c. 98. For fliers, see the documents referred to in notes 41 and 45 below.

15. *STC* 14077c. 43.

16. *STC* 14077c. 6–16, 23. It might be objected that as woodcuts these do not properly count as "cheap print." That can be debated. Cf. comments on the similar issue in Germany in F. Eisermann, "Mixing Pop and Politics: Origins, Transmission and Readers of Illustrated Broadsides in Fifteenth-Century Germany," in K. Jensen, ed., *Incunabula and Their Readers: Printing, Selling, and Using Books in the Fifteenth Century* (London: British Library, 2003), 163.

17. See e.g., Oxford, Bodleian Library, MS Rawl.D.403, fols. 1v, 2v (fol. 3v is also a devotional print but without an indulgence).

18. *STC* 14077c. 64.

19. For Continental printing of this kind (including reference to the Newton sheet), see D. C. Skemer, *Binding Words: Textual Amulets in the Middle Ages* (University Park, PA: Pennsylvania State University Press, 2006), 222–232.

20. Reproduced in E. Duffy, *Marking the Hours: English People and Their*

Prayers, 1240-1570 (New Haven, CT, and London: Yale University Press, 2006), 134.

21. *STC* 14077c. 146. See also R. N. Swanson, "Prayer and Participation in Late Medieval England," *Studies in Church History*, 42 (2006): 130–131, 139.

22. See, e.g., *STC* 14077c. 1–5.

23. See, e.g., *A Gloryous Medytacyon of Jhesus Crystes Passyon* (London: Richard Fakes, ?1523), *STC* 14550; *STC* 14077c. 148.

24. See pp. 92-93.

25. Swanson, "Letters," 47–48.

26. See, e.g., fragments now in the library of Christ's College, Cambridge. The only reference to them in C. Sayle, "Cambridge Fragments," *The Library*, 3rd ser., 2 (1911): 349–350, mentions a single piece, but in fact there are several.

27. *STC* 14077c.68A, which was destroyed in a fire at Packington Hall in 1978.

28. G. Oliver, *Lives of the Bishops of Exeter and a History of the Cathedral; with an Illustrative Appendix* (Exeter, UK: William Roberts, 1861), 249.

29. Needham, *Printer and the Pardoner*, 81–82; R. N. Swanson, "Caxton's Indulgence for Rhodes, 1480–81," *The Library*, 7th ser., 5 (2004): 195.

30. Swanson, "Caxton's Indulgence," 195–197 (a complete copy of *STC* 14077c. 107c); London, BL MS Add. 4719/2 (not in *STC*).

31. BL MS Add 4719/2.

32. Some of the pardons for the guild of Our Lady at Boston were printed with the equivalent of "15___" or "152_" as the date, allowing the final figures to be added (or not) on purchase.

33. This is especially notable with indulgences which appeared in different issues over several years, such as those for the Boston guild of Our Lady and for Santo Spirito. Other pardons appeared in limited issues, presumably with shorter sale periods. Printed indulgences with gaps for a precise date of sale to be inserted should perhaps be distinguished from those that bear a full date (see, e.g., Duff and Hellinga, *Printing in England*, nos. 214–220, suppl. 20–22), which follow the manuscript practice of copies being sent out for sale already fully dated.

34. W. H. Frere and W. M. Kennedy, eds., *Visitation Articles and Injunctions of the Period of the Reformation*, 3 vols., Alcuin Club Collections, 14–16 (London, New York, Bombay and Calcutta, 1910), 2:304. In the mid-1540s, a Calais chaplain reported that he still possessed a stash of confessional letters for

Rome's Santo Spirito Hospital—was he holding onto them in the hope that he might still have an opportunity to sell them? See J. S. Brewer, J. Gairdner, and R. H. Brodie, eds., *Letters and Papers, Foreign and Domestic, of the Reign of Henry VIII*, 23 vols. in 38 (London: Her/His Majesty's Stationery Office, 1862–1932), 15: no. 37.

35. John Strype, *Ecclesiastical Memorials Relating Chiefly to Religion and the Reformation of It, and the Emergencies of the Church of England under King Henry VIII., King Edward VI., and Queen Mary I*, 3 vols. in 6 (Oxford: Clarendon Press, 1822), 2/i:283. Obviously, such documents would rot if buried, but if entombed with their owners aboveground, they might last longer; for a handwritten pardon so recovered, see C. A. J. Armstrong, *England, France, and Burgundy in the Fifteenth Century* (London: Hambledon Press, 1983), 156.

36. Swanson, "Caxton's Indulgence," 198–199; R. N. Swanson, "A Rounceval Pardon of 1482," *Archives*, 30. no. 113 (Oct. 2005):51–54.

37. For a vernacular publicity document of 1404 for Holy Cross Hospital, Colchester, see BL Stowe ch.603.

38. A role most obvious in BL Sloane charter xxxii. 15, 27 (both for the Hospitallers); see also BL MS Harley 211, fol. 101v (for St. Mary in the Sea at Newton in Cambridgeshire).

39. Needham, *Printer and the Pardoner*, 44–45; BL MS Egerton 2886, fols. 144r, 172r.

40. R. N. Swanson, "Fund Raising for a Medieval Monastery: Indulgences and Great Bricett Priory," *Proceedings of the Suffolk Institute of Archaeology and History*, 40 (2001–2004):1–2.

41. *STC* 14077c. 59G.

42. Oxford, Bodleian Library, MS Lat.Misc.c.66, fol. 17v.

43. See, e.g., entries of dual occupation in F. Collins, ed., *Register of the Freemen of the City of York from the City Records, vol. I: 1272–1558*, Surtees Society, 96 (1897), 194, 229 (Ed. Sotheby, questor alias chapman; William Smyth, haberdasher and questor). See also Swanson, *Indulgences*, 210–211, 220, 433–435. On peddlers, see J. Davis, "'Men as March with Fote Packes': Pedlars and Freedom of Movement in Late Medieval England," in P. Horden, ed., *Freedom of Movement in the Middle Ages*, Harlaxton Medieval Studies, 15 (Donington, UK: Shaun Tyas, 2007), 137–156.

44. There is, of course, no way of telling when or by whom the leaflet and almanac were united.

45. *STC* 14077c. 41, reproduced in N. Orme and M. Webster, *The English Hospital, 1070–1570* (New Haven, CT, and London: Yale University Press, 1995), 124.

46. Ibid., 247–248.

47. York Minster Archives, H3/1, fol. 122r.

48. The collecting methods are outlined in A. T. Gaydon, ed., *Victoria County History: Shropshire*, vol. 2 (London: Published for the Institute of Historical Research by Oxford University Press, 1973), 137–138.

49. Shrewsbury, Shropshire Archives, LB5/.

50. *STC* 14077c. 61.

51. See p. 88.

52. The problem is to some extent similar to that of Beverley Minster. Limited evidence survives for the minster's indulgence distributions from c. 1300 to the 1530s, but the only mention of confessional letters occurs in a printed sixteenth-century publicity schedule: *STC* 14077c. 26.

53. Cf. general comments on the transition from manuscript to print in D. McKitterick, *Print, Manuscript and the Search for Order, 1450–1830* (Cambridge, UK: Cambridge University Press, 2003), 9–10, 47–48. The latest handwritten confessional letter I have seen is from 1526, for the hospital of Burton Lazars (Exeter, Devon Record Office, 312M/TY.195), but others may have been produced into the 1530s.

54. A. M. Erskine, ed., *The Accounts of the Fabric of Exeter Cathedral, 1279–1353*, Devon and Cornwall Record Society, n.s. 24, 26 (1981–1983), 2:218, 274, 282–283, 285, 288, 290; J. C. Colchester, ed., *Wells Cathedral Fabric Accounts, 1390–1600* (Wells, UK: Friends of Wells Cathedral, 1983), 12, 18, 24, 31, 38; R. N. Swanson, "Contributions from Parishes in the Archdeaconry of Norfolk to the Shrine of St. Thomas Cantilupe at Hereford, ca. 1320," *Mediaeval Studies*, 62 (2000): 191.

55. Swanson, "Letters," 43. Other "bureaucratic" texts were also produced as forms; see A. J. Slavin, "The Tudor Revolution and the Devil's Art: Bishop Bonner's Printed Forms," in *Tudor Rule and Revolution: Essays for G. R. Elton from His American Friends*, ed. D. J. Guth and J. W. McKenna (Cambridge, UK: Cambridge University Press, 1982), 7–8.

56. N. F. Blake, "Manuscript to Print," in Blake, *William Caxton and English Literary Culture* (London and Rio Grande, OH: Hambledon Press, 1991), 285–289. In the absence of readily available multiple printed copies, hand-copying continued to be used: McKitterick, *Print*, 47–48; R. N. Swanson, "A Small Library for Pastoral Care and Spiritual Direction in Late Medieval England," *Journal of the Early Book Society*, 5 (2002): 196–197.

57. STC 14077c. 48, illustrated in Swanson, *Indulgences*, 460.

58. As no early publicity schedules survive which demonstrate overlap between production in print and manuscript, it is impossible to say whether a similar pattern applied to their production.

59. Swanson, "Caxton's Indulgence," 196–199.

60. STC 14077c. 151–152. On these Cambridge documents, see O. Treptow, *John Siberich: Johann Lair von Siegberg*, ed. J. Morris and T. Jones, Cambridge Bibliographical Society Monographs 6 (Cambridge, UK: Cambridge Bibliographical Society, 1970), 30, 58–59.

61. S. Gee, "The Coming of Print to York, c. 1490–1550," in P. Isaac and B. McKay, eds., *The Mighty Engine: The Printing Press and Its Impact* (Winchester, UK: St. Paul's Bibliographies, and New Castle, DE: Oak Knoll Press, 2000), 80–81, 83–84. In addition to the material cited, there is the purchase of three hundred printed briefs for the indulgences associated with the hospital of St. Thomas, Micklegate, noted in York City Archives, C102:3, in 1533 to 1534, presumably from a York printer.

62. STC 14077c. 26–35, 41, 61, 69. That Beverley turned to Pynson in London rather than to a York printer is suggestive. As noted, that documents survive is not proof that they were formally issued by those bodies they purport to represent. A unique surviving confessional letter is in each case the only indication that the Ludlow palmers' guild and the hospital of St. Thomas at Salisbury used printed documents (STC 14077c. 61, 69); their commissioning and purchase are not visible in the surviving accounts, but there is no reason to challenge their authenticity.

63. STC 14077c. 24.

64. Cf. D. R. Carlson, "A Theory of the Early English Printing Firm: Jobbing, Book Publishing, and the Problem of Productive Capacity in Caxton's Work," in W. Kuskin, ed., *Caxton's Trace: Studies in the History of English Printing* (Notre Dame, IN: University of Notre Dame Press,

2006), 45–48, 52. (I would temper his comments about printed indulgences at 47.) The issue of jobbing printing, the necessity for printers to undertake small jobs, and the profitability of these jobs is discussed with greater chronological breadth in Stallybrass, "Little Jobs," 315–341, although he would challenge the use of the label of "jobbing printer" for Caxton, seeing him rather as a printer "who tried to balance the rapid cash flow that came from job printing against the speculations they made when printing books" (ibid., 335).

65. While this article focuses on indulgence-related printing, other similar products, including ballads and maybe royal proclamations, also provided small-scale contracts and thereby fit into the picture (as Stallybrass indeed asserts, with specific reference to Pynson: "Little Jobs," 324–345—material cited elsewhere in the present article extends his list of Pynson's post-1523 minor printing, notably for the Boston guild).

66. Windsor, St. George's Chapel archives, XV.59.1, m.10d.

67. Needham, *Printer and the Pardoner*, 44–45.

68. York City Archives, C102:3.

69. Ibid., CB3, 188.

70. Ibid., 189.

71. *STC* 14077c. 27–35, 91–99 (this list can now be expanded). See also comments on Pynson's prioritizing of minor contracts in Stallybrass, "Little Jobs," 324.

72. BL MS Egerton 2886, fols. 209r, 228r, 241v, 260v–261r, 264v, 299v, 303r (Pynson is not always identified as the printer). See also Brewer, Gairdner, and Brodie, *Letters and Papers*, 3/ii: no. 3015.

73. BL MS Egerton 2886, fols. 299v, 303r. From the pricing, I assume that the three thousand "small briefs" produced for fifteen shillings are the same as "jubilees." The documents detailed at fol. 303r were significantly cheaper than the other batch.

74. With a unit cost of just under a halfpenny, the parchment letters may push at the limit of the category of single-sided "cheap print" because their printing costs were higher than those of contemporary ballads. To exclude them would, however, be an arbitrary choice.

75. Oxford, Bodleian Library MS Bodley 123, fols. 149r–v.

76. For the letters, see *STC* 14077c. 114–115.

77. Information about this is scattered through the guild accounts, now among the Westminster Abbey Muniments.
78. York City Archives, CB3, 188, 241.
79. Swanson, *Indulgences*, 191–193, 454.
80. Ibid., 188.
81. These may be represented by the fragments of *STC* 14077c. 84 (their issuer is wrongly identified), which in their overlaps are textually identical to the document cited in note 82 below. *STC* suggests a date of ?1520, but the printed date could be either 1520 precisely or 152_.
82. BL MS Add. 4719/2 (not in *STC*).
83. Exeter, Devon Record Office, Chanter 15, fols. 61r–v; see also Swanson, *Indulgences*, 457.
84. Swanson, *Indulgences*, 174–175.
85. The sense of inspection is most evident in the Santo Spirito documents and some of the confessional letters for the Boston guild. A small fragment bound into Cambridge University Library F152.b.6.3 is a similar attestation, now visible only under ultraviolet light. (Listed in *STC* at 14077c. 84, but I am not convinced that the two fragments are actually separated parts of the same document. There is no textual overlap to validate a link.) The Boston guild publicity leaflet, *STC* 14077c. 35, also has signs of such examination.
86. BL Sloane ch.xxxii.27.
87. J. B. Gleason, "The Earliest Evidence for Ecclesiastical Censorship of Printed Books in England," *The Library*, 6th ser., 4 (1982): 137–138, 140–141.
88. London, National Archives, SC7/64/6 (not identified in *STC*). The inserted name is no longer legible or recoverable.
89. STC 14077c. 124.
90. Axton and Happé, *Plays of John Heywood*, 96–107.
91. Ibid., 100.
92. See P. Needham, "The Customs Rolls as Documents for the Printed-Book Trade in England," in Hellinga and Trapp, *The Cambridge History of the Book in Britain, vol. III, 1400–1557*, 159.

WORKS CITED

A Gloryous Medytacyon of Jhesus Crystes Passyon. London: Richard Fakes, ?1523.

Armstrong, C. A. J. *England, France, and Burgundy in the Fifteenth Century.* London: Hambledon Press, 1983.

Axton, R, and P. Happé, eds. *The Plays of John Heywood.* Cambridge, UK: D.S. Brewer, 1991.

Blake, N. F. "Manuscript to Print." In his *William Caxton and English Literary Culture.* London and Rio Grande, OH: Hambledon Press, 1991.

Brewer, J. S., J. Gairdner, and R. H. Brodie, eds. *Letters and Papers, Foreign and Domestic, of the Reign of Henry VIII,* 23 vols. in 38. London: Her/His Majesty's Stationery Office, 1862–1932.

Cameron, K. W. *The Pardoner and His Pardons: Indulgences Circulating in England on the Eve of the Reformation, with a Historical Introduction.* Hartford, CT: Transcendental Books, [1965].

Carlson, D. R. "A Theory of the Early English Printing Firm: Jobbing, Book Publishing, and the Problem of Productive Capacity in Caxton's Work." In *Caxton's Trace: Studies in the History of English Printing,* edited by W. Kuskin. Notre Dame, IN: University of Notre Dame Press, 2006.

Colchester, J. C., ed., *Wells Cathedral Fabric Accounts, 1390–1600.* Wells, UK: Friends of Wells Cathedral 1983.

Collins, F., ed., *Register of the Freemen of the City of York from the City Records, vol. I: 1272–1558,* Surtees Society 96 (1897).

Davis, J. "'Men as March with Fote Packes': Pedlars and Freedom of Movement in Late Medieval England." In *Freedom of Movement in the Middle Ages,* edited by P. Horden, Harlaxton Medieval Studies, 15. Donington, UK: Shaun Tyas, 2007.

Duff, E.G., and L. Hellinga. *Printing in England in the Fifteenth Century: E. Gordon Duff's Bibliography with Supplementary Descriptions, Chronologies and a Census of Copies by Lotte Hellinga.* London: British Library with the Bibliographical Society, 2009.

Duffy, E. *Marking the Hours: English People and their Prayers, 1240-1570.* New Haven, CT, and London: Yale University Press, 2006.

Eisermann, F. "Mixing Pop and Politics: Origins, Transmission and Readers of Illustrated Broadsides in Fifteenth-Century Germany." In *Incunabula*

and Their Readers: Printing, Selling, and Using Books in the Fifteenth Century, edited by K. Jensen. London: British Library, 2003.
Erskine, A. M., ed. The Accounts of the Fabric of Exeter Cathedral, 1279–1353, 2 vols., Devon and Cornwall Record Society, n.s. 24, 26 (1981–1983).
Frere, W. H. and W. M. Kennedy, eds. Visitation Articles and Injunctions of the Period of the Reformation, 3 vols., Alcuin Club Collections, 14–16. London, New York, Bombay and Calcutta, 1910.
Gaydon, A. T., ed. Victoria County History: Shropshire, vol. 2. London: Published for the Institute of Historical Research by Oxford University Press, 1973.
Gee, S. "The Coming of Print to York, c. 1490–1550." In The Mighty Engine: The Printing Press and Its Impact, edited by P. Isaac and B. McKay. Winchester, UK: St. Paul's Bibliographies, and New Castle, DE: Oak Knoll Press, 2000.
Gleason, J. B. "The Earliest Evidence for Ecclesiastical Censorship of Printed Books in England." The Library, 6th ser. 4 (1982): 135-141.
Hellinga, L. "Printing." In The Cambridge History of the Book in Britain, vol. III, 1400–1557, edited by L. Hellinga and J. B. Trapp. Cambridge, UK: Cambridge University Press, 1999.
Hughes, P. L., and J. F. Larkin, eds., Tudor Royal Proclamations, 3 vols. New Haven, CT, and London: Yale University Press, 1964-1969.
McKitterick, D. Print, Manuscript and the Search for Order, 1450–1830. Cambridge, UK: Cambridge University Press, 2003.
Needham, P. The Printer and the Pardoner: An Unrecorded Indulgence Printed by William Caxton for the Hospital of St. Mary Rounceval, Charing Cross. Washington, DC: Library of Congress, 1986.
Needham, P. "The Customs Rolls as Documents for the Printed-Book Trade in England." In The Cambridge History of the Book in Britain, vol. III, 1400–1557, edited by L. Hellinga and J. B. Trapp. Cambridge, UK: 1999.
Oliver, G. Lives of the Bishops of Exeter and a History of the Cathedral; with an Illustrative Appendix. Exeter, UK: William Roberts, 1861.
Orme, N., and M. Webster, The English Hospital, 1070–1570. New Haven, CT, and London: Yale University Press, 1995.
Pollard, A. W., and G. R. Redgrave, A Short-Title Catalogue of Books Printed in England, Scotland, and Ireland, and of English Books Printed Abroad,

1475–1640, 3 vols., 2nd ed., rev. W. A. Jackson, F. S. Ferguson, and K. F. Pantzer. London: Bibliographical Society, 1976–1991.

Sayle, C. "Cambridge Fragments." *The Library*, 3rd ser. 2 (1911): 336-339.

Skemer, D. C. *Binding Words: Textual Amulets in the Middle Ages.* University Park, PA: Pennsylvania State University Press, 2006.

Slavin, A. J. "The Tudor Revolution and the Devil's Art: Bishop Bonner's Printed Forms." In *Tudor Rule and Revolution: Essays for G. R. Elton from His American Friends*, edited by D. J. Guth and J. W. McKenna. Cambridge, UK: Cambridge University Press, 1982.

Stallybrass, P. "'Little Jobs': Broadsides and the Printing Revolution." In *Agent of Change: Print Culture Studies after Elizabeth L. Eisenstein*, edited by S. A. Baron, E. N. Lindquist, and E. F. Shevlin. Amherst, MA: University of Massachusetts Press, 2007.

Strype, John. *Ecclesiastical Memorials Relating Chiefly to Religion and the Reformation of It, and the Emergencies of the Church of England under King Henry VIII., King Edward VI., and Queen Mary I*, 3 vols. in 6. Oxford: Clarendon Press, 1822.

Swanson, R. N. "Contributions from Parishes in the Archdeaconry of Norfolk to the Shrine of St. Thomas Cantilupe at Hereford, ca. 1320." *Mediaeval Studies* 62 (2000): 190-218.

Swanson, R. N. "Letters of Confraternity and Indulgence in Late-Medieval England." *Archives* 25 (2000): 40-57.

Swanson, R. N. "Fund Raising for a Medieval Monastery: Indulgences and Great Bricett Priory." *Proceedings of the Suffolk Institute of Archaeology and History* 40 (2001–2004): 1-7.

Swanson, R. N. "A Small Library for Pastoral Care and Spiritual Direction in Late Medieval England." *Journal of the Early Book Society* 5 (2002): 99-120.

Swanson, R. N. "Caxton's Indulgence for Rhodes, 1480–81." *The Library*, 7th ser. 5 (2004): 195-201.

Swanson, R. N. "A Rounceval Pardon of 1482." *Archives* 30 no. 113 (Oct. 2005): 51-54.

Swanson, R. N. "Prayer and Participation in Late Medieval England." *Studies in Church History* 42 (2006): 130-139.

Swanson, R. N. *Indulgences in Late Medieval England: Passports to Paradise?* Cambridge, UK: Cambridge University Press, 2007.

Thomas, H. "An Indulgence Printed by Pynson, 1491." *British Museum Quarterly* 9 (1934): 32-33.

Treptow, O. *John Siberich: Johann Lair von Siegberg*, edited by J. Morris and T. Jones. Cambridge Bibliographical Society Monographs, 6. Cambridge, UK: Cambridge Bibliographical Society, 1970.

Writing Fame: Epitaph Transcriptions in Renaissance Chaucer Editions and the Construction of Chaucer's Poetic Reputation

ARNOLD SANDERS

While examining two copies of Stow's 1561 Chaucer edition[1] at the Garrett Library Collection of the Sheridan Libraries at Johns Hopkins University, I discovered that each of them contained a manuscript transcription of the verses on Chaucer's tomb, the marble structure Nicholas Brigham paid to erect at Westminster in 1556. Though one transcription is far more complete than the other, both appear to have been written in early-modern hands and both are located in places suggesting that their writers considered the epitaphs the "termini" of Chaucer's works. In the first one, a single quatrain from the epitaph is traced in now-faint brownish ink with red capitals on the verso of folio 378, the colophon leaf, just below its sarcophagus-like printer's ornament.[2] The other, copied in black ink, stands just below the printer's title announcing "Thus endeth the workes of Geffray Chaucer" and before the beginning of Lydgate's works (fol. 355v).[3]

The occurrence of the same kind of annotation in two different hands in two copies of the same Chaucer edition seemed astonishing and suggestive. In 1999, Joseph Dane and Alexandra Gillespie reported finding two more tomb-verse transcriptions at the Huntington Library and at the Harry Ransom Center.[4] Dane's Huntington discovery was a complete version of the tomb verses on the title page of a 1550 reprint of the Thynne edition, located beneath another sarcophagus-like printer's ornament. Gillespie's Ransom Center discovery in a copy of the 1561 Stow Chaucer has a similarly complete version on the colophon leaf below the printer's device, exactly where I found the first copy in the Garrett collection. Because the texts of all four inscriptions differ from each other and from surviving printed transcriptions, they do not seem to have been copied from the same source or to be the work of even modestly skilled scribes.[5]

Nor are these four the only annotations of their type in early Chaucer editions. A few months after finding the Garrett Library transcriptions, I found another in a 1532 Thynne edition at the Folger Shakespeare Library. That annotation had already been reported the previous year by Alison Wiggins, who also found two additional epitaphs inscribed in other Folger copies of the 1532 and 1561 editions.[6] Based on the Wiggins survey of fifty-two Renaissance copies of Chaucer's collected works in England and America and on copies examined by Dane, by Gillespie, and by me, these seven epitaph transcriptions appear to be the only kind of extended annotation that occurs so frequently.

If the manuscript epitaphs have been found in an eighth of these fifty-six Renaissance Chaucers, it seems likely that we would find more now that we know what we are looking for. This article advances a hypothetical explanation for the social behaviors which may have produced these annotations and reexamines the publishing history of Chaucer's collected works in light of that hypothesis. This leads to new potential explanations for the destruction of the carved verses on the tomb itself and to another possible connection between the tomb and the collected works of Edmund Spenser, whose interest in associating himself with Chaucer is well established. I also request readers' assistance in seeking further examples of the tomb-verse transcriptions in Chaucer editions published between 1532 and 1598.

In brief, I believe these annotations may represent early-modern English readers' participation in the construction of Chaucer's poetic fame by means of behaviors that resemble the social practices of cult worship of the saints. Those behaviors included pilgrimage, profound meditation upon relics of the dead, taking away representative artifacts from ceremonial sites, especially tombs, and study of the saints' words and deeds, both those authorized by the Church and apocrypha circulated in collections such as Jacobus de Voraigne's *Legenda aurea*.⁷ By the eighteenth century, all four of those cult-like behaviors had become a commonly accepted part of English secular literary culture, with the Poet's Corner in Westminster Abbey as its focal point.

The transmission of the tomb-verse-annotation custom to later owners of early Chaucer editions appears to have passed through an important stage in which Chaucer's "Englishness" and his status as an originator of high English literature were consolidated, finding expression in three important print events: the front matter of Thomas Speght's late-seventeenth-century Chaucer editions (1598, 1602, 1687), the engraving of the tomb in Elias Ashmole's 1650-to-1651 alchemical anthology, and the reproduction of a similar tomb engraving on the frontispiece of Edmund Spenser's *Collected Works* (1679).⁸ These editions represent two important groups of specialist readers in the late seventeenth century who seem to have played a role in steering the quasi-religious social practices of a generation or two earlier toward their completely secular form. The secular antiquarians and "hermetic philosophers," early students of the medieval past, helped preserve the text of the verses even as Chaucer's physical tomb apparently began to crumble in a mysterious process we may finally be able to explain. Continued popular dialogue about Chaucer's tomb and editions of his collected works also seems to have caught the attention of editors, printers, and booksellers, because they added the verses and images of the tomb to later Chaucer editions.

The tomb verses themselves, which are reproduced at the end of this article, differ from typical English funerary inscriptions of this era which have been studied by Nigel Saul in that they do not ask for intercessory prayers for the deceased.⁹ They do identify the poet by name and date of death, as would be traditional, but their primary concern is Chaucer's fame, his status as "thrice-greatest English poet." They also take pains to identify the tomb's sponsor, Brigham, and the year of its construction, as if memorializing the tomb itself. The verses seem intended to remind onlookers of what Saul calls "the deceased's place in the social pecking-order," a kind of biographical inscription he finds increasingly common in tombs constructed in the 1500s.¹⁰ Unlike those epitaphs that celebrate a knight's most famous battles, a squire's ancestry, or a married couple's tally of years lived faithfully together, Chaucer's epitaph concentrates his entire identity into his fame as an English poet.[11] In addition, the plane-relief, full-length portrait of Chaucer seems an unusual departure from tomb iconography after 1538.[12] The inscriptions and Chaucer's graven image would be ideally designed, however, to help visitors associate Chaucer's poetry with the tomb's spectacular presence, and they may help to explain the use made of those verses by readers and printers.

The earliest hand in which the tomb verses are inscribed appears to be Dane's Huntington discovery in the 1550 reprint of Thynne.[13] Both Garrett Library copies of the Stow 1561 edition that I examined appear to be in a late-sixteenth-century or early-seventeenth-century secretary hand. Gillespie's 1561 Stow discovery in the Ransom Center is described as a "mixed secretary italic" hand associated with other annotations from "[Matthew] Parker's circle," including Stow himself.[14] Wiggins's Folger discovery in a 1550 Thynne reprint is "written in an Elizabethan secretary hand by one Edward Muckelston," and her 1561 Stow discovery in the same collection "was apparently added by William Sandbrook around 1635."[15] Perhaps the most astonishing evidence of the tomb-verse tradition's survival is the annotation of Wiggins's Folger discovery in a 1532 Thynne edition, "apparently added during the eighteenth century by William Latton, a fellow of Wadham College, Oxford" by transcription from one of two printed sources.[16] By this time, the significance of both Chaucer's works and his tomb had been translated into something far different from what they were two centuries earlier, but the same reader behaviors were being elicited by them.

So far, the epitaph annotations in Chaucer's collected works from 1532 to 1561 have been studied as evidence of reader response to the text (Wiggins) and of the writers' choice of copy text from the tomb itself or from print editions by Camden and Speght (Dane and Gillespie).[17] Wiggins goes so far as to suggest that they represent "a persistent tradition of transcribing, circulating, and re-copying these lines," and traces the provenance of the three copies she discovered to households in Cheshire, Shropshire, and Lincolnshire.[18] She does not speculate upon what might have motivated that tradition, however, nor its possible influence on later print editions of the works and its apparent persistence for centuries. These annotations may be just a small sample of a more widespread pattern of interactions among readers, editors, and printers during the period when Chaucer manuscripts were being replaced by print editions. Early-modern vernacular English printers, with their significant "sunk costs" and geographically limited customer base, had to listen closely to what readers said they wanted in order to remain profitable. These manuscript annotations may have helped astute printers to make wise marketing decisions about what a proper Chaucer edition should contain.[19]

Even the earliest tomb inscriptions certainly should not be read as evidence that the English people actually began to worship Chaucer as a supernatural being. The readers who wrote the tomb inscriptions into their copies of Chaucer may well have been responding to a politically interesting vagueness affecting cultural expressions of profound respect and admiration that we also see asserted in praise of Chaucer's language as an original foundation of Englishness.[20] Christopher Cannon describes the myth-making process by which poets and critics from Lydgate to the current era have claimed that Chaucer and Chaucer's works "purified" or even "originated" English as we know it.[21] These claims of Chaucer's linguistic and national originality may also have encouraged readers' visits to his tomb and their reverent annotation of his text with its words.

Elizabethan readers' interaction with their Chaucer editions and the tomb verses may also shed light upon English governments' persistent struggles to control their subjects' religious practices. Alexandra Walsham notes that Elizabethan clergy "were dealing with a populace which had been baptized Catholic" and which had a "nostalgia for the ritual protection which had been supplied by the pre-Reformation Church."[22] Jesuit missionaries to England invoked the superior "thaumaturgic" powers of the Old Religion's saints as evidence of its superiority over the leaner liturgy of the upstart schismatics. Nevertheless, Reformation critiques of these practices appear to have produced significant cultural resistance to the saints' worship. The Roman Church's "crisis of canonization" between 1523 and 1588 resulted in no new saints being made during the period as the Church was formulating its response to attacks on the cult of the saints as "superstition." This encompasses the period in which the first editions of Chaucer's collected works were printed and almost precisely brackets Brigham's construction of the tomb in 1556. The poet's tomb and writings thus become available to English readers at a time when ancient, popular religious practices involving pilgrimage, relics, and study of saints' words suddenly had no acceptable public outlet.

Chaucer's poetic influence and his early-modern fame have also drawn critical attention from literary scholars, who attend closely to the part played by increased English linguistic nationalism in the adornment of Chaucer's tomb and praise of his works. Edwin Benjamin points out that Chaucer himself was the first poet in English to write specifically about poets' posthumous reputations in *The House of Fame*, in which the pillars adorning the temple to the poem's fickle goddess bear the images of the writers Josephus, Statius, Homer, Vergil, Ovid, Lucan, and Claudian.[23] As early as 1993, Seth Lerer argues that Chaucer's first tomb poem, composed by Stephano Surigone and reprinted by Caxton in the 1478 *Boethius*, was evidence that the printer appropriated the poet's tomb, texts, and authority in a way that already identified Chaucer as a humanist "laureate," a titular father of his language's literature and object of readers' veneration.[24]

We may be able to read in the diversity of modern views of the Renaissance reception of Chaucer some sense of the poet's capacity to appeal to both Protestant and Roman Catholic readers in that era. In 1995, for instance, Derek Pearsall analyzes the circumstances of Brigham's erection of the new tomb to investigate whether the merchant was appropriating Chaucer's fame for the Counter-Reformation.[25] In 1998, John Watkins argues that Thynne's 1532 edition specifically allied itself with Henry VIII's political ideology to create a "Protestant Chaucer," following the lead of John Foxe's declaration that the poet was "a right Wicleuian."[26] Nevertheless, Alexandra Gillespie and Greg Walker argue that the same edition was not Protestant but rather patriotic.[27]

Amid such a tug-of-war between the English and Roman Churches, both trying to construct a "Chaucer" to suit their causes, Protestant and Catholic English readers may have turned to Chaucer to bridge a difficult cultural gap, seeking some common ground upon which to base their "Englishness."[28] His most popular work was inextricably connected with both the practice of religious pilgrimage to the shrine of an English saint and satire upon religious corruption and the abuse of clerical privileges. If recusant Catholics copied out the Latin verses, they may have been interested in Chaucer as "one of us," the poet of pilgrimage and of the Parson's sermon on penance. Protestant annotators might share nostalgia for the inscription language, associated as it was with the Old Religion's comforting liturgy and with learned authority. The editions' juxtaposition of Chaucer's authentic anticlerical satires with the apocryphal "Plowman's Tale," first added to the *Works* in 1542, seven years after its solo publication, also allowed Protestant readers to claim Chaucer as an ally in their battle against Rome.

Perhaps around the time of John Stow's last reprinting of Thynne's edition in 1561, Stow and other members of the antiquarian scholarly movement, along with students of alchemical lore, entered the social system that brought readers to copy the tomb verses. For these researchers, the addition of the verses to a print edition would encourage respect for the poet as a founding figure in English history and a scholar of arcane lore. As secular devotees to Chaucer's tomb and works, John Stow and Elias Ashmole performed important services to those who still may have approached the tomb with atavistic religious behaviors in mind. They also enabled printers to publish the inscriptions' text and underwrote production of Robert Vaughan's first engraving of the tomb.

In this way, the cultural reception of Chaucer and his works differs from that of any other medieval poet. The pattern of readers' annotations reveals a concern for the poet's tomb and fame that seems actively to link their interests with the material survival and completeness of the poet's works.[29] Following the growth of readers' and editors' interest in Chaucer's collected works, popular attention to other authors' Westminster tombs in the following two centuries became increasingly commonplace, and tomb tourism at Poet's Corner began to take on its current cultural significance.[30] In a curious inversion of the modern literary anthology, abbey tourist guides gathered together images of the authors' tombs, together with their inscribed memorial texts, so that visitors could serially direct their attention to the postmortem remains of the masters of the English canon.

Readers' annotation practices in older editions may have become known to printers and would have strongly implied what kinds of new content would sell new editions. In fact, we can observe the tomb verses' migration from readers' manuscripts to the type set for later editions.[31] The content and location of the annotations suggest what early-modern readers believed to be a "complete" Chaucer edition and what production and ownership of such a book meant to the poet's growing fame as a kind of ancestral figure for the English language and "Englishness."

As early as the preface to Caxton's second edition of *Canterbury Tales*, printers represented Chaucer's reputation and his works as contested ground. Alexandra Gillespie points out specific kinds of printed annotations that emerged when the earliest Chaucer editions were read amid post-Reformation government censorship of Catholic content.[32] She also speculates that later editions may have been influenced when public Catholic religious practices returned during Mary's reign. Thomas Prendergast observes, however, that Stow's 1561 edition, printed only three years after Mary's death, ignores Brigham's tomb and prints only the Surigone-Caxton verses.[33] Prendergast suspects Stow was responding cautiously to the new government, but it seems equally likely that Stow gave readers what they had asked for in the past.

The four manuscript tomb verses so far discovered in copies of Stow's edition may bear witness to increased public interest in the abbey, which may have redirected Stow's own research. In his 1598 *Survey of London*, Stow reports extensively on Brigham's monument and reproduces its inscriptions. Of all of the 1561 Chaucers, Gillespie's Ransom Center copy is the most interesting, because it had been annotated by Stow himself and later by Matthew Parker, a member of whose circle provided the tomb-verse annotation.[34] From Stow's notes, the epitaph seems to have made its way into Speght's Chaucer edition of the same year in which Stow's *Survey* was published.[35] By that point, the Brigham inscriptions had become a standard element of Chaucer's collected works, much like the Chaucer portrait and the "hard word" glossary, which Speght also introduced. John Speed's engraving of the author's portrait for the frontispiece of the 1598 edition already shows the poet standing, somewhat incongruously, upon a tomb identified as that of the poet's son, Thomas, and Thomas's wife, Matilda.[36] This image might be said to begin the visual mingling in print of the poetic and mortuary aspects of the author.

Elias Ashmole's *Theatrum chemicum Britannicum* (published from 1651 to 1652) played the next crucial role in establishing Chaucer's tomb as a subject of secular admiration when he published Robert Vaughan's engraving of the tomb with the main verses clearly legible beside Chaucer's portrait. Ashmole's "Prolegomena" explicitly articulates the "tomb = text" metaphor when describing his readers' interaction with the works he reprinted. Ashmole not only calls the authors' texts their "Monuments," but also treats the text-monuments as the metaphorical source of the alchemical treasures his text purports to purvey:

> Wherefore you that love to converse with the *Dead*, or consult with their *Monuments*, draw near: perhaps you may find more benefit in them, then the *Living*; There you may meet with the *Genii* of our *Hermetique Philosophers*, learne the Language in which they woo'd and courted *Dame Nature*, and enjoy them more freely, and at Greater *Command*, (to satisfy your *Doubts*) then when they were in the *Flesh*, For, they have *Written* more then they would *Speake*; and left their *Lines so Rich*, as if they had dissolved *Gold* in their *Inke*, and clad their *Words* with the *Soveraign Moysture*. (sig. [B4])

Since the days of G. L. Kittredge and S. Foster Damon, the Renaissance view of Chaucer as an alchemical student has been well known, though the number of those scholars who actually believed the poet was a practicing adept remains in debate.[37] Ashmole's notes specifically assert that he reprints the "Canon's Yeoman's Prologue and Tale" "to let the *World* see what a notorious *Cheating* there has beene ever used, under pretence of this true (though Injur'd) *Science*," but also "to shew that *Chaucer* himselfe was a *Master* therein."[38] Then he draws the antiquaries and previous editors into his proofs, naming Speght, and the antiquaries Bale and Leland as his guarantors of Chaucer's life of study among the "Friers Carmelites of Lynne" to become "*Universally learned*."[39]

Ashmole gives no specific reason the tomb engraving appears at the foot of the last page of the *Theatrum chemicum*'s reprinting of *Hermes Bird*, facing the beginning of the Canon's Yeoman's prologue, but he does draw attention to the tomb itself, noting that "The *Picture of Chaucer* is now somwhat decay'd, but the *Graver* has recovered it after a Principall left to *posterity* by his worthy Schollar *Tho. Occleve*."[40] There he quotes the *Regiment of Princes* verses from MS BL Harley 4866 which specifically defend the making of Chaucer's image by comparing it with those of the saints: "The ymages þat in þe chirche been, / Maken folk þenke on god & on his seyntes, / Whan þe ymages þei be-holden & seen." This gesture helps to move the textual and tomb representations of Chaucer further along the path to secular or metaphorical sainthood.

During the following two centuries, the tomb underwent a period of curious celebrity in English culture. In 1721, John Urry's edition of Chaucer's works finally included the tomb engraving with the verses on its title page, as well as reproducing the text in its entirety in the preface, completing the transformation of readers' handcrafted annotations to the mise-en-page of mass-produced artifacts. As printers and editors adopted readers' analogous association, "fame = tomb and tomb = text," the tomb contained and editions memorialized the poet's bodily and textual remains as complete and somehow sacred constructions whose secular residue was that elusive but powerful phantom, "fame." In fact, the actual tomb's social or ethical power seems to have been considered potent enough to oversee and guarantee oaths sworn to secure loans.[41] Like the tomb's image and inscriptions, the text of Chaucer's works could also manifest the poet's absent presence and the poet's fame by a process similar to that by which saints' relics operated. Just as the Church had declared since the eighth century that "relics had the power of reproducing themselves," so the press could reproduce potentially infinite copies of Chaucer's works.[42] Translations of the tomb inscriptions to print editions accomplish the same ends for Chaucer's text as the ceremonial translation of the saint's remains to the site of viewers' veneration, in this instance, a Latin memorial imposed upon a collected body of Middle English poetry.

Even as the tomb poems influenced the content of Chaucer's printed works, copying the epitaphs may have altered the tomb. Copying the text from someone else's annotation or a new print edition would be the easiest way to obtain the text, but some annotators, like so many Canterbury pilgrims, may have carried their editions to Westminster to copy the epitaphs on the spot, perhaps helping to wear away the marble inscriptions while tracing the stone letters with their hands. Speght, writing his edition's preface only forty-six years after the tomb's construction, notes that the "verses written about the ledge" of the monument ("*Si rogites quis eram*") were "clean worne out." This would be peculiarly rapid erosion of a marble inscription that was protected from rain and other natural forces by its location within the abbey.⁴³ In fact, the damage may be explained by visitors' tactile devotional practices authorized for sacred pilgrims by the Roman Church.

Alexandra Walsham cites instances in which the Church sanctioned worship of "secondary" or "associative" relics, and between 1615 and 1640 printed books were credited with performing miraculous cures in their authors' names.⁴⁴ The Christian worship of "brandea," including "touch relics," dates to the earliest days of the Church, and in England, worship of saints' relics, including physical contact with their tombs and reliquaries, was especially active until the late 1530s.⁴⁵ Even today, secular visitors to public monuments continue to practice unconsciously the ancient rituals by touching specific portions of public statues. At the F.D.R. Memorial in Washington, D.C., for instance, the brightness of the president's forefinger and knee, and the shiny ears and nose of Fala, Roosevelt's Scottish terrier, testify to the secularized traces of religious ritual in our interaction with modern monuments.⁴⁶ Secular and increasingly nationalistic attention to relics derived from poets, composers, and philosophers resulted in the hideous disinterment and plundering of remains thought to be John Milton's in 1790 and in the popular veneration of skulls said to belong to Joseph Haydn (until 1954), Emanuel Swedenborg (to 1958), and Friedrich von Schiller (to 1965).⁴⁷

Readers used to the "hands-off" curatorial instructions of modern libraries and museums might find outrageous the suggestion that generations of visitors to Westminster Abbey had been handling Chaucer's tomb. Constance Classen points out, however, that caretakers of early museums and collections often encouraged visitors to touch their artifacts, including objects in the Tower of London and the abbey. Although the coronation chairs of the Chapel of St. Edward the Confessor were forbidden to visitors, and the German tourist Zacharias Conrad von Uffenbach was forced to refrain from scraping a souvenir from the Stone of Scone, he was allowed to handle a famous sword to judge its weight and reports numerous tactile details of artifacts he handled on his tour of English historical sites.⁴⁸ Samuel Pepys records that when visiting the abbey on his birthday, he was invited to kiss the mouth of the mummified body of Henry V's queen, Katherine, and did so.⁴⁹

Westminster Abbey's sixteenth- and seventeenth-century visitors to Chaucer's tomb inscriptions may have been influenced more than those of later generations by the saints cults' emphasis on physical contact with objects that had absorbed what has been called "the holy radioactivity" of the saint.[50] In the 1620s, the Church officially authorized worshippers of the proto-saint Bishop Frances de Sales to "carry away fragments of stone scraped from his tomb."[51] The physical location of the first verses said to have vanished from Chaucer's tomb, those "about the ledge," may have rendered them more vulnerable to deliberate removal.

Even innocent tracing, however, might have been sufficient to erode the rest of the letters, given the material from which the tomb may have been constructed.[52] If we can trust surviving descriptions, the tomb was carved from "Petworth Marble," a stone that geologists call "large 'Paludina' marble," after the fossil shells embedded in its calcite matrix.[53] Widely used since Roman times for interior monuments, including those at Canterbury Cathedral, Petworth marble is "easily weathered by acid rain," which dissolves the matrix and allows the shells to fall out.[54] One source of acid-bearing liquids in the abbey could have been the human sweat deposited by visitors' hands tracing inscriptions as they copied them out. The chemistries of sweat and acidic rainwater are similar. Ordinary, preindustrial rainwater could reach an acidic pH of 5.0 to 5.6 (7 being neutral), which is strong enough to erode marble, and sweat from the palm of the hand may have a pH between 4.9 and 6.4.[55] In exterior locations subject to centuries of rain, the marble's calcite ($CaCO_3$) interacts with carbonic acid (H_2CO_3) created when CO_2 in the atmosphere dissolves in rainwater.[56] Human hands effectively deposit a similar "acid rain" directly upon the marble they touch. As more of the calcite matrix gave way, the inscriptions would have become more difficult to read and the need to hand-trace them would increase.

The erosion of the tomb by those copying its verses may have occurred quite quickly, which may suggest that additional sources of accelerant may have been available in the abbey's atmosphere. Two years before Speght's editorial comment on the tomb verses' dilapidation, Edmund Spenser's 1596 homage to Chaucer in Book IV, canto ii, of *The Faerie Queene* may already have been referring to their erosion in his famous praise of the poet whose fame he sought to emulate:

> But wicked Time that all good thoughts doth waste,
> And workes of noblest wits to nought out weare,
> That famous moniment hath quite defaste,
> And robd the world of threasure endlesse deare,
> The which mote haue enriched all vs heare.
> O cursed Eld the cankerworme of writs,
> How may these rimes, so rude as doth appeare,
> Hope to endure, sith workes of heauenly wits
> Are quite deuourd, and brought to nought by little
> bits? (stanza 33)

Although these verses function perfectly well as Spenser's literary allusion to Chaucer's own comments on the impermanence of all reputations and the peculiar vulnerability of literature to meaning-loss by linguistic change (in *The House of Fame* [ll. 1144–1147] and *Anelida and Arcite* [10–14]), the images could also have functioned as an insider's mournful jest about the state of the actual tomb's engravings in the decade in which Spenser wrote.[57] Damage to the inscriptions appears to have continued unabated over the next two centuries until nearly all the verses were illegible.[58]

Spenser's careerist identification of his work with Chaucer's may also have played yet another role in the growth of modern tomb tourism when aristocratic patrons paid to bury Spenser near his poetic "father," with a similarly inscribed memorial. An 1818 account of the deterioration of Chaucer's tomb notes that Spenser's nearby tomb had also become "decayed" before being replaced in 1778.[59] Depending upon the materials from which the original tomb was constructed, it is possible that Spenser's ambition had fatal consequences for his own monument, even as his works memorialized the decay of Chaucer's.[60] Printers of Spenser's works also appear to have originated the inclusion of the tomb engraving with the author's *oeuvre*. The first folio of Spenser's *Collected Works*, printed in 1679 by Henry Hills for Jonathan Edwin, uses his Westminster Abbey tomb for the frontispiece. The success of this edition in establishing Spenser's poetic fame may in turn have influenced the title-page layout devised for Urry's 1721 Chaucer edition.

Little work has been done to date on the practice of representing poets' tombs rather than their portraits on title pages and frontispieces, but the

1679 Spenser page layout suggests a direct relationship between the tomb and the collected works that may owe a debt to the earlier practices of Chaucer's readers and printers. More importantly, further inspection of surviving copies of early-modern Chaucer editions may reveal additional instances of tomb inscriptions that might provide ownership evidence to help determine whether these annotation practices were linked to identifiable persons with common geographical or social ties.[61] The evidence, in manuscript and print, suggests a complex and evolving set of relationships among printers, readers, poets, the tombs, their makers, and their keepers. The same social forces that wore away the tombs' marble letters may also have set them forever in cold type and black ink.

Goucher College

Acknowledgments

I wish to thank Earle Havens, Johns Hopkins University curator of rare books, and his assistant, Amy Kimball, for their unflagging assistance, encouragement, and advice regarding this research. Steven Galbraith, curator of rare books and manuscripts at the Folger Shakespeare Library, also generously gave me access to materials from the Folger collection and directed me to Alison Wiggins's study. A previous version of this article, delivered at an Early Book Society session at the 44th Medieval Institute International Congress, benefited from comments and questions by several persons, especially Derek Pearsall. Finally, two anonymous reviewers for the *Journal of the Early Book Society* offered many valuable suggestions and corrections, for which I am extremely grateful.

APPENDIX

Joseph Dane's and Alexandra Gillespie's transcription of the monument's original verses:

> Qui fuit Anglorum vates. Ter maximus olim
> Galfridus Chaucer. conditur hoc tumulo
> Annum si queras domini si tempora mortis

ecce nota subsunt. que tibi cuncta notant. 25 octobris anno
    domini 1400

Chaucer occubuit sed corpore, cetera magnis
post cineres virtus vincere sola facit. ICB

recquies erumnarum mors
N. Brigham hos fecit musarum nomine sumptus. 1556

[The "verses about the ledge"]
Si rogites quis eram forsan te fama docebit
quod si fama negat mundi quia gloria transit
Hec monumentie lege.

Garrett Library Stow Chaucer, 1561, shelfmark PO1850 1561 QUARTO (EST 5075, the John Work Garrett copy)[62]

Qui fuit Anglor<um> vates ter maximus, olim:
Galfridus Chaucer, conditur hoc Tumulo
Ann<um>, si queras domini: si tempora, Mortis:
ecce: nota, subsunt: [que?] tibi cuncta, notant.
Æ<um>mar<um> requies, Mors.
N: B[ri?]gam: hos fecit [?musarum sumptus]
        1556

Garrett Library Stow Chaucer, 1561, shelf mark PO1850 1561a QUARTO (EST 5076, the Tudor and Stuart Club copy)[63]

The wordes writtin a bout Chaucers
tombe ſtone in Weſt<minster>
Si rogites quis eram, forſan te fama docebit
   quod ſi fama negat, mundi quia gloria tranſit
      hec monumenta lege

~~Qui fuit Anglorum~~ Chaucers epitaphe [written over cancelled first line]
written in West<minster> upon his tombe
Qui fuit Anglon vates ter maximus olim
   Galfridis Chaucer conditur hoc tumulo
An<n>um ſi queras d<omi>ni si tempora mortis
   ecce nota ſubſunt, qui tibi cuncta notant
     25 octob<e>r a<n>o D<omi>ni <u>1400</u>

Ærrumar<um> requies mors
N: Brigham hos fecit musſar<um> <nomine>
   sumptus 1556   } wordis[?] also writtin
                                  upon chaucers stone

NOTES

1. The most complete inscription is located on folio 355v of *The woorkes of Geoffrey Chaucer : newlie printed, with diuers addicions, whiche were neuer in print before: with the siege and destruccion of the worthy citee of Thebes, compiled by Ihon Lidgate, monke of Berie: as in the table more plainly doeth appere.* (STC 5076), Sheridan Library shelf mark PO 1850 1561a QUARTO. The shorter version is located at the foot of the colophon page verso (378v) of *The workes / of Geffrey Chaucer ; newly printed with diuers addicions, whiche were neuer in print before; with the siege and destruccion of the worthy citee of Thebes, compiled by Ihon Lidgate, monke of Berie: as in the table more plainly doeth appere,* (STC 5075), Sheridan Library shelf mark PO1850 1561 QUARTO. Features which distinguish the copy of EST 5075 from EST 5076 are found on the general title page ("workes" vs. "woorkes"), and the 5075 copy's woodcut illustrations before the pilgrim descriptions in the *General Prologue* front matter (which 5076 lacks). The title pages match Anne Hudson's and Joseph Dane's descriptions of the "king in counsel" engraving for STC 5075 and the armorial engraving for STC 5076, but the title page of the STC 5075 copy was no longer truly integral with the binding. Anne Hudson, John Stow (1525?-1605)," in *Editing Chaucer: The Great Tradition*, ed. Paul G. Ruggiers (Norman, OK: Pilgrim, 1984), 57;

Joseph Dane, "In Search of Stow's Chaucer," in *John Stow (1525-1605) and the Making of the English Past: Studies in Early Modern Culture and the History of the Book*, edited by Ian Gadd and Alexandra Gillespie (London: British Library, 2004), 154. The STC 5075 title page leaf was sewn into the binding upon a vertical repair at the gutter that extends from top to bottom. The remaining leaf appears to be of the same level of browning and wear as the adjacent leaves, but no further evidence of its relationship to this copy can be given. Folio 355, upon which the inscription is found, is integral to the gathering in which it is sewn, as well as could be observed. The title page of STC 5076 is integral to its gathering, as is folio 378, upon which its inscription is found.

2. For my transcription and Joseph Dane's reconstruction of the verses he discovered, see the Appendix. Digital color images of the Sheridan Library copies can be viewed at "Writing Fame: Manuscript Chaucer Epitaphs in Renaissance Editions of Chaucer's Collected Works," http://faculty.goucher.edu/eng330/Kzoo%202010/kalamazoo_2010.htm.

3. That manuscript epitaph also stands beside the printer's reproduction of the earlier Surigone-Caxton memorial verses, possibly indicating the annotator's intention to "correct" or update the older verses.

4. Joseph Dane and Alexandra Gillespie, "Back at Chaucer's Tomb: Inscriptions in Two Early Copies of *Chaucer's Workes*," *Studies in Bibliography* 52 (1999): 89–96.

5. The first Garret Library copy annotator's attempt to simulate medieval manuscript rubrication completely misunderstands the function of red letters, using them not to indicate beginnings of verses, actions performed in the Mass, or responsories but rather for irregular capitalization and punctuation marks, for example, the lowercase "d" of "domini." The second copy's annotator, apparently working in haste and without planning the mise-en-page, overwrote the first line of the second set of verses with a description of their location before going on to transcribe them.

6. Alison Wiggins, "What Did Renaissance Readers Write in Their Printed Copies of Chaucer?," *The Library* 9.1 (2008): 3–36.

7. For a broad survey of these practices throughout Europe, see Wilfrid Bonser, "The Cult of Relics in the Middle Ages," *Folklore* 73.4 (1962): 234–256. A description of English cult practices in this period is given in

Eamon Duffy, *The Stripping of the Altars: Traditional Religion in England, 1400–1580* (New Haven, CT: Yale University Press, 1992).

8. Speght's editions are STC 5077, 5080, the 1687 edition being considered by the STC a reprint of 5080. Spenser's 1679 collected works edition appears to have no STC number. Ashmole, Elias. *Theatrum chemicum Britannicum: Containing Severall Poeticall Pieces of our Famous English Philosophers, Who Have Written the Hermetique Mysteries in Their Owne Ancient Languge.* London: J. Grismond for Nath. Brooke, 1652. Rpt. Kila, MT: Kessinger, 1991.

9. Nigel Saul, *English Church Monuments in the Middle Ages: History and Representation* (Oxford: Oxford University Press, 2009), 343–352.

10. Ibid., 359, 357–359.

11. Ibid., 357, 359, 361.

12. Henry VIII's Injunctions of 1536 and 1538 "ordered the removal of images attracting pilgrimages or offerings." See Nicholas Orme, "Church and Chapel in Medieval England," *Transactions of the Royal Historical Society* 6th ser., 6 (1996): 75–102, 100.

13. Dane and Gillespie report that this appears to be "a nearly contemporary secretary hand"; Joseph Dane and Alexandra Gillespie, "Back at Chaucer's Tomb: Inscriptions in Two Early Copies of *Chaucer's Workes*," *Studies in Bibliography* 52 (1999): 89–96, 89.

14. Ibid., 95.

15. Alison Wiggins, "What Did Renaissance Readers Write in Their Printed Copies of Chaucer?" *The Library* 9.1 (2008): 3–36, 19.

16. Ibid.

17. Although Connell does not mention the manuscript tomb verses, he does note the later rapid multiplication of poets' tombs with verses memorializing their literary achievements, beginning with seventeenth-century monuments to Spenser (1620) and Cowley (1667) and leading to the eighteenth-century memorials to "both the recently deceased (such as Prior, Gay, Gray, Goldsmith, and Johnson), as well as retrospective monuments to Dryden (1720), Butler (1721), Jonson (c. 1723), Milton (1737), and Shakespeare (1740)"; Philip Connell, "Death and the Author: Westminster Abbey and the Meanings of the Literary Monument," *Eighteenth-Century Studies* 38.4 (2005): 557–585, 559.

18. Wiggins, "What Did Renaissance Readers Write," 20.
19. In this analysis of the early-modern printer's business sense, I follow the entrepreneurial view of the English book trade developed by A. S. G. Edwards, Martha Driver, and David Carlson, especially Carlson's "theory of the early English printing firm," as a corrective to the aristocratic-patronage model of early-modern publication. Carlson's study of job printing in Caxton's era strongly suggests how customer-oriented the printer's publishing decisions had already become because of the need to keep the presses busy. Competitive pressures in the following century would intensify printers' economic motives for publication. A. S. G. Edwards, "From Manuscript to Print: Wynkyn de Worde and the Printing of Contemporary Poetry," *Gutenberg-Jahrbuch* (1991): 1430–1438, and "Poet and Printer in Sixteenth Century England: Stephen Hawes and Wynkyn de Worde." *Gutenberg-Jahrbuch* (1980): 82–88. Martha Driver, "Ideas of Order: Wynkyn de Worde and the Title Page," in *Texts and Their Contexts: Papers from the Early Book Society*, ed. Julia Boffey and V. J. Scattergood(Dublin: Four Courts Press, 1997): 87–146; *The Image in Print: Book Illustration in Late Medieval England and Its Sources* (London: British Library, 2004), and "Mapping Chaucer: John Speed and the Later Portraits." *Chaucer Review* 36.3 (2002): 228–249. David Carlson, "A Theory of the Early English Printing Firm: Jobbing, Book Publishing, and the Problem of Productive Capacity in Caxton's Work," in *Caxton's Trace: Studies in the History of English Printing*, ed. William Kuskin, (Notre Dame, IN: University of Notre Dame Press, 2006): 35–68.
20. The cult-like aspect of the tomb-verse annotations, beginning in an era in which religious observances were under intense government scrutiny, remains difficult to understand and explain. The annotation practices might indicate some unconscious blurring of distinctions between behaviors appropriate only for sacred persons or objects and those accepted in use for very high-status secular persons or objects. Such ambiguity already existed in the language itself. In fifteenth- and sixteenth-century English, "to worship" also had secular usages which the *O.E.D.* defines as "To honor; to regard or treat with honor or respect" (ca. 1300–1578) and "To treat with signs of honor or respect; to salute, bow down to" (ca. 1380–1601). Readers of Sir Thomas Malory often encounter "worship" in descriptions of the correct reward for proper knightly conduct and even "disworship" as a synonym

for opprobrium or abuse. All *O.E.D.* usage examples of "disworship" occur ca. 1400–1600.

21. Christopher Cannon, "The Myth of Origin and the Making of Chaucer's English," *Speculum* 71.3 (July 1996): 646–675.

22. Alexandra Walsham, "Miracles and the Counter-Reformation Mission to England," *Historical Journal* 46.4 (2003): 779–815, 813.

23. Edwin Benjamin, "Fame, Poetry, and the Order of History in the Literature of the English Renaissance," *Studies in the Renaissance* 6 (1959): 64–84, 66.

24. Seth Lerer, *Chaucer and His Readers: Imagining the Author in Late-Medieval England* (Princeton, NJ: Princeton University Press, 1993), 153–163.

25. Pearsall, Derek. "Chaucer's Tomb: The Politics of Reburial." *Medium Aevum* 64 (1995): 51–73.

26. John Watkins, "Wrastling for This World": Wyatt and the Tudor Canonization of Chaucer," in *Refiguring Chaucer in the Renaissance*, ed. Theresa M. Krier (Gainesville, FL: University Press of Florida, 1998), 23–25.

27. Alexandra Gillespie, *Print Culture and the Medieval Author: Chaucer, Lydgate, and Their Books, 1473–1557* (Oxford: Oxford University Press, 2006); Greg Walker, *Writing under Tyranny: English Literature and the Henrican Reformation* (Oxford: Oxford University Press, 2005), 56 ff.

28. This was only the beginning of a process of secular cultural "worship" of Chaucer and other famous English poets. See Connell, "Death and the Author," esp. 557–558, for the complete eighteenth-century flowering of this patriotic, literary, and funerary association.

29. Gillespie, *Print Culture*, 229–230, observes that no such monument is certainly known to exist for John Lydgate, although a rubbing of words from his tombstone was reported in 1777, and the words may have been copied on the flyleaf of an unrelated manuscript in a fifteenth-century hand. The monk of Bury St. Edmunds may have attracted no such cult-like attention in Protestant England because he was too much like the saints of old.

30. Connell, "Death and the Author," 559–633, traces the eighteenth-century flowering of Westminster tomb tourism. This article contributes to his study by examining relations between early-modern print editions and their readers as they create the need for later guide books such as Jodocrus Crull, *The Antiquities of St. Peters, or the Abbey Church of Westminster: Containing all*

the Inscriptions, Epitaphs, &c. upon the Tombs and Grave-Stones... (London: by J. N. for John Morphew, 1711); and David Henry, *An Historical Account of the Curiosities. Of London and Westminster* (London: J. Newbery, 1753 [1754]), STC N25777.

31. As Dane and Gillespie, "Back at Chaucer's Tomb," point out, actual visits to the tomb would not have been necessary for the verses' reproduction. Discovery of the tomb verses printed in post-1598 editions would also have encouraged readers to remedy their omission in older editions by adding them. Thus reader responses to the tomb inscriptions may have influenced and been influenced by the printers' decisions in ways that may add to recent studies of early-modern printing practices by Edwards and Driver. Readers' influence on printers' book-design decisions might offer a new, more "collaborative" way to see the earlier breakthroughs in English publishing by Caxton, especially his prologues and epilogues describing interactions with his customers. This approach may also add to Edwards's study of editions of Stephen Hawes's poems, in which de Worde used custom woodcuts to identify and sell a contemporary poet's work, and Driver's work on de Worde's reinvention of the title page and John Speed's portrait of Chaucer; see Edwards, "Poet and Printer," 82–88; and Driver, "Ideas of Order," 87–146; Driver, *The Image in Print*; and Driver, "Mapping Chaucer: John Speed and the Later Portraits," 228–249.

32. Gillespie, *Print Culture*, 186–228.

33. Thomas A. Prendergast, *Chaucer's Dead Body: From Corpse to Corpus* (New York: Routledge, 2004), 53–54.

34. Dane and Gillespie, "Back at Chaucer's Tomb," 95.

35. As Derek Pearsall notes, the Chaucerian content of Speght's edition is "firmly within [the Thynne-Stow] tradition of reprint-with-augmentation," but its main contribution to the emerging idea of Chaucer's "Collected Works" is "the beginnings of an editorial apparatus"; Derek Pearsall, "Thomas Speght (ca. 1550–?)," in *Editing Chaucer: The Great Tradition*, ed. Paul G. Ruggiers (Norman, OK: Pilgrim, 1984), 71–92, 71. Thus the tomb verses and the portrait on Thomas Chaucer's tomb (see text accompanying note 33) are part of what Speght thought to be his most important addition to the received text.

36. Driver, "Mapping Chaucer," 228–249.

37. Pauline Aiken, "Vincent of Beauvais and Chaucer's Knowledge of Alchemy," *Studies in Philology* 41.3 (1944): 371–389, 387; Robert M. Schuler, "The Renaissance Chaucer as Alchemist," *Viator* 15 (1984): 305–333, 316–317.

38. Elias Ashmole, *Theatrum chemicum Britannicum: Containing Severall Poeticall Pieces of our Famous English Philosophers, Who Have Written the Hermetique Mysteries in Their Owne Ancient Languge* (London: J. Grismond for Nath. Brooke, 1652; rpt. Kila, MT: Kessinger, 1991), 467. An anonymous reviewer questioned an earlier draft's characterization of Ashmole's logic as "tortured" when he uses Chaucer's satire of alchemical frauds as evidence that Chaucer was an alchemist, "given that Chaucer claims arcane alchemical knowledge at the end of the CYT and does not seem to be joking." According to Larry D. Benson's notes in the *Riverside Chaucer*, the preponderance of critical opinion in the late twentieth century seems to assume that Chaucer thought, as some modern readers do, that alchemy was "absurd" or at least that he was "skeptical," "unconsciously prophetic in warning against an incipient dehumanizing technology," or "convinced of the evil of science." *The Riverside Chaucer*, ed. Larry Benson (Boston: Houghton Mifflin, 1987), n. 948. As I reread those confident assertions, I am stricken with the suspicion that we have all fallen victim to our modern version of treating the adaptable Chaucer as "one of us." This time, he seems a twentieth-century scientist rather than a heretical practicing alchemist. Because we cannot know Chaucer's own beliefs but only that Ashmole treated him as a fellow practitioner, I would follow Benson to "the calmer views of [Derek] Brewer ... that Chaucer does not take an extreme position but has objections on the practical and religious grounds that the ignorant non-scientist should leave the science alone." *The Riverside Chaucer*, ed. Larry Benson (Boston: Houghton Mifflin, 1987), n. 948.

39. Ashmole, *Theatrum chemicum Britannicum*, 471.

40. Ibid., 472.

41. Prendergast, *Chaucer's Dead Body*, 1.

42. Bonser, "Cult of Relics," 236.

43. John Urry, in a footnote discussing the verses in his prefatory "Life of Geoffrey Chaucer," invents a completely unfounded explanation: "These Verses were probably written upon a Ledge of Brass, which may have been

fixed upon the Marble Table, but is now taken away, and not upon the Stone itself, there being no footsteps of any writing upon the edge of it"; sig. [e2], n. t.

44. Walsham, "Miracles and the Counter-Reformation," 798, points out that "secondary relics" might include objects such as a handkerchief used to retrieve parts of a martyr's body from the ashes."

45. Andre Grabar, *Martyrium*, 3 vols. (Paris: Collège de France, 1944–1946), 343 ff.; Ernst Kitzinger, "The Cult of Images in the Age before Iconoclasm," *Dunbarton Oaks Papers* 8 (1954): 83–150, 115–119; John Crook, *The Architectural Setting of the Cult of the Saints in the Early Christian West* (Oxford: Oxford University Press, 2000), 6–39 and 210–241, esp. 238–239.

46. As a resident of the Washington, D.C., region, I have often visited the memorial and witnessed countless examples of this behavior. To see the results of visitors' highly directed attention to specific parts of this sculpture, visit www.flickr.com and enter the search terms "FDR" and "Fala." For a single example, see http://www.flickr.com/photos/clockwerks/1392865964/.

47. Allen Walker Read, "The Disinterment of Milton's Remains," PMLA 45.4 (1930): 1050–1068; Ronald Finucane, *Miracles and Pilgrims: Popular Beliefs in Medieval England* (New York: St. Martin's Press, 1995), 29–30.

48. Constance Classen, "Museum Manners: The Sensory Life of the Early Museum," *Journal of Social History* 40.4 (2007): 895–914, 889.

49. Ibid., 902. Sculpture's aesthetic qualities, in particular, were thought by many seventeenth- and eighteenth-century visitors to be best understood by touch; ibid., 901–903. Classen draws our attention to the quasi-religious motivation for visitors' desire to touch artifacts with religious or nationalistic associations and notes that the shift to hands-off curation in England seems not to have taken place until the nineteenth century; ibid., 908.

50. Finucane, *Miracles and Pilgrims*, 26.

51. Walsham, "Miracles and the Counter-Reformation," 786.

52. Dane notes that the verses "about the ledge" were never mentioned in the earliest surviving versions of the transcription, and "later versions are dependent on Camden or the 1602 Speght," leading him to suspect that they were already on a previous, pre-Reformation monument whose stone was used to frame Chaucer's tomb; Joseph Dane, "Who Is Buried in Chaucer's Tomb? Prolegomena," *Huntington Library Quarterly* 57 (1994): 98–123,

114. This might help explain the rapidity of their erosion, but any obliteration of stone carving on a marble surface in a cathedral's protected interior requires some accelerant.

53. John Ashurst and Francis G. Dimes, *Conservation of Building and Decorative Stone* (London: Elsevier-Butterworth-Heinemann, 1990; rpt. 2004), 114. For the shells' resemblance to the modern "periwinkle," Petworth marble and the related Purbeck stone are sometimes colloquially called "winklestone."

54. Roger Birch, *Sussex Stones: The Story of Horsham Stone and Sussex Marble* (np: Roger Birch, 2006), 45 and 44. Floor slabs and exterior monuments were more likely to be constructed from Purbeck marble, also mined in Sussex from earlier Jurassic deposits which are more resistant to acidified liquids. See the Reverend F. H. Arnold, *Petworth: A Sketch of Its History and Antiquities, with Notices of Archaeological Interest in Its Vicinity* (Petworth, UK: A. J. Bryant, 1864), 80.

55. Mark J. Patterson, Stuart D. R. Galloway, and Myra A. Nimmo, "Variations in Regional Sweat Composition in Normal Human Males," *Experimental Physiology: Translation and Integration* 85:6 (November 2000), 871.

56. Philip A. Baedecker and Michael Reddy, *The Erosion of Carbonate Stone: Laboratory and Field Investigation,. USGS: Science for a Changing World*, April 15, 2003, http://wwwbrr.cr.usgs.gov/projects/GWC_Crystal/erosion/index.html (March 24, 2010).

57. Edmund Spenser, *Spenser: The Faerie Queene*, ed. A. C. Hamilton (New York: Longman, 1980), 440, n. Stanza 33 and Stanza 33, ll. 6-9.

58. Nineteenth-century descriptions suggest that all of the letters were almost completely obliterated before the 1850 campaign to restore the tomb. Prendergast, *Chaucer's Dead Body*, 87–96. In 1808, a letter to *The Gentleman's Magazine* by "G.W.L." laments that the tomb is in a "mutilated state" and declares that "the inscription is almost defaced, and the Monument has suffered much through neglect"; "G.W.L." [Letter to "Mr. Urban"], *The Gentleman's Magazine*, November 1808, 974–975. "G.W.L." may be self-consciously echoing the same provocative verb, "defaced," Spenser chose to conflate the wearing out of "workes" of "heavenly wits" with Time's destruction of a "famous moniment." More suggestive still is Edward Wedlake Brayley's 1818 judgment that of the plane-relief carvings on the monument,

"the arms of Chaucer are along distinguishable, through the partial decomposition and crumbling state of the marble: *the same arms may be traced* in an oblong compartment at the back of the recess, where also, are some remains of the [Brigham epitaph] inscription, now almost obliterated from similar circumstances"; Edward Wedlake Brayley, *The History and Antiquities of the Abbey Church of St. Peter, Westminster, including Notices and Biographical Memoirs of the Abbots and Deans of that Foundation*, vol. 2 (London: J. P. Neale, 1818), 2:265; emphasis added. Brayley appears to describe his own continuation of the erosion process when, frustrated by others' damage to the inscriptions, he hand-traces the remaining fragments of text and armorial bearings. Of the Chaucer portrait, which Brayley says was "similar to that engraved in [Chaucer's] printed Works," presumably referring to Urry's title page, "not a vestige is left"; ibid., 2:265.

59. Brayley, *History and Antiquities*. The replica of the original was paid for by subscriptions and reproduced what is alleged to be Spenser's original epitaph:

> HEARE LYES (EXPECTING THE SECOND COMMINGE OF OUR SAVIOVR CHRIST JESUS) THE BODY OF EDMOND SPENCER THE PRINCE OF POETS IN HIS TYME WHOSE DIVINE SPIRRIT NEEDS NOE OTHIR WITNESSE THEN THE WORKS WHICH HE LEFT BEHINDE HIM. HE WAS BORNE IN LONDON IN THE YEARE 1553 AND DIED IN THE YEARE 1598. Restored by private subscription 1778.

After Spenser's burial in Westminster Abbey in 1599 at the expense of the Earl of Essex, in 1620 Ann Clifford, countess of Dorset, Pembroke, and Montgomery, paid to erect the monument near Chaucer's, engraved with the claim that "THE WORKS WHICH HE LEFT BEHINDE HIM" are the "WITNESSE" of the poet's "SPIRRIT."

60. One problem with this hypothesis arises from the fact that the tradition of sumptuous folio editions of Spenser's work never quite became established after the 1679 edition by Henry Hills for Jonathan Edwin. The multivolume octavo and other small-format editions by Jacob Tonson took the place of

folio editions in 1715, 1742, 1750 and were followed by reprints by John Hughes in 1758 and J. Bell in 1777–1778, the year of the new tomb. Their frontispieces usually contain engravings of a "laureate" Spenser surrounded by female figures representing Faith, Justice, etc., rather than images of his tomb, but these circumstances are not those which appear to have motivated the annotators of Renaissance Chaucer folio editions. If I am correct that readers' motives for copying the tomb verses into their collected editions depended on the association of the single folio volume with the tomb, these multi-volume editions would offer less attractive sites upon which to copy the verses. Nevertheless, the inscriptions were described as having been obliterated by 1798, only a century after the folio collected works edition was published and 158 years after the inscriptions were carved, so once again, some accelerant seems to be required to explain the indoor weathering of the stone. See Francis R. Johnson, *A Critical Bibliography of the Works of Edmund Spenser Printed before 1700* (Baltimore, MD: Johns Hopkins Press, 1933), 53–56, for a description of the first collected works.

61. Scholars with access to early-modern editions of Chaucer's collected works, especially those published between 1532 and 1598, are encouraged to share their evidence at the ChaucerEdMSS Wiki, "Chaucer Tomb Epitaph MSS in Early Modern Chaucer Editions: A Survey of Surviving Copies," at http://chauceredmss.wikispaces.com/. Summaries of evidence indicating either the absence or the presence of the tomb inscriptions will help us better determine how common or rare the seven known inscriptions are and what provenance evidence is available for each of those that survive.

62. In both transcriptions, my angle brackets expand scribal ligatures. The red ink remains more legible than the rest, which has faded to light brown. This annotation corresponds roughly with the text quoted by Dane and Gillespie, but skips from the quatrain about Chaucer to the line commemorating Brigham. The irregularly rubricated capitals and haphazard punctuation suggest the writer was not Latin literate but was familiar in passing with the general appearance of rubricated manuscripts.

63. The John Work Garrett copy inscription's curly brackets enclose both sides of the epitaph, itself, and a single curly bracket encloses the right side of Brigham's line. I have been unable to reproduce the reversed "N" of Brigham's line in digital text. The annotation's relative closeness to the Dane-

Huntington Wilbraham text, its careful attention to exactly where verses were located, its cancelled line, and other signs of hasty composition, suggest this also may have been copied directly from the tomb at Westminster.

WORKS CITED

Aiken, Pauline. "Vincent of Beauvais and Chaucer's Knowledge of Alchemy." *Studies in Philology* 41.3 (1944): 371–389.

Arnold, Reverend F. H. *Petworth: A Sketch of Its History and Antiquities, with Notices of Archaeological Interest in Its Vicinity.* Petworth, UK: A. J. Bryant, 1864.

Ashmole, Elias. *Theatrum chemicum Britannicum: Containing Severall Poeticall Pieces of our Famous English Philosophers, Who Have Written the Hermetique Mysteries in Their Owne Ancient Languge.* London: J. Grismond for Nath. Brooke, 1652. Rpt. Kila, MT: Kessinger, 1991.

Ashurst, John, and Francis G. Dimes. *Conservation of Building and Decorative Stone.* London: Elsevier-Butterworth-Heinemann, 1990. Rpt. 2004.

Baedecker, Philip A., and Michael Reddy. *The Erosion of Carbonate Stone: Laboratory and Field Investigations. USGS: Science for a Changing World.* April 15, 2003. http://wwwbrr.cr.usgs.gov/projects/GWC_Crystal/erosion/index.html (March 24, 2010).

Benjamin, Edwin B. "Fame, Poetry, and the Order of History in the Literature of the English Renaissance." *Studies in the Renaissance* 6 (1959): 64–84.

Birch, Roger. *Sussex Stones: The Story of Horsham Stone and Sussex Marble.* Np: Roger Birch, 2006.

Bonser, Wilfrid. "The Cult of Relics in the Middle Ages." *Folklore* 73.4 (1962): 234–256.

Brayley, Edward Wedlake. *The History and Antiquities of the Abbey Church of St. Peter, Westminster, including Notices and Biographical Memoirs of the Abbots and Deans of that Foundation,* vol. 2. London: J. P. Neale, 1818.

Cannon, Christopher. "The Myth of Origin and the Making of Chaucer's English." *Speculum* 71.3 (1996): 646–675.

Carlson, David R. "Alexander Barclay and Richard Pynson: A Tudor Printer and His Writer." *Anglia* 113 (1995): 283–302.

———. "A Theory of the Early English Printing Firm: Jobbing, Book

Publishing, and the Problem of Productive Capacity in Caxton's Work." In *Caxton's Trace: Studies in the History of English Printing*, ed. William Kuskin. Notre Dame, IN: University of Notre Dame Press, 2006, 35–68.

Chaucer, Geoffrey. *The Riverside Chaucer*. Ed. Larry Benson. Boston: Houghton Mifflin, 1987.

———. *The workes of Geffray Chaucer newly printed, wyth dyuers workes whiche were neuer in print before: as in the table more playnly dothe appere. Cum priuilegio*. London: by [Nicholas Hill for] Rycharde Kele, [1550?] STC 5072 [Folger Shakespeare Library copy]

———. *The workes of Geffrey Chaucer, newlie printed, with diuers addicions, whiche were neuer in print before; with the siege and destruccion of the worthy Citee of Thebes, compiled by Ihon Lidgate, Monk of Berie. As in the table more plainly doeth appere. 1561*. London: John Stow, 1561. STC 5075 [Garrett Library Collection of the Sheridan Libraries, John Work Garrett copy].

———. *The workes of Geffrey Chaucer, newlie printed, with diuers addicions, whiche were neuer in print before; with the siege and destruccion of the worthy citee of Thebes, compiled by Ihon Lidgate, Monk of Berie. As in the table more plainly doeth appere. 1561*. London: John Stow, 1561. STC 5076 [Garrett Library Collection of the Sheridan Libraries, Tudor and Stuart Club of Johns Hopkins University copy].

———. *The WORKS of Geoffrey Chaucer: Compared with the Former Editions, and Many Valuable MSS. Out of which, Three Tales are added which were never before Printed / by John Urry, Student of Christ-Church, Oxon. Deceased; Together with a GLOSSARY By a Student of the same College. To the Whole is prefixed The Author's LIFE, newly written, and a PREFACE, giving an Account of this Edition*. London: Bernard Lintot, 1721.

Classen, Constance. "Museum Manners: The Sensory Life of the Early Museum." *Journal of Social History* 40.4 (2007): 895–914.

Connell, Philip. "Death and the Author: Westminster Abbey and the Meanings of the Literary Monument." *Eighteenth-Century Studies* 38.4 (2005): 557–585.

Crook, John. *The Architectural Setting of the Cult of the Saints in the Early Christian West*. Oxford: Oxford University Press, 2000.

Damon, S. Foster. "Chaucer and Alchemy." *PMLA* 39.4 (1924): 782–788.

Dane, Joseph. "In Search of Stow's Chaucer." In *John Stow (1525-1605) and the Making of the English Past: Studies in Early Modern Culture and the History of the Book*, edited by Ian Gadd and Alexandra Gillespie, 145-155. London: British Library, 2004.

——— "Who Is Buried in Chaucer's Tomb? Prolegomena." *Huntington Library Quarterly* 57 (1994): 98–123.

Dane, Joseph, and Alexandra Gillespie. "Back at Chaucer's Tomb: Inscriptions in Two Early Copies of *Chaucer's Workes.*" *Studies in Bibliography* 52 (1999): 89–96.

Driver, Martha. "Ideas of Order: Wynkyn de Worde and the Title Page." In *Texts and Their Contexts: Papers from the Early Book Society*, ed. Julia Boffey and V. J. Scattergood. Dublin: Four Courts Press, 1997, 87–146.

———. *The Image in Print: Book Illustration in Late Medieval England and Its Sources*. London: British Library, 2004.

———. "Mapping Chaucer: John Speed and the Later Portraits." *Chaucer Review* 36.3 (2002): 228–249.

Duffy, Eamon. *The Stripping of the Altars: Traditional Religion in England, 1400–1580*. New Haven, CT: Yale University Press, 1992.

Edwards, A. S. G. "From Manuscript to Print: Wynkyn de Worde and the Printing of Contemporary Poetry." *Gutenberg-Jahrbuch* (1991): 1430–1438.

———. "Poet and Printer in Sixteenth Century England: Stephen Hawes and Wynkyn de Worde." *Gutenberg-Jahrbuch* (1980): 82–88.

Finucane, Ronald. *Miracles and Pilgrims: Popular Beliefs in Medieval England*. New York: St. Martin's Press, 1995.

Gillespie, Alexandra. *Print Culture and the Medieval Author: Chaucer, Lydgate, and Their Books, 1473–1557*. Oxford: Oxford University Press, 2006.

Grabar, Andre. *Martyrium*. 3 vols. Paris: Collège de France, 1944–1946.

"G.W.L." [Letter to "Mr. Urban"]. *The Gentleman's Magazine*. November 1808, 974–975.

Hackel, Heidi Brayman. *Reading Material in Early Modern England: Print, Gender, and Literacy*. Cambridge, UK: Cambridge University Press, 2005.

Hudson, Anne. "John Stow (1525?-1605)" In *Editing Chaucer: The Great Tradition*, ed. Paul G. Ruggiers. Norman, OK: Pilgrim, 1984, 53–70.

Johnson, Francis R. *A Critical Bibliography of the Works of Edmund Spenser Printed before 1700*. Baltimore, MD: Johns Hopkins Press, 1933.

Judson, Alexander C. *The Life of Edmund Spenser*. Baltimore, MD: Johns Hopkins University Press, 1945.

Kitzinger, Ernst. "The Cult of Images in the Age before Iconoclasm." *Dunbarton Oaks Papers* 8 (1954): 83–150.

Krier, Theresa M., ed. *Refiguring Chaucer in the Renaissance*. Gainesville, FL: University Press of Florida, 1998.

Lerer, Seth. *Chaucer and His Readers: Imagining the Author in Late-Medieval England*. Princeton, NJ: Princeton University Press, 1993.

Orme, Nicholas. "Church and Chapel in Medieval England." *Transactions of the Royal Historical Society*. 6th ser., 6 (1996): 75–102.

Patterson, Mark J., Stuart D. R. Galloway, and Myra A. Nimmo. "Variations in Regional Sweat Composition in Normal Human Males." *Experimental Physiology: Translation and Integration* 85.6 (2000): 869–875. http://www.ncbi.nlm.nih.gov/pubmed

Pearsall, Derek. "Chaucer's Tomb: The Politics of Reburial." *Medium Aevum* 64 (1995): 51–73.

———. "Thomas Speght (ca. 1550–?)." In *Editing Chaucer: The Great Tradition*, ed. Paul G. Ruggiers. Norman, OK: Pilgrim, 1984, 71–92.

Prendergast, Thomas A. *Chaucer's Dead Body: From Corpse to Corpus*. New York: Routledge, 2004.

Read, Allen Walker. "The Disinterment of Milton's Remains." *PMLA* 45.4 (1930): 1050–1068.

Saul, Nigel. *English Church Monuments in the Middle Ages: History and Representation*. Oxford: Oxford University Press, 2009.

Schuler, Robert M. "The Renaissance Chaucer as Alchemist." *Viator* 15 (1984): 305–333.

Spenser, Edmund. *The Works of that Famous English Poet, Mr. Edmund Spenser*. London: by Henry Hills for Jonathan Edwin, 1679.

———. *Spenser: The Faerie Queene*. Edited by A. C. Hamilton. New York: Longman, 1980.

———. *Works: A Variorum Edition*. Edited by Edwin Greenlaw, Charles Grosvenor Osgood, and Frederick Morgan Padelford. Baltimore, MD: Johns Hopkins University Press, 1932–1949.

Walker, Greg. *Writing under Tyranny: English Literature and the Henrican Reformation.* Oxford: Oxford University Press, 2005.

Walsham, Alexandra. "Miracles and the Counter-Reformation Mission to England." *Historical Journal* 46.4 (2003): 779–815.

Watkins, John. "Wrastling for This World": Wyatt and the Tudor Canonization of Chaucer." In *Refiguring Chaucer in the Renaissance*, ed. Theresa Krier. Gainesville, FL: University Press of Florida, 1998, 21–39.

Wiggins, Alison. "What Did Renaissance Readers Write in Their Printed Copies of Chaucer?" *The Library* 9.1 (2008): 3–36.

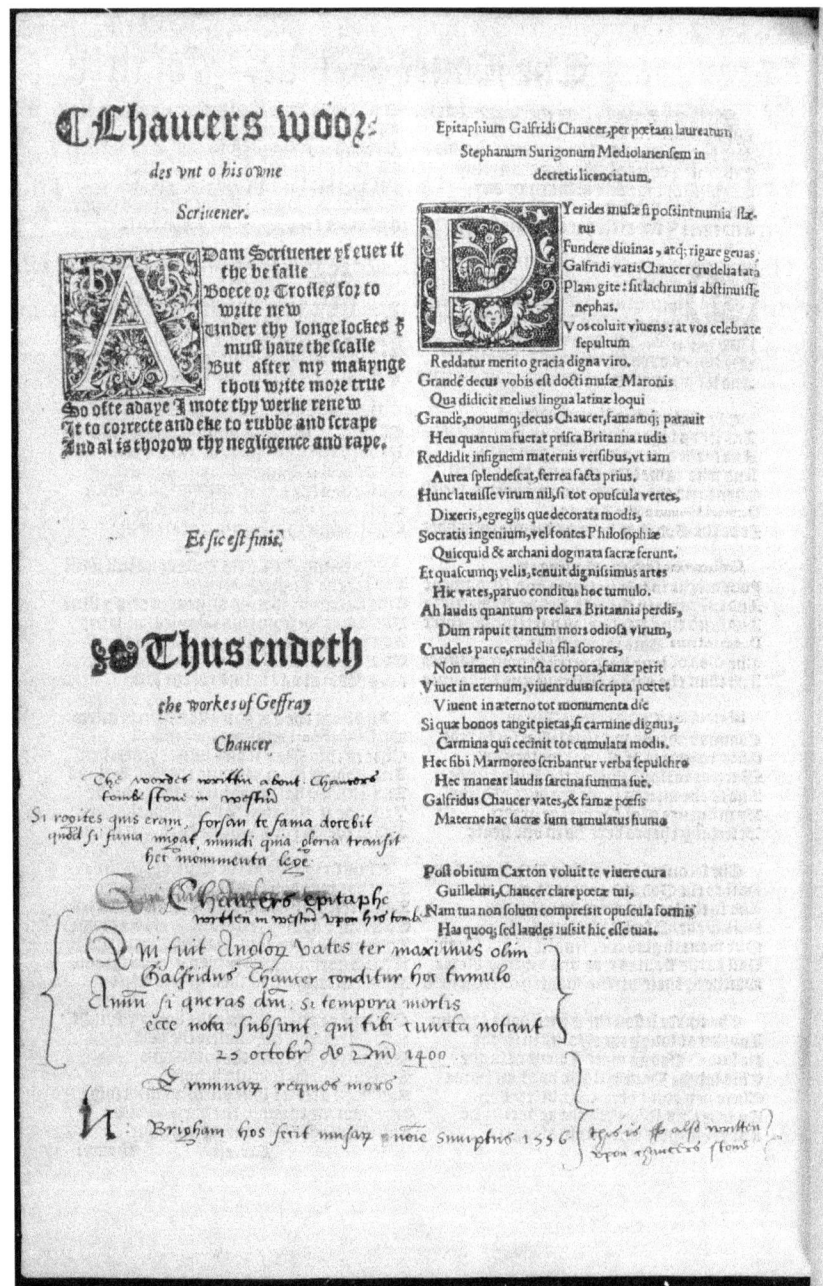

Figure 1. Folio 355v of *The woorkes of Geoffrey Chaucer* (STC 5076), Sheridan Library shelf mark PO 1850 1561a QUARTO.

Figure 2. Folio 378v of *The workes of Geoffrey Chaucer* (STC 5075), Sheridan Library shelf mark PO 1850 1561 QUARTO.

Figure 3. Close-up of folio 378v of *The workes of Geoffrey Chaucer* (STC 5075), Sheridan Library shelf mark PO 1850 1561 QUARTO.

Nota Bene: Brief Notes on Manuscripts and Early Printed Books

Highlighting Little-known or Recently Uncovered Items or Related Issues

Pre-Fifteenth-Century Scribes Copying Middle English in More than One Manuscript

RALPH HANNA

One of the most impressive (and potentially significant) current manuscript research projects is that devoted to medieval scribes. This is housed at the University of York and headed by Linne R. Mooney and Simon Horobin.[1] In the main dedicated to fifteenth-century copying, it seeks to isolate the work of scribes clearly professional because attested in multiple manuscripts. The researchers are particularly interested, as a variety of references below will indicate, in identifying hands responsible for the promulgation of what would become national Scripture, the writings of Chaucer and company. The Scribes Project is also engaged in undertaking further identifications of these copying individuals and their careers.

This note offers a provisional prequel to Mooney and Horobin's impressive efforts. I present an initial listing that will point to what precedes their project, pre-1400 scribes engaged in copying more than one book. However, my goals are limited: I seek to identify only those persons responsible for at least one English book, although they may be recorded elsewhere copying other languages.

This limitation is, of course, necessary, given the nature of English scribal culture for the greater part of the Middle Ages, the long stretch from circa 700 to the period I survey. Mooney and Horobin survey the first period in which English materials held a place remotely comparable to those in Latin and French (which still appear vastly more frequently in fifteenth-century books than does English). But the scribes I survey below represent a considerably broader range of engagements, even in those books they copy containing English. Here numbers 1, 7-10, and 12 in my listing would testify to the polylingual mix typical of medieval England. Including scribes not engaged with English, given the relative scarcity of such materials before 1400, would swell the number of individuals to be listed a very great deal.

This would particularly be the case for the period between 700 and 1200. During this era, books and bookmaking may be strongly, if not nearly exclusively, associated with monastic environments. In this situation, individuals might spend a generation copying volumes for their house and its library, and such repeated hands, including ones working before the Conquest (and a few copying Old English), have long been a center of studies. Among the scribes I list here, numbers 7 to 10 and 19 exemplify such book-production by members of regular orders. (Moreover, numbers 11, 13, 17, and 18 might be construed generically similar, since they may well have been cathedral canons.) Similarly, in the years after 1200, the growth of Oxbridge threw together men with a need for books and a capacity for copying them. Like the monastic situation, most such copying will not include English, but it would again extend any list of professional scribes a great deal.[2] Ultimately, a database of medieval English scribes will need to expand well beyond even the already extensive archive envisioned by Mooney and Horobin.

Yet even this skeletal listing of thirteenth- and fourteenth-century scribes does present at least one feature of interest. The Mooney-Horobin project is inspired by Ian Doyle and Malcolm Parkes's important showing of the interconnection of hands at work on important Chaucer and Gower manuscripts just after 1400.[3] Doyle and Parkes focus on one important conjunction, the development, in the hands of a very few individuals, of a recognizable "English canon," a set of masterworks that now stand at the head of modern conceptions of English literature. But repetitions of major texts, or those deemed particularly important, among professionals scarcely began in 1400, and it is informative to see that manuscripts communicating Chaucer and Gower. were engaged in replacing an earlier library of "literarily worthwhile" objects, themselves subject to repeated copying by the scribes I have listed below.

Here one can point to a range of texts. Four of the scribes in my list (numbers 3, 10, 16, and 19) engaged with *Ancrene Riwle*. This work seems always to have been perceived as a central spiritual classic (scribe 3's version is a particularly tendentious effort at copying the text for the laity, rendering it more explicitly for general use rather than simply that of enclosed women). As the selections published as *A Tretyse of Loue* should remind us, the *Riwle* was still considered useful reading in the age of printing. Perhaps a more surprising text to find the object of repeated copying, given its failure to attract modern attention, is *The South English Legendary* (among the work of numbers 2, 3, and 16). But until well into the fifteenth century, this provided the authoritative entré into holy lives (and perhaps especially those of English holy persons).

The preceding examples are, of course, thirteenth-century texts (s. xiii in. and xiii ex., respectively). With them might be joined the non-English, but extraordinarily influential—one suspects that it lurks in the background of a prominent Northern tradition of instructional verse texts in English— *Manuel des Péchés* of William of Waddington (selections copied by scribes numbers 9 and 12). But notions of canon did not remain static through the fourteenth century, and some of the later scribes in the list point toward more recent texts deemed worthy of repeated copying. Thus, Richard Rolle, who remained a mainstay of religious culture through the later Middle Ages (but was printed only exiguously), also appears prominently here (numbers 9, 16, and 17). Three of the scribes (numbers 4, 14, and 16), all at the very end of the period, copied William Langland's *Piers Plowman*, interestingly, each of them a different version. Langland thus would stand as a forerunner for (and probably a figure ousted from a central cultural position by) the circulation of that imaginative writing in English originally sketched out by Doyle and Parkes.

Finally, a number of regional texts have some prominence in the record I here assemble. Specifically London materials occur in the oeuvre of scribes numbers 1, 3, 5, 6, and 16. At the very end of the period I survey, four of the scribes, all of them provincial (numbers 15-18; the text generally bypassed London), testify to the great grey eminence of fifteenth-century studies, *The Prick of Conscience*. From modern efforts to ignore it, one would scarcely guess that this text, one of those imitators of Waddington to which I have alluded above (and again inspired by Anglo-Norman materials), survives in more than half again as many copies as *The Canterbury Tales*. But, like Rolle's "Form of Living" and Latin *Emendatio vitae*, the text may be more integral to medieval English intellectual and spiritual life than any more literary outpouring.

My list of scribes, to which I would be grateful for additions since I am sure I have overlooked a good deal, follows. Bold numbers following simple references to manuscripts are cross-references to the scribe entries in the list wherein the manuscript is cited; the entries themselves appear in alphabetical order connected with the earliest or most important pre-1400 manuscript written by each scribe. This list is limited in one respect: I adhere to the shapes of original manuscripts, not modern library bindings. As a consequence, in conceiving a scribe as appearing in more than one book, I have ignored dispersed fragments of the same original manuscript, although I note these as appropriate.

Aberystwyth, National Library of Wales, MS Peniarth 383D **4**

1 Cambridge, Cambridge University Library, MS Gg.iv.32, fols. 2-5, 21-47, 51-76, 81-104: "Andrew Horn's scribe," a London professional and legal writer, 1310s and 1320s.

The book mainly presents Latin texts of use to a parish priest, with brief English and Anglo-Norman verse and prose instructional materials at fols. 21-24^v.

The scribe also copied London, Corporation of London Records Office, MS Cust. 6, fols. ii, 1-84, 86-102, 173-86.[4]

Cambridge, Cambridge University Library, MS Ii.i.15 **8**

2 Cambridge, Corpus Christi College, MS 145: a west Berkshire/north Gloucestershire professional scribe, s. xiv in. (probably 1310s).

A copy of *The South English Legendary*.[5]

The scribe also copied Leicester, Wyggeston Hospital, MS 18 D 59, the wrapper (a deposit at the Archives Department, Leicester City Museum; a fragment from *The South English Legendary*).[6]

London, British Library, MS Egerton 2891 (*The South English Legendary*)

Nottingham, Nottingham University Library, MS Mi WLC/LM/38, another fragmentary leaf from *The South English Legendary*.[7]

3 Cambridge, Magdalene College, MS Pepys 2498: a London professional, s. xiv med./xiv³/⁴.

A large anthology of early London prose translations, with a heavily redacted version of *Ancrene Riwle*.[8]

The scribe also copied London, British Library, MS Harley 874 (the prose Apocalypse, an early London prose translation also in the preceding; a fragment of a *South English Legendary* text).[9]

Oxford, Bodleian Library, MS Laud misc. 622 (*South English Legendary* selections, *Titus and Vespasian*, *Alisaunder*).[10]

Cambridge, Trinity College, MS B.1.45 **10**

4 Cambridge, Trinity College, MS B.15.17: "Early London Scribe B," s. xiv/xv. *Piers Plowman* B and Rolle's "Form of Living."[11]

Cambridge, Trinity College, MS R.3.8 **17**

5 Dublin, Trinity College, MS 69, fols. 1-64, 73-83: a South Coast professional scribe, s. xiv ex. (the manuscript includes an ownership inscription perhaps associable with Londoners who died shortly after 1400).

Mostly given over to early London prose translations (the prose Psalter and Apocalypse), and shorter London prose of s. xiv ex. (some items shared with Oxford, University College, MS 97). A second scribe, in similar language, succeeds on fol. 83ᵛ and copies *The Prick of Conscience*, southern recension.

The scribe also copied Princeton, NJ, Scheide Library, MS M.143 (the prose Psalter), a reduced facsimile at Sotheby's, 21 November 1978, lot 547 (50-52).

Durham, Durham Cathedral Muniments **9**

Durham, Durham University Library, MS Mickleton and Spearman 27 **17**

6 Edinburgh, National Library of Scotland, MS Advocates 19.2.1: a London professional, c. 1330

A large anthology, especially rich in romances (including, among texts appearing elsewhere here, *Alisaunder* and the "Short Metrical Chronicle").[12]

Hereford, Hereford Cathedral, MS O.i.iv **7**

Leicester, Wyggeston Hospital, MS 18 D 59 **2**

London, British Library, MS Additional 22283 **16**

London, British Library, MS Additional 24059 **9**

London, British Library, MS Additional 35287 **4**

7 London, British Library, MS Additional 46919, about one-quarter of the ensemble, along with notes and marginalia passim: William Herebert OFM, prior of the Hereford convent, fl. s. xiv in.

A trilingual anthology, especially rich in works of Nicole Bozon, but also Walter of Bibbesworth's grammar and Malachi of Ireland's "De venenis." Composed of about a dozen booklets (and missing others once present, one with "The Proverbs of Hending" and other English verse). Most of these bear Herebert's notes, but the book also includes, in his hand, his translations of Latin hymns into English verse, some recipes, and scattered English phrases in his sermons.[13] Herebert also copied notes, marginalia, and annotations in Hereford, Hereford Cathedral, MS O.i.iv (Bernard of Clairvaux).

London, British Library, MS Cotton Nero A.ix + MS Egerton 3133 (materials relating to Franciscan history)

London, British Library, MS Royal 7 A.iv (Hildebert of Lavardin, letters)

London, British Library, MSS 7 F.vii + viii (Roger Bacon, *Opus maius*)

Oxford, Bodleian Library, MS Rawlinson C.308 (Bede, *De ratione temporum*)

8 London, British Library, MS Arundel 57, fols. 13-96, with a table in the lower margin, fols. 2-4: Dan Michel of Northgate, monk of St Augustine's Abbey, Canterbury, fl. c. 1300-40.

Michel's *Ayenbite of Inwyt* and shorter texts.[14]

Michel also copied Cambridge, Cambridge University Library, MS Ii.i.15 (Latin science), flyleaves, notes, lombards, and supplied headings in rubric and crayon

London, British Library, MS Cotton Vespasian A.ii, fols. 2-10 (planetary tables, ascribed to Roger Bacon; originally the head of the next book but two)

London, British Library, MS Sloane 1754, fols. 1^v-47, 205-37, and perhaps 174^v-204 (Latin science, a few scattered English words), as well as a variety of notes and marginalia and some supplied headings

Oxford, Bodleian Library, MS Bodley 464, fols. 58-206 (and notes elsewhere) (Latin science, probably copied shortly after 1300, not 1318).[15]

Oxford, Corpus Christi College, MS 221, flyleaves and fols. 2-66 (Latin moralized science).[16]

9 London, British Library, MS Arundel 507, fols. 16-81: Richard of Sedgebrook, monk of Durham (d. 1396 or 1397).

A trilingual commonplace book, mainly excerpts from Rolle and Rolleana, but also from Waddington's *Manuel*, an Anglo-Norman history of the cross, and excerpted Richard of St Victor, *Benjamin minor*.[17]

Sedgebrook also copied Durham, Durham Cathedral, extensive entries in various priory accounts, and an entry for his family members in the *Liber Vitae*

London, British Library, MS Additional 24059, fols. 1-14, 15^v, 20-22^v, 61-62^v (Latin annals added to Durham historical materials)

London, College of Arms, MS Arundel 25, fols. 4^v-31^v (Latin lives of Cuthbert and Becket)

Although these last two books are datable (post-1381 and post-1384, respectively), neither has appeared in catalogues of such volumes.

10 London, British Library, MS Cotton Cleopatra C.vi, fol. 199 and numerous additions passim: an Augustinian canon (not necessarily, given that his language reflects the King's Lynn area, at Canonsleigh, Devon), s. xiii ex.

The scribe corrected, and added a few texts (lyric snatches, a sermon) around, a text of *Ancrene Riwle*.[18]

The scribe also copied Cambridge, Trinity College, MS B.1.45, fols. 24^{rv}, 41^v-42 (much the same texts as added in the previous, with an additional sermon), facsimile Dobson between 110 and 111.

11 London, British Library, MS Cotton Galba E.ix, fols. 4-48: a North Yorkshire scribe, s. xiv ex.

"Scribe 1," responsible for *Ywain and Gawain* and *The Seven Sages*.[19]

The scribe also copied London, British Library, MS Cotton Tiberius E.vii, fols. 1-81 (*Speculum Vitae*), "scribe 1" of that manuscript.

London, British Library, MS Cotton Nero A.ix **7**

London, British Library, MS Cotton Nero A.xiv **19**

London, British Library, MS Cotton Tiberius E.vii **11**

London, British Library, MS Cotton Vespasian A.ii **8**

London, British Library, MS Egerton 2891 **2**

London, British Library, MS Egerton 3133 **7**

London, British Library, MS Harley 273 **12**

London, British Library, MS Harley 874 **3**

London, British Library, MS Harley 1205 **17**

12 London, British Library, MS Harley 2253, fols. 49-140: legal/professional scribe, Ludlow, c. 1314-49.

A trilingual anthology (English lyrics and political/historical poems, *King Horn*, "The Proverbs of Hending"), available in full facsimile, N. R. Ker, ed., *Facsimile of British Museum MS. Harley 2253*, EETS, o.s. 255 (London, 1965).[20]

The scribe also copied London, British Library, MS Harley 273, fols. 181ᵛ-97 (portions of Waddington's *Manuel* and *Le purgatoire de S. Patrice*)

London, British Library, MS Royal 12 C.xii, passim (trilingual, including the English "Short Metrical Chronicle").[21]

Shrewsbury, Shropshire Records and Research Centre, about forty legal documents (a few elsewhere)

13 London, British Library, MS Harley 4196, fols. 133-64: a North Yorkshire scribe, s. xiv ex.

"Scribe 3," responsible for the "sanctorale" of the "expanded" *Northern Homily Cycle.*

The scribe also copied London, British Library, MS Cotton Galba E.ix (number **11** above), fols. 50-75 (poems of Laurence Minot, verse "Gospel of Nicodemus," "The Book of Shrift" [an excerpt from *Cursor Mundi*]), "scribe 3" of that manuscript.

London, British Library, MSS Royal 7 A.iv, 7 F.vii + viii **7**

London, British Library, MS Royal 12 C.xii **12**

London, British Library, MS Sloane 1754 **8**

London, College of Arms, MS Arundel 25 **9**

London, Corporation of London Records Office, MS Cust. 6 **1**

14 London, University of London Library, MS S.L.V.88: "Early London Scribe D," s. xiv/xv.
Piers Plowman C; see number **4** above.[22]

Manchester, John Rylands University Library, MS Eng. 50 **17**

New Haven CT, Yale University Library, MS Osborn fa.45 **4**

Nottingham University Library, MS Mi WLC/LM/38 **2**

Oxford, Bodleian Library, MS Bodley 464 **8**

15 Oxford, Bodleian Library, MS Eng. poet. a.1, the contents table, fols. a-h and passim; "John," perhaps, following a note at British Library, MS Additional 22283, fol. 38, John Scriveyn, a Lichfield professional scribe, s. xiv ex. or s. xiv/xv.

There is a full facsimile, A. I. Doyle, ed., *The Vernon Manuscript* (Cambridge, 1987); it also includes many images from London, British Library, MS Additional 22283 (see the next).

The scribe also copied Oxford, Trinity College, MS 16B (*The Prick of Conscience*, Lichfield recension), where he is "scribe 1," alternating with another scribe.

Stratford-upon-Avon, The Shakespeare Birthplace Library, Lord Leigh's deposit, cartulary of Stoneleigh (a Cistercian abbey in Warwickshire)

Wells-next-the-sea (Norfolk), Holkham Hall, the earl of Leicester, MS 668 (*The Prick of Conscience*, Lichfield recension), like Trinity, as "scribe 1," in frequent alternation with another hand.

16 Oxford, Bodleian Library, MS Eng. poet. a.1, the main hand; a north Worcestershire professional scribe, perhaps employed in Lichfield, s. xiv ex.[23]

The scribe also copied London, British Library, MS Additional 22283, fols. 62-115, 135-52, where he is "scribe 2/B." The first stint includes a run of texts shared with Oxford, University College, MS 97; the second, the same Rolle and some of the same Hilton the scribe copied in his other volume.[24]

Oxford, Bodleian Library, MS Eng. poet. e.17 **17**

Oxford, Bodleian Library, MS Laud misc. 622 **3**

17 Oxford, Bodleian Library, MS Rawlinson A.389, fols. 1-20, 25^v-31^v, 85-104^v: a Lichfield professional scribe, s. xiv ex. or s. xiv/xv.

"Scribe 1," who copies Rolle, both Latin and English; and Richard Maidstone's penitential psalms. See Hanna, *English Manuscripts*, 171-74, with facsimile as plate 2.

The scribe also copied Cambridge, Trinity College, MS R.3.8 (*Cursor Mundi*, southern recension)

Durham, Durham University Library, MS Mickleton and Spearman 27 (Latin Statutes)

London, British Library, MS Harley 1205 (*The Prick of Conscience*, Lichfield recension)

Manchester, John Rylands University Library, MS Eng. 50 (*The Prick of Conscience*, Lichfield recension)
  perhaps Oxford, Bodleian Library, MS Eng. poet. e.17, fols. 9-12 (Maidstone, fragments)

Oxford, Bodleian Library, MS Rawlinson C.117 **8**

Oxford, Bodleian Library, MS Rawlinson C.308 **7**

18 Oxford, Bodleian Library, MS Rawlinson poet. 175, fols. 55^v-133: a North Yorkshire scribe, s. xiv ex.
  "Scribe 2," who copied *The Northern Passion*, "The Book of Shrift" (an excerpt from *Cursor Mundi*), *The Seven Sages*, and other texts; his companion, responsible for the opening portions, with *The Prick of Conscience*, appears to be of shared training.
  The scribe also copied London, British Library, MS Harley 4196 (number **13** above), fols. 206-58 (verse "Gospel of Nicodemus," *The Prick of Conscience*), "scribe 5" of that manuscript.
Oxford, Corpus Christi College, MS 221 **8**

Oxford, Trinity College, MS 16B **15**

Princeton NJ, Scheide Library, MS M.143 **5**

Shrewsbury, Shropshire Records and Research Centre **12**

Stratford-upon-Avon, The Shakespeare Birthplace Library, Lord Leigh's deposit, cartulary of Stoneleigh **15**

Wells-next-the-sea (Norfolk), Holkham Hall, the earl of Leicester, MS 668 15

19 Worcester, Worcester Cathedral Library, MS F.174: "the tremulous hand," a local monk, s. xiii$^{2/4}$.
  Ælfric's grammar, verse fragments, including "The debate of the body and the soul."[25]

The scribe also provided Latin and Middle English glosses in more than twenty Worcester Cathedral Priory manuscripts[26].

He may also have copied London, British Library, MS Cotton Nero A.xiv (*Ancrene Riwle*).[27]

Oxford University

NOTES

1. The website for this Arts and Humanities Research Council project, examining all medieval and early modern manuscripts of works by Geoffrey Chaucer, John Gower, William Langland, John Trevisa and Thomas Hoccleve, is available as *Late Medieval English Scribes* at http://www.medievalscribes.com

2. For a few prominent examples of studies outlining production behaviours in a single house (and thus, scribes who copy more than one book), see R. A. B. Mynors, *Durham Cathedral Manuscripts to the End of the Twelfth Century* (Oxford, 1939); Elaine M. Drage, 'Bishop Leofric and Exeter Cathedral Chapter (1052-1070): A Reassessment of the Manuscript Evidence' (unpublished Oxford University D.Phil. thesis, 1978 [Bodleian MS D.Phil. e.2650]); Rodney M. Thomson, *Manuscripts from St Albans Abbey, 1066-1235*, 2 vols (Woodbridge, 1982); Teresa Webber, *Scribes and Scholars at Salisbury Cathedral, c. 1075-c. 1125* (Oxford, 1992); Jennifer H. Sheppard, *The Buildwas Books: Book Production, Acquisition and Use at an English Cistercian Monastery, 1165-c. 1400*, Oxford Bibliographical Society, 3rd ser., vol. 2 (1997). For an introduction to the University book-scene, with passing references to a few scribes writing in more than one book, see M. B. Parkes, 'The Provision of Books,' *The History of the University of Oxford: ii Late Medieval Oxford*, ed. J. J. Catto and Ralph Evans (Oxford: OUP, 1992), 407-83.

3. 'The Production of Copies of the *Canterbury Tales* and the *Confessio Amantis* in the Early Fifteenth Century', in *Medieval Scribes, Manuscripts and Libraries: Essays Presented to N. R. Ker*, ed. M. B. Parkes and Andrew G. Watson (London: Scolar Press, 1978), 163-210.

4. See P. R. Robinson, *Catalogue of Dated and Datable Manuscripts c. 888-*

1600 in London Libraries, 2 vols (London: British Library, 2003), 1:32-33, with facsimile, 2: plate 44 (no. 20).

5. See Charlotte D'Evelyn and Anna J. Mill, eds, *The South English Legendary*, 2 vols, Early English Text Society, o.s. 235 and 236 (London, 1956 [hereafter EETS]), with reduced facsimiles as frontispieces to both volumes.

6. For this and the next two items, see Manfred Görlach, *The Textual Tradition of the South English Legendary*, Leeds Texts and Monographs n.s. 6 (Leeds: University of Leeds, 1974), 113, 92, and 117, respectively.

7. See Thorlac Turville-Petre and Dorothy Johnston, "Image and Text: Medieval Manuscripts at the University of Nottingham" (Nottingham: Nottingham University, 1996), item 6, with a reduced facsimile.

8. See A. Zettersten, ed., *The English Text of the Ancrene Riwle, Edited from Magdalene College, Cambridge MS Pepys 2498*, EETS, o.s. 274 (London, 1976), xvii-xviii, with facsimile as frontispiece.

9. See Elis Fridner, ed., *An English Fourteenth Century Apocalypse Version...*, Lund Studies in English 29 (Lund: University of Lund, 1961), with reduced facsimile as frontispiece.

10. See G. V. Smithers, ed., *Kyng Alisaunder*, EETS, o.s. 227 (London, 1952), with reduced facsimile as frontispiece.

11. The whole is available in CD-ROM facsimile as "The Piers Plowman Electronic Archive," 2, ed. Thorlac Turville-Petre and Hoyt N. Duggan (Ann Arbor MI, 2000). See further Simon Horobin and Linne R. Mooney, "A *Piers Plowman* Manuscript by the Hengwrt/Ellesmere Scribe and its Implications for London Standard English," *Studies in the Age of Chaucer* 26 (2004), 65-112. I include this item and number **14** below because of scholars' general sense that they are early surviving works of their copyists—in this case, Adam Pynkhurst, active from the 1380s; see Mooney, "Chaucer's Scribe," *Speculum* 81 (2006), 97-138. At least two other *Piers Plowman* manuscripts have been noted as resembling the scribal hand here: British Library, MS Additional 35287 (B Version); and "The Holloway fragment" (C Version; now New Haven CT, Yale University, Beinecke Library, Osborn fa45); and see further Estelle Stubbs, "A New Manuscript by the Hengwrt/Ellesmere Scribe? Aberystwyth, National Library of Wales, MS. Peniarth 383D," *Journal of the Early Book Society* 5 (2002), 161-68, with an indistinct facsimile (Chaucer's *Boece*). Study of both these and the scribe's remaining oeuvre belongs, however, to Mooney's project.

12. See the full facsimile, Derek Pearsall and I. C. Cunningham, eds, *The Auchinleck Manuscript: National Library of Scotland Advocates' MS. 19.2.1* (London: Scolar Press, 1979). There this individual is identified as scribe 1, responsible for about 70% of the surviving volume, composed as twelve booklets. The difficulty of "scribe 6"/booklet 7 portions (fols. 268-77) is not altogether effectually addressed in Alison Wiggins, "Are Auchinleck Manuscript Scribes 1 and 6 the Same Scribe?...", *Medium Ævum* 73 (2004), 10-26. Given a variety of differences in production (not to mention a large initial at the head without parallel elsewhere in the book), this portion is possibly better taken as materials the scribe prepared for another manuscript.

13. See Stephen R. Reimer, ed., *The Works of William Herebert OFM*, Studies and Texts 81 (Toronto: Pontifical Institute of Mediaeval Studies, 1987), 7-9, with a facsimile as frontispiece and further references to other reproductions, esp. the 1949 Robinson's sale catalogue.

14. See Pamela Gradon, ed., *Dan Michel's Ayenbite of Inwyt, Volume II...*, EETS, o.s. 278 (London, 1979), 1-4. Facsimiles appear at C. E. Wright, *English Vernacular Hands from the Twelfth to the Fifteenth Centuries*, Oxford Palaeographical Handbooks (Oxford: OUP, 1960), plate 12; Andrew G. Watson, *Catalogue of Dated and Datable Manuscripts c. 700-1600 in the Department of Manuscripts, the British Library*, 2 vols (London: British Library, 1979), 1:88 and 2:plate 222 (no. 435).

15. See Watson, *Catalogue of Dated and Datable Manuscripts c. 435-1600 in Oxford Libraries*, 2 vols (Oxford: OUP, 1984), 1:16, with facsimile at 2:plate 159 (no. 90).

16. On Dan Michel's library, donated to his monastic house, see Bruce C. Barker-Benfield, *St Augustine's Abbey, Canterbury*, 3 vols, Corpus of British Medieval Library Catalogues 13 (London, 2008), particularly the summary, 3:1851-54, with notice of further brief examples of Michel's hand in a variety of contexts. On Michel's annotations in Oxford, Bodleian Library, MS Rawlinson C.117, see Wilbur R. Knorr, "Two Medieval Monks and Their Astronomy Books: MSS. Bodley 464 and Rawlinson C.117," *Bodleian Library Record* 14, iv (1993), 269-84, with facsimiles.

17. See Ralph Hanna, *The English Manuscripts of Richard Rolle: A Descriptive Catalogue* (Exeter: Exeter University Press, 2010), 85-89, with a facsimile as plate 3. For Sedgebrook, see A. J. Piper, "Biographical Register of Durham

Cathedral Priory (1083-1539)," *The Durham Liber Vitae*, ed. David and Lynda Rollason, 3 vols (London: British Library, 2007), 3:271-72.

18. See E. J. Dobson, ed., *The English Text of the Ancrene Riwle Edited from B.M. Cotton MS. Cleopatra C.vi*, EETS, o.s. 267 (London, 1972), esp. xlvii-iii, cxl-viii, with facsimile between 316 and 317.

19. See Albert B. Friedman and Norman T. Harrington, eds, *Ywain and Gawain*, EETS, o.s. 254 (London, 1964), with facsimile as frontispiece.

20. See Carter Revard, "Scribe and Provenance," in *Studies in the Harley Manuscript*, ed. Susanna Fein (Kalamazoo MI: Medieval Institute Publications, 2000), 21-109, with reduced facsimiles of all the legal documents.

21. See E. J. Hathaway et al., eds, *Fouke le Fitz Waryn*, Anglo-Norman Text Society 26-28 (Oxford: OUP, 1975), with detailed discussion of the book and its construction at xliv-liii, and facsimile as frontispiece.

22. For the foundational view that engagement with the poem should be associable with the early career of this prolific Chaucer- and Gower-scribe, see Charles A. Owen's report on Jeremy J. Smith's still unpublished dissertation, "Pre-1450 Manuscripts of the *Canterbury Tales*: Relationships and Significance," *Chaucer Review* 23 (1988), 1-29, at 25-26 n.5. But see further Simon Horobin and Daniel W. Mosser, "Scribe D's SW Midlands Roots: A Reconsideration," *Neuphilologische Mitteilungen* 106 (2005), 289-305.

23. See the previous; the book is an enormous religious anthology, including texts of *The Northern Homily Cycle, Prick of Conscience*, and *Speculum Vitae*, as well as works of Rolle and Hilton, copies of *Ancrene Riwle, Piers Plowman* A, and several texts from *The South English Legendary*.

24. For the first stint, see A. I. Doyle, "University College, Oxford, MS 97 and its relationship to the Simeon Manuscript (British Library Add. 22283)," *So meny people longages and tonges*, ed. Michael Benskin and M. L. Samuels (Edinburgh: Middle English Dialect Project, 1981), 265-82.

25. See Christine Franzen, *The Tremulous Hand of Worcester...* (Oxford, 1991), with abundant facsimiles of various aspects of the oeuvre.

26. For a convenient listing, see N. R. Ker, *Medieval Libraries of Great Britain: A List of Surviving Books*, 2nd edn, Royal Historical Society Guides and Handbooks 3 (London: Royal Historical Society, 1964), 206 n.3.

27. See Franzen, "The Tremulous Hand of Worcester and the Nero Scribe of *Ancrene Riwle*," *Medium Ævum* 72 (2003), 13-31.

Documents and Books: A Case Study of Luket Nantron and Geoffrey Spirleng as Fifteenth-Century Administrators and Textwriters

DEBORAH THORPE

Upon his return to England in the aftermath of the Hundred Years War, Sir John Fastolf embarked upon a program of property acquisition in East Anglia. Caister Castle, on the coast of Norfolk, was one of the properties he acquired and began to improve and by 1448 it was a complete, furnished, impressive castellated residence. However, Caister was not Fastolf's *residence* until 1454. From 1438 until 1454 he spent the majority of his time at "Fastolf Place" in Southwark. Caister could not manage itself, though, so Fastolf endowed it with a full complement of servants, and tasked local men with advising him and representing him in legal cases held in Norwich, Yarmouth and King's Lynn. One such man was his "chaplain" Thomas Howes. Though Howes was "chaplain" in job-title, and though he was indeed responsible for religious elements of daily life at Caister, Howes was more than what we might today deem a "chaplain." Thomas Howes managed Fastolf's other servants, directed his non-resident legal advisors, and dispatched goods to Fastolf in London. Howes's administrative tasks were so diverse that he had his own administrative assistant, a man named Geoffrey Spirleng. It is with Geoffrey Spirleng that this examination of the work of junior clerks will begin. Spirleng went on to write a copy of *The Canterbury Tales*, together with his son Thomas. However, this did not happen until at least thirty years after he began to work as an assistant to Thomas Howes. This article will examine Spirleng's early work in the circle of Sir John Fastolf, and his progression up a kind of career ladder within the circle. Finally, it will attempt to relate the clerkly work that Spirleng did for Howes with his later literary output.

The second man with whom this article is concerned is one with the unusual name of Luket Nantron. Nantron was a native of Paris, and his name first appears in the corpus of letters and documents associated with Sir John Fastolf in 1455 and 1456. His given name was possibly an anglicization in the same way that the Italian merchant Carlo Gigli was referred to as Karoll Giles within the Fastolf circle.[1] In contrast with Spirleng, Nantron was mostly connected with Fastolf's interests in London, as he worked alongside Fastolf's London-based receiver Christopher Hansson.[2] However, his work with Hansson highlights some similarities between Nantron and Spirleng, as both men were assisting more senior members of Fastolf's circle. Like Spirleng, Nantron performed general and apparently mundane clerkly duties, but unlike Spirleng he appears to have first become associated with Fastolf during Fastolf's time in the service of John Duke of Bedford (b. 1389 to d. 1435) in France. Both of these men produced "literary" work as the scribes of manuscript books, and carried out this work alongside their duties as clerks writing documents and letters. There are two letters in the *Paston Letters* corpus from one of the family's scribes, William Ebesham, to John Paston II in which he listed his scribal output and asked for payment for the work (letters 751 and 755). In these lists he grouped together his administrative work ("wrytyng of the prué seal" and "witnesses") with his work as a copyist of books (seven quires of the "great book," a "book of physyke"). He was also responsible for book decoration (he asked for payment for "rubrissheng of all the booke"). This valuable document gives information about how written administration and the writing of literature related to each other in the Paston circle. Unfortunately, no such account exists for Sir John Fastolf and his scribes. Therefore, this article will look for similar information indirectly by piecing together alternative sources of evidence.

This article draws together circumstantial and palaeographical evidence concerning Spirleng and Nantron as men who began their writing careers in the circle of Sir John Fastolf. Both of these men began drafting letters and documents, and ended their careers having produced high-prestige literary books (one of them within a few years of having been trained in basic writing skills). This will be a study of life as a young, junior, or inexperienced clerk within Fastolf's circle of men. The evidence that it will unearth and interpret will add to our scant knowledge about how scribes were trained, and about the milieu from which copyists of major literary works were drawn.

In 1448, when he was just twenty-two years old, Geoffrey Spirleng moved from room to room around Caister Castle making an inventory of its contents.[3] He recorded everything from the copious number of items of clothing in Fastolf's wardrobe, to the vestments in the chapel, to the brass pots in the kitchen. Among the most interesting items entered into the inventory by Spirleng were the seventeen books stored in the "stewe hous," or bath room, next to Fastolf's chamber. Spirleng listed these books by their title and, where relevant, their author and it was possibly he who underlined each of the titles for emphasis. Spirleng was eager to stamp his identity on the inventory: the confirmation that it was he who wrote the document comes from his inscription on the vellum cover of the book into which the leaves of the inventory were bound. This inventory was not Geoffrey Spirleng's earliest piece of written work for Sir John Fastolf, though it was his most substantial. A year earlier he wrote his earliest extant letter in the capacity of assistant to Thomas Howes.[4] From this point onwards, when letters passed from Thomas Howes, Walter Shipdham and William Cole, to Fastolf, the letter was usually co-addressed from Spirleng and was in his hand.[5] When letters passed in the opposite direction, from Fastolf to his receivers in Norfolk, Walter Shipdham and William Cole, Fastolf always included Thomas Howes in the address.[6] This was the medieval predecessor of an email from a company Director to his or her executives, copied to the Office Manager for his information. The letters were never co-addressed to Howes' assistant Geoffrey Spirleng. However, circumstantial evidence within these letters reveals Spirleng's close involvement with documents associated with Fastolf and his interests.[7] Thus it is conceivable that Geoffrey Spirleng was responsible for the storage of this correspondence between Fastolf and his Norfolk-based associates. Indeed, the numerous times that the letters mention Spirleng fetching documents for Fastolf suggest that it was he who best knew how and where written information was stored.[8]

The earliest extant work of Luket Nantron as clerk dates from almost a decade after Spirleng began his career. However, the nature of the work was similar. In a letter tentatively dated by Norman Davis to November 1456, Fastolf told John Paston that he had received a letter from William Barker, written in Nantron's hand, regarding his servants at the manor of Cotton.[9] William Barker, like Thomas Howes, was a servant of Sir John Fastolf. Therefore Nantron, like Spirleng, was writing letters on behalf of another man regarding the management of Fastolf's properties and servants. Nantron stands out among Fastolf's writers due to the evidence that he acted as a scribe for men who were themselves competent and practiced writers. He wrote for William Barker, who was scribe of twelve letters from Fastolf (making him Fastolf's second most prolific scribe). He also acted as a scribe for another of Fastolf's associates, Henry Winsdor, apparently of the Chancery.[10] Windsor wrote to John Paston, excusing himself for using "Luket" as his secretary but he "had no leiser" to write the letter himself (letter 574, lines 7 to 8). The fact that these men delegated work to Nantron suggests that he was working at the bottom of a hierarchy of scribes, or at least that he was more accustomed to doing general clerkly work such as drafting letters. In contrast, Spirleng was writing for Thomas Howes, who hardly ever wrote an autograph letter, and when he did it was in an unsophisticated hand that suggests he was not a well-practiced writer.

In the case of Spirleng, Richard Beadle has already speculated about how he gained his clerkly skills. He has postulated that the close working relationship between Thomas Howes and his young assistant suggests that Spirleng may have been trained by Howes. As an alternative he suggested that Spirleng might have been schooled "in business and estate management of the kind that was available, for example, in Oxford."[11] A third possibility, which Beadle did not suggest, is that Spirleng received his training in London, and since Fastolf was living in London in the 1440s it is quite possible that he encountered the young Spirleng there.[12] This article will look more closely at the inventory, Fastolf Paper 43, along with Spirleng's earliest letters, in an attempt to make a more definite statement about his training. Nantron's development as a clerk has been discussed less than Spirleng's. Up until now there has been no evidence of his work as a scribe of documents and letters: it was only the indirect circumstantial details discussed above that indicated that he ever did this kind of work. This article will present new palaeographical evidence of Nantron's work. These samples of the inexperienced Nantron's hand have the potential to enrich our knowledge of the training undertaken by inexperienced scribes within a gentry circle.

Spirleng's inventory, Fastolf Paper 43, is a neat piece of work that contains few corrections (see figure 1). The scribal work was much more carefully executed than the work of William Worcester in the same inventory, which was done in order to update the inventory in 1454. This suggests that Spirleng drafted the inventory before copying it neatly. This appears especially likely when the document is compared with other record-keeping documents such as Oxford, Magdalen College, Fastolf Paper 25, an account roll from 1444 to 1445 which was scrawled on a narrow strip of paper. Perhaps Spirleng also produced rough notes on scraps of vellum or paper before copying them into this neat book. However, the fact that Spirleng left a significant amount of blank space for certain rooms suggests that he intended the document to be a work in progress. The competence of Spirleng's scribal work in this document makes it difficult to make statements about the way in which he was trained. There is no evidence, either, that Spirleng had any assistance in compiling this inventory: his work was not checked or corrected, and the only other hand in this book is William Worcester's, added a decade later.

Luket Nantron's earliest piece of documentary work is very different from Spirleng's carefully-written inventory. Oxford, Magdalen College, Fastolf Paper 48 is a draft petition by Sir John Fastolf concerning the dispute between himself and Huw Fastolf over the estate of Bradwell in Suffolk. There is no date on the document, but since the dispute was being discussed in letters around 1455 to 1456, it is likely that the petition was written around then.[13] The first forty-six lines of the petition were written by Nantron and the rest was written by a second scribe.[14] The second scribe also corrected Nantron (see figures 2 and 3). He made the odd superscript addition, and corrected short phrases within the first forty-six lines. Nantron made some basic drafting mistakes, such as omitting the regnal year in the formula "yere of the Regne of kyng herry the sext with ought any thyng yeldyng." In this case, the correcting scribe inserted "xxxi" superscript to indicate the missing year. On occasions, the correcting hand made additions, supplementing information that he believed was missing from the work of the first scribe. For example, he altered "...the summe of vi^{xx} x marc wheche is xx li more than ever the seyd wentworth offered for the same..." to "...the summe of vi^{xx} x marc wheche is xx li more than ever the seyd wentworth **or any odir**/ offered for the same..." (my emphasis). He also clarified Nantron's work where Nantron had written that the profits of Bradwell should go to John Paston and Sir John Fastolf by adding "& the king not þerof." By making these kinds of clarifications, the correcting scribe made the requests of the petition clearer and more legally sound. The final kind of minor correction was to make small alterations to the phrasing of the petition. For example, he altered "the patent<u>is</u>" to "the \seyd/ patent<u>is</u>" by inserting the phrase "the seyd" superscript, and he changed "the seyd Paston" to "[the seyd] Paston," by cancelling the phrase "the seyd." The application of the prefix "said" to a noun or proper noun was something in which Nantron evidently still needed guidance, which again indicates that he was a novice scribe. Later in the document the correcting scribe made more major corrections, crossing out lines 44 to 46 of the first scribe's work and replacing them with superscript corrections.[15] Finally, he took over the drafting of the petition and went on to write the rest of the document. Years after this document was written by the inexperienced Nantron, Henry Windsor moaned to his associate John Paston, that he had to deal with documents that had been drawn up by an inept scribe: "And also, sir, [William Worcester] hath caused me to examyn olde and mony records writon by som frenshman concernyng the manoir of Dedham, that was a comberouse labour for these copies were full defectif..." (letter 574, lines 11 to 5). It is mere speculation, since no palaeographical evidence exists to back up the suggestion, but it is possible that the inexperienced French scribe Windsor referred to was Luket Nantron. If this were the case, then Nantron had a hand in even more documents than have been referred to in this article.

Fastolf Paper 48 is the first document to be uncovered that contains significant internal evidence about how scribes were trained within this circle of men. It appears from the petition that the second scribe supervised the drafting of this document, allowing the first to write forty-six lines before stopping him to check the work and make alterations. For some reason, the second scribe decided to take the work away from the first and write the rest of the petition himself. Considering he had needed to correct three whole lines of the first scribe's work, perhaps he decided that the first scribe was not proficient enough to complete the task, or that it was more time-efficient to do the work himself. Comparing the scribal work of the correcting scribe with letters in the *Fastolf Letters and Papers* corpus has revealed the identity of the correcting scribe. The man who was supervising Luket Nantron was William Barker, the scribe who wrote the second-highest number of letters for Sir John Fastolf after William Worcester.[16] This identification arises from similarities between the corrections and Fastolf Paper 26, a letter that Barker wrote on behalf of his master Sir John Fastolf (figure 4). Barker in figure 4, and the correcting hand of figure 3 both wrote the same looped **d** (fig. 3, line 3 "trowbled", fig. 4, line 7 "payed"), **f** (fig. 3, line 6 "of", fig. 4, line 11 "for"), sigmoid s (fig. 3, line 6 "this", fig. 4, line 12 "was"), looped **w** (fig. 3, line 7 "wheche", fig. 4, line 7 "wherefore"), loose anglicana **e** (fig. 3, line 8 "bille", fig 4, line 1 "where"), **k** (fig. 3, line 9 "kyng", fig. 4, line 4 "lyke"), looped **b** (fig. 3, line 9 "beyng", fig 4, line 3 "bille"), **p** with a very long descender (fig. 3, line 11 "put", fig. 4, line 5 "prisoner"), **y** (fig. 3, line 13 "they", fig. 4, line 10 "compleyneth"), and long s (fig. 3, line 13 "seyd". fig. 4, line 13 "present").[17]

Moving on to other written pieces that concern Luket Nantron and William Barker, there are two letters in the *Paston Letters* corpus that contain exactly the same information, with only minor variations in wording. One is folio 35 of British Library, Ms. Additional 39848, and the other is folio 36 (letter 538 in Davis's edition). The first version of the letter was composed on 25th January 1456 from Fastolf to John Paston and Lady Whytyngham, and the second version was written five days later to Lady Whytyngham alone. Norman Davis attributed the copies to two different unidentified hands. The version on folio 35, as Norman Davis stated in the headnote to the letter in his edition, was formally written and was sent to its recipient judging by the appearance of the dorse of the letter. The second version was corrected by William Worcester and was also sent.

It appears from a comparison of these two letters with other samples of the work of Fastolf's scribes, that the version on folio 35 was written by Luket Nantron, and that the version on folio 36 was written by William Barker. The fact that it was the version that was written by William Barker that was corrected by William Worcester is surprising considering Barker's seniority to Nantron. However, this does make sense when one considers that Nantron's version was probably intended for Paston's information alone, whereas Barker's version was actually going to be sent to Lady Whytyngham.[18] It was because of this that William Worcester, as Fastolf's diligent secretary, felt it necessary to get involved and make corrections. This means that minor corrections are preserved in Barker's version that do not appear in Nantron's. For example, Barker's letter reads "right likly \ys/ to be," while Nantron's reads "right lykly to be." That Luket Nantron would write the version of the letter that was intended for Paston's records, whereas Barker would write the final version to be sent to its final recipient is most logical in the context of the hierarchy that is emerging in this study.

So it seems that Luket Nantron, an inexperienced scribe in the mid-1450s, was tasked by William Barker with basic clerkly duties as part of his training. Then, as his career progressed he was utilised by both Barker and other servants of Fastolf to carry out the mundane scribal work that they did not have the time to do themselves. Is there similar circumstantial evidence about the training of Geoffrey Spirleng? There is certainly evidence that Spirleng spent most of his working hours with Thomas Howes in 1447/8. In 1447, Howes sent Spirleng to Martham to make genealogical enquiries connected with his dispute over the estate of Titchwell (letter 961, line 68). In December 1448, the two men went together to Norwich to try to get a copy of a document related to Titchwell (letter 964, lines 5 to 7). A month later Spirleng was doing the "foot work" to retrieve some metal clasps that had been asked for by Fastolf (letter 965, lines 25 to 28). And of the four letters that were addressed from Howes in 1447 to 1449, three were written by Geoffrey Spirleng. There was no mention of Spirleng being trained by Thomas Howes, but this shows that the two men were certainly working together, and that Spirleng was certainly Howes's assistant.

Looking at the three extant letters written by Geoffrey Spirleng might reveal more about how he as a young scribe gained and developed his ability to write. Magdalen College, Hickling 140, is a remarkably neat letter. It is peppered with his own interlinear alterations, but these are mainly minor one-word corrections (such as the alteration of "gef credence to this for it hath..." to "gef credence to this \writing/ for it hath..."). There is a line that has been entirely crossed out, and individual words that have been eliminated in the same way. Spirleng corrected his own grammar in Magdalen College, Titchwell 158, dated to January 1440: he altered "we fynde also" to "we found also." However, neither of these two early letters stand out as the work of an inexperienced trainee scribe, and they were not corrected by any other man. So though there is evidence that Spirleng worked within the Fastolf circle in a junior position, there is no evidence that he gained his ability to write within the circle. This supports Richard Beadle's suggestion that Spirleng entered the circle having already been trained in business and estate management.[19] Indeed, Beadle has also pointed out that Spirleng's personal accounts reveal that he must have been of "some standing," as his annual stipend was 40 shillings, "a handsome wage for a clerk at the outset of his career," especially as he was provided with accommodation at Caister Castle.[20] Despite having the foundations of a high status, it appears that the young Geoffrey Spirleng required guidance in the interpersonal skills that a man needed to function within a gentry circle. Fastolf wrote: "...I pray you to do sende for William Cole... and that Geffrey Spyrlyng forbere hym and gefe non occasion to displese hym" (letter 990, line 52). William Cole was an important man as Fastolf's chief auditor, and thus Fastolf was concerned with ensuring that his young clerk did not upset him. This may indicate either that Cole was especially temperamental, or that Spirleng had yet to develop his skills of discretion. Fastolf demonstrated that he was used to men taking sides against him after being upset by one of his associates: "...I vndrestand that Robert Norwych wolle not occupie as vndreshyreff, because that Jenneys had geve hem langage that was not hys plesure..." (letter 1006, lines 5 to 6). So the busy Sir John Fastolf felt that a potential confrontation between Geoffrey Spirleng and William Cole warranted his sending a special instruction to Spirleng's supervisor, Thomas Howes.

Even if Geoffrey Spirleng was not trained to write "in-house," it appears that his first written work within a gentry household context was done for Sir John Fastolf. So both he and Luket Nantron did their first administrative and epistolary written work within the circle of Fastolf. Both of these inexperienced clerks went on to write manuscript books. This article will now turn to the relationship between their early clerkly work and this later output as the writers of manuscript books.

It is Luket Nantron's hand in London, College of Arms, Ms. M.9 that makes it possible to identify his hand in Fastolf Paper 48 (see figure 5). The text in this manuscript is *Basset's Chronicle*, a "plain soldierly account of the wars" that was intended as a presentation piece for Sir John Fastolf. It was composed by Peter Basset and Christopher Hansson, who were, according to Louise Campbell's catalogue of manuscripts in the College of Arms, "both men serving with English garrisons in the Maine district of France in the years covered by the chronicle."[21] Campbell described the hand of *Basset's Chronicle* as "possibly" that of Luket Nantron. The manuscript itself contains a heading, written by William Worcester, which lists all of the men involved in the writing of the *Chronicle*. Among these is "*luket Nantron natus de Parys vnus de clericis Johannis ffastolf.*" As Nantron was the only man described here by Worcester as a "clerk," it seems likely that he was the scribe of the text in the College of Arms manuscript. It is by comparing the palaeographical features of this manuscript with those of the draft petition Fastolf Paper 48 that it can be stated that the drafting clerk was the same man who wrote *Basset's Chronicle*. Both the clerk of the petition, and the scribe of *Basset's Chronicle* used a very tall capital **A** (fig. 2, line 1 "and," fig 5, line 1 "avaint"), they wrote an identical **g** (fig. 2, line 1 "greet," fig 5., line 36 "grant"), the symbol they used to abbreviate "sir" was the same (fig. 2, line 5 "sir," fig. 5, line 14 "sir"), as was the biting "de" (fig. 2, line 7 "founde," fig. 5, line 4 'de'). The **p** written in each manuscript has the same looped hook (fig. 2, line 9 "put," fig. 5, line 17 "piquet"), and the **h** (fig. 2, line 10 "the," fig. 5, line 32 "henry"), capital **B** (fig. 2, line 11 "Bradwell," fig. 5, line 16 "Baron"), **y** (fig. 2, line 11 "conceyue," fig. 5, line 33 "Gyugy"), and 2-shaped **r** (fig. 2, line 11 "creature," fig. 5, line 37 "Bellencombre") are all identical.

Basset's Chronicle was not completed by the time of Fastolf's death in 1459, which dates Nantron's hand in the text to the period immediately preceding this date.[22] K.B. McFarlane suggested that Nantron not only contributed towards this text in the capacity of scribe, but that the words were his own, and that it was in fact he who led its composition.[23] So the palaeographical evidence in this chronicle, combined with that in documents written in the mid-1450s, reveals that Nantron did high prestige work as a textwriter, and possibly as a composer, just two or three years after he was having his basic drafting work corrected by William Barker.

Nantron's foray into the composition and writing of literature appears to have been an isolated event. His duties were primarily the practical "clerkly" duties associated with the management and protection of Fastolf's properties. Christopher Hansson and Luket Nantron sustained their working relationship for years after they collaborated on *Basset's Chronicle*. After writing the *Chronicle*, they returned to the practical duties associated with collecting revenues and administering Fastolf's will after his death.[24] There was a fourth man involved in *Basset's Chronicle*: Fastolf's secretary, William Worcester. His work in the *Chronicle* also demonstrates the parallels between administrative and literary written work. Worcester stated, in the title to the *Chronicle*, that he was the corrector of the text: *"per diligenciam Willelmi Wircestre."* I have identified Luket Nantron's hand in a petition from Worcester to James, bishop of Norwich, which was corrected by William Worcester himself (letter 1049, probably 1472). Finally, I have found Luket Nantron once more in British Library, Ms. Sloane 4, a compilation of medical recipes that was made after Fastolf's death. This collection is dominated by the hand of William Worcester, whose work was added to by numerous sixteenth-century readers. However, there is another contemporary hand in the manuscript, which wrote a text that spans folios 29r to 35v, beginning *"summa de crisi et criticis diebus...."* Palaeographical features identify the hand as Luket Nantron, and since each of the dated texts in this manuscript were dated between 1468 and 1471, it seems that this is a example of Nantron's text hand when he was an older man. It is neat, with relatively few mistakes, but interestingly there is once again evidence that his work was checked and amended. This evidence is in the margin of folio 30v, where William Worcester drew a symbol which signified that continuation of the text at this point could be found where he had drawn a corresponding symbol on folio 35v. Perhaps Worcester was re-organizing the text as it was originally laid out by Nantron?

So the training and supervision of Luket Nantron appears to have been an ongoing process: he was being corrected in the 1450s by William Barker as might be expected for an inexperienced scribe, but he was also being supervised in the 1470s. Luket Nantron gained his writing skills through drafting petitions, but he applied his ability to write, with apparent ease, to the production of a literary manuscript just a few years later. Having produced this one-off piece of work, he returned to the clerkly duties he was apparently most accustomed to. Luket Nantron, it seems, was a junior clerk whose connections with the military man Christopher Hansson made him the logical choice as scribe of *Basset's Chronicle*. He was first and foremost a clerk and assistant, but his work demonstrates his flexibility as a writer within the Fastolf circle.

There is no evidence that Geoffrey Spirleng was scribe of any manuscript book during Fastolf's lifetime: perhaps he was too busy. There is a five-year hiatus in evidence concerning Geoffrey Spirleng in the Fastolf letters and papers between 1450 and 1455. While this is frustrating for scholars attempting to track his early career, it does make his rise through the ranks of Fastolf's circle even more striking when one compares his duties before and after the hiatus. There is one letter from the mid-1450s that shows that Spirleng had moved on from his work as the scribe of letters for Thomas Howes, and was by this time writing for Fastolf himself (letter 547, written in 1455). This does not necessarily mean that there had been an improvement in his abilities—his early work shows that he was a competent clerk from the outset of his career. However, it does show that he was by this time working closer to Fastolf himself, and it was perhaps this proximity that allowed Fastolf to spot his potential. Indeed, Spirleng was by the late-1450s acting as an auditor for Fastolf (see letter 572). Anthony Smith has highlighted the importance of this role by pointing out that Fastolf's auditors gave him the means to monitor the performance of his other officials.[25] We have already seen the care with which Fastolf treated William Cole, his chief auditor.

Spirleng, in his later career, became one of Fastolf's most peripatetic servants, travelling around East Anglia, and as far as Yorkshire, in the course of his duties (letters 558, 569, 883, and 585). Though in 1458 he spent eight weeks living with Fastolf, he also spent "iij quarters of a yeere after" apart from him, probably drawn away by the demands of managing Fastolf's interests around the country (letters 603, lines 8 to 9 and lines 37 to 38). Spirleng's importance among Fastolf's circle of men is apparent in a letter that Spirleng himself wrote in 1460, two years after Fastolf's death: he testified that at Halloween 1458 he was with Fastolf, and that Fastolf told him what he wanted to do with his lands after his death. Not only did Fastolf apparently confide in Spirleng, but he seems to have listened to what he had to say: "And thanne it fortuned me to syt sadly and noted these wordys, and in maner he toke a conceyt in me of some woordys þat softely I answered in..." (letter 603). Spirleng's writing indicates that by this date he had gained the interpersonal skills that he apparently lacked as a younger man: he knew that to remain in the favor of the irascible Fastolf he had to speak "softely." This information demonstrates how far Spirleng had progressed within Fastolf's circle since he had joined it as the young assistant to Thomas Howes. He had travelled up the hierarchy so much that his evidence became integral in the dispute over Fastolf's will.

The only evidence of Geoffrey Spirleng's work as a textwriter dates from twenty years after Fastolf's death. Glasgow University Library, Huntarian Ms. U.1.1, a copy of *The Canterbury Tales*, was written by Geoffrey and his son Thomas Spirleng during the time that he was in residence in Norwich acting as common clerk to the city of Norwich. Richard Beadle has argued that Spirleng's "daily association at Caister with cultivated and bookish men like William Worcester and Stephen Scrope" probably "left its mark" by encouraging Spirleng to develop literary leanings.[26] There is no written evidence that Spirleng read, was read to, owned, or copied, any literary books during his time in the service of Sir John Fastolf. However, he certainly encountered books, and the list of Fastolf's books in Fastolf Paper 43 demonstrates that he knew Fastolf's book collection well, as he listed its authors and titles diligently. Just as Nantron's work in *Basset's Chronicle* suggests a connection between literary and administrative work, due to the ease with which he switched between the two modes of writing and the working relationships that transferred between literary and administrative work, Spirleng's work in Huntarian, Ms. U.1.1 also suggests parallels between clerkly work and the work of a textwriter. In Spirleng's case, this is due to the palaeographical features of the *Canterbury Tales* manuscript. Though the manuscript was copied to a higher degree of neatness than Fastolf Paper 43, and the manuscript has an appropriate two-column layout, the appearance of the page reflects Spirleng's training as a clerk. The rubricated titles are similar to the titles of Fastolf Paper 43, which break the document down into Caister's constituent rooms (see figure 1). Spirleng divided the text of the *Canterbury Tales* with the same paraph marks, giving the page the same visual aspect. In fact, apart from the enlarged rubricated initials, there is not much to visually separate the two modes of writing. By the time that Spirleng wrote Huntarian, Ms. U.1.1 he was an expert writer: Manly and Rickert pointed out that compared to Thomas, Geoffrey's hand in the manuscript "is the freer and more graceful." He also made numerous corrections to his son's work, for example, on folio 101, where Thomas omitted a passage and Geoffrey provided it in the margin.[27] This evidence demonstrates that a man who had been trained in administrative clerkly work could turn his hand to literary production with relative ease. Of course, the production of manuscripts within Fastolf's circle had degrees of formality. So when Fastolf wanted an expensive decorated book like Oxford, Bodleian Library, Laud Misc 570, he turned to Ricardus Franciscus who it seems was working within a circle of textwriters and decorators in London.[28] However, books like Laud Misc 570 were exceptional cases: in the case of *Basset's Chronicle*, and Spirleng's *Canterbury Tales*, it seems that a man who was trained for the written tasks of a clerk was also prepared to write manuscript books if it were required of him. That these men seemingly fit in the production of such books around their day-to-day administrative tasks is evidence for the lack of a divide between the two types of duty. Both Luket Nantron and Geoffrey Spirleng were well-trained and flexible scribes who were required and willing to apply their ability to write to whatever was demanded of them. This mirrors what existing scholarship has revealed about other writers of literary texts whose hands are found in administrative documents, such as Adam Pinkhurst,[29] Ricardus Franciscus,[30] and the Hammond Scribe.[31] Where this study differs is in being able to track two scribes' careers from their very beginnings through to their latest stages. We are able to see Geoffrey Spirleng as a young, inexperienced clerk, and follow him up the hierarchy within Fastolf's circle. Then we can see him moving beyond this after Fastolf's death and reaching the pinnacle of his career, being appointed city clerk and training own son, Thomas, to write. Luket Nantron's biography is less complete: it is not possible to track it in the same way as Spirleng's. Nevertheless, we can see in him as a man whose primary work was as an administrator, but who turned his hand at least once to writing high quality manuscript books.

Centre for Medieval Studies, University of York.

NOTES

1. See Norman Davis ed., *Paston Letters and Papers*, part 2, (Oxford: Oxford University Press, 2005), letter 574. All further references to letters and documents in this edition will be presented in parentheses, along with letter number and line number where relevant. Letter numbers 421 to 930 refer to part 2. It was Jonathan Hughes who identified the Italian name behind the anglicization: Jonathan Hughes, "Stephen Scrope and the Circle of Sir John Fastolf: Moral and Intellectual Outlooks," in *Medieval Knighthood IV. Papers from the Fifth Strawberry Holl Conference, 1990*, edited by C. Harper-Bill and R. Harvey (Woodbridge: Boydell Press, 1992), 109-46, 132.
2. A receiver was responsible for collecting his master's revenues, such as rent paid by his tenants. For some written evidence of Christopher Hansson's activities in this capacity see Oxford, Magdalen College, Fastolf Paper 51, an account roll by Christopher Hansson of rents due to Sir John Fastolf.
3. Oxford, Magdalen College, Fastolf Paper 43.
4. Richard Beadle and Colin Richmond eds., *Paston Letters and Papers of the Fifteenth Century*, part 3, (Oxford: Oxford University Press, 2005), letter number 961. All further references to letters and documents in this edition will be presented in parentheses, along with letter number and line number where relevant. Letter numbers 931 to 1051 refer to part 3.
5. See for example letters 964 and 965 in Beadle and Richmond's edition.
6. This point was made by Richard Beadle in "Geoffrey Spirleng (c.1426 to c.1494): a Scribe of the *Canterbury Tales* in his Time," in *Of the Making of Books: Medieval Manuscripts, Their Scribes and Reader: Essays Presented to M. B. Parkes*, edited by P. R. Robinson and Rivkah Zim, 116 to 46 (Aldershot: Scolar Press, 1997), 122. See letter 962 in Beadle and Richmond's edition as an example.
7. See, for example, letter 964 which records Spirleng attempting to get hold of a document related to Titchwell dispute. Or 965 which documents his attempt to find a will at the manor of Titchwell.
8. For example, letter 964, line 9, and letter 965, lines 25 to 28.
9. "...I receyvid by Henre Hannson on Thorsday last passid at iii after none certeyn lettres, amonges whiche I receyvid on from William Barker writen

of Lukettes hand." See Norman Davis ed., *Paston Letters and Papers*, part 2, (letter 569, lines 2-3).

10. "*de cancellaria domini Regis*" (letter 574, lines 1 to 8).

11. Beadle "Geoffrey Spirleng,"123.

12. I am grateful for this suggestion, which was made to me by Professor Linne Mooney. Very little is known about the training of clerks in London. Thomas Frederick Tout wrote about the potential ways that these men could have been trained in "Literature and Learning in the English Civil Service in the Fourteenth Century," *Speculum*, 4, (October 1929): 368- 369.

13. November 15, probably 1456: "...I shuld haue disseasid Ser Hue Fastolf of þe manere, where as I haue sufficient evidences preuyng a trewe saale and purchace..." (letter 569, lines 20 to 32).

14. Nantron did not inscribe his name on this document. The identification of his hand comes from comparison with Nantron's hand in *Basset's Chronicle*, which will be discussed later in this article.

15. He crossed out: "...wheche evedently apperith by the bille put in to the parlement Remaynyng with the lordes as by the surmys of the seyd sir philipp [...] with that for iij C marc the seid ser philipp hath hadde þe day xvjC [...]" and wrote superscript to the deleted passage, "...þe seyd fastolff and past men wer advayled ther by iii ton this day and [...] but the seid ffastolf wrongfully trowbled for the seyd oranoir wheche is his owen enheritances and that nowtwithstandyng yes compelled in the [...] to paye xx li ... of the seyd ciix li wheche is surmitted by this bille shuld growe to the kyng."

16. In c.1485, Barker wrote that upon Fastolf's death, he had been "late howshold servaunte be the space of xxi yere wyth Syr John Fastolf, Knyght, dysseysid" (letter 925, lines 6 to 16).

17. Line numbers here refer to the line number within the figure, rather than the line number of the original document.

18. This practice of sending a copy to Paston for his records was described by Beadle and Richmond in the headnote to letter 1035 in their edition: "in common with other Fastolf letters of this period, this exists as a copy forwarded to Paston and Bokkyng, presumably at the same time the original was sent to the primary addressee."

19. Beadle "Geoffrey Spirleng," 122.

20. These personal accounts are now Oxford, Magdalen College Archives, EP 176/9. Beadle "Geoffrey Spirleng," 122.
21. Louise Campbell, *A Catalogue of Manuscripts in the College of Arms* (London: College of Arms, 1988), 129.
22. Benedicta J. H. Rowe, "A Contemporary Account of the Hundred Years War from 1415 to 1429," *English Historical Review* 41 (1926): 504 to 513 (513).
23. K. B. McFarlane, "William Worcester: A Preliminary Survey," in *England in the Fifteenth Century: Collected Essays*, edited by K. B. McFarlane, 199 to 224 (London: Hambledon, 1981), 211.
24. In 1461, Clement Paston wrote to John Paston I promising him five marks and assuring him that, "...þe remnawnte I trow I xall gett vp-on Cristofire Hanswm and Lwket" (letter 116, lines 38 to 39). Then in a letter written after 1466, Fastolf's executors claimed: "Item, dictus Johannes recepit per manus dicti Tome Howys, Willelmi Paston, Thome Playter, Thome Plummer de London, scryvaner, **Christofori Hansson**, armigeri, et **Luce Nantron** ad diuersas vices tam Londonijs quam in Suthwerk..." (letter 906).
25. Anthony Smith, "Aspects of the Career of Sir John Fastolf 1380-1459." (D. Phil dissertation, Oxford University, 1982), 63 to 64.
26. Beadle "Geoffrey Spirleng," 10.
27. John Manley and Edith Rickert, *The Text of* The Canterbury Tales, *Studied on the Basis of all Known Manuscripts*, Volume I: Descriptions of the Manuscripts, (University of Chicago Press: Chicago and London, 1940), 187.
28. Martha Driver looked at the several manuscripts copied by Franciscus that demonstrate repeated co-operation between certain scribes and artists, and concluded that these connections "imply the existence of a coterie of artists who, like the Fastolf master and Richardus, worked in the fifteenth century." Martha Driver, "'Me fault faire': French Makers of Manuscripts for English Patrons." In *Language and Culture in Medieval Britain. The French of England, c.1100-c.1500*. Edited by Jocelyn Wogan-Browne et al. (York Medieval Press, 2009), 431.
29. For more information about Adam Pinkhurst, see Linne R. Mooney, "Chaucer's Scribe," *Speculum* 81 (2006): 97–138.
30. For more information about Ricardus Franciscus, see Driver, "'Me fault faire': French Makers of Manuscripts for English Patrons."

31. For more information about the Hammond Scribe, see Linne Mooney, "More Manuscripts Written by a Chaucer Scribe," *The Chaucer Review* 30:4 (1996) and Mooney, "A New Manuscript by the Hammond Scribe Discovered by Jeremy Griffiths," in *The English Medieval Book: Essays in Memory of Jeremy Griffiths*, edited by Tony Edwards, Ralph Hanna and Vincent Gillespie (London: British Library, 2000), 113-23.

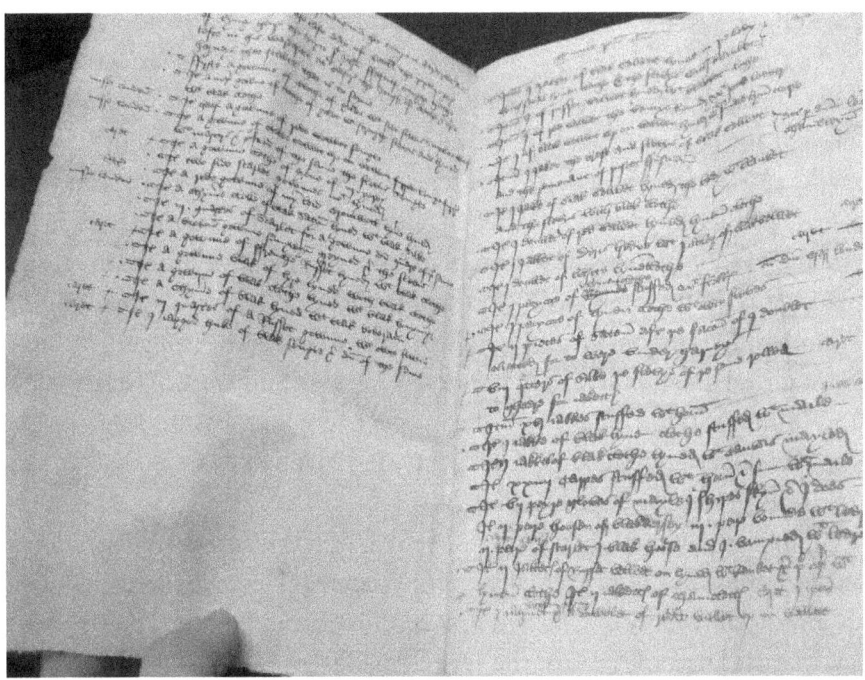

Figure 1. Inventory of Caister Castle in Norfolk, 1448. In the hand of Geoffrey Spirleng. Oxford, Magdalen College, Fastolf Paper 43. By permission of the President and Fellows of Magdalen College, Oxford.

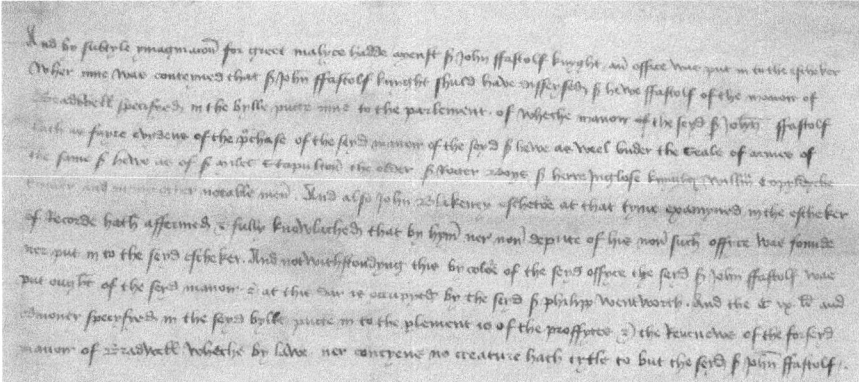

Figure 2. Lines 10-20 of a draft petition by Sir John Fastolf, in hand of Luket Nantron. Oxford, Magdalen College, Fastolf Paper 48. By permission of the President and Fellows of Magdalen College, Oxford.

Figure 3. Lines 41-55 of a draft petition by Sir John Fastolf. Lines 1-4 in hand of Luket Nantron, corrections and remainder of the text in hand of William Barker. Oxford, Magdalen College, Fastolf Paper 48. By permission of the President and Fellows of Magdalen College, Oxford.

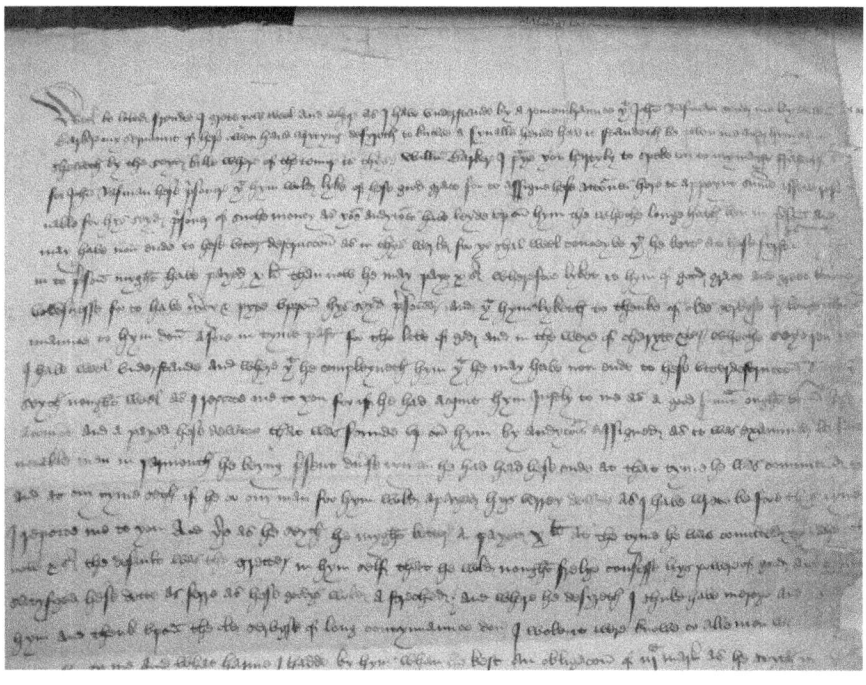

Figure 4. The hand of William Barker in a letter from Sir John Fastolf. Oxford, Magdalen College, Fastolf Paper 26. By permission of the President and Fellows of Magdalen College, Oxford.

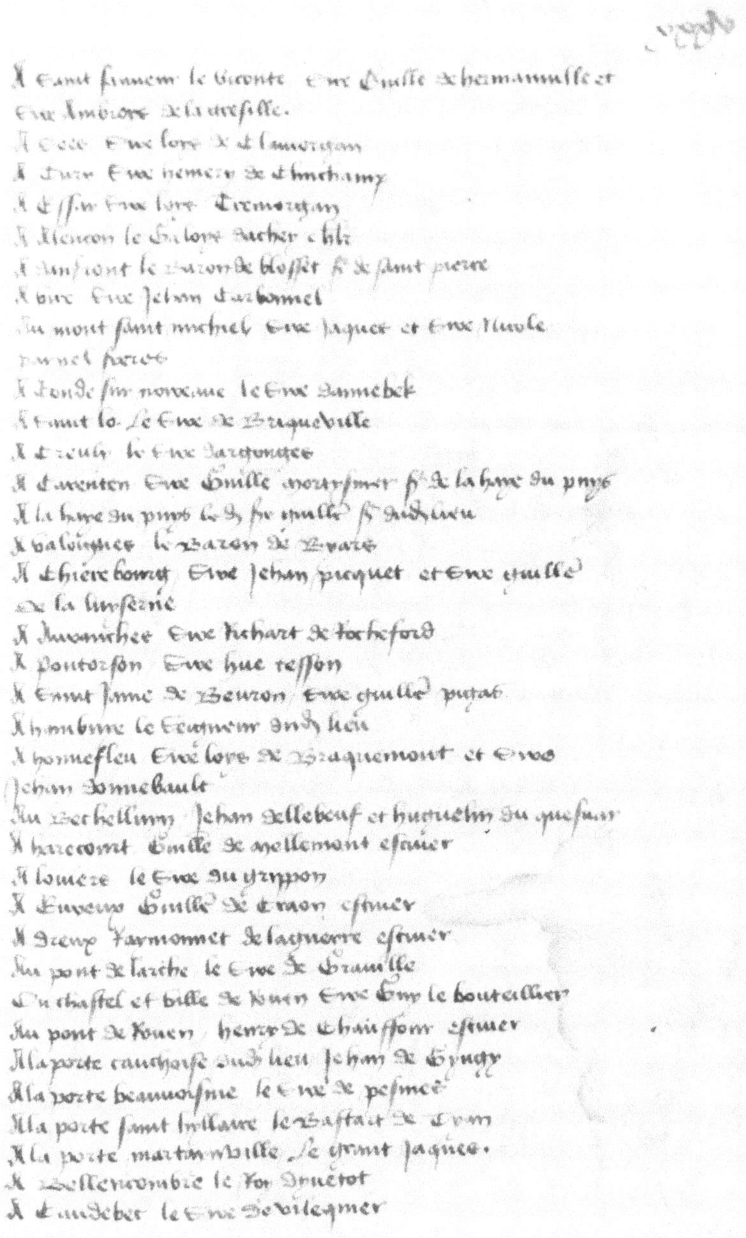

Figure 5. The hand of Luket Nantron in *Basset's Chronicle*. London, College of Arms, MS m.9, folio 35 recto.

The Middle English Cooking Recipes in New York Public Library Whitney MS 1

PAUL ACKER

New York Public Library, Whitney MS 1 consists of fifteen vellum leaves and contains a selection of Middle English cooking recipes written down in the first half of the fifteenth century,[1] probably *c*.1425. The first group of recipes on folios 1 to 12r, here called *Cures*[2] *of Metis* (*The Cooking of Food*), appears in other manuscripts under the title *The Forme of Cury*, that is, the (proper) *Method of Cookery*,[3] or more loosely, *How to Cook*.[4] The collection as excerpted in the Whitney MS provides recipes for dishes running from "Firmenty" or frumenty, "a dish of boiled, hulled wheat, resembling a modern wheat porridge or pilaff,"[5] through "Puerate" or peverade (later poivrade), a pepper sauce for veal or venison.[6] Porridges and vegetarian pottages were the first courses served in medieval English aristocratic menus; accordingly *The Forme of Cury* begins with a dozen recipes for such dishes.[7] The Whitney MS skips five of these (see note 6) but retains stewed turnips, herbs in broth, pottage of onions, pottage of squash (courgettes), rice in broth, and mushrooms and leeks in broth.[8] Only the frumenty is thickened with almond milk, according to Constance Hieatt and Sharon Butler a feature that "came from the East, either via Spain and/or Italy or as direct importations by returning Crusaders."[9]

Heavier meat dishes came next on the menu and next in *The Forme of Cury*'s recipes, beginning with various organ meats in broth, then preparations for veal, chicken and other fowl, kid, rabbit, hare, pork, mutton and lamb followed (after some more meatless dishes) by fish and seafood.[10] The meatless recipes include some for unexpectedly familiar dishes, including salad (field greens with oil and vinegar), ravioli, and macaroni and cheese.[11]

According to the headnote in one manuscript of *The Forme of Cury*, the recipe collection is organized so as first to teach one "to make commune potages and commune mettis for howshold as þey shold be made craftly and holsomely. Aftirward it techiþ for to make curious potages & meetes and sotiltees for alle manere of states both hye and lowe" (British Library, MS Additional 5016).[12] As Hieatt and Butler point out,[13] our modern practice of ending a meal with dessert descends from this medieval practice of saving the delicacies (the "curious and subtle" dishes) for last, although medieval menus incorporated dainty savory dishes as well as sweet ones. The final section of *The Forme of Cury*, recipes numbers 153 to 205 as printed in Hieatt and Butler, presents recipes for the later courses, including fritters, tarts, custards and ending with *ypocras* (modern hippocras) or spiced wine.[14] A number of the dishes in this final section are listed as appropriate for third courses in surviving medieval menus, such as a menu for meat days printed as Menu 3 in Hieatt and Butler,[15] which lists as its third- and second-to-last items *daryols* (custard tarts, see *Forme of Cury* number 191) and *flampoyntes* (tartlets filled with ground pork, see *Forme of Cury* number 192).[16] Working back from this final section, we find *Forme of Cury* recipes number 151 and 152 are brief notes on roasting cranes and herons, then peacocks and partridges.[17] These more exotic fowl (along with woodcocks, plovers, larks, mallards, teal and snipe) were served as second and third courses on the menus printed in Hieatt and Butler, before the pastry dishes.[18] Prior to these directions for roasting fowl, *Forme of Cury* recipes numbers 139 to 150 are all for sauces, from *poivrade* or pepper sauce (the final recipe in the Whitney MS selection contained on fols. 1-12r) through "Lombard" or honey-mustard sauce.[19]

In order to round off my bibliographical description thus far, I provide a transcription followed by a modern English translation of the first and last recipes from *The Forme of Cury* as contained in Whitney MS 1, fols. 1 and 12r:[20]

[f. 1] *Here begynnes [Cu]res of metis.*[21]
Firmenty. Tak clene whete and ~~breke~~ bre hijt in a mort*er* all w[e]lle and sethe hijt in wat*ur* til hijt breke & þanne wasch

MIDDLE ENGLISH COOKING RECIPES 219

hijt clene. Þanne take hijt vp & late hijt cole and take good broth and swet milke of almaynus & temper hijt with many olkes of eyrn rawe and saferen and kast þeretoo salt & late hijt nout b[o]il & aftur þanne þat eyrn ben caste þereto. With venysun oft or with fatte metoun ffresch & serue hijt foorþe.

Here begins The Cooking of Food.
Frumenty. Take clean wheat and pound it thoroughly in a mortar [to remove the hulls]. Boil it in water until it bursts and then wash it clean. Then take it off [the fire] and let it cool. Take good broth and sweet almond milk and mix it with several raw egg yolks and saffron, add salt. Do not let it boil after the eggs have been added. Serve it forth with venison or with fresh fatty mutton.[22]

[f. 12] *Puerate for vel and veneson.* Tak bred & frie hit ynne grees & drauh hit vp with broþ & vinegur. Cast þerto & pouder of pepur & salt & seþ hit on þe fuyre & boile hit a luytel & messe hit forþe.

(*Poivrade for veal and venison.* Take bread and fry it in grease and cut it up in broth and vinegar. Add ground pepper and salt, set it on the fire and boil it a little; serve it forth.)

On folio 12 of Whitney MS 1, a second group of recipes begins with a new rubricated incipit, "Here begynnes aires," with "aires" again a miswriting for "cures" (see note 2). Running from folios 12-15r, these recipes are mainly taken from a collection elsewhere entitled *Diversa Servicia* (Oxford, Bodleian Library, Douce MS 257).[23] Another manuscript, Bodleian Ashmole MS 1444, likewise preserves a sampling of the *Diversa Servicia* recipes and is there entitled *Curye on Inglysch*, that is, *Cookery in English*—as against Anglo-Norman, the principal language used for recording recipes in England in the early fourteenth century. The Whitney MS shares twenty-two recipes with the Ashmole MS (cf. *Diversa Servicia* numbers 4-16, 18-22, 24-26 and 65), but also includes 14 *Diversa Servicia* recipes not in the Ashmole MS (cf. *Diversa Servicia* numbers 2-3, 17, 23, 60-61, 63-64, 66-69 and 74), for a total of thirty-six recipes.[24] The complete *Diversa Servicia*, by contrast, runs to ninety-two recipes.

The first two recipes in the Whitney selection of *Diversa Servicia* tell how to roast cranes, herons, peacocks and partridges (*Diversa Servicia* nos. 3 and 4).[25] The last two recipes tell how to prepare eels in broth and roasted lobster.[26] The (brief) lobster recipe reads as follows in the Whitney MS:

> [f. 15] [*Lopister(s)*][27] schal be rostud in here schalus and in an ouun or be a fuyre vndur a panne and etun with vinegur &c.
>
> ([*Lobsters*] should be roasted in their shells in an oven or beside a fire under a [roasting] pan and eaten with [wine] vinegar etc.)

The Whitney recipes sometimes occur out of order by comparison with the Douce manuscript,[28] and the Whitney manuscript interpolates two recipes and appends four others. On fol. 12v, after Hieatt recipe *Diversa Servicia* no. 9, the Whitney MS interpolates a recipe for Saracen sauce (miswritten *Samfarayn*). It is made of almonds and wine and garnished with pomegranate seeds:

Whitney interpolated recipe 1

> [f. 12v] *Samfarayn*[29] Tak almownes & blanche hem & frie hem in oile olyue & seþun bray hit in a morter. Temper hit vp with almowne milke & good wyne & þrid part schal be good sugur. And ȝef hit be not þik, tak a littul of mayne de floure or with floure of ris & coloure hit with alk [Hieatt & Butler: alconet]. Flerische hit with powngarnettus abouen & serue hit forþ.
>
> (*Saracen sauce*. Take almonds and blanch them and fry them in olive oil. Then grind them in a mortar and mix with almond milk, good [red] wine and

a third part fine sugar. If it is not thick [enough],
take a little wheat starch or rice flour. Color it with
alkanet [a red dye] and garnish it with pomegranate
seeds on top; serve it forth.)[30]

On fol. 13r, after Hieatt and Butler recipe no. 12,[31] the Whitney MS records a recipe "For *geree*," a close variant of its earlier recipe on f. 12 for *Egredowce* (aigre-doux, sweet and sour fish;).[32] I transcribe both versions below for comparison:

Whitney interpolated recipe 2

[f. 13] *For geree.*[33] Tak luces or tenches and schred hem
smal and fry hem. Tak vinegur & þrid part of sugur &
mise þe oynons and a litul ale and buyle al togedir & cast
þerynne mas and clowes & quibubbus and serue hit forþ.

(*Aigre-doux*. Take luce [pike] or tench [a type of
fish] and shred them small and fry them. Take
vinegar and a third part of sugar, mince the onions
with a little ale and boil them all together. Add
mace, cloves and cubebs and serve it forth.)

[Compare f. 12] *Egredowce*. Tak luces or tenches & hew
hem on gobbetus & frie hem yn oile & seþ hem. Tak vinegur
& þrid part sugur & mise oynons smal & boile hit toged-
er & cast þerto clowes of mas quibibbes & dres hit forþe.

(*Aigre-doux*. Take luce or tench & cut them into
pieces and fry them in oil and boil them. Take vinegar
and a third part sugar, mince onions finely & boil it
together; add cloves, mace, cubebs and serve it forth.)

After the recipe for lobster transcribed above (no. 75 in the Douce 257 *Diversa Servicia* collection), the Whitney MS appends four more recipes not textually related to any of those in *Curye on Inglysch* or *Diversa Servicia*, nor to any in other major published collections.[34] Recently, however, Hieatt[35] has published some similarly anomalous recipes from British Library MS Sloane 1108, and it turns out that two of the Whitney appended recipes are closely related to two in Sloane, and a third is more broadly similar. To conclude my bibliographical description of Whitney MS 1, I provide transcriptions and translations of these four appended recipes.

Whitney appended recipe 1

[f. 15] *Flawnus in lentu*n. Tak past and mak a cofyng & ful him ful of mayn milk & blanche almown*us* cast þ*er*ynne poud*ur* of ging*ur* & of safrenne & bake him &c.

(Lenten tarts. Take dough and make a pie shell and fill it with wheat starch, milk and blanched almonds. Add powdered ginger and saffron and bake.)

This recipe is broadly similar to but briefer than a recipe for lenten tarts in Douce 257 (not in the Whitney MS);[36] it is closer to a recipe in BL Harley 279,[37] and closer still to a recipe in British Library MS Sloane 1108:[38]

[Compare Sloane 1108:] *Flawnes in lentoun*. Take almond mylke and do it in a cofyn of past, and blanched almondes and poudre of gyngere, & coloure it with safroun, and bake it and serve it forth.

(Lenten tarts. Take almond milk and put it in a pie shell and [also] blanched almonds and powdered ginger. Color it with saffron and bake it and serve it forth.)

Whitney appended recipe 2

[f.15] *Spynes of fisch*. Tak good fisch and hew him on peces and þe liuoure with*al* and mak a cofyn & do hit þ*er*ynne and grind ginger & pep*ur* & safrenne & cast þeron and couer hit and bake hit &c.

([*Fish tart.*] Take fresh fish and cut it in pieces with
the liver and make a pie shell and put it therein.
Add ground ginger, pepper and saffron, cover it
and bake it, etc.)

The recipe is mislabeled "spynes," since a *spinee* is properly a stew flavored with powdered hawthorn blossoms (Old French *espinee*), as in *Diversa Servicia* number 46[39] (not in the Whitney MS) and *The Forme of Cury* no. 58.[40] This recipe instead calls for fish baked with its liver and spices in a pie shell and is not closely paralleled by any other recipes I have seen.[41]

Whitney appended recipe 3

[f. 15] *Porpeys fresch* schul be hewen on gobbet*us* with þe blod so þenne grind ging*er* & pep*ur* & bred or wyne & ale buyle hit &c.

(*Fresh porpoise* should be cut into pieces and boiled
with the blood. Grind ginger, pepper, bread or wine
& ale; boil it, etc.)

The preparation, if not the choice of meat, is quite similar to a recipe in the *Diversa Servicia* called "Hares in talbots",[42] which reads as follows in the Whitney MS, f. 12v:[43]

[Compare Whitney f. 12v] *Hare yn talbot* schold be hewen ynne gobettus al rawe & soden w*ith* ale & blod[44] & bred & pep*ur* & ale & grinde toged*ur* [with, underdotted] & temp*er* hit w*ith* þe selue broþ & boile hit & salt hit & serue hit forþe.

(*Hare in broth* should be cut raw into pieces &
boiled with all the blood. [Take] bread, pepper &
ale and grind together. Mix it with the same broth
& boil it. Salt it and serve it forth.)

Closer in both preparation and contents, however, is a recipe from Sloane MS 1108:[45]

> [Sloane 1108:] *Purpeyce en cyve.* Purpayce in cyve shal be hewun in gobettes, blode and al sothen. Grynde peper, brede and wyne or ale and boile it and do þerto, and þanne serve it forth.
>
> (Porpoise in onion sauce[46] should be cut in pieces [with] the blood and all [of it] boiled. Grind pepper, bread and wine or ale and boil it and add thereto, and then serve it forth.)

Whitney appended recipe 4

> [f. 15v] *Tart ?permusan.*[47] Tak past of white flouer & mak a good cophyn. Tak floure of almownes and fresch samowne & turbut and haddoc & gurnard & luces & elus maces & clowes & quibubbus and ginger canel & datus & safrenne and mayn de flour & floure of ryse & do al in wo couyn. Tak reysones & tak tak [*sic*] oute þe kurnellus & drop þerynne & good almownd milk & plawnt hem abouenne in þe tart & blanche almown[es] also fruit & bake hit wele &c.
>
> ([*Fish tart*]. Take white flour dough and make a good pie shell. Take almond flour and fresh salmon, turbot, haddock, gurnard, luce and eels; mace, cloves, cubebs, ginger, cinnamon, dates, and saffron, wheat starch and rice flour and put it all in one (?) pie shell. Take grapes and remove the seeds, drop therein and [also] good almond milk and place them on top of the tart with blanched almonds and [dried] fruit and bake it well.)

This recipe is broadly similar to those for fish tarts in *The Forme of Cury*[48] and in BL Harley MS 279,[49] although both of those also include stuffed eel.

A slightly more comparable recipe is printed in Austin,[50](Tart de ffruyte), from Harley MS 4016; the Harley recipe in turn closely resembles a fish tart recipe from Sloane 1108:

> [Sloane 1108, f. 15v][51] *Tartez de pessoun*: Take fygges and sethe hem in wyne, and grynde hem smal; and þanne take hem up into a vessell, and take poudre of peper and canel and cloves and mace and grete resens, and fry hem in oyle and cast hem þerto. And make fayre low cofyns and so couche þe stuff þerynne, and plante above prunys and kut dates, and kytte fayre fresshe salmoun in peces, or ellys fresshe elys, and perboile hem and couche þeron. And kever þe cofyns with þe same paste, and endorre þe cofyns withoute with safroun and with water, or els with safroun and almonde mylke, and set hem in þe ovyn and lete hem bake; and þenne serve hem forth.

> (Fish tarts. Take figs and boil them in wine and grind them small; and then take them up into a pot, and take ground pepper and cinnamon and cloves and mace and large raisins, fry them in oil and add them thereto. And make good, shallow pie crusts and place the ingredients therein, and set on top prunes and chopped dates, and cut good, fresh salmon in pieces, or else fresh eels, and parboil them and add them on top. And cover the pie shells with the same dough, and gild the outside of the pie crusts with saffron and water, or else with saffron and almond milk, and put them in the oven and let them bake; and then serve them forth.)

Bon appetit!

Saint Louis University

NOTES

1. The manuscript is thus dated in Constance B. Hieatt and Sharon Butler, eds. *Curye on Inglysch: English Culinary Manuscripts of the Fourteenth Century (Including the* Forme of Cury), Early English Text Society, s.s. 8 (London: Oxford University Press, 1985), 18. Since the handwriting employs Anglicana graphs rather than secretary ones for the letters *d, g* and *w*, I would date it more narrowly to *c.* 1425. NYPL Whitney MS 1 is the sole medieval manuscript in the Whitney Cookery Collection, bequeathed by Helen Hay Whitney (1875-1944), widow of Harry Payne Whitney (1872-1930). Lewis M. Stark, "The Whitney Cookery Collection," *Bulletin of the New York Public Library* 50 (1946): 103-126, reports that the collection has 17 MSS and over 200 printed cookery books. It has not previously been noted that prior to Whitney, the MS belonged to Walter Sneyd of Keele Hall (1809-1888; his bookplate, f. i^v), whose MSS were catalogued by Sir Thomas Phillipps, *Additional MSS. in the Possession of the Revd. Walter Sneyd, of Denton House, Oxon., acquired since the printing of his former Catalogue by Sir Thomas Phillipps, Bart. in 1837,* [Middle Hill, ?1863], p. 1, as number 34, "Old English Receipts for Cookery, 4to, vellum"; and by Alfred J. Horwood, "The Manuscripts of the Rev. Walter Sneyd, of Keele Hall, Co. Stafford," *Third Report of the Royal Commission on Historical Manuscripts* (London: HMSO, 1872), Appendix, 287-90, esp. p. 290, as "A small vellum 4to volume, contains 15 leaves of cookery receipts, in English." Sneyd's MSS were sold at Sotheby's Dec. 16-19, 1903 (Dec. 16, Lot 214, Ancient Recipes in English Cookery, 15 leaves; sold to Edwards): see *Catalogue of a Selected Portion of the Valuable and Choice Illuminated and Other Manuscripts and Rare Early Printed Books, the Property of the Late Rev. Walter Sneyd,* 16 Dec. and 3 following days (London: Sotheby's, 1903).

2. The rubricated and smudged heading atop f. 1 appears to read: "Here begynnes Aires of metis"; the incipit to the second recipe collection (see below) definitely says: "Here begynnes aires." I assume "aires" in both cases is a mistranscription for "cures" (the Whitney headings are often miscopied; cf. *Capes for Rapes* [turnips] on f. 1, *Drineus for Brineus* on f. 13v). Since Hieatt in *A Gathering of Medieval English Recipes* (Turnhout: Brepols, 2008), 132, despaired of reading the heading (and did not report

the later incipit), the Whitney recipe collections are here given titles for the first time.

3. Hieatt and Butler, *Curye on Inglysch*, p. 20.

4. *The Forme of Cury* is edited as Part IV of Hieatt and Butler, *Curye on Inglysch*, pp. 93-145. For a description and bibliography of *The Forme of Cury* and other Middle English cooking recipe collections, see George R. Keiser, *Works of Science and Information. A Manual of the Writings in Middle English 1050-1500*. Ed. Albert E. Hartung, vol. 10 (New Haven: Connecticut Academy of Arts and Sciences, 1998), 10.3678-80, 3885-93. For a more broadly European list, see Terence Scully, *The Art of Cookery in the Middle Ages* (Woodbridge: Boydell, 1995), 257-60.

5. Hieatt and Butler, *Curye on Inglysch*, 190; see their *Forme of Cury* recipe number 1, p. 98.

6. Recipe number 139 in Hieatt and Butler, *Curye on Inglysch*, 129. Their edition, based on British Library MS Additional 5016 supplemented by other MSS (including Whitney), totals 205 recipes. The Whitney MS contains Hieatt and Butler recipes 1, 7-44, 46-55, 58-65, 70-81, 85, 87-94, 98, 101-02, 106-07, 109-15 (and 113 variant, Elus in sorrey, f. 10), 122-27, 129-37, and 139 for a total of 107 recipes (see Hieatt and Butler's table, pp. 93-97).

7. See Hieatt and Butler, *Curye on Inglysch*, 4. Two surviving medieval menus, one from *c.* 1400 (printed Hieatt and Butler, 39), begin with frumenty (with venison). On fish days, frumenty was served with porpoise: see Anne C. Wilson, *Food and Drink in Britain from the Stone Age to Recent Times* (New York: Harper, 1974), 31; Scully, *Art of Cookery*, 38; or see the recipe in *Forme of Cury* number 70, Hieatt and Butler, *Curye on Inglysch*, 114; Whitney MS 1, f. 6v. On pottages, see further Wilson, 199-208.

8. I give these in the Hieatt and Butler order; MS Whitney recipes 1-6 correspond to Hieatt and Butler *Forme of Cury* recipes 1, 7, 9-12, 8.

9. Hieatt and Butler, *Curye on Inglysch*, 7.

10. The first and second courses on feast days especially would have also offered meats (boar's head, venison) roasted on spits (see Scully, *The Art of Cookery*, 6-7, 94), for which recipes were not always deemed necessary (but see below on roast peacock, Hieatt and Butler, *Curye on Inglysch*, 85 on roast swans, and Constance B. Hieatt, *An Ordinance of Pottage: An Edition of the Fifteenth Century Recipes in Yale University's MS Beineke 163* (London:

Prospect, 1988), 91-95 for roast birds, rabbit, kid, veal and venison). The division in recipes between meat and fish dishes reflects the need for the latter on Christian fast days (see Wilson, *Food and Drink* 30-32); the menus in Hieatt and Butler, 40-41 differentiate between "flesh" and fish days.

11. See recipes numbered 78, 94 and 95, respectively, in Hieatt and Butler, *Curye on Inglysch*, 115, 118-19, the last omitted from the Whitney MS but appearing in other MSS of *The Forme of Cury*. On ravioli, see Barbara Santich, "The Evolution of Culinary Techniques in the Medieval Era," *Food in the Middle Ages*, ed. Melitta Weiss Adams (New York: Garland, 1995), 61-81 at 74-75; on pasta and macaroni, see Reay Tannahill, *Food in History*, rev. ed. (New York: Three Rivers, 1988), 234-37.

12. Cited Hieatt and Butler, *Curye on Inglysch*, 20. By *sotiltees* is meant in particular dishes that masquerade as something they are not, such as castles made of pastry (see Hieatt and Butler, 142-3, *Forme of Cury* recipe number 197).

13. Hieatt and Butler, *Curye on Inglysch*, 5.

14. Hieatt and Butler, *Curye on Inglysch*, 132-45. On hippocras as a last course, see Scully, *The Art of Cookery*, 135, 148-49. For recipes for hippocras, see Paul Acker, "Texts from the Margin: Lydgate, Recipes and Glosses in Bühler MS 17," *The Chaucer Review* 37.1 (2002): 59-85 at p. 67.

15. Hieatt and Butler, *Curye on Inglysch*, 40.

16. These two *Forme of Cury* recipes are edited in Hieatt and Butler, *Curye on Ynglysch*, 141. See also the menus from BL Sloane 442 in Hieatt, *Ordinance of Pottage*, 110, and her comment (16-17) relating them to the sequence of recipes in the *Forme of Cury*.

17. Hieatt and Butler, *Curye on Inglysch*, 131-2.

18. Hieatt and Butler, *Curye on Inglysch*, 40-41.

19. Hieatt and Butler, *Curye on Inglysch*, 129-31.

20. The texts differ somewhat in wording but not substantially in content from the *Forme of Cury* recipes nos. 1 and 139, ed. Hieatt and Butler, *Curye on Inglysch*, pp. 98 and 129. In the following transcriptions, I expand abbreviations with italics. Letters in square brackets are supplied where the original is cropped or effaced. NYPL Whitney MS 1 is reproduced with permission.

21. MS *Aires*, see note 2.

22. Medieval recipes were not as specific about amounts of ingredients and cooking times as we would like. For a recipe for frumenty adapted for modern use, see Hieatt et al., *Pleyn Delit: Medieval Cookery for Modern Cooks* (Toronto: U of Toronto, 1996), number 47. The recipes in Hieatt, *Ordinance*, are given in both Middle English and adapted modern English versions; for frumenty, see p. 40 (ME) and 129 (modern adaptation).

23. Hieatt and Butler, *Curye on Inglysch*, 59-79. The title of this collection has been given variously as *Universa Servisa* in Laurel Braswell, *A Handlist of Douce Manuscripts containing Middle English Prose in the Bodleian Library, Oxford, The Index of Middle English Prose*, gen. ed. A. S. G. Edwards, vol. 4 (Cambridge: D.S. Brewer, 1987), 51; *Diuersa Servisa* in Keiser, *Works of Science*, 3888; and *Diuersa Servicia* in Hieatt & Butler, 62. The MS incipit (Douce 257, f. 86) reads "hic incipiunt diuersa seruicia tam de carnibus quam de pissibus." The *Diuersa Seruicia* (or *Diversa Servicia*) had earlier been edited by Samuel Pegge as "Ancient Cookery" in an addendum to his edition of *The Forme of Cury* (London: Society of Antiquaries, 1780), 91-122.

24. London, British Library, Sloane MS 1108 also has a comparable sampling, with *Diversa Servicia* recipes 1-2, 5, 7, 10-14, 16-19, 22, 25, 29, 32 (variant), 46, 60-62, 64-65 and 67 (see Hieatt, *A Gathering of Medieval English Recipes* [Turnhout: Brepols, 2008], 99-101).

25. Hieatt and Butler, *Curye on Inglysch*, 62; cf. *Forme of Cury* recipes 151 and 152, ed. Hieatt and Butler, pp. 131-32.

26. The final recipe is mislabelled "Tench in cyue," that is, tench (a fish) in onion sauce (a recipe for which appears in *The Forme of Cury*, number 123, ed. Hieatt and Butler, *Curye on Inglysch*, p. 126). But the text of the recipe (in which the creature is cooked in its shell), as well as comparison with *Diversa Servicia* recipe number 75 (Hieatt and Butler, p. 76), shows that lobster is intended (Hieatt *Gathering*, 133 n4 suggests "crab"; failing to recognize the Whitney recipe as a version of *Diversa Servicia* number 75).

27. Hieatt & Butler, 76.

28. The Whitney MS contains Hieatt and Butler recipes 2 (occurs after *Diversa Servicia* number 69, not noticed by Hieatt and Butler, *Curye on Inglysch*, but corrected in Hieatt *Gathering*, 133), 3-26, 60 (occurs after number 6), 61 (occurs after number 11, not noticed by Hieatt and Butler, but corrected in Hieatt *Gathering*, 133), 63 (occurs after number 13), 64 (occurs after

number 14), 65-69 and 74-75 (75 not noticed by Hieatt and Butler, noticed but not identified as number 75 in Hieatt *Gathering*, 133) for a total of 36 recipes from the *Diversa Servicia* collection (see Hieatt and Butler's table on pp. 59-61, to which the Whitney MS should be added as a witness for *Diversa Servicia* recipes 2, Pise of Almayne; 61, Rapy; and 75, Lopister). See also the list of headings from this part of the Whitney MS in Hieatt, *Gathering*, 133.

29. See Hieatt & Butler 86, *Saunc Sarazine*.

30. Textually this recipe is nearly identical with one from a different collection edited by Hieatt and Butler as *Utilis Coquinario* (number 16, p. 86). There is also a recipe for *Sawse Sarzyne* in *The Forme of Cury* (Hieatt number 86, p. 117, skipped in the Whitney MS) which adds rose hips. Hieatt (*Gathering*, 132) found the Whitney heading "samfarayn" puzzling (which it is), and was thus unable to identify this sauce.

31. Hieatt and Butler, p. 64.

32. Hieatt and Butler number 60, p. 74. The Whitney MS had also recorded a recipe for *Egredouce* (for rabbit or goat) in its *Forme of Cury* section, f. 2v (Hieatt number 23, pp. 102-03).

33. *Sic*, not *Egre* as Hieatt transcribes (*Gathering*, 133), but doubtless a corruption of *Egre(douce)*.

34. Comparing extant Middle English culinary recipes has now been made considerably easier by the publication of Constance B. Hieatt, et al., *Concordance of English Recipes: Thirteenth through fifteenth Centuries* (Tempe: Arizona Center for Medieval and Renaissance Studies, 2006). These previously unedited Whitney recipes are not indexed there but comparable published recipes can be sought out under their lemmata, e.g. Flaun in Lent for the first Whitney appended recipe. The recipes subsequently edited in Hieatt *Gathering* are concorded on pp. 155-170. These include the appended Whitney recipes and those from Sloane 1108.

35. *A Gathering of Medieval English Recipes* (Turnhout: Brepols, 2008).

36. Hieatt & Butler, *Diversa Servicia*, number 86, p. 78. The recipe in Douce 257 is related to one in BL Harley 5401, ed. Constance B. Hieatt, "The Middle English Culinary Recipes in MS Harley 5401," *Medium Ævum* 65 (1996): 54-71, number 12, p. 58.

37. Number 41, p. 46 in Thomas Austin, ed., *Two Fifteenth-Century Cookery Books*, Early English Text Society, o.s. 91 (London: Trübner, 1888).

38. Hieatt, *Gathering*, p. 100.
39. Hieatt and Butler, p. 71.
40. Hieatt and Butler, p. 110.
41. Hieatt, *Gathering*, 134 mistranscribes *licour* for MS *liuoure*, obscuring the particular nature of this dish. *Forme of Cury* number 97 (Hieatt and Butler, p. 119), *Gynggaudy*, combines fish with their livers and stomachs but places them in green-colored gelatin. Cf. also "Haddok yn gyve" (Hieatt, *Ordinance*, number 176, p. 101), which adds the liver and pouch but serves the fish on a charger. For other fish tarts, see below under Whitney appended recipe 4.
42. Hieatt and Butler *Diversa Servicia* number 9, p. 63.
43. There are also longer versions of hares in talbots in *Forme of Cury* number 25 (Hieatt and Butler, p. 103) and *Ordinance of Pottage* number 31 (Hieatt, *Ordinance*, p. 46).
44. Hieatt & Butler, p. 63: al þe blod.
45. Hieatt *Gathering*, 100.
46. Hieatt suggests that the onions, while not specified, might be inferred from the preceding recipe, *Tench de cyve*.
47. On f. 15, the scribe started to write *Ta[rt]* at the bottom of the page. The heading on 15v is not clearly legible, but Hieatt, *Gathering*, 132 reads "Tart permusan," and compares a similar, unpublished recipe heading from Oxford, Corpus Christi College MS 291. I consulted this manuscript, and on its table of contents, f. 2, recipe number 14 reads "Tart*is* permusoun" (or per-nísou*n*?). At the bottom of f. 12v the scribe has written "Tartis p*er* muson," but unfortunately a page has been ripped out (as Hieatt notes) and only the end of the recipe remains: "... hem & colour hem bake hem & ȝeue foryȝ."
48. Number 178, Hieatt and Butler, p. 138.
49. Thomas Austin, ed., *Two Fifteenth-Century Cookery Books*, Early English Text Society, o.s. 91 (London: Trübner, 1888). no. vj, pp. 47-48.
50. Austin, p. 98.
51. Hieatt, *Gathering*, 98.

A Record Identifying Thomas Hoccleve's Father

ESTELLE STUBBS AND LINNE MOONEY

Until now, nothing has been known of the origins of Thomas Hoccleve, poet and clerk of the Office of the Privy Seal from 1387 to 1426. None of his biographers has much to say about his origins, and his most recent biographer, John Burrow, sums up our ignorance as follows:

> There are no references in his poetry, or naturally enough, in the documents to his origins, his childhood, or his youth. The surname perhaps points to his—or his family's—origin in the village of Hoccliffe, Bedfordshire.[1] His own language, as displayed in the three manuscripts of his poems that he himself copied, belongs to an early fifteenth-century type of London English, which is consistent with what we know of his adult life; but this does not rule out the possibility that he was born and brought up at Hockliffe, some fifty miles north-west of London.[2] Nothing is known of his family.[1]

However, with so many records of medieval deeds now searchable through online databases, we have found a record that might offer our first clues to his parentage. Records of the ownership of a property on Ironmonger Lane show that Thomas Hoccleve was the son of William Hoccleve ("Occlyf"), citizen and Draper of London.[2] This is very likely to be the poet since "Occlyf" or "Hocclyff" was an uncommon surname and because the spelling "Occlyff" or "Occlyf" was a common variant for the poet's surname in documents relating to him, particularly those dated to this period, between 1401 and 1409: in this period the documents of Burrow's appendix spell his surname without initial **H** "Occlyve," "Occlive," "Occlyf," "Occlyffe," "Occleve," "Occliffe" in 14 out of 21 instances.³

The property in question was a small shop with solars above it, designated parcel 6 of the property recorded as St Martin Pomary 95; together with parcel 7 it occupied land that is now numbers 16 to 19 Ironmonger Lane. The lane lay in the parish of St. Martin Pomary, in the Cheap Ward, and this property would be on the west side of Ironmonger Lane in the first block north of Cheapside. Across the street would be the portion of the Hospital of St. Thomas of Acon that by 1403 was leased to the Mercers' Company for their hall.⁴ Parcel 6 was purchased in 1380 by Maud Holbech (widow of William Holbech, d. 1365-7) and her second husband Hugh Southern, who were occupying the property already at the time of the purchase. The record then reads,

> Maud died in 1392-3 and left these properties to Thomas son of William Occlyf, formerly citizen and draper, for the term of his life and then to be sold. In 1408 Thomas surrendered the properties to Maud's executors, who included Stephen Speleman and in 1415 sold 6 to Henry Halton, citizen and grocer. 6 was now described as a shop with solar(s) over measuring 10 1/2 ft. (3.2 m.) next to the street, 10 ft. (3.05 m.) at its W. end, 14 ft. 3 in. (4.34 m.) on its S. side and 14 ft. 2 in. (4.32 m.) on its N. side.⁵

This little record of a property left to Thomas Hoccleve for use during his lifetime is intriguing because it names no connection between Maud Holbech and Thomas Hoccleve: was there some tie of blood between them or was their relationship simply a business transaction? That is, the Hustings record does not explain either that Thomas was related to Maud, or had some claim on the property, or paid for its use. If merely a business transaction, Hoccleve would have paid Maud during her lifetime or her executors after her death for the use of this property after her death for the period of his own life thereafter. Perhaps Hoccleve as a young clerk was investing in London property for rental income. It seems unlikely that he would have made this transaction to put a roof over his own head, since in 1392 he lived with the other bachelor clerks of the Office of the Privy Seal in Clifford's Inn.

The year 1408 when he surrendered the property to Maud's executors instead of continuing to hold it for life was around the time when we presume he must have married, so this would be precisely when he *would* need to provide a home for himself and his wife. Burrow notes that "[the] marriage evidently took place some time between 1399 and 1411 (the date of the *Regiment*)."[6] We know that he was unmarried in 1399 because the annuity he received from Henry IV in that year was granted for life or until Henry should promote him to an ecclesiastical benefice with income of £20 per year (*"ad terminum vite ipsius Thome, vel quousque ipse ad beneficium ecclesiasticum sine cura valoris viginti librarum per annum per nos fuerit promotus"*).[7] He could not be expected to be promoted to such an ecclesiastical benefice if not in major orders (the priesthood), and could not be a priest if married. Burrow marks the date of the *Regiment* as the *terminus ad quem* for the marriage because Hoccleve there says that he has married, having waited long for a benefice and not received one (lines 1447-56).[8] In fact the second granting of an annuity, in 1409, should mark the *terminus ad quem* since this second grant raising his annuity does not offer the alternative of his being promoted to an ecclesiastical benefice, stating that he is simply to receive it throughout his life (*"durante vita sua"*).[9] It is possible, then, that he sold his holding in Ironmonger Lane back to Maud's executors in 1408 in order to raise money for his marriage or for the purchase of a house for his own habitation.

While it still holds such mysteries for us, this little record of a property transaction *does* tell us one important fact: it gives us a likely parentage for Thomas Hoccleve, that is, that he was born of a London citizen, William Hoccleve, and one who was a member of one of the city's wealthiest and most prestigious livery companies, the Drapers. Since the companies did not begin to keep lists of their members until the 1390s, we would not have known of William Hoccleve, or "Occlyff," except through deeds and other

City documents like Maud's will of 1392. This document of 1392 indicates that by that time William had apparently died: he was *formerly* citizen and draper.

We know that Hoccleve had already entered into service in the Office of the Privy Seal by 1387, at least five years before the date of this document: why had he not followed his father into the City?[10] Perhaps his clerical inclination had been recognized early: we know of Hoccleve's early interest in books from Guy de Rouclyf's having left him a book on the Trojan War in his will of 1392,[11] and Burrow remarks that the bequest "suggests that he [Hoccleve] was already known there [in the Office of the Privy Seal] as something of a reading man."[12]

It is something to know that Thomas Hoccleve had in fact been a Londoner all his life: his father would almost certainly have been born a Londoner to have been a freeman of the City and a member of the Drapers' Company, so the family must have migrated to the capital from Hoccliffe, Bedfordshire, before the poet Hoccleve was born.

NOTES

1. J. A. Burrow, *Thomas Hoccleve*, Authors of the Middle Ages series, 4; English Writers of the Late Middle Ages series (Aldershot, Hants: Variorum/Ashgate Publishing, 1994), 1-2. Burrow's notes refer to the introduction to F. J. Furnivall, ed., *Hoccleve's Works, Vol. I: The Minor Poems in the Phillipps MS. 8151 (Cheltenham) and the Durham MS. III.9*, EETS, e.s. 61 (1892), li-lxx and vii-viii respectively.

2. *Historical Gazeteer of London before the Great Fire: Cheapside: Parishes of All Hallows Honey Lane, St Martin Pomery, St Mary le Bow, St Mary Colechurch, and St Pancras Soper Lane*, ed. D. J. Keene and Vanessa Harding (London: Institute for Historical Research, 1987), 150-59, as accessed through *British History Online*, URL: http://www.british-history.ac.uk; the description of transactions regarding this property are drawn from the following original sources: Hustings Rolls 63(176), 90(13), 93(106), 95(99), 96(209), 115(40), 122(22), 143(33); GL [Guildhall Library], MS 25121/1766; *Cal SPMR 1381-1412*, [*Calendar of the Plea and Memoranda Rolls*] pp. 126-7.

3. Burrow, *Thomas Hoccleve*, Appendix, pp. 33-49, documents 10, 12, 13, 16,

17, 19, 20, 23, 24, 25, 26, 27, 29, 30 on pp. 36-40, with a smattering of later instances in which it is spelled similarly, without the initial **H**, documents 34 in 1412, 39 and 40 in 1415, 53 in 1420, 60 in 1423, and 67 in 1425(?), on pp. 41-49.

4. See Linne R. Mooney, "Chaucer's Scribe," *Speculum* 81 (2006), 109-10 and n. 50.

5. *Historical Gazeteer*, as n. 2 above.

6. Burrow, *Thomas Hoccleve*, 12.

7. Burrow, *Thomas Hoccleve*, Appendix, 34, document 6.

8. These line references from the edition of Frederick J. Furnivall, *Hoccleve's Works, Vol. III: The Regiment of Princes A.D. 1411-12 from the Harleian MS. 4866, and Fourteen of Hoccleve's Minor Poems from the Egerton MS. 615*, EETS, e.s. 72 (1897).

9. Burrow, *Thomas Hoccleve*, Appendix, 39-40, document 28, quoted from p. 40.

10. Burrow, *Thomas Hoccleve*, 2.

11. Burrow, *Thomas Hoccleve*, 9 and Appendix, 33, document 3.

12. Burrow, *Thomas Hoccleve*, 9.

Lord Rivers and Oxford, Bodleian Library, Ms Bodley 264: A *Speculum* for the Prince of Wales?

OMAR KHALAF

The purpose of this essay is to shed light on the possible use of Oxford, Bodleian Library MS Bodley 264 in a rather obscure period of its life. A new hypothesis is here proposed: it involves Anthony Woodville, second Earl Rivers (*c.* 1440 to 1483) and the role of the codex in the education of his nephew, Edward IV's son and the future Edward V. MS Bodley 264 is famous among scholars of medieval French literature and philology as it contains one of the most valuable recensions of the *Roman d'Alexandre*; yet it is also notable for the presence of the only extant copy of the Middle English alliterative poem known as *Alexander and Dindimus*. The manuscript results from the bringing together of three distinct units: the first is a collection of French poems on the gests of Alexander the Great, among which the *Roman* is the most famous; the second is represented by *Alexander and Dindimus*,[1] while the last contains a French re-elaboration of Marco Polo's *Milione*, known as *Livre du Grant Caam*.[2] A note on fol. 208r reveals that the core of the manuscript, represented by the *Roman* group, is dated to 1338. *Alexander and Dindimus* and *Caam* are later interpolations. Originally, the English poem was conceived as an independent unit: transmitted in a single *quaternio* (fols. 209r-216v), it is datable on linguistic grounds to the fifteenth century.

Alexander and Dindimus deals with the epistolary exchange between

Alexander the Great and Dindimus, king of the Indian people called Bragmans. The two sovereigns allegorically embody the conflict between two cultural models: Alexander's, materialistic and aimed at earthly power, and Dindimus's, ascetic and spiritual. The story is the following: in his campaign to the East, Alexander enters the easternmost regions of India. His first encounter is with the Gymnosophists (here incorrectly called Bragmans), who live in poverty and meditation. Alexander decides to spare them and claims that he would fulfill anything they desire: they demand eternal life, the only thing Alexander cannot grant even for himself; they ask him why he desires to submit the whole peoples of the world, since life is so short. Alexander answers that he must accomplish the fate gods have planned for him and continues his journey. At the bank of the river Phison, impossible to wade except on certain months of the year, Alexander sees some men on the opposite side and sends a message to their king Dindimus. Here, a long epistle exchange between the two takes place. In the first letter, Alexander asks Dindimus to tell him about his customs, as his people are known all over the world for their wisdom. Dindimus answers that they do not farm, hunt or fish; they do not use fire, they live in caves and they die at an indefinite age. They do not wear any clothes and their women do not use make-up to appear fairer. They always tell the truth, and have never threatened anybody or fought with any people. By contrast, he accuses Alexander of being wicked and a liar and strongly condemns his cruel exercise of power, his love for war and his faith in false gods. Finally, he gives the major classic divinities typically earthly faults, like greed, lust and falsehood. Alexander claims that Dindimus has no right to criticize his behavior and way of life since his is so miserable. According to the Macedonian, his people live like animals and ignore earthly joys. Dindimus answers that human life is nothing but a passage and that Alexander's deeds do not increase God's glory, but his own pride. He cannot drink the gold he continually longs for, and the Bragmans behave more wisely than he because they trample on it as on any other kind of stone. Dindimus goes on reproaching Alexander, telling him that he does not realize he lives in error, and that he is doing a favor to him in showing his mistakes. Alexander closes the exchange answering that they live in an island in the middle of a river like prisoners: in this way, God decreed for them a miserable life.

After this, he erects a white marble pillar as the extreme boundary of his empire, and comes back with his troops. The debate between Alexander and Dindimus has no winners. The latter does not manage to change the former's mind and convince him to modify his way of life; on the other hand, Alexander abandons the idea of invading the land of the Gymnosophists. The suspension of either implicit or explicit moral judgment urges the reader to make a synthesis between the two models proposed in the poem, drawing the best from each of them.

As Skeat[3] and Magoun[4] demonstrated, no redaction of the *Roman* reports the exchange between Alexander and Dindimus. Consequently, the inclusion of the English poem has been interpreted as a result of what can be considered a scribal error, on the basis of the assumption that the *Roman* contained a lacuna.[5] From a codicological point of view, *Alexander and Dindimus* and *Caam* seem to constitute a unitary entity: the copyist's hand is the same and so is the illustrator's. The copyist, taking advantage of a blank column left in the *Roman* section (fol. 67r), wrote a colophon which refers the reader to the Middle English poem.[6] This proves that the collection of texts in the codex results from conscious choices, aimed at satisfying a precise need that has been a matter of debate among scholars. Grady[7] states that the structure of the codex is to be intended as a vernacular imitation of an anthology of Latin texts, whose presence in England is witnessed by a number of manuscripts containing Julius Valerius's *Epitome*, the *Collatio Alexandri cum Dindimo* and the *Epistola Alexandri ad Aristotelem*. Apart from some doubts that a potential interchangeability between *Caam* and the *Epistola* can arise,[8] if the interpolator had planned to imitate the order of the Latin texts—each independent of the others—the colophon that invites the reader to stop to read the pseudo-*Epitome*, to switch to the pseudo-*Collatio*, and then to come back to that point would not be comprehensible. Another interpretation of the anthology has been given by Evans, who describes Bodley 264 as one of the clearest examples of *compilatio*, i.e., the process of arranging different literary materials in a manuscript.[9] In this case, it has cohesive purposes and determines a final effect of unity among the parts, but it cannot account for the reasons that urged the compiler to modify the structure of the manuscript.

The history of the codex, as reconstructed from the signatures and the notes of possession found within it, reveals that it formed part of the libraries of important personages of fifteenth- and sixteenth-century England.[10] Peculiarly significant is the period when it was in the hands of the Woodville family,[11] after its purchase by Richard, the first Lord Rivers, and particular attention will be paid to the function this manuscript might have had during that particular moment of its life.[12]

It is not easy to determine whether the codex came into Richard's possession in its ultimate form or without *Alexander and Dindimus* and *Caam*. Nevertheless, the evidence at this point suggests that the interpolation can hardly be subsequent to the Woodvilles' ownership.[13] According to the two editors of *Alexander and Dindimus*,[14] the poem was originally composed in the fourteenth century, even though several specific phonological and morphological tracts reveal a fifteenth-century superstrate, due to the copyist's activity. Moreover, the possession note on the flyleaf placed at the end of the codex suggests that the Woodvilles owned it complete, with *Alexander and Dindimus* and *Caam* inserted into the present binding. The actual use of the manuscript by any other specific member of the family has never been considered or verified; yet the first line of a hardly readable inscription on fol. 274r seems to provide the proof that it passed into the hands of another notable member of the Woodvilles: Anthony, Richard's first-born and second Lord Rivers. It reports the name "ARiverys," written in a chancery hand typical of the second half of the fifteenth century. The initial represents a rather peculiar capital "R" which seems to be merged with a capital "A," forming a sort of monogram indicating Rivers' name. This can be related to the one found in a signature in London, British Library, MS Harley 80, fol. 59r (see Appendix, plate 3) and in the possession note on fol. 1r of London, British Library, MS Harley 4431, a manuscript containing several works by Christine de Pisan and supposed to be written by Christine herself.[15] The prestige of Bodley 264 is intimately related to the power reached by the Woodvilles: its possession symbolized the acquisition of a new social and political role, which began with Richard's marriage with Jacquetta of Luxemburg, and reached its apex in the following generation, with Anthony and his sister Elizabeth. Moreover, the literary inclinations developed by Anthony during his lifetime and his role in the Prince of Wales's education corroborate the hypothesis that the codex was actually part of his library. Anthony succeeded his father and also succeeded in keeping all the titles and privileges granted to the family, despite the temporary breakdown of the Yorkist party which Richard supported. He married Elizabeth, heir of the Baron of Scales, and in 1473 he was appointed Governor to the Prince of Wales's household. After his wife's death, he also became a member of Parliament as Baron of Scales. When Edward IV died in 1483, he was charged with taking his nephew, the future Edward V, to London. Along the way, he fell victim to a plot organized by the Duke of Gloucester—the future Richard III—who imprisoned him and had him executed in Pomfret (or Pontefract) Castle in June of that year.

Renowned as a model of moral and chivalric virtues, Rivers held many eminent offices: he was ambassador to France and Rome, and Governor of the Isle of Wight. He followed Edward IV into exile to the Low Countries and eventually participated in his successful attempt to regain power. He reached the height of his prestige when appointed Lord Protector to the Prince of Wales.[16] Ethics was a central aspect of his literary work:[17] the translations Rivers made in those years and which were printed by Caxton—the *Dicts and Sayings of the Philosophres*, the *Cordyale*, and Christine de Pisan's *Moral Proverbs*[18] and *Livre du Corps de Policie*[19]—aimed at satisfying the need to offer the young prince a range of texts written in his native language and dealing with edifying and moral concepts on which Anthony could base his educational program.[20]

In addition to this, it is probable that Rivers used some material already present in his family library: this may have been the case of Bodley 264, whose characteristics could fit his needs very well. The aesthetic value of the manuscript could justify its introduction into the court and the themes contained in the texts—especially in the Middle English poem—match some of the key concepts on which Rivers founded his educational program. The search for the right balance between morality and glory which characterizes *Alexander and Dindimus* would undoubtedly be an interesting argument for anybody in charge of educating a future king to govern wisely and rightfully. If seen in this light, the ultimate structure of the manuscript can be matched—at least as far as the *Roman* and *Alexander and Dindimus* are concerned—to a mirror for princes.[21] A thematic parallelism can be established between Rivers' translation of Christine de Pisan's *Livre de Corps de Policie* and *Alexander and Dindimus*. In fact, the two kings' debate matches most of the topics discussed in first part of the *Livre*, such as the ruler's virtue[22] (and, mostly, the balance between it and the search for glory)[23] and good governance.[24] Moreover, the second part of the *Livre* gives instructions for the good exercise of knighthood, which can be seen valuably applied in Alexander's chivalric adventures narrated in the *Roman* group of Bodley 264. In the light of this evidence, it is possible to suppose that Anthony, aware of Alexander's role in the tradition of the *exempla*, probably wanted to improve the prince's consciousness on the exercise of power by adding to a text that can be considered "technical" as the *Livre* is, a literary product which is more engaging from the point of view of narrative structure, but likewise pregnant with didacticism like the Bodley anthology. The use of poetry for the transmission of certain messages should not be considered strange or irrelevant to the literature of the *speculum principum*, which escapes any attempt of definition or classification: as Genet states, "political theory [...] is found in nearly all forms of literary work."[25] In the Bodley anthology, Rivers found merged all the most important characteristics of a ruler: his courage on battlefields (like Alexander in the *Roman*), but also his moral rectitude and piety (like Alexander in the English poem). The figure of Anthony himself matched this ideal: he was brave in battle—many sources remember the joust won against the Bastard of Burgundy and the extravagance of his garb—but at the same time pious and devout: he goes on pilgrimage to Santiago de Compostela in 1473; he is titled by the Pope "defenseur du siège apostolique," and on the day of his execution, he is told to wear a hair shirt under his luxurious clothes.[26]

In light of these considerations, then, it is possible to consider Bodley 264 a compilation of texts that could be used for the education of the future sovereign. They concentrate on one exemplary king of the past, and mixing up adventures and moral reflection, use the formula of entertainment to convey edifying messages. In fact, the content of the manuscript answers coherently to what Edward IV requested for the education of his son. The texts contained in the Bodley anthology can be considered "suche noble stories as behoveth a prince to understand and knowe," and particularly in the case of the Middle English poem, they are able to lead to right and virtuous conversations, for which Anthony Rivers can be considered undoubtedly one of the fittest men of his times.

Ca' Foscari University Of Venice

APPENDIX

Here, the inscriptions of Anthony Rivers found in his manuscripts are shown. They show the initial monogram "AR" in different styles.

Oxford, Bodleian Library, MS Bodley 264, fol. 274r: the first graphic element of the inscription is a typical chancery capital "A" bound with the "R" of "Ryverys." By kind permission of the Bodleian Library.

© The British Library Board. London, British Library, MS Harley 4431, fol. 1r: the capital inscription clearly shows the "AR" monogram used by Anthony Rivers.

Reproduction of the signature in a charter found in London, British Library, MS Harley 80: similarly to the Bodley inscription, this signature shows the "AR" monogram, with the "A" used as ornamental element.[27]

NOTES

1. The traditional title given by the first editors of the poem, *Alexander B*, is due to the hypothesis that this text was part, together with the so-called *Alexander A* (or *The Romance of Alisauder*), of a longer alliterative poem on the gests of Alexander of Macedon. Cf. M. Trautmann, *Über Verfasser und Entstehungszeit einiger alliterirender Gedichte des Altenglischen* (Halle, 1876), 18-19; W. W. Skeat, *Alexander and Dindimus, or the Letters of Alexander to Dindimus* (Early English Text Society Extra Series 31, Milford: Oxford University Press, 1863), xi-xii; F. P. Magoun, *The Gests of King Alexander of Macedon: with introduction, notes, appendices and index* (Cambridge: Harvard University Press, 1929), 113; T. Turville-Petre, *The Alliterative Revival* (Cambridge:, Boydell & Brewer, 1978), 31. This paper does not intend to give a definitive answer to this question; however, since the topic of the discussion will be the relationship of this text with its codicological environment, I think it is preferable to consider it a single poem and to refer to it as *Alexander and Dindimus*.
2. An investigation of the codex, with special reference to illuminations, is found in K. Scott, *Later Gothic Manuscripts 1390 – 1490. II, Catalogue and Indexes*, (Turnhout: Harvey Miller Publishers, 1996).
3. Skeat, ix.
4. Magoun, 13.

5. However, the choice to insert the English poem in that specific point of the *Roman* might find a simple explanation: that section of the French poem deals with Alexander's adventures in India and his encounter with marvellous things. The chapter ends with the story of four old Indian men who tell Alexander of three miraculous springs with the power to rejuvenate, make men live forever and make them come back from the dead. Probably, the episode's setting and the figures of the four old wise men inspired the interpolator to insert Alexander and Dindimus just at this point.

6. "Here fayleth a prossesse of þis romance of Alixandre, þe which prossesse þat fayleth e schulle fynde at þe ende of þis bok ywrete in Engelyche ryme; and whanne ȝe han radde it to þe ende, turneþ hedur aȝen and turneþ ovyr þis lef and bygynneþ at þis reson, 'Che fu el mois de May que li tans renovele'; and rede forþ þe romance to þe ende whylis þe Frenche lasteþ." Cf. Scott, 69.

7. F. Grady, "Contextualizing Alexander and Dindimus," *The Yearbook of Langland Studies* 18 (2004), 81-106.

8. Moreover, the Middle English recension of the *Epistola* contained in Worcester, Cathedral Library MS F.175, edited by V. DiMarco & L. Perelman, *The Middle English Letter of Alexander to Aristotle* (Amsterdam: Rodopi, 1978), witnesses that the Latin text still circulated in medieval England. In my opinion, this fact makes the hypothesis of substitution advanced by Grady unlikely.

9. M. J. Evans, *Rereading Middle English Romance: Manuscript Layout, Decoration, and the Rhetoric of Composite Structure* (Montreal: McGill-Queen's University Press, 1995), 5-7.

10. Cf. P. Meyer, "Étude sur les manuscrits du Roman d'Alexandre," *Romania* 11 (1882), 290-301.

11. The events related to the origin, the social rise and the sudden decline, as well as the dubious morality of the Woodvilles have been object of contrasting judgments both in the past as well as recently. In particular, Anthony has always been the object of particular attention; starting with Thomas More, *The History of King Richard the Third* (Bloomington:, Indiana University Press, 2005) and Shakespeare in the tragedy *Richard III*, which characterize him as a positive figure, up to P. M. Kendall, *Richard III: The Great Debate* (New York: Norton, 1965), who distinguishes Anthony's piety and moral value against the excessive ambition of the rest of the Woodvilles. On the

other hand, G. Richardson, *The Popinjays* (Ripponden: Pennine, 2000), 92, in his invective against this family, defines Anthony as "a mass of contradiction," who could hardly balance his ascetism and courtly life. The climax of the family's road to power was reached with the wedding between Richard and Jacquetta of Luxemburgh, in 1462, when King Edward IV married Elizabeth, Richard's daughter. Anthony was the one who most enjoyed the results, but only for a short time. In fact, he became the Governor of the household of the Prince of Wales, the future Edward V, until the coup of the dead king's brother, the Duke of Gloucester, who would execute Anthony, imprison the nephews and rise to the throne with the name of Richard III.

12. The Woodvilles' ownership is recorded in a note on fol. 274r: "Cest livre est a monseignour Richart de Widevielle, seignour de Rivieres, ung des compaignons de le tres noble ordre de la jartiere, et ledist seigneur acetast ledist livre l'an de grace mille .ccclxvi., le premier jour de l'an a Londres, et le v an de la coronation de tres victorieux roy Eduard quart de che non, et le second de la coronation de tres vertueuse royne Elyzabeth, l'endemain du jour de sainct More."

13. K. Harris, "Patrons, Buyers and Owners: the Evidence for Ownership and the Rôle of Book Owners in Book Production and the Book Trade," in J. Griffiths and D. Pearsall eds., *Book Production and Publishing in Britain 1375-1475* (Cambridge: Cambridge University Press, 1989, 163-199), 175, suggests that the addition was made before Richard's purchase in 1466, on the basis of Scott's analysis of the illustrations of the poem, made by a hand "more typical of the late 14th than of the early 15th century" (Scott, 70).

14. Skeat, 26; Magoun, 94.

15. For a comparison of the three inscriptions, see Appendix, plate 1.

16. The instructions Edward IV gave him regarding the education of the prince were recorded in the seventeenth century in British Library, MS Sloane 3479, on fol. 53v: "no man sitt at his bord, but suche as shalbee thought by the discrecion of the saide Erle Riviers. And that then bee read before him suche noble stories, as behoveth a Prince to understand, and knowe, and that the communycacions, at all tymes in his presens, bee of vertue, honour, connynge, wisdome, and dedys of worship, and of no thinge that should move or stere him to vices." M. Kekewich, "Edward IV, William Caxton, and Literary Patronage in Yorkist England," *The Modern Language*

Review 3, 1971, 481-487, 486.

17. Caxton himself, in his epilogue to the *Cordyale*, writes about him: "he semeth that he conceiveth wel the mutabilite and the unstablenes of this present lyf, and that he desireth with a greet zele and spirituell love, our goostlye help and perpetuel salvacion, and that we shal abhorre and utterly forsake thabominable and dampnable synnes, which comunely be used now a dayes; as pride, perjurye, terrible swering, thefte, murdre, and many other." W. J. B. Crotch, *The Prologues and Epilogues of William Caxton* (Early English Text Society Series 176, London:, Oxford University Press, 1928), 39.

18. Cf. Crotch.

19. Cf. D. Bornstein, *The Middle English Translation of Christine de Pisan's Livre du Corps de Policie* (Heidelberg:, Winter, 1977), 31-36.

20. In fact, in the dedicatory preface to the only extant witness of the *Dictes*—London, Lambeth Palace Library MS 265, dated back to 29th December 1477—Rivers states that the aim of his translation was the education of his pupil (Kekewich, 486). Moreover, in the epilogue to the *Cordyale*, Caxton lists these three texts as part of the didactic material used by Anthony for his nephew's education. See S. Bentley, *Excerpta Historica: or, Illustrations of the English History* (London:, Bentley, 1831), 245. Such attention to the ethics of power is characteristic of medieval political thought: John of Salisbury's *Policraticus*, for instance, gives ample space to this matter. However, the concern with morality as related to the exercise of power saw a great development in the fifteenth century thanks to Italian humanism, whose attention to moral philosophy and ethics surely influenced the concept of kingship from the beginning of the century. See J. Canning, *A History of Medieval Political Thought, 300-1450* (London and New York:, Routledge, 2005), 114; 185.

21. Many moralizing texts written in other cultural areas such as Germany, France and Italy testify to a broad use of Alexander as exemplary figure related to the concept of liberality which lasts until Renaissance. See G. Cary, *The Medieval Alexander* (Cambridge: Cambridge University Press, 1956) 260; 272; 358-368. In relation specifically to literary tradition in medieval England, starting from Latin texts like John of Salisbury's *Policraticus* (1159 ca.) and Gerald of Wales' *De Instructione Principis* (1220 ca.), Alexander is presented as a model of royal virtue worthy to be imitated (Cary, 108; 158-160). Chronologically nearer to Anthony and Edward V, also Thomas Hoc-

cleve's *Regement of Princes* (1410 ca.) resorts to episodes related to Alexander for didactic purposes (vv. 2300-2338). Thomas Hoccleve, *The Regiment of Princes*, Kalamazoo, Medieval Institute Publications, 1999, http://www.lib.rochester.edu/camelot/teams/hoccfrm.htm (21 December 2010).

22. Chapters II, "Here after it [the chapter] speketh of vertuous felicite"; XV, "Of the humayne pite of a prynce"; XVI, "Of the mekenesse and debonerte in a prynce"; XVIII, "Houghe a prynce shulde not be proude thoughe fortune favoureth him neuer so moche"; XIX, "Houghe the good prynce ought to loue iustyce"; XXVI, "Howe it longeth to a prince to be wise and prudente in eloquence"; XXVIII, "Houghe it is a conuenabill thyng to a prynce to behaue himselfe goodly"; XXX, "How the good prynce ought to fle lecherye"; XXXI, "Howe the good prince shulde kepe himself frome angre."

23. Chapter XXXIII, "Howe the good prince whiche undirstondith hymself that he dothe his devoire in all vertues ought resonablye desire the lawde and glorie."

24. Chapters VIII, "Of the observaunces and the lawe that a good prynce ought to holde"; IX, "Houghe a good prynce ought to be resembled to a good shepherde"; X "Yet of the same"; XI "The loue that the good prince ought to haue to his subiectys"; XXI, "Houghe a good prynce notwithstondyng that he be debenoir and meke ought to be dradde and doubted"; XXVIII, "Houghe euery good prynce ought to be diligent to occupie himself in the necessiteis of his londe or realme."

25. J.-P. Genet, *Four English Political Tracts of the Later Middle Ages* (London: Offices of the Royal Historical Society, University College London, 1977), vii.

26. Cf. *inter alios* Bentley, 244-5 and Richardson, 9.

27. Bentley, 242.

Manuscripts of "A Prince out of the North"

NICOLE CLIFTON

"A Prince [or "A King"] out of the North shall come" is a fifty-line verse prophecy about James I and VI, which survives in seventeen manuscripts. Until recently, it was misunderstood as a medieval work, in part because most manuscripts attribute it to Merlin. *A Manual of the Writings in Middle English* includes these lines among "Unpublished Merlin Prophecies," although in fact they were published by Hales and Furnivall in 1868.[1] The original *Index of Middle English Verse* and *New Index of Middle English Verse* both included "A Prince."[2] The electronic *iMEV*, however, remedies past errors by omitting this early modern piece.[3] Topical references and manuscript contexts both fix "A Prince" firmly in the 1620s, with some antiquarians collecting or copying it later in the seventeenth century.

Alastair Bellany and Andrew McRae include this prophecy in *Early Stuart Libels*, where they discuss it as a response to the Spanish Match (the proposed union between Prince Charles and the Infanta of Spain).[4] *Early Stuart Libels* and the *Union First Line Index of English Verse*[5] between them list fifteen copies of "A Prince" held in five libraries. To these, I can add two more: Washington, DC, Folger MS L.b. 670, a single sheet in the hand of George More,[6] and Cambridge, Cambridge University Library MS Ee.V.36, a small manuscript volume that collects several pages of prophecies.[7] The More manuscript appears in the Folger's card file of first lines. Its omission from the *Union First Line Index* is surely an oversight. The Cambridge

University Library manuscript, however, appears to have gone unnoticed by collectors of verse libels.

Bellany and McRae note that "A Prince" had "an uncertain status in manuscript culture" and consider that some of its readers, like John Rous, "took the poem seriously as prophecy," rather than treating it as a political libel.[8] The seventeen manuscripts containing this verse vary their placement of the poem: some accompany it with political libels, some with prophecies, and some with other popular verses, while others combine it with collections of loose sheets that may have been the original "separates" on which this and other verses circulated. The Cambridge manuscript is another that seems to take the prophecy seriously, and like John Rous, its scribe corrects it with reference to other copies.

Cambridge, CUL Ee.V.36 measures 210 x 160 mm, with a dark green marbled binding. It has forty-six numbered folios and two flyleaves. The main hand is small, neat, partly cursive italic with some secretary forms, which inscribes a variety of prophecies on the first eight folios. "A Prince" appears on folio one, with a marginal note: "fathered on Merlin but how true I know not." Below it appears a Latin prose prophecy ("Surget Rex ex natione illustrissimi Lilij"). The first eight leaves contain a variety of prophecies in English and Latin. Many have either dates in the 1620s or clear topical allusions to events of that decade. After folio 8v, the pages are blank through folio 46r. On folio 46v, a very current hand records a recipe involving fine castor sugar and flour. The page is darkened in places, as if this had been the outermost page for some time. It appears that this writer compared his collected prophecies to other versions, because on 8r, the writer indicates that two entries have been copied from others' manuscripts: John Rous and T. Greenwood.

John Rous (c.1584 to 1644), known as a diarist and Suffolk clergyman, studied "A Prince" with a scholar's care, recording it in London, British Library, Additional MS 28640, with annotations and notes on the two other copies he had seen. In his marginal notes, Rous spells out the initials CJS appearing in line 4: "Charles James Stuart" (f. 101). He also indicates variants in the text, gives additional lines from other copies, and comments on the need for changes: "this staffe is lame you see," he says of line 37 ("the seas and being past"). Rous also says "Merlin in Latin hath nothing that is like hereto," and notes, "In the beginning of Merlins prophecie which I bought, there was written this prophecie, conteining as much as both these copies & no more." This comment suggests that there may be, or may have been, a copy of Geoffrey of Monmouth's prophecies with "A Prince" copied into it.[9]

Although Matthew Steggle suggests that BL Add. 28640 was "an earlier portion of the diary," based on the contents dealing with the Spanish Match controversy,[10] some of the other contents seem to indicate a later effort to collect documents from this time, or at least that Rous left space to add further notes and commentary as it became available. Folio 100 contains two notes which Rous dates to 1622, as well as a prophecy attributed to "a plaine man" in Norwich, 1602. Following "A Prince," Rous mentions Thomas the Rimer's prophecy and on the next page gives the Lily prophecy,[11] with a note that it was printed in 1642. Rous studies prophecies seriously, not only collecting them but adding variants and commentary.

Rous matriculated at Emmanuel College, Cambridge, in 1598. If there is a Cambridge connection among Rous, the writer of CUL Ee.V.36, and "T. Greenwood," then the last may be the Thomas Greenwood who matriculated as a sizar in 1581, took a BA between 1584 and 1585, and gained an MA in 1588.[12] Subsequently he was rector of Castor in Norfolk, of Clipsham in Rutland, and of Beccles, Suffolk, from 1608 until his death in 1638. The Suffolk position would put him about forty miles from John Rous's parish of Santon Downham. There were also three men by the same name who matriculated at Oxford in the same period: one each in 1586 (a Yorkshire man), 1590 (Oxford city), and 1601 (Somerset).[13]

"A Prince" is the lead item in CUL Ee.V.36, a collection of prophecies; clearly this copyist valued it as prophecy rather than as political commentary. Aside from John Rous's diary, other books (as opposed to bound collections of loose sheets) containing these verses downplay their prophetic significance. Sir Francis Castillion, the son of Elizabeth I's Italian tutor, living quietly in Benham, Berkshire, entered "A Prince" in his book of letters, verses, reading notes and other miscellaneous material.[14] Castillion placed it on the reverse of a page containing seven paragraphs about the Council of Trent (230). He appears to have copied these from Nathaniel Brent's 1620 translation (STC 21761) of Paolo Sarpi's scurrilous account of the Council (London, 1619; STC 21760). On the whole, Castillion's interests are more literary than either political or prophetical. Around the time he is most likely to have written the prophecy (1621), he also took extensive notes on Philip Sidney's *Arcadia* and on Erasmus's *Enchiridion*, the latter of which he addressed to his son, who was eighteen in that year. Castillion does not ignore happenings at court but seems more closely interested in events that directly concern his family.

"A Prince" appears in more explicitly political contexts in several other personal miscellanies, often with the same accompanying material. This implies that these verses circulated together, perhaps as part of the newsletters that conveyed information about Parliamentary proceedings and other news.[15] Two manuscript books in the Folger Shakespeare Library in Washington, DC, Folger V.b.303 and V.a.275, as well as Oxford, Bodleian Library MS Tanner 88, include on the same leaf a series of prognostications for the years 1620 to 1630 (but omitting 1621). Tanner 88 is a collection of loose sheets of varying sizes that have been bound together; two different copies of "A Prince" appear on fol. 252v and fol. 253r. Immediately preceding "A Prince," fol. 252r contains "The Emperor Ferdinands letter to Baltazar 19 Octob 1621," while fol. 253v has the list of dates and predictions that have been copied into the Folger books along with "A Prince." Possibly the Tanner 88 pages are original separates sent out by newsagents in London, while the copyists of Folger V.b.303 and Folger V.a.275 found the material interesting enough to warrant writing it out in their books of political news, reports of speeches in Parliament, letters attributed to famous figures, and similar items.

Folger MS V.b.303 is written by various hands, and items are dated at various points between about 1550 and 1650. A seventeenth-century hand lists the contents at the beginning of the book, but focuses on the items of political or topical import. The table of contents does not include the collection of prophecies entered on pages 231 to 232, so they were either entered later or considered unimportant compared to the other items. Three of the prophecies, including "A Prince," clearly comment on actual events, while the other three are full of vague forebodings and animal imagery borrowed from Geoffrey of Monmouth.

Folger MS V.a.275, written by schoolmaster George Turner, also focuses on documents relating to news and politics, such as speeches in Parliament and lists of the King's ships for 1635 and 1636.[16] Besides "A Prince" and the predictions for the decade of the 1620s, both this book and Folger V.b.303 include the arraignment of Robert, Earl of Essex, and both are much concerned with English relations with Spain. Turner's book, however, includes more poetry, including poems by Thomas Carew and Ben Jonson, as well as many occasional and comic verses. Although the presence of the articles drawn up for the marriage of Prince Charles and the Spanish Infanta suggests worries about the Spanish Match, "A Prince" does not appear with the articles. Rather, it occurs with two other prophecies on page 176, following a table for reckoning wages, and pages 177 to 81 contain a variety of comic and literary verses. This section may simply have been a convenient place to record short pieces, perhaps after other items were copied.

Leeds, University of Leeds, Brotherton Library MS Lt q 9 similarly places "A Prince" among verses of various types, including epigrams and anagrams on people's names. Its political relevance is implied by the presence on the facing page of "A writing found at ye court at Whitehal .1619." (f. 64). Most of the manuscript contains material of practical use for the Yorkshire family to whom the book belonged: accounts, recipes, sermon notes, a form for drawing up indentures and another for wills. Dated entries mostly range from 1640 to 1659. While the manuscript does include a parliamentary petition from 1628 and a speech of Prince Charles from 1620, these were probably transcribed well after the 1620s, out of historical rather than topical interest.

Other manuscripts obscure the topical significance of "A Prince." New Haven, Yale University, Beinecke Library, Osborn MS b197 is a collection of poetry by both canonical and amateur versifiers.[17] It includes several items related to the Spanish Match, such as "Vpon Prince Charles & ye D. of Buckingames/ Goeing into Spaine," seventy pages before "A Prince"[18]; a song about Charles's return from Spain, including the lines "But shall be treason to be sober /On the fift day of October"[19]; and other similar material dated to the early 1620s, scattered throughout the book. However, the immediate context for "A Prince" is two love poems: it appears between George Withers' "Shall I wasting in despair"[20] and Sir Robert Ayton's "I loved thee once, I'll love no more."[21]

Similarly, the Percy Folio (London, British Library, Additional MS 27879) places "A Prince" among ballads and love poems: preceding it are such works as "Lady Bessye,"[22] "Are women faire,"[23] "I dreamed my love,"[24] "A Cavilere,"[25] and, following the prophecy, "Maudline"[26] and "Come pretty wanton."[27] In this copy, "yclept" (line 4) is spelled "Jcilippedd," suggesting that the scribe did not recognize this archaic word, while the surrounding contents imply that the compiler did not understand the historical import of the poem. The Percy Folio does contain a variety of ballads recounting historical events, but these all appear much earlier in the manuscript. In this and in Osborn MS b197, the prophecy is assimilated to "established literary culture";[28] by the time the Percy Folio was copied, "A Prince" may have had antiquarian (rather than either literary or topical) value.

Compared to many of the political and satirical verses of the 1620s, "A Prince out of the North" is mild and uncontroversial. It is not insulting or scurrilous; its description of the king is neutral to flattering; it does not clearly name any other political figure. The "foo from East" is a vague threat, not plainly associated with any particular conflict, and could refer either to a Christian ruler or to the Turks at the borders of Christendom. That is, when read against events of the early 1620s, the foe is clearly the Holy Roman Empire, but the prophecy as a whole is sufficiently vague as to be susceptible to multiple readings once removed from its initial context, which in turn may contribute to its preservation in a variety of manuscript settings as later readers responded more to its prophetic elements than to its topical references.

Northern Illinois University

APPENDIX

Table of manuscripts of "A Prince Out of the North"

Place, library	Shelfmark, folio	Context
Cambridge, Cambridge University Library	CUL Ee.V.36, f.1r	8 leaves of prophecies; edited with reference to John Rous.
Leeds, University of Leeds	Brotherton Lt q 9, f. 63v	Family miscellany.
London, British Library	Additional MS 27879, f. 239r	"Percy Folio."
London, British Library	Additional MS 28640, f. 107r	John Rous's diary; edited with reference to other copies
London, British Library	Harley 7332, f. 28r	Loose sheets bound together.
London, British Library	Sloane 1479, f. 6r	Verse miscellany.

New Haven, CT, Yale University, Beinecke Library	Osborn b197, p. 174	Verse miscellany.
New Haven, CT, Yale University, Beinecke Library	Osborn fb69, p. 229	Personal miscellany and letter book of Sir Francis Castillion.
Oxford, Bodleian Library	Ashmole 423, f. 263r	Loose sheets bound together; many letters to William Lilly.
Oxford, Bodleian Library	Eng. poet. c. 50, f. 26v	Verse miscellany; "James Leigh" and more than one "Thomas Gardiner" write their names in this book.
Oxford, Bodleian Library	Rawl. poet. 26, f. 67r	Loose sheets and individual gatherings bound together.
Oxford, Bodleian Library	Tanner 88, f. 252v	Loose sheets bound together.
Oxford, Bodleian Library	Tanner 88, f. 253r	Loose sheets bound together.
Washington DC, Folger Shakespeare Library	Folger STC 14344, copy 3	Complete *Works* of James I; on title page, in hand of Jean l'Oiseau de Turval, rector of St. Martin Orgar.
Washington DC, Folger Shakespeare Library	Folger MS V.a.275, p. 176	Personal miscellany: verse and political documents.
Washington DC, Folger Shakespeare Library	Folger MS V.b.303, p. 232	Political documents.
Washington DC, Folger Shakespeare Library	Folger MS L.b.670	A single sheet in the hand of George More.

NOTES

1. *A Manual of the Writings in Middle English*, ed. Jonathan Severs and Albert Hartung, 11 vols (New Haven: Connecticut Academy of Arts and Sciences, 1967-), 5. 1521. *Bishop Percy's Folio Manuscript: Ballads and Romances*, ed. John Hales and Frederick J. Furnivall, 3 vols (London: Trubner, 1868), 3. 371-2. Furnivall's notes place "A Prince" around the beginning of the Thirty Years' War, and indicate the enthusiasm expressed by English Protestants for the Elector Palatine's cause.

2. Number 52 in *The Index of Middle English Verse*, ed. Carleton Brown and Rossell Hope Robbins (New York: Columbia UP, 1943); *Supplement to the Index of Middle English Verse*, ed. Rossell Hope Robbins and John L.

Cutler (Lexington: University of Kentucky Press, 1965); and *A New Index of Middle English Verse*, ed. Julia Boffey and A. S. G. Edwards (London: British Library, 2005).

3. *The iMEV: An Open-Access, Web-based Edition of the Index of Middle English Verse, prototype site*, ed. Linne R. Mooney, Daniel W. Mosser, and Elizabeth Solopova, http://www.cddc.vt.edu/host/imev/index.html (accessed 5 October 2010).

4. Alastair Bellany and Andrew McRae, eds., "Early Stuart Libels: an edition of poetry from manuscript sources," online edition, *Early Modern Literary Studies* Text Series I (2005), http://purl.oclc.org/emls/texts/libels/ (accessed 4 October 2010). On the Spanish Match and other events of the early 1620s, see Thomas Cogswell, *The Blessed Revolution: English Politics and the Coming of War, 1621-1624* (Cambridge: Cambridge University Press, 1989).

5. *Union First Line Index of English Verse*, online edition, ed. Carolyn W. Nelson et al., Folger Shakespeare Library, June 2010, http://firstlines.folger.edu/ (accessed 4 October 2010), hereafter *UFLI*.

6. Edited by Nicole Clifton, "A Seventeenth-Century Prophecy of Merlin," *Folger Shakespeare Library*, summer 2005, http://www.folger.edu/html/folger_institute/mm/EssayNC.html (accessed 5 October 2010).

7. *A Catalogue of the Manuscripts Preserved in the Library of the University of Cambridge*, ed. Henry Richards Luard, 5 vols (Cambridge: Cambridge University Press, 1856-67), 2. 252.

8. "Early Stuart Libels," http://www.earlystuartlibels.net/htdocs/spanish_match_section/Ni3.html (accessed 5 October 2010).

9. The rector of St. Martin Orgar (London), Jean l'Oiseau de Turval, entered a copy of "A Prince" on the title page of his copy of the complete *Works* of James I, now Folger Shakespeare Library, STC 14344, copy 3.

10. Matthew Steggle, "Rous, John, (*bap.* 1584, *d.* 1644)" in *Oxford Dictionary of National Biography*, online ed., ed. Laurence Goldman (Oxford: Oxford University Press, 2004-10), http://www.oxforddnb.com/view/article/24174 (accessed 10 October 2010).

11. The "Lily" prophecy was popular in both its English and its Latin versions. The English text, beginning "A lille rayning in the best parte of the worlde shalbe moved like vnto the seede of a lyon" is given by Sharon L. Jansen, in *Political Protest and Prophecy under Henry VIII* (Woodbridge:

Boydell and Brewer, 1991), 127. The Latin text begins *"Lilium regnans in nobile parte mundi manebit contra semen leonis,"* printed in Lesley Coote's *Prophecy and Public Affairs in Later Medieval England* (York: York Medieval Press, 2000), 97. Coote discusses nearly twenty manuscripts that include this prophecy in various contexts. The British Library catalogue description folds this entry into "other verses," giving item two of British Library Add. 28640 as "Prophecy of Merlin: 'A Prince out of the North shall come,' and other verses, *etc.*, relating to James I., f. 9 b." http://www.bl.uk/catalogues/manuscripts/HITS0001.ASP?VPath=html/15750.htm&Search=28640&Highlight=F (accessed 21 January 2011).

12. J. Venn and J. A. Venn, *Alumni Cantabrigienses*, 2 parts in 10 vols (Cambridge: Cambridge University Press, 1922-54).

13. Joseph Foster, *Alumni Oxoniensis*, 4 vols. (Nedeln, Lichtenstein: Kraus Reprints, 1968).

14. New Haven, CT, Yale University, Beinecke Library, Osborn MS fb69; the prophecy appears on page 229.

15. For discussion of these, see Harold Love, *Scribal Publication in Seventeenth-Century England* (Oxford: Clarendon, 1993); Andrew McRae, *Literature, Satire and the Early Stuart State* (Cambridge: Cambridge University Press, 2004); Kevin Sharpe, *Reading Revolutions: The Politics of Reading in Early Modern England* (New Haven: Yale University Press, 2000).

16. This manuscript has been missing since 5 November 1991; I have consulted the microfilm.

17. On verse miscellanies in general, see Mary Hobbs, *Early Seventeenth Century Verse Miscellany Manuscripts* (Aldershot, UK: Scolar Press, 1992) and Arthur Marotti, *Manuscript, Print, and the English Renaissance Lyric* (Ithaca: Cornell University Press, 1995).

18. *Union First Line Index* reference number Osborn W0633 (page 104).

19. *UFLI* ref. no. Osborn T0559 (pages 63-5).

20. *UFLI* ref. no. Osborn S0378 (page 174).

21. *UFLI* ref. no. Osborn I0262 (page 175).

22. *UFLI* ref. no. britlib04205 (ff. 231-238v). Helen Cooper discusses "Lady Bessy" in "When Romance Comes True," *Boundaries in Medieval Romance*, ed. Neil Cartridge (Cambridge: Brewer, 2008), 13-27.

23. *UFLI* ref. no. britlib01045 (f. 238v).

24. *UFLI* ref. no. britlib05634 (f. 239).
25. *UFLI* ref. no. britlib11541 (f. 239).
26. *UFLI* ref. no. britlib01721 (f. 240v-241v).
27. *UFLI* ref. no. britlib02532 (f. 241v).
28. Andrew McRae, "The Literary Culture of Early Stuart Libeling," *Modern Philology* 97.3 (2000): 364-92, at 383.

Descriptive Reviews

ALEXANDRA BARRATT
Anne Bulkeley and her Book: Fashioning Female Piety in Early Tudor England. A study of London, British Library, MS Harley 494.
Turnhout, Belgium: Brepols, 2009. xii, 275 pp.

British Library MS Harley 494 is an interesting and complex manuscript, and it is good to have it made available in such a handsome and well-produced volume. It is to be hoped that it does not vanish as quickly as *The Commonplacebook of Robert Reynes of Acle* (edited by C. Louis and published in New York by Garland in 1980). Barratt gives a detailed description of the manuscript, explores its dating and ownership, argues for its deliberate compilation, and provides a rich historical and literary context for its contents. The complexity of the contents presents a major challenge about how best to organize this "book about a book."

The introduction skilfully integrates developments in scholarly understanding of women's literate practices with the author's own successive encounters with the manuscript. Chapter one covers the physical make-up of the book, although the only reference to the binding, probably the Virgin and Child binder of Winchester (dates not given), is slipped into the later discussion of ownership. The main scribe is identified as Robert Taylor who worked for the Birgittines at Syon Abbey and also copied the *Myroure of oure Ladye* for them, but sixteen other hands are identified as contributing to the book, and Barratt would like to think that these might be Birgittine. Contents by the Birgittine monks Richard Whitford and William Bonde would point to a date in the 1530s, but the piece by Maria van Oisterwijk cannot have been available before 1531/2 and the fact that the word "pope" is written on folio 31 suggests a date before 1535 when Cromwell ordered all such references to be erased (as this one is). The elucidation of the identity of Anne Bulkeley, mother and daughter, is fascinating and convincing; their identity also explains the obvious Birgittine connections of the manuscript. Hidden in this first chapter (11-13) is a useful summary list of the contents and hands of the collection.

The second chapter looks at the context from which the book came, the Birgittine "textual community." Indeed, Barratt would like to be able to prove that "the supervisor of the whole exercise may have been Richard Whitford" of Syon; his contributions to the collection are discussed in the following chapter. This one looks at the history of the two communities associated with the manuscript, Syon and Amesbury priory, and at related early sixteenth-century religious history in England, including the Holy Maid of Kent and developments in eucharistic doctrine. The next chapter looks at the main texts: the *Dyurnall: for deuoute soules* (which neither White nor Rhodes attributes to Whitford, 78 n5); Whitford's *A werke of preparacion… vnto communion* (Barratt has used the adapted Wayland edition of 1537); meditations during Mass derived from William Bonde's *Pilgrymage of perfeccyon*, and pieces by continental women visionaries, Mechtild of Hackeborn and Maria Van Oisterwijk, noting the comparative absence of St. Birgit's writings. It offers fascinating analysis and comparison of texts and is prefaced by a survey of noble women's pious practices of the late fifteenth and early sixteenth century.

Having looked at the major source authors, the fourth chapter looks rather at comparable types of manuscript sources: Books of Hours and *preces privatae*, in particular the Burnet Psalter (Aberdeen University Library MS 25) and in more detail, London, Lambeth Palace MS 3600 (a comprehensive list of contents is given, 127–131, and both have a color plate). The chapter is prefaced by a general survey of the early sixteenth-century development of the printed primer. While there are similarities between MS Harley 494 and the Burnet psalter, there appears to be a closer connection with Lambeth Palace MS 3600. All the prayers in Anne Bulkeley's book for which sources have been found are English translations from the Latin, but does this suggest "a stringent if covert enforcement of orthodoxy by the compiler(s)," as stated on page 149? Might it not rather be a recognition that her Latin was not fluent?

The final chapter considers "Dominant devotional themes and modulations," looking at "The sacralization of time and daily life," suggesting that the whole collection moves through the day, and in more detail at the *Dyurnall*, already discussed in chapter 3. "The Sacraments" relates the two items (24, 25) on confession to similar texts and goes on to review texts concerned with Holy Communion, a significant concern of the book, especially how to behave at Mass and the notion of spiritual communion, supplementing earlier discussion of the main texts. "Passion devotions" concentrates on the Wounds and Blood of Christ, looking again at Maria van Oisterwijk's devotion (item 15). "The Name of Jesus" provides some background to the devotion in England, notes the use of the Sacred Monogram at the head of a few pages, claiming it as particularly Birgittine, but fails to relate the repetition of "Jhesu" at the end of item 15 (by Whitford) to the Jesus Psalter, often attributed to him. Items 5, 7, 19 to 23, 26 and the end of 28 show that devotion to the Blessed Virgin was important to Anne Bulkeley; the angels make less impression and named saints apart from St. Anne (the owner's name saint) are conspicuous by their absence.

An annotated transcription of the manuscript is given in the appendix. Divided somewhat arbitrarily into thirty-three items, each is usually provided with notes on the source and a commentary that includes identification of the hand; any Latin is translated and glossarial notes provided if necessary.

It is good to have the text of this manuscript made available, and Barratt has provided a wealth of contextual material as well as identifying the probable owners. Some might question the inclusion of some of that contextual material such as the amount of attention given to Elizabeth Barton or to printed primers. The organization of the book makes it difficult to use, however, since items are frequently discussed in different chapters. The lack of an index means that one has to hunt through the chapter references. The topics addressed in chapter five might better have been attached to the main discussion of each item, thus reducing the amount of irritating cross-referencing. On some pages, there are "scribal errors" (see 46, 56, 64, 110; on 167, the reference to item 33 should read 32; the reference on 39 should be to the Fifteen Oes, and sadly A.I. Doyle has never been awarded a professorship). Omitted from the bibliographies are Cré, *Vernacular mysticism*, and Hennessy (152, n37), and Durham, Ushaw College MS 10 cited on page 243 has escaped the list of manuscript sources.

J. T. Rhodes, Durham University

**JAMES P. CARLEY, ED. and TRANS.
with the assistance of CAROLINE BRETT**
John Leland: De uiris illustribus: On Famous Men.
British Writers of the Middle Ages and the Early Modern Period, 1.
Toronto: Pontifical Institute for Mediaeval Studies;
Oxford: Bodleian Library, 2010. pp. 868; 8 plates.

Having perused this volume, the reader is somewhat startled not to find James Carley himself cited last (since Leland attempted chronology) among these "uiris illustribus." Carley's task of sifting, elucidating, and describing John Leland's method of working, his strengths and weaknesses, his relationships to people (both contemporary and long dead) and to places and, above all, to books, is meticulous and scholarly. It is also fascinating, and I read the 160-page Introduction at one sitting, rather as if it were an historical novel, even though it is dense, closely argued, and sometimes complex. Added to this is, of course, the task of transcribing and translating the text, which clearly engaged much of Carley's time. (Although he gives due credit to Caroline Brett for the initial transcription and translation, her work was much revised by Carley himself.) The text and translation (*en face*) cover a further 815 pages, with 593 entries, beginning in obscurity with block entries for the Druids, Bards, Vates and Flamines, thereafter dealing with individual famous men, and ending with the similarly obscure (to me) Robert Widow.

Leland's task was to rescue these men (*de feminis illustribus nihil est*) from obscurity (not all needed it—Chaucer, for example). The immediate reason was to further Henry VIII's arguments for the early independence of Britain from the Pope, but that was effectively lost in Leland's fascination for the texts themselves, particularly for those which show the elegance of style and perspicuity of wit which he himself deployed (and which Carley translates, seemingly so effortlessly). Carley explains with clarity the various journeys that Leland made from monastic house to monastic house, garnering information on volumes held in their libraries and elsewhere, sometimes garnering the volumes themselves. In writing up a work which previously failed to find the light of day (and which Carley has now resurrected from its variously mangled stages of existence), Leland's method was to cite the man and then his works. For someone like Tatfrith (bishop of Whitby) little could be said; for others like William of Malmesbury, for example, more information was available (padded out by a digression, which Leland later deleted, castigating his *bête noire*, Polydore Vergil, for omitting William from his *Historia Anglica*). The entry on Chaucer, whom Leland admired for his style (in words which were still the basis of Chaucer appreciation well into the twentieth century), is fascinating. Doubtless Carley will elucidate in the second volume of explanatory notes, but one is curious now about the sources for Chaucer's birth in Oxfordshire or Berkshire (presumably the Ewelme connection, which Leland mentions later), his education at Oxford, and his later life in France. Much of the entry is dedicated to Leland's quoting his own epigrams in praise of Chaucer, but Chaucer's canon is stated (including the *Origenes*, presumably from Chaucer's own statements, rather than from having found any trace of the work itself) and the elegy hung next to his tomb in Westminster Abbey.

However, the major interest for readers of *JEBS* will be in the books rather than the men: the manuscripts that Leland found, and where he found them, such as Ecgberht's at Salisbury, Lawrence of Durham's at Durham, and Stephen Langton's "which were extant even recently in the library of Stratford, near the banks of the river Lea" (plus one work "which was moved from Canterbury to Oxford, where I once found it in Canterbury College"). Some of these books were certainly appropriated by Leland for himself (as also for the King), such as his copy of Anselm's letters ("*ueteri quidem illo*"), those he took (for himself as well as the King) from St. Augustine's Canterbury, and those extant today, such as British Library MS Cotton Faustina B. IX and Bodleian MS Digby 96 (pp. lxxxvi, xci). Indeed one wonders whether those books said to be stolen before Leland saw them were in fact concealed as his reputation passed around the monasteries (as happened in the Marian commissions of 1557).

Carley's Introduction is divided into three sections: I. Life and Works (A. Leland's Life, B. The New Year's Gift as Curriculum Vitae, C. His Surviving Writings, 1. Manuscript Presentation Volumes, 2. Works Printed in Leland's Lifetime, 3. Writings Edited and Printed after his Death, 4. The Editions of the *Itinerary* and the *Collectanea*); II. "Infynyte treasure of knowledge": The *De uiris illustribus* (A. Leland's Perusal of and Diligent Search through Monastic Libraries, 1. The Sequence of Journeys and the Booklists, 2. Later Library Visits and the Welsh Itinerary, B. Stages of Compilation, 1. Sources, 2. Leland and Polydore Vergil, C. Leland's Prose Style); III. The Editions (A. The Manuscript, B. John Bale's Epitome, C. *Commentarii de scriptoribus Britannicis*, ed. Anthony Hall (Oxford 1709), D. The Present Edition). The first section gives the known facts of his life, the dates during which he worked on the *De uiris illustribus*, and his surviving writings. The dates are ascertained from what Carley suggests was a New Year's gift to the King in 1544 (not 1546, as Bale suggested), which outlines his completed project, the *Antiphilarchia*, and the other "completed" project (so Leland indicates, with an economy of truth), the *De uiris illustribus*. Carley deduces two stages to the latter work, from 1535 to 1537 and from 1543 to 1546 (after which Leland became insane). Carley details Leland's published poetry and the publication of his prose works by, or through, others, most notably John Bale's *The laboryouse journey & serche of Johan Leylande* (1549) and Thomas Hearne's *Joannis Lelandi antiquarii de rebus Britannicis collectanea* (1715) and *The Itinerary of John Leland the Antiquary* (issued between 1710 and 1712). The second section is a masterly reconstruction of Leland's *modus operandi* in relation to, first, his journeys (starting in 1533, when he set out to perform the King's business and only the lesser houses faced dissolution, and ending six years later, when their cause was lost) and, secondly, his writing up of the project. In the third section Carley tackles the manuscript and what others have made of Leland's work, such as Bale's "personalized transcript" (p. cxxxvii) (Cambridge, Trinity College MS R.7.15), in which he "tried to reconcile his own researches - quite apart from his own theological position - with Leland's" (p. cxlviii), Anthony Hall's publication of 1709,

Thomas Tanner's of 1748 (thirteen years after Tanner's death), and, finally, Carley's own edition, thankfully not published posthumously. (Although it has, unsurprisingly, taken over thirty years from conception to completion, the reader will be aware of how much else Carley has produced during this period.)

This handsome and scholarly volume carries its 150-plus pages of Introduction and 800-plus pages of text with great aplomb. Huge as it is, it is easy to handle and to read, although the non-Latinate reader may have some difficulties where passages remain untranslated (generally, Carley assumes that simple, short citations can remain in Latin, but much is translated within the Introduction, as well, of course, as the whole of the text). The manuscript (Oxford, Bodleian Library MS Top. gen. c. 4) is illustrated by eight plates, chosen to demonstrate Leland's mind-boggling revisions, deletions, and additions. There are four Appendices: Houses for which Leland compiled library lists; Stages of development of the *De uiris illustribus*; Changes in the spelling of Leland's Latin names (rather an *idée fixe* with Leland); Physical constitution of the manuscript. A Selected Bibliography is followed by a List of Authors (i.e. entries). There is no comprehensive List of Persons and Places. A second volume of Notes is planned. Carley must be proud of, as his readers are grateful for, a tremendous achievement.

Sue Powell, University of Salford

MARGARET CONNOLLY
The Index of Middle English Prose. Handlist XIX: Manuscripts in the University Library, Cambridge (Dd-Oo).
Cambridge: D. S. Brewer, 2009. lx + 467 pp.

As Kari Anne Rand rapidly catalogues Cambridge's college libraries for *IMEP* (see review in this volume, 233-34), Margaret Connolly has been engaged in the onerous task of cataloguing the University Library. The shelfmarks Dd-Oo render four times the number of Parker Library manuscripts containing Middle English prose, besides four times as many inspected but found to contain none. Further comparison between the Parker and the University Libraries would be invidious, and pointless. Connolly's is a major achievement and she is to be congratulated for accuracy, consistency, and (certainly) perseverance.

There is little need for a history of CUL, given the several that exist already, most recently that given by Peter Clarke in his edition of the early catalogues of the University and College libraries (reviewed *JEBS* 2009: 268-270). Having cited these, Connolly allows herself just a few pages to set the scene: the earliest catalogue dates from 1424 to 1440; benefactions augmented the collection to around 600 volumes by the early sixteenth century, although Marian depredations (or were the books hidden?) reduced the number to 163 by 1557; further benefactions (notably Parker himself, the impeached Laud, and Richard Holdsworth, Master of Emmanuel) increased the collection in the sixteenth and seventeenth centuries; this was capped in the early eighteenth century when George I donated the 30,000 volumes (1,790 manuscripts) of John Moore, bishop of Ely. The 1750s saw the development of the shelving and cataloguing system still in use: Aa-Cc printed books, Dd-Mm manuscripts acquired by that date, Nn manuscripts acquired later that century, Oo the last of the western manuscripts before the nineteenth century catalogue. Later manuscripts have been assigned to the Additional category (see review in this volume, 235-236).

The Middle English prose manuscripts overwhelmingly contain religious works, and all the important works are there: Nicholas Love's *Mirror of the Blessed Life of Jesus Christ* (two manuscripts); Hilton's *Scale* (three, one complete) and *Mixed Life; the Cloud of Unknowing* (three); Rolle (several manuscripts of several works); sermons, including the Wycliffite dominical cycle and Mirk's *Festial* (four, one complete—Connolly suggests five, but, in fact, Gg.vi.16 is not a *Festial*, although it is related to the Revision of the *Festial*); *The Charter of the Abbey of the Holy Ghost* and *The Abbey* itself (two of each); *Speculum Christiani* (four); *The Lay Folks' Catechism* (two); *The Pore Caitiff* (five, two complete); and so on. Everything one might expect is there (including the unique copy of the unfortunate Reginald Pecock's *Repressor*). Among secular texts, *The Canterbury Tales* is represented by several manuscripts, of which four contain the essential prose Tales of Melibee and of the Parson. There are translations, scientific and linguistic works, and practical pieces galore, particularly recipes and prescriptions.

It is the tendency of reviewers to look at the material they know best. In this case, Connolly is meticulous in acknowledging my having sent her descriptions of three *Festial* manuscripts (which can barely have lightened her load). In the one full manuscript (which I did not send), *Festial* sermons are listed in full with accurate incipits and explicits (not, sadly, always the case in *IMEP* editions: see *JEBS* 2003, 204-208). Spot-checking of other manuscripts has not revealed errors, and indeed errors were not expected. The volume ends with the usual Indices: Macaronic (A: Latin and English, B: French and English), Incipits, Reverse Explicits, Rubrics and Titles, and General (very useful, even including an entry for "book owner inscriptions"). Connolly is to be congratulated on a work of major scholarship—and the largest *IMEP* published to date.

Sue Powell, University of Salford

JOSEPH A. DANE
*Abstractions of Evidence in the Study of
Manuscripts and Early Printed Books.*
Burlington, VT: Ashgate, 2009.
viii + 176 pp. 8 black and white illus.

Joseph A. Dane's *Abstractions of Evidence in the Study of Manuscripts and Early Printed Books* is a challenging but uneven collection of nine essays, four of which were previously published from 1993 to 2000. Discounting, for a moment, the introduction and conclusion, the volume contains essays organized into two broad divisions: those primarily concerning manuscripts and those mainly about early printed books. On manuscripts, Dane includes essays that consider: the number of possible editions of *Everyman*; Gg.4.27's version of "The Prologue to Chaucer's *Legend of Good Women*"; issues relating to the staging of medieval dramas including *La Seinte Resureccion*, *Le Jeu de Robin et Marion* and *Le Jeu du Pelèrin*; and the existence of the Wakefield Master. The second part of the collection considers: facsimile editions; the differences between individual copies of early printed books; Colard Mansion's 1476 edition of *Boccaccio's De Casibus*; the works of Caxton the printer and Caxton the writer; and the book collection of Leander van Ess.

Dane's greatest strength is in his ability to quantify uncertainty in the realms of the bibliographical, the editorial and the textual. In his discussion of "The Prologue to Chaucer's *Legend of Good Women*," for example, he challenges the notion that Gg.4.27's version of the Prologue represents a separate textual tradition rather than a singular reading preserved in a singular manuscript. In the chapter on Caxton, Dane explores the increasing gulf being created between Caxton's work as a printer and Caxton's work as a writer. A lot of Dane's work raises some fascinating points, or spontaneously leads to detailed thought experiments and mental puzzles: which Caxton, for example, is responsible for the errors in Caxton?

The book's greatest weakness is that it is not a unitary composition. It is too obviously a collection drawn together from a variety of articles that although allied are not different aspects of the same whole or progressions to any given point in an overall argument. The attempts made to forge an artificial coherence—the charmless introduction and conclusion, and a variety of headlinks—do nothing to fashion a consistent text, and, indeed, I think that the attempt lessens the impact of each individual essay.

Dane further fails to refer to or cite much current scholarship. In an eight-page bibliography of principal works cited, only six items were published in the last decade. As nearly half of the book's contents are reprinted articles, I cannot entirely fault Dane for being unable to see the future, but in some cases, it might have been advisable to revisit the past. For example, the world of Chaucer scholarship in 1993 is not the world of Chaucer scholarship today, and as interesting as Dane's take on Gg.4.27 is, his points are largely moot. The great digital edition projects on Chaucer and Langland, for example, have completely rewritten many of the assumptions that Dane addresses. Similarly, Dane's apt criticisms of EEBO's production standards are less biting in light of the incredible variety of individual high resolution digital copies of early printed books now available on the Web. Overall, however, the book will be of interest to the serious textual scholar, and Dane's writing style is an acerbic treat.

Carl James Grindley,
Eugenio María de Hostos Community College, CUNY

ORIETTA DA ROLD and ELAINE TREHARNE, EDS.
Textual Cultures: Cultural Texts.
Essays and Studies New Series 63.
Cambridge: D. S. Brewer, 2010. xii + 221 pp.

Elaine Treharne's brief introduction to this essay collection acknowledges the rapid growth of scholarly interest in the history of the book and the sociology of texts. The ten essays which follow offer discussions of texts (manuscript, print, and digital), and technologies (broadly understood) from the earliest period to the present day, though the main concentration of the volume is on the medieval era.

We begin in the eleventh century with Erika Corradini's discussion of the composite nature of homiliaries from that time. She draws particular attention to Cambridge, Corpus Christi College MS 421, which was typical of other homiliaries in that it had a long life: repeatedly updated and expanded, it was still in use at end of the eleventh century, one hundred years after its creation, though, ironically, as she observes, its cultural and intellectual value was preserved by disrupting its original codicological integrity. Julia Crick's contribution, "The Power and the Glory: Conquest and Cosmology in Edwardian Wales," cautions against conflating textual and physical origins. She argues that Exeter, Cathedral Library MS 3514, must be seen as a Welsh book, because it was read and at least partly copied in conquered Wales. Various tables, appendices and plates make this essay seem longer than it is; the plates are of excellent resolution in which even the glosses might be deciphered with a magnifying glass.

Co-editor Orietta da Rold offers some preliminary observations on manuscript production before Chaucer, reminding us (44) that, despite our collective efforts, "There is still much mystery surrounding the origins of many manuscripts, their mode of production, and who wrote them, and for whom." Arguing that there is greater evidence for English manuscript production than we might imagine between 1100 and 1400, da Rold suggests some lines of enquiry relating to scribal activities and writing environments, providing in an appendix a list of some fifty-seven thirteenth- and fourteenth-century manuscripts which might be used as a testing ground. A. S. G. Edwards considers how the celebrated Ellesmere manuscript of the *Canterbury Tales* contributes to our textual and cultural understanding of the poem itself. Rehearsing what we know about this magnificent manuscript and its handlers, Edwards demonstrates that Ellesmere has been linked to elite bibliophile circles from its earliest history, with the consequence that its privileged environment has limited its textual influence.

A very long contribution by Martin K. Foys and Whitney Anne Trettien, "Vanishing Transliteracies in *Beowulf* and Samuel Pepys's *Diary*," might usefully have been split into two complementary essays. After a theoretical start there is a very good analysis of the presence and significance of runes in *Beowulf* which includes an illuminating discussion of how these might have been received by the poem's original audience: perhaps these strange and mysterious symbols would have seemed commonplace to the poem's original readers and listeners? Continuing in the same vein, the editors consider Pepys's use of shorthand in his seventeenth-century diary, and the way that this was bowdlerized in nineteenth-century editions of the text. Things get fairly technical in David L. Gants's account of "Descriptive Bibliography and Electronic Publication." He argues that in order to overcome a deep distrust of inherently unstable electronic formats we need to achieve a framework for designing bibliographical descriptions of electronic editions by finding "the digital equivalent of paper, type, collators and documentation" (126), because, while the requisite tools for the digital bibliographer differ from those used by the student of the book, the scholarly goals remain the same.

Ralph Hanna returns us to more familiar ground in his account of one of the central manuscripts which has formed perceptions of vernacular Lollardy: Oxford, Bodleian Library, MS Bodley 647. He extends existing descriptions of this thematic miscellany in an appendix to his essay and traces its progress before its entry into the Bodleian. Robert Romanchuk's essay, "The Idea of the Heart in Byzantium and the History of the Book," is less codicologically based but instead takes up the idea of the *heart* as a trope for the book, examining metaphors of the book-like heart (for example, the earth of the heart, the eyes and ears of the heart, the tablets of the heart) found in writings from the Eastern Christian Roman Empire and also in the Latin tradition (St Augustine's book of the heart).

Perhaps the most interesting and informative contribution is Margaret M. Smith's discussion of the color red as a textual element during the transition from manuscript to print. Using as a case study Johannes Nider's *De morali lepra* printed by Ulrich Zel in 1470, Smith analyzes the rubrication in seven of the surviving copies. She finds that each one is different and concludes that rubrication was a complex business, governed partly by personal interpretation. She argues that this variability was a factor in the demise of rubrication, along with the expense of two-color printing. Finally, Liberty Stanavage brings our attention to medieval drama by problematizing textual authority in the York Register of the Corpus Christi cycle (British Library MS Additional 35290). Drawing upon ideas current in New Philology, Stanavage challenges the notion that this manuscript contains a fixed and final text; instead she argues that the medieval sense of a codex was far from static, and that in its openness to additions and alterations it in many ways resembles a modern hypertext.

This wide-ranging and stimulating collection of essays is provided with a basic index but regrettably has no separate listing of the manuscripts cited.

Margaret Connolly, University of St Andrews

A. C. DE LA MARE and LAURA NUVOLONI
Bartolomeo Sanvito: The Life and Work of a Renaissance Scribe, edited by Anthony Hobson and Christopher De Hamel. The Handwriting of the Italian Humanists, II. Association Internationale de Bibliophilie, 2009. 464 pp, color illustrations.

Members of the Early Book Society who have attended conferences in the past will remember Professor de la Mare (1932-2001) with affection, both for her generosity as a scholar and her prowess at croquet. Tilly, as she was universally known, was famed for her ability to recognize from among the many fifteenth-century hands writing the new humanist script that of an individual as if it were an old friend's from whom a letter had just arrived. Chief among these "friends" was Bartolomeo Sanvito (1433-1511), one of the most active and famous scribes of his day whose work was much in demand by wealthy patrons. For many years de la Mare had collected materials for a study of Sanvito's career (an account of her odyssey is provided elsewhere by Laura Nuvoloni, "The Scribe and the Scholar: Bartolomeo Sanvito and Prof. Albinia de la Mare," *Bulletin du Bibliophile* [2005], part 2, 247-70), and at her untimely death left copious notes, which Nuvoloni has supplemented and prepared for publication in the present handsome volume.

The core of *Bartolomeo Sanvito: The Life and Work of a Renaissance Scribe* is a catalogue of 123 manuscripts described in chronological order, plus addendum. The earliest entry (Oxford, Bodleian Library, D'Orville 166) contains a copy of Tibullus, *Elegiae,* by an unknown Paduan scribe, later corrected by Sanvito. An *ex dono* inscription records that it was given to him in

October 1452, and "quite probably soon after" (104) Sanvito added a quire containing Pseudo-Ovid, *Epistola Sapphus*, which he had copied himself. The last entry (Biblioteca Apostolica Vaticana, Vat.lat. 5326) is a copy of Fra Giovanni Giocondo's *Sylloge*, catalogue of ancient inscriptions, datable *c*. 1509. The addendum features a recent discovery copied much earlier in Sanvito's career, *c*. 1460 (Rome, Biblioteca Casanatense 924), important because it contains copies of Petrarch's *Canzoniere* and *Trionfi* derived directly from the poet's autograph drafts. Each manuscript is illustrated in color, some by plates of more than one folio. The catalogue is preceded by four introductory essays: de la Mare's account of Sanvito's career (15-38: a translation of her essay, "Bartolomeo Sanvito, copista e miniatore," in the exhibition catalogue *La miniatura a Padova Medioevo al Settecento* [1999]; Scott Dickerson, "Chronology" (39-62), based on his research for documentary evidence for Sanvito's life; Ellen Cooper Erdreich, "Bartolomeo Sanvito as Illuminator" (63-86); and Anthony Hobson, "Sanvito's Bindings" (87-99). Four appendices (of marginal sigla commonly used by Sanvito with approximate date of their first use; the principal sequences of colored capitals he employed; of signatures, catchwords and ruling patterns he adopted; and of manuscripts wrongly attributed to him), are followed by notes to the essays and catalogue, and a bibliography. An Index of Manuscripts and General Index complete the volume.

Sanvito's earliest manuscripts are written in the *littera antiqua* developed by the Florentine humanists, Niccolò Niccoli and Poggio Bracciolini, but his fame is linked to his cursive "italic" hand, the "bouncing lightness and dancing quality" (102) of which soon attracted the great and the good. His influential clients included Pope Sixtus IV, Cardinals Giovanni d'Aragona and Francesco Gonzaga, Matthias Corvinus and Lorenzo de' Medici. The only Englishman to acquire one of Sanvito's manuscripts was John Tiptoft, earl of Worcester, who brought home a copy of Juvenal and Persius (Oxford, Bodleian Library, Auct. F. 5. 4) from his student days at Padua. Sanvito chiefly copied classical texts, some several times (six copies of Cicero's *De officiis* are known, and five each of Suetonius, *Vitae Imperatorum* and Eusebius/Jerome, *Chronici Canones*), and was concerned that the texts he produced should be as correct and authoritative as possible. Thus he possibly used the fifth-century Codex Mediceus of Virgil (Florence, Biblioteca Medicea-

Laurenziana 39.1) as his exemplar for London, British Library, King's MS 24. As well as the many manuscripts he copied, he often supplied rubrication and epigraphic capitals in manuscripts written by other scribes, and, while not as good an artist as he was a scribe, he collaborated with other artists, particularly Gaspare da Padova.

Sanvito began his career working for a notary. Yet, unlike other humanist scribes who were accustomed to writing documents which it was normal practice to date and sign, Sanvito did not date and sign most of his work. It was only towards the end of his life that he began to do so. His "pocket" editions of Cicero were produced between December 1494 and February 1500. The short interval between a copy of *De oratore*, dated 20 December 1499, and a copy of the Tusculan Disputations, dated 10 February 1500, shows that it took him about seven weeks to produce a small volume of 200 to 300 pages in italic script with simple decoration. He signed his late work with his initials B. S. and a drawing of an ivy leaf, possibly because a copycat scribe, Jacopo Questenberg, was producing volumes in exactly the same style and format. Only two volumes, the Evangeliary and Epistolary (Padua, Biblioteca Capitulare, E 26-27) written and illuminated by Sanvito to give to the collegiate church of Santa Giustina in Monselice, where he had become a canon shortly before his death, are signed in full.

Thus the identification and dating of Sanvito's *oeuvre* depends on a close and careful study of the palaeography and codicology of manuscripts now widely dispersed in many collections. Meticulous analysis enabled de la Mare to establish a chronology of his output. She traced not only the development of his handwriting, but observed features such as changes in his ruling techniques, changes in his way of writing ligatures, and how from *c*. 1459 to 1461 Sanvito began to sign quires with letters of the alphabet (a system found in late Antique and Carolingian manuscripts) rather than using catchwords. Around 1464 to 1466 he employed a new abbreviation for *quam*, and later in life, *c*.1506, he began to adopt a new system of punctuation (our modern system with commas, semi-colons, apostrophes and full-stops), that Aldus had begun to use in his edition of Pietro Bembo's *De Ætna* (1495/6). Similarly, Sanvito's style of decoration changed over time, from simple white-vine initials to three-dimensional faceted initials to epigraphic Mantegnesque initials with classical acanthus leaves.

Based on de la Mare's observations, the catalogue entries are organized into several groups according to the period in which Sanvito produced them. Each group of entries is preceded by an analysis of Sanvito's handwriting at that time, followed by detailed descriptions of the manuscripts. Unless a manuscript is specifically dated by a colophon, the date assigned to one is rightly given in square brackets, indicating the degree of caution necessary when dating an undated codex. Nevertheless, a compilation of Sallust's histories (Rome, Biblioteca Casanatense 1443) is said to date "[22 October 1455]"; this is too precise. The manuscript, in quires of ten, was copied by three scribes; however, it appears from its description that the three collaborated only in the first part (or fascicule) of the manuscript, quires 1-7, containing the *Catiline*. Sanvito himself copied only fols. 16-24 (part of quires 2-3). The text ended on fol. 65v, leaving the last five leaves of quire 7 (fols. 66-70) blank, with no catchword on fol. 70v. The main item, the *Jurgurtha*, in the remaining quires, 8-23, is written entirely by Hand C on palimpsest leaves and the date (fol. 206v) properly relates only to it. I would therefore prefer to express the date for the volume as a whole (and Sanvito's stint) as *c*.1455.

A note at the beginning of *Bartolomeo Sanvito* (14) draws attention to the fact that de la Mare's chronological divisions do not always coincide with those derived by Scott Dickerson from archival sources. Given that dating a manuscript on palaeographical and art-historical grounds is always an exercise in judgement, what is remarkable is how little her suggested datings differ from those supplied by Dickerson. A manuscript of Propertius with the Sanvito family's coat of arms (Deventer, Stadsarchief en Athenaeumbibliotheek 11 D 4 Kl) was dated by de la Mare *c*.1453-4; Dickerson redates it *c*.1454-7. She dated the dedication copy to Mathias Corvinus of Alessandro Cortese's *Laudes bellicae* (Wolfenbüttel, Herzog August Bibliothek 85.1.1 Aug. 2⁰) to 1487 or 1488; Dickerson redates it to the first half of 1488. The only major discrepancy is in the case of a book of hours with Mantuan calendar (Harvard University, Houghton Library, Typ 213) containing added prayers to be spoken by "Ysabella," presumably Isabella d'Este, wife of Francesco Gonzaga, marquis of Mantua. Was this manuscript presented to Isabella on her betrothal to Francesco in 1480 (Dickerson, pp. 49-50, who identifies it with a book of hours known to have been commissioned by Marquis

Federico Gonzaga in 1479) or on her marriage to Francesco in 1490 (de la Mare and see 427 n12 arguing from text and decoration for the later date)?

The skilful preparation of the catalogue makes it impossible to determine how much is derived from de la Mare's notes and how much is due to Nuvoloni's own research. Together with the essays the volume constructs a comprehensive account of Sanvito's career. The care taken over its production (even the binding bears Sanvito's monogram "BS" and characteristic ivy leaf in gold tooling on the front cover) ensures that it will represent, as hoped, a worthy "monument to the skills and scholarship" (Hobson's foreword, 7) of a generous and humane scholar.

Pamela Robinson, Institute of English Studies, University of London

A. S. G. EDWARDS, ED.
Tudor Manuscripts, 1485-1603. English Manuscript Studies 1100-1700, 15. London: The British Library, 2009. vi + 280 pp.

As usual with volumes in the English Manuscript Studies series, *Tudor Manuscripts* has no introduction, but we learn from the dust jacket that it is published to mark the 500th anniversary of Henry VIII's accession. The volume contains ten essays of somewhat mixed quality, followed by the editor's regular survey of English manuscripts sold at auction the previous year. The principle of arrangement appears to be broadly geographical, in that the essays move from south to north in terms of subject-matter—from London to Scotland. They variously address matters of content, compilation, authorship, textual transmission, circulation, and, throughout, the nature of manuscript culture.

The collection opens strongly with three authoritative contributions: Jason Powell, "Marginalia, Authorship, and Editing in the Manuscripts of Thomas Wyatt's Verse," Julia Boffey, "London, British Library, Add. MS 18752: a Tudor hybrid book?" and Carole Meale, "London, British Library, Harley MS 2252: John Colyns' 'Boke': Structure and Content." Powell is editing Wyatt's complete works for OUP, and writes with expert knowledge of the main poetical manuscripts. He brings out how much they differ, both generically and in regard to ascription of authorship, and stresses the need for us to understand the potential uses of anonymity in Henrician manuscript culture. Boffey presents a detailed physical analysis of a miscellany volume, part manuscript, part printed, which comprises eleven different sections of widely differing date, likely to have been assembled into a composite volume in the earlier sixteenth century—perhaps also by someone associated with the Henrician court. The lyrics added to the book at this time, distributed over several of the sections, are to be the subject of a separate article. Meale's long essay, very valuable, is a revision of a chapter in her unpublished 1984 PhD thesis. She first discusses all aspects of the work that the London merchant John Colyns put into his substantial compilation, which was centred around two pre-existing booklets containing Middle English romances, and which can be dated to *c*. 1525 to 1539. There then follows a detailed catalogue of all ninety-one items in the manuscript. Information about the relevant scribal hand is lacking, but otherwise this is exemplary work.

The following two essays—before we move north—are somewhat less satisfactory. There is a good deal of very useful detail in Joyce Boro, "Miscellaneity and History: Reading Sixteenth-Century Romance Manuscripts," but her count of eleven such manuscripts needs to be reduced by two in terms of the actual date of copying of the romances (one other manuscript now lacks the two that it once contained), and her attempted division of the manuscripts into two generic groups is inconsistent. Tamara Atkin writes on "Manuscript, Print and the Circulation of Dramatic Texts: a Reconsideration of the Manuscript of *The Marriage of Wit and Wisdom*," arguing that the sole (manuscript) witness to this play, dated 1579, was probably written to resemble a contemporary printed play text rather than having been copied from a printed text now lost. She may well be right, but her main reason for rejecting the latter is what she calls "the degree of scribal error" (158), for which she presents no evidence.

The North of England is represented by Pat Naylor, "Scribes and Secretaries of the Percy Earls of Northumberland, with Special Reference to William Peeris and Royal MS 18 D.11." This is an accomplished and unfailingly interesting piece of work, first making the case for the scribe and decorator of items added to two existing Percy manuscripts *c*. 1516 to 1532 being the same person, and then very plausibly identifying him as the fifth Earl of Northumberland's secretary, William Peeris. Naylor, whose knowledge of manuscripts associated with the Percies—and their various secretaries—is clearly extensive, provides just the right amount of detail for her purposes.

Tudor Manuscripts is completed by four essays on Scottish subjects. Jane Griffiths, "Exhortation to the Reader: the Glossing of Douglas's *Eneados* in

Cambridge, Trinity College MS O.3.12," is a little over-argued for what it is able to demonstrate. Griffiths draws attention to the two very different styles of annotation in the manuscript, contrasting what are accepted as Douglas's own, subtle comments on matters of interpretation of his source with the practical sententiousness that appears in the margins elsewhere, and which is also a feature of Copland's 1553 edition of the *Eneados*. But Griffiths' argument that the Trinity manuscript illustrates these different approaches in conflict is weakened by there being only four rather trivial glosses of the latter type, amounting in total to no more than twenty-four words. Cathy Shrank's essay, "Manuscript, Authenticity and 'evident proofs' against the Scottish Queen," is a very different kind of enquiry, investigating the problematic status of manuscripts, especially holographs, in terms of providing evidence for legal purposes. While manuscripts were valued as appearing to preserve the immediacy of oral testimony, there could be difficulties regarding their authenticity. Shrank's valuable case study concerns documents used against Mary Queen of Scots.

Priscilla Bawcutt, "The Authorship of James VI and I's *Amatoria*: The Manuscript Evidence," is an enjoyable, expertly written contribution, deploying textual and linguistic as well as manuscript evidence to demonstrate the strength of James's claim to be the sole author of the poems known as the *Amatoria*, though Bawcutt acknowledges that the occurrence of Thomas Erskine's name in one of the relevant manuscripts, following the poems, remains unexplained. Joanna M. Martin and Katherine A. McClune, "The Maitland Folio and Quarto Manuscripts in Context," finally provide a fresh analysis of these two verse miscellanies, in which they discuss, inter alia, their overlapping contents, ordering, and structure, and their affinities with other manuscripts. They include a detailed annotated list of the Maitland poems known to have had an English circulation or provenance, raising numerous questions about textual transmission.

Overall, *Tudor Manuscripts, 1485-1603* is a very worthwhile collection. It concludes with the expected indexes, and — in terms of materials — benefits from the heavyweight production standards associated with the English Manuscript Studies series. There are, however, relatively frequent proofing errors in the form of missing words and letters.

Oliver Pickering, University of Leeds

JOHN BLOCK FRIEDMAN
*Brueghel's Heavy Dancers: Transgressive Clothing,
Class, and Culture in the Late Middle Ages.*
Syracuse, NY: Syracuse University Press, 2010. 361 pp.

In its title, John Block Friedman's latest generous and erudite book, *Brueghel's Heavy Dancers: Transgressive Clothing, Class, and Culture in the Late Middle Ages*, presents readers with an intriguing riddle: who are these "heavy dancers," and what does the sixteenth-century Pieter Brueghel have to do with the late Middle Ages? For readers encountering the title on the book's dust jacket, the riddle is partially solved but also deepened. The title is set over a detail from one of Brueghel's most recognizable paintings, *The Wedding Dance* (1566); visible behind "Heavy Dancers" (given in a squat and heavy orange font), Brueghel's dancers are noticeably massive, and situated in the background above the book's subtitle, the male dancer's stuffed codpiece serves as a fitting illustration of the word "transgressive." Still, one thinks of Brueghel's paintings, as Friedman soon concurs, as quintessentially early modern, their detailed depictions of everyday life as exemplifying the new era's turn toward all things human. But as Friedman also quickly explains, paintings like *The Wedding Dance* are at least as medieval as they are early modern, for their visual motifs—of drunkenness, of inappropriate dress, of overt sexuality, to name a few—refer to a venerable literary and artistic tradition that reflects a fascination on the part of medieval aristocracy with the supposed excesses of the lower classes and their exotic manners and pastimes.

In this way, Brueghel's work makes a felicitous point of departure for Friedman's central project in *Heavy Dancers*: an examination of an earlier, medieval literary and artistic preoccupation with rustics, of which Brueghel's *The Wedding Dance* is only a late attestation, focusing on that tradition's semiotics of clothing in particular. The arc of the book's seven chapters takes readers from the thirteenth to the sixteenth century and from the bucolic realm of the Old French pastourelle, and the humble clothing its shepherdesses customarily wear and the finery they fervently desire, to the dystopic domain of German anti-peasant satire with its crowds of brawling villagers decked out above their station in spurs and buttons and detachable sleeves. Along the way, two chapters are given to Chaucer's *Canterbury Tales*: one explicates the clothing of both the Miller and the saucy heroine of his tale, Alison, to reveal satiric portraits of crass social climbers; a second focuses on the *General Prologue* portrait of the Yeoman as a send-up of the "faux heraldry" (199) affectation popular among ambitious late-medieval townspeople. Across these studies, Friedman provides meticulous histories and descriptions of a broad spectrum of literary genres and aspects of material culture. This in itself would make *Heavy Dancers* an extremely informative work of scholarship; what makes the work truly illuminating are Friedman's consistent reminders that his interest in all of the "stuff" of the book—from caps to shoes and from arrows to *aumonières*—is in its significance a system of representation, and, beyond that, a system that alleges rustic transgression even as it reveals aristocratic fear of and voyeuristic preoccupation with the same.

Of particular interest to readers of the *Journal of the Early Book Society* will be the numerous short studies of medieval manuscripts that Friedman weaves into this analysis. He turns to deluxe Books of Hours most often, reading from their images—especially those of the Labors of the Months—clear documentation both of the sartorial coding of class and of beliefs about the habits of the lower classes on the part of these books' upper-class owners. Just one example of Friedman's magisterial use of this material is his survey of images of the labors of January and February in three celebrity Books of Hours, the *Très Riches Heures* of Jean Duc de Berri, the Grimani Breviary, and the Hennessy Hours, which depict rustic urchins urinating from doorways, adults warming their genitals before the fire as well as a prominently displayed codpiece worn by peasant chopping wood. Given the otherwise "heightened realism" (66) of these scenes, Friedman argues, it is likely that such behaviors were understood by viewers of these images as the norm for peasants even as the inclusion of such imagery in these prayer books hints at an appetite for such information among their elite owners.

While the art and literature Friedman examines in this book take the habits and clothing of the lower classes as their subject, the same tradition also offers the aristocracy idealized, reassuring images of themselves. Those exquisitely appareled hunting parties passing by "obedient and unfestive peasants before their houses" (280) pictured in Simon Bening's Books of Hours, for instance, portend a world in which the poor naturally know their place and are unable, congenitally, to countenance aspirations for wealth or elegance. Through its examination of the view from both sides of the late-medieval class divide, and from several points in between, *Heavy Dancers* thus shows that clothing is the very "fabric" of class envy, anxiety, and, for the upper class, hopes for enduring privilege; moreover, its innovative and interdisciplinary methodology is bound to enable further valuable work in this area.

Martha Dana Rust, New York University

RALPH HANNA

The English Manuscripts of Richard Rolle: A Descriptive Catalogue.
Exeter: University of Exeter Press, 2010.
xlv + 264 pp. 8 black and white plates.

This author-based manuscript bibliography is devoted to "Rolle in English" (xxiv); it enumerates both Richard Rolle's English writings and those of his Latin writings which were translated into English (Latin versions of the English writings are also noted). This is an unusual type of book, and among Middle English writers only Chaucer has received similar treatment. Rolle was recognized as a major spiritual author in the later Middle Ages in England, a contemporary status that is reflected by the number of manuscripts quantified in this volume. The catalogue lists 122 manuscripts (the numeration actually runs to 123 because the recent relocation of one manuscript means that number 67 is now a vacant entry). Four of these manuscripts are now bilocated, two conveniently enough in collections in London (one codex that is now in two parts finds itself in two different collections in the British Library), but two others are now split between Dublin and Yale in the first instance, and Tokyo and California in the second. Ralph Hanna has personally examined all but six of these manuscripts, and the volume as a whole represents a quarter of a century's worth of research and note-taking and visits to libraries, a project begun in the era when it was unimaginable that digitized versions of manuscripts could ever be accessible from our own desks. Yet, despite all his labor and diligence, Hanna cautions against accepting this as a full listing of all of the manuscripts of all of Rolle's English works, pointing out that more copies of Rolle's prologue to the Psalter may still lurk in the under-investigated manuscripts of the Wycliffite Psalter.

In his Introduction, Hanna provides an overview of the canon of works associated with Rolle, largely following and acknowledging the early twentieth-century research of Hope Emily Allen, but extending and emending her lists in the light of more recent discoveries. He adds one text to the canon, the *Lessouns of Dirige*, and discusses the problematic authorial status of various short texts (meditations, lyrics, exempla), that have been ascribed to Rolle. Hanna also highlights an area of even greater complexity: that of dealing with works which were habitually adapted, altered, and interpolated, and distinguishing texts from quotations. Noting that the excerpting and appropriation of Rolle's texts was a regular and substantial feature of Rollean transmission, Hanna confesses to making arbitrary distinctions in his cataloguing of such extracts, largely because, had he *not* done so, he would have had to take on the immense task of describing a large number of late medieval religious miscellanies. The pragmatics of this decision are entirely justified, though it does also highlight the pressing need for attention to this overlooked category of later vernacular manuscripts. Nevertheless, with this exception, the catalogue offers a great deal of information about the circulation of Rolle's works, constituting a database that could be used to determine which of Rolle's works were distributed most numerously and widely, in which regional areas, and in what types of manuscript contexts.

In the "Notes on Editorial Procedure" that preface the catalogue itself Hanna acknowledges that he has not provided the "full-fledged palaeographical accounts" which are customary in this type of work. Instead he has been concerned to give "an abbreviated sequence of topics of use to scholars whose interests are predominantly literary rather than codicological" (2). Individual entries begin with an overview of the physical composition and layout of the manuscript, its date and scribal hand(s), before proceeding to list its contents, collation, decoration, dialect, provenance, and binding. For further information (all of these sections are necessarily brief), the reader is directed to existing published descriptions and discussions. I would have welcomed more information about provenance. Hanna generally attends only to the medieval and early modern evidence of manuscript provenance and does not attempt to track modern sale catalogue movements. There is thus less information to be gleaned here than there might be about the afterlives of Rolle's works, and because his writings were almost wholly ignored by the early printers and did not emerge in print until their rediscovery in the nineteenth century, more attention to traces of ownership and readerly activity in the manuscripts in the intervening period would be illuminating. Hanna does, however, include a very helpful list of references to some twenty-seven lost copies of Rolle's works represented by entries in wills and inventories from the fifteenth to eighteenth centuries (xxv-xxxviii).

This will be an invaluable volume, obviously useful to those interested in its named author and his works, but also to all those engaged with later Middle English religious texts and their manuscript contexts. There is a great deal of information here about the material culture of later medieval Yorkshire. Hanna's recent editorial work in publishing Rolle's *Uncollected Prose and Verse* (Early English Text Society, Original Series 329, 2007), and the anonymous *Speculum Vitae* (Early English Text Society, Original Series 331 and 332, 2008), has reminded us of the rich tradition of spiritual writing that emanated from this region in the fourteenth and fifteenth centuries. The primary focus in the present volume on the physical repositories in which that tradition has been preserved, at least in the case of its pre-eminent author, allows us an insight into later medieval book production that is not focused on the metropolitan environs of London, and which is all the more welcome because of that.

Margaret Connolly, University of St Andrews

E.A. JONES and ALEXANDRA WALSHAM, EDS.
Syon Abbey and its Books: Reading, Writing and Religion c. 1400–1700.
Woodbridge: The Boydell Press, 2010. xvi + 267 pp.

CLAES GEJROT, SARA RISBERG, and MIA ÅKESTAM, EDS.
Saint Birgitta, Syon and Vadstena. Papers from a Symposium in Stockholm 4–6 October 2007.
Stockholm: Kungl. Vitterhets Historie och Antikvitets Akademien, 2010. 301 pp.

This year has seen the welcome publication of two volumes devoted to Birgittine concerns, both resulting from symposia; in the case of Exeter the conference took place in 2005, while the Stockholm one occurred two years later. They complement each other well and, relatively speaking, there is little overlap between them. The Exeter volume contains a small number of rather lengthy essays, with a matching introduction by the editors (1–38). This introduction is much more expansive than normally found in edited collections and is all the better for that; indeed, as the subtitle demonstrates, it is really an essay in itself, "Introduction: Syon Abbey and its Books: Origins, Influences and Transitions." Not only does it serve to introduce the individual essays but, even more importantly, it attempts to provide a history of Syon and its scholarship. The eight essays that follow deal with different aspects of the abbey in medieval and post-medieval times; they are subdivided into sections as follows: I "Brothers and Sisters": Peter Cunich, "The Brothers of Syon, 1420–1695," and Virginia R. Bainbridge, "Syon Abbey: Women and

Learning *c.* 1415–1600"; II "Syon Abbey and the Book Trade": Vincent Gillespie, "Syon and the English Market for Continental Printed Books: The Incunable Phase," and C. Annette Grisé, "'Moche profitable unto religious persones, gathered by a brother of Syon': Syon Abbey and English Books"; III "The Bridgettines in Exile": Claire Walker, "Continuity and Isolation: The Bridgettines of Syon in the Sixteenth and Seventeenth Centuries," and Caroline Bowden, "Books and Reading at Syon Abbey, Lisbon, in the Seventeenth Century"; and IV "History and Memory": Claes Gejrot, "The Syon Martiloge," and Ann M. Hutchison, "Syon Abbey Preserved: Some Historians of Syon."

The Stockholm volume by contrast has a very short preface (only two pages) and so devotes the time to a longer, and more eclectic, selection of short essays. The twenty essays are not subdivided into sections but, broadly speaking, the first third covers Syon, the second third Vadstena, and the remaining third other Birgittine convents, topics, and portraits. The essay are as follows: Topher Martin, "The History of Syon Abbey"; Richard Farrant, "The Birgittine Abbey of Syon. The Archaeological Evidence"; Virginia Bainbridge, "Who Were the English Birgittines? The Brothers and Sisters of Syon Abbey 1415–1600"; Susan Powell, "Syon Abbey as a Centre for Text Production"; Laura Saetveit Miles, "Scribes at Syon. The Communal Usage and Production of Legislative Manuscripts at the English Birgittine House"; Ann M. Hutchison, "Richard Whitford's *The Pipe or Tonne, of the Lyfe of Perfection*: Pastoral Care, or Political Manifesto?"; Elin Andersson, "Vadstena 1427: The Visit of the Syon Brothers"; Elisabet Ragner, "Monastic Vision and Archaeology. Vadstena Abbey Revisited"; Eva Lindqvist Sandgren, "Book Illumination at Vadstena Abbey"; Jonas Carlquist, "Learning among the Nuns at Vadstena Abbey"; Ingela Hedström, "Hand in Hand. Scribes and Books among the Vadstena Nuns"; Inger Lindell, "Christine Hansdotter Brask. A Vadstena Nun and Her Use of Writing"; Karl G. Johansson, "The Birgittines and the Bible. On the Use of the Pentateuch Paraphrase at Vadstena Abbey"; Marko Lamberg, "Authority through Gendered Role Models. The Case of Late Medieval Monastic Literature at Naantali"; Martin Berntson, "Reformation and Counter-culture in Maribo Abbey"; Olle Ferm, "King Magnus and his Nickname 'Smek'"; Janken Myrdal, "The Revelations of Saint Birgitta and Everyday Life in the Fourteenth Century"; Nina Sjöberg, "Gender in Heaven and on Earth according to the Revelations of Saint Birgitta"; Jan Svanberg, "The Earliest Image of the Future Saint Birgitta"; Elisabeth Hallgren, "Birgitta's Character. A Debate around 1900."

For a reviewer who has read both these volumes in turn it is inevitable that s/he will start to weigh up the opposing merits and deficiencies (which are few) in each of these volumes. Both volumes are well produced and it is a cause for celebration that the publisher of the Stockholm volume saw fit to allow the inclusion of so many color plates (in total, there are some forty images, of which the vast majority are in color). The index in the Exeter volume makes us think how beneficial a similar index would have been for the Stockholm volume, while conversely the cumulative bibliography in the Stockholm volume reminds us of how useful such a bibliography would have been in the Exeter volume.

From the contents lists above, it will be immediately apparent that the Exeter volume has an overall cohesiveness that is lacking in the Stockholm collection. This is particularly apparent towards the end of the Stockholm volume when some essays are included, which, though interesting in themselves, have not much bearing on the subject. Yet in an odd way the thematic unity in the Exeter volume is more apparent than real as one of the essays is a reprint from 2005 (Gillespie). Admittedly, the essays themselves are exemplary and most of the contributors are masters of their areas. They treat their subjects comprehensively and even the most incisive summary of each could not do justice to the lengthy, wide-ranging and detailed scholarship. However, when the book is read as a whole, what is most obvious is the failure of the editors to make an effort to include cross-reference. In the overall scheme of things this is only a minor point but the trouble is that unless a reader reads every word of every essay, s/he is in danger of missing out on material that could be followed up or of getting a partial account of a subject treated more fully elsewhere (and the fact that there is an index does not answer the problem, or at least only partially so). There are various cases of this lack of cross-reference throughout the volume; for example, Cunich (40, n. 5) would have benefited from a cross-reference to Gejrot's chapter on the Syon *Martiloge*; Bainbridge (86) makes a novel suggestion (though without any evidence) about the likelihood of a Sr. Magdalena Baptista Boeria (professed by 1518) having helped to prepare the printed *Orcherd of*

Syon, though in her essay Grisé shows no knowledge of this (132–3); while Walker (173, n. 63) should really have a cross-reference to Hutchison's discussion of an especially knotty issue (242–6). The editors might also have been a little more pro-active in reconciling duplication; for instance, Cunich (58), essentially gives an abbreviated account about donations to Syon by the brothers that is found more expansively in Gillespie (122–5).

In the Stockholm volume there is not the same sense of duplication or missed cross-references; this may be in part because the essays are considerably shorter. Yet in the midst of a few insubstantial essays there is considerable scholarly substance. In their different ways the contributors highlight areas of particular interest. These range widely and include a biographical sketch of Syon personnel (Bainbridge), detailed detective work to uncover manuscripts and incunabula associated with Syon before and after 1519 (Powell), and a painstaking evaluation of the significance of the annotation in a Whitford text (Hutchison). Yet fascinating as these essays are, from this reviewer's perspective it has to be said that it is the discussion of Vadstena and other continental convents that is most captivating. While much is already known about Syon, for an English-speaking audience what is most important is to gain access to the sort of scholarship about Vadstena that has long been available only in Swedish circles. This is where the true merit of this volume lies. In reading these essays we gain, for instance, an insight into the purpose of table books in promulgating regulations and rituals (Carlquist), the precise patterns of illumination in Vadstena (Lindqvist Sandgren), and examples of the handwriting of particular nuns (Hedström and Lindell), a subject long made popular by Monica Hedlund (in Swedish and, to a lesser extent, in English).

Minor criticisms aside, when viewed together (or apart), these volumes make a worthy contribution to the area of Birgittine scholarship and both sets of contributors and editors are to be heartily congratulated on their work.

Veronica O'Mara, University of Hull

JOHN N. KING, ED.
Tudor Books and Readers: Materiality and the Construction of Meaning.
Cambridge: Cambridge University Press, 2010.
xviii + 270. 18 black and white illus., 13 tables.

This collection of essays edited by John N. King considers books in what he calls – after the lengthenings of other periods – the "long Tudor period" (2). The length is rewardingly great: the material surveyed stretches for 150 years from Caxton's printing of the *Recuyell* at Ghent in 1473 to the First Folio of Shakespeare's plays in 1623. Readers of *JEBS* might be encouraged to lengthen their interests, too, already stretching to the Reformation, by browsing this book, for although some of its topics fall later than the purview of this *Journal*, the book's ideas, in particular, would prove useful for people working on earlier periods. Much recent research has crossed the divide between 1350 and 1550, but has often paused, or argued for a break, at the Reformation; this book crosses that divide firmly and shows what we might learn from so doing.

Two chapters which say a lot about the lengthy Tudor period before 1550 seem more useful to specialists in its latter part, who want to look backwards: namely, the potted history of Tudor books in King's introduction (2-10) which, with just a few errors at the earlier end, is extremely useful as a framework for the later case-studies in this collection; and Lotte Hellinga's short summary of early printing (15-22), which is fine but of course surpassed by her recent full-length *William Caxton and Early Printing in England* (2010). The first chapter that should be essential reading for students of early Tudor printing is by Joseph A. Dane and Alexandra Gillespie. Typical of this book's invitation to look further afield for new ideas, though, their chapter invites reading alongside the subsequent one by Steven K. Galbraith on Elizabethan and Jacobean printing. Taken as a pair, these chapters have the largest implications for thinking about printing, or indeed for thinking about the size and material form of manuscripts, in any period. Together they debunk ideas that smaller formats such as quartos were always "cheap" and larger ones such as folios always prestigious or expensive. Dane and Gillespie usefully remind us not to assume the significance of bibliographical or material facts, such as cost or format, in a simplistic way (29). However, both chapters remind us of the importance of other material qualities: durability and the length of texts (42, 63, 66). And they not only dispose of lazy assumptions and categories; they also propose helpful new hypotheses and categories, such as Galbraith's three reasons for using folio format (48-49), that further studies in other media and eras might go on to test and develop. Continuing this collection's titular focus on "Materiality," Elizabeth Evenden's chapter similarly stresses material concerns (79: the need to fill space) but also, similarly, considers immaterial things—ideas, ambitions—and the lack of material practicality in making Foxe's *Book of Martyrs* (68, 72). This is a productive balance that exemplifies the broadmindedness needed in all studies of the history of the book.

There is a similar breadth of ideas exemplified in Alexandra Walsham's chapter on animadversions and rebuttals. This chapter balances detailed archival and bibliographical facts with thoughtful political and religious history, and is distinguished by its alertness to the multiple possibilities open to writers, printers, readers and annotators. Though Walsham's material is largely Elizabethan, historians of the book and of reading in any period could learn much here about the wealth of explanations they might essay—and the breadth of research that underpins such subtlety. John N. King's own chapter, a study of banderols and captions in Foxe's *Book of Martyrs*, their contents, typefaces and means of transmission, is similarly excellent in its avoidance of reductive explanations. (He also considers early Tudor precedents briefly: 197-99.)

There are other useful questions, which historians of reading might want to consider, whatever their period of specialism, in a pair of case-studies by

Andrew Cambers and Jason Scott-Warren of late Elizabethan readers. They explore sensitively questions of fact specific to their case-studies but also questions of method and evidence in general—say, what one can or cannot learn from marginalia (230) or from book-lists (230)—in a way typical of this thought-provoking collection of essays.

These last two chapters do differ from some of the other chapters, though, in attending to lots of manuscript evidence. For one divide crossed but not fully bridged by this collection is that between manuscript and print. The focus is primarily on printed books—or on print culture in the broadest sense, as in chapters by Douglas A. Brooks and Cyndia Susan Clegg—and it will prove very useful for people studying that medium. When the focus is on manuscript material, it is often on manuscript additions to printed books (as in captions to illustrations or marginalia) or on documents which record people's use of printed books (in inventories or diaries). But thereby King's *Tudor Books and Readers: Materiality and the Construction of Meaning* achieves admirable focus and coherence, which is difficult in a collection of essays, and makes clear its usefulness to specialists but also, as suggested here, to thoughtful readers among the scholarly community in general.

Daniel Wakelin, University of Cambridge

ANNE LAWRENCE-MATHERS and PHILIPPA HARDMAN, EDS.
Women and Writing, c.1340-c.1650. The Domestication of Print Culture.
York: York Medieval Press, 2010. 231 pp.

    This collection of eleven essays concentrates on the transition from manuscript to print as illustrated by a range of works in which women were involved in various ways. Its main purpose is to address the question of female participation in "literary production" in the broadest sense of the term, a question the editors rightly say has not been sufficiently dealt with to date. They have thus decided to "recover women's engagement with texts more broadly" by examining the contribution, not only of authors, but also of "translators, copyists and readers." Some would argue that nowadays the author/translator distinction is far more blurred, since translation is seen as creation rather than as a secondary, inferior activity. The Introduction's claim that one of the essays "tackles head on" the "disputed issues" concerning the relative merits of women's translations is in fact a little dated, such issues having been discredited by writers on women translators over the past decade. Copyists, letter writers and readers, however, still occupy rungs further down the literary ladder, despite playing a crucial role in the history of the book, and Lawrence-Mathers and Hardman have done well to examine their contribution to early modern literary production via domestic modes of expression and dissemination.

    In several essays, the domestic sphere is represented by compilations of various sorts. Phillipa Hardman, in "Domestic Learning and Teaching: Investigating Evidence for the Role of 'Household Miscellanies' in Late-Medieval

England," discusses five manuscript household miscellanies: the Auchinleck, Thornton, Findern, Heege and Rate. She argues that they played a role in the education of young children, for which women were largely responsible since it took place in the home. However, as she also says, there is very little documentary evidence of exactly how they were used, given the paucity of annotations, discretion as to ownership, and commentary on whether they were read aloud in groups or silently in private. Not surprisingly, then, the importance of the link between women and these miscellanies remains implicit rather than explicit. A second essay, "Domesticating the Calendar: The Hours and the Almanac in Tudor England" by Anne Lawrence-Mathers, also suffers from some uncertainty as to the particular pertinence of the documents to women, since primers and almanacs were owned and annotated by men, too, although they did contain information that concerned the household, diet, and horticulture. A different kind of compilation is treated by Adam Smyth. In "Commonplace Book Culture: A List of Sixteen Traits," he widens the genre by increasing the number of traits previously used to define the commonplace book; this enables him to include a more diverse range of texts and activities, one that demonstrates women's agency in what has always been a genre associated with university-educated males. The essay is well structured and argued, listing the sixteen proposed traits one by one and discussing the eleven that he considers pertinent to women.

Two essays deal with women's correspondence. James Daybell, in "Women, Politics and Domesticity: The Scribal Publication of Lady Rich's Letter to Elizabeth I," studies women's participation in scribal publication and court politics as seen in Penelope Rich's 1599 plea to the queen for mercy for her brother, the earl of Essex. The "private" and the "public" intersect in many ways, as Daybell demonstrates, not least in the passage from manuscript to print and from traditionally female social activities such as familial letter writing to political intervention in court circles by means of formal correspondence, not so usually associated with women. Graham Williams, in "Joan Thynne, her scribe and her letters to her son," confines his discussion to familial correspondence, as his title suggests, but explores the question of why Joan, literate and the author of much correspondence, chose to have a scribe write these particular letters. In a wider context, he asks what impact this corpus of letters, unusual in its dual authorial/scribal nature, has had on linguistic features, thus being of value to both historical linguists and students of rhetoric and epistolary composition.

Family relationships are further explored in essays by Elizabeth Heale and C. B. Hardman. In "Fathers and Daughters: Four Women and their Family Albums of Verse," Heale discusses women's participation in copying and transmitting, as well as perhaps composing, verse in the late sixteenth and early seventeenth centuries. This, however, constitutes what another contributor calls "creative licence," for it is unclear how much actual input these women had in producing these verse albums, which are found in: British Library MS Add. 36529 signed by John Harington's daughters, Ellina and Francis; the Pepys Library Maitland Quarto containing verse either copied by or for Richard Maitland's daughter Mary; and Edinburgh University, MS Laing III. 444, that includes a prose work copied by Sir John Davies's daughter, Lucy. C. B. Hardman, in "The Book as Domestic Gift: Bodleian Ms Don.C.24," discusses a collection of poems by Nicholas Oldisworth presented by him to his wife in 1644 and then passed on to his second daughter, Margaret, who adds a collection of recipes to the manuscript.

Of the remaining four essays, two deal very clearly with the domestic sphere. Alison Wiggins's "Frances Wolfreston's *Chaucer*" discusses the ownership of William Thynne's 1550 edition of *The workes of Geffray Chaucer* by the women of the Wolfreston family. The volume contains manuscript marginalia and underlinings, demonstrating female engagement with a literary text within a domestic context, although, as Wiggins points out, these cannot in all certainty be attributed to the women owners. Moreover, the annotations of an identified male reader muddy the waters somewhat. Female authorship is not, however, in any doubt when it comes to the annotated volume of life-writing discussed by Alice Eardley in "'like hewen stone': Augustine, Audience and Revision in Elizabeth Isham's 'Booke of Rememberance'." Here the domestic element is represented by Elizabeth's family audience but also, more tellingly, by the changes she wrought in borrowing from St. Augustine's *Confessions*, transplanting the public events recounted there into the private sphere of her own similar experiences.

Domestic links, although present, are more tenuous in the remaining two essays, both of which are nevertheless excellent. Gemma Allen's perceptive "'a briefe and plaine declaration': Lady Anne Bacon's 1564 translation of the *Apologia Ecclesiae Anglicanae*" argues convincingly that although the translation was executed in the domestic sphere of Bacon's home, it was clearly intended as a very public work, engaging with one of the foremost issues of the day, the legitimization of the Church of England. Anna Bayman's "Female Voices in Early Seventeenth Century Pamphlet Literature" demonstrates how the *querelle des femmes* moved from clerical and literary debate through learned humanist tracts and popular literature to pamphlets, where it was articulated in terms similar to those used to criticize print. The association of male pamphleteering with "railing" was widened, through the publication of pamphlets on the "woman question" that now afforded space to female speech, to include shrewishness and scolding. These, perhaps, provide the domestic context that is presented more explicitly in other contributions to the volume.

Brenda M. Hosington, Université de Montréal and University of Warwick

SUSAN POWELL, ED.
John Mirk's Festial *edited from British Library MS Cotton Claudius A.II.*
Vol. 1. Early English Text Society, o.s., 334.
Oxford: Oxford University Press for the Early English Text Society,
2009. 550 pp.

Probably written toward the end of the 1380s, John Mirk's *Festial* was conceived as a resource for the humble English homilist, providing him with sixty-four "off-the-shelf" vernacular sermons for the major feasts of the Church calendar. Twenty-one manuscripts transmit the text in two main versions. Group A, preserved in thirteen manuscripts, follows the chronology of the Church year (beginning on Advent Sunday), whereas Group B, in eight manuscripts, transmits a rearrangement of a Group A text into *Temporale* and *Sanctorale* cycles (with significant textual modifications as well). Four manuscripts also attest to a post-1434 revision of a Group B text, while another Group B text served as the basis for the roughly two dozen early printed editions from 1483 to 1532. (For the record, STC 17973.5 was not printed by Wynkyn de Worde, but rather for him by an unidentified printer active between 1515 and 1520; similarly, I would attribute STC 17972 to Robert Copland.) Added to this mix are nineteen manuscripts containing material extracted, or otherwise derived, from the *Festial*, a number sure to grow as scholars become increasingly familiar with Mirk's influential compilation. As one might expect from a popular preaching manual transmitted for more than one hundred fifty years, the corpus of variants is huge and the relationships correspondingly complex. Powell proves herself to be a deft handler of this textual Rubik's cube, and her edition will become the essential starting-point for any discussion of Mirk and his "treti [that] speketh alle of festis" (3).

A handful of remarks in Mirk's three known works constitute his only biography. He was a canon regular and eventually prior of the Augustinian abbey of Lilleshall in Shropshire, and his *floruit* has recently been pushed back about twenty years, from *c.* 1403 to *c.* 1380 (xxi). Powell contextualizes such meager information by exploring the history of Augustinian canons in England, the foundation of Lilleshall (an Arrouaisian house), and the scholarly inclinations and output of other members of this high-profile order (xxii–xxv). As she points out, Mirk's entire corpus—the *Instructions for Parish Priests* (in English rhyming couplets) and *Manuale sacerdotis* (in Latin), in addition to the *Festial*—can be understood as a kind of educational program for parish priests, reflecting the pastoral concerns and pedagogical mission of the Augustinians (xxv–xxviii). A zeal for preaching characterizes Mirk's personal contribution to this enterprise. What Mirk lacked in intellectual prowess, Powell explains, he made up for in energy and expressive sensitivity (xxv). His skills can be glimpsed in his treatment of his source material. Broadly speaking, Mirk derives his homilies from the *Legenda aurea* (almost exclusively for the *Sanctorale* cycle) and lifts additional matter primarily from John Beleth's *Rationale divinorum officiorum* (for the *Temporale* sermons). His standard practice is to summarize the legends in his own words, reducing their length, simplifying their structure, and adding *narrationes* and *exempla* as needed—all for the sake of the semi-literate preacher and his unlettered flock. The quirky but exuberant nature of this free adaptation emerges from Powell's comparison of the Ascension Day sermon to its source in the *Legenda aurea* (xxxiii–xxxv). Somewhat less clear is whether any of these modifications, especially the abridgments, could be attributed to Mirk's use of an idiosyncratic manuscript of the *Legenda aurea*.

Understandably, Powell devotes most of her introduction to the textual transmission of the *Festial*, building on the previous research of Martyn F. Wakelin (1967). She accepts the conventional division of the manuscripts into two groups, with textual primacy assigned to Group A. (These conclusions are based on full collations of the prayer, the prologue, and sermons 2, 14, 24, 34, 39, and 56—with the complete corpus of variants to appear in volume two—plus an informal collation of the remaining material.) Powell goes on to discuss the filiation of the texts within each group (lxiii–lxxxiii), identifying broad relationships among all the witnesses: ABC, aDFI, DEFG, HIJK, abeg, cdfh, and so forth. Owing to the extent of variation, Powell refrains from drawing a stemma, although a neo-Lachmannian approach, with its focus on shared errors, could prove extremely helpful, if not crucial, in such cases as: *(venit) ad ostium crebris ictibus pulsans* → *beat upon the gate so hard* → *bade open the gate so hard* (lxii; cxvii). Lacking Powell's intimate knowledge of the sources, I am in no position to dispute her conclusions, although it strikes me that some of the more intractable problems of filiation might be solved if one supposed that Group A and Group B texts descend, via separate hyparchetypes, from a single common ancestor. Hence, the Group B features in Group A witnesses—like the Group A features in Group B witnesses—come largely from the archetype, not (necessarily) from the "intensive inter-copying" (cx) of different *Festial* texts. Depending on its relationship to the archetype, moreover, C could transmit the original arrangement of Mirk's sermons, the service-book order having been retained by this single Group A witness and by the hyparchetype of the Group B texts, but altered in a hyparchetype of the remaining Group A texts. Accordingly, the amplifications in Group B texts would have to be treated as omissions from various hyparchetypes of Group A texts. Since I have not subjected the corpus of variants to a thorough analysis, however, I shall defer to Powell's formidable arguments in support of her own position. Doubtless the raw textual data in volume two will decide the matter.

Powell chooses British Library MS Cotton Claudius A.II as the base text for her edition. Notwithstanding its problematic textual strata, this manuscript, as she points out, is the earliest, the most conscientiously assembled, and the most complete witness of the *Festial*, while its three main hands can be localized to Staffordshire, which shares its western border with Mirk's home county of Shropshire (cxx–cxxi). Powell's description of the manuscript is a tour-de-force of codicology (lxxxiii–cx), and her embedded analysis of the five hands is at once meticulous and comprehensive (lxxxvii–civ). The editorial outcome is a Claudius A.II version of the *Festial*, transcribed according to EETS norms and sparingly amended with reference to the most closely related manuscripts, with rejected base-text readings at the foot of the page and explanatory remarks in a separate section at the end of the transcription. Readers can consult the edition knowing that Powell has left nothing to chance.

Like Mirk himself, Powell has a passion for communicating her message and a commitment to helping others understand the complexities of her subject. Her modern-day *treti*, which combines great learning and old-fashioned hard work, sets a high standard for those who might follow in her footsteps. We can only hope that volume two appears soon. Meanwhile, Powell has given us a powerful piece of scholarship to think about.

Joseph J. Gwara, United States Naval Academy

RALUCA L. RADULESCU and CORY JAMES RUSHTON, EDS.
A Companion to Medieval Popular Romance
Cambridge: D.S. Brewer, 2009. xiv + 209 pp.

In a 1986 essay, Stephen Knight quipped that Middle English verse romances are the "ugly ducklings of medieval English studies" ("The Social Function of the Middle English Romances," in David Aers, ed., *Medieval Literature: Criticism, Ideology and History* [Brighton: Harvester Press, 1986], 99–122, 99). Perhaps this was so in 1986—but not today. Raluca L. Radulescu and Cory James Rushton's collection of essays represents another (welcome) addition to a series of recent edited collections examining the so-called "popular romances": the biennial Romance in Medieval Britain conference (whose proceedings have been regularly published since 1991); Ad Putter and Jane Gilbert's *The Spirit of Medieval English Popular Romance*; and *Pulp Fictions of Medieval England: Essays on Popular Romance*, edited by Nicola MacDonald. In an age of Formalism, critics had to hedge and plead in order to justify serious engagement with the few "popular" verse romances thought worthy of critical attention (*Sir Orfeo* always being the diamond in the rough). One hopes that this recent critical interest signals a new willingness to engage with popular romance—one of the primary mediums of entertainment in late medieval England.

The volume opens with the editors' Introduction, which surveys recent work on popular romance. Radulescu and Rushton also provide a brief meditation on the difficulties inherent in applying the term "popular" to any medieval narrative. They ultimately resolve that "in this Companion we define 'popular romance' as those texts in Middle English, sometimes with origins in Anglo-Norman versions, which show a predominant concern with narrative at the expense of symbolic meaning. Such texts appear to have been widely read or heard, but have subsequently been ignored by scholarship as less worthy of study than the equivalent productions by Chaucer or the *Gawain-poet*" (7). Rosalind Field's "The Material and the Problems" provides a suitable first chapter, for it picks up on the editors' discussion of the difficulties inherent in assessing the "popular" nature of Middle English romance. Field pays particular attention to the mixing of seemingly high and low registers in Anglo-Norman romance, and how such mixing is often preserved in the Middle English adaptations of these texts. Ultimately, Field demurs from making any totalizing claims about the nature of popular romances, for "The problem is not that there is so little to say about anonymous, conventional works, but there is so much" (29–30). Radulescu's own contribution to the volume, "Genre and Classification," follows nicely on from Field's. Radulescu, like Field, wrestles with how to classify this body of narratives, ultimately offering what she calls the "[t]hree main characteristics of the popular romance genre": a focus on social and family concerns, the central position occupied by strong female characters, and "the self-consciousness of the narratives, whether expressed at the level of criticism against courtly or chivalric values or cultural taboos" (40).

The next two chapters will be of most interest to readers of *JEBS* and to book historians in general. The first, Maldwyn Mills and Gillian Rogers's "The Manuscripts of Popular Romance," offers a concise overview of the circulation of romance. This chapter comprises, more properly speaking, two distinct single-author chapters joined into one. Mills contributes the section on "Medieval Manuscripts of Popular Romances," while Rogers writes the section on the Percy Folio. Mills draws attention to the diversity of manuscript contexts, arguing that such diversity replicates the diversity of narrative forms that comprise the corpus of popular romances. The usual suspects—e.g., the Lincoln Thornton Manuscript, the Findern Anthology, British Library Cotton Caligula a.2, Cambridge University Library Ff.2.38, and Bodleian Ashmole 61—feature centrally in Mills's discussion. Rogers then devotes attention specifically to the Percy Folio Manuscript, a seventeenth-century compilation of, among other things, Middle English romance. She characterizes the compiler of this manuscript as interested in things both current and antiquarian, with the romances exemplifying the latter. Rogers traces several major themes that underlie the Percy romances, adding the interesting observation that many of the non-romance items, particularly the ballads, shared similar themes with the romances. The second chapter most likely to interest readers of *JEBS* is Jennifer Fellows's "Printed Romances in the Sixteenth Century." Fellows examines the early printed editions of the romances found in Cambridge University Library MS Ff.2.38, demonstrating the variety of ways in which printers—primarily Wynkyn de Worde and William Copland—treated their texts. As she shows, there was no absolute rule for how printers handled such romances: sometimes they followed the source texts faithfully, and at other times they abridged and emended rather more liberally.

The next two chapters consider the ideological underpinnings of popular romance. Thomas H. Crofts and Robert Allen Rouse examine the complex ways in which *nationalism*—itself a fraught term, as they note—is inflected in these texts, ultimately concluding that each text presents a different ideal of both the nation and the foreign Other and thus each must be read on its own terms. Following this chapter, Joanne Charbonneau and Désirée Cromwell discuss issues of gender raised by popular romances, concluding that "It is not a simple case of male dominance and hierarchical importance, but a complicated nexus of male and female desires" (106). After these interrelated chapters, the collection turns to another pair of chapters sharing similar concerns—this time, concerns about form. First is Ad Putter's "The Metres and Stanza Forms of Popular Romance." Rather than advancing any particular argument, this chapter masterfully synthesizes the panoply of metrical forms one encounters in Middle English romance into a clear and concise summary—as such, it forms recommended reading for graduate students preparing for exams or for faculty preparing to teach advanced courses in search of a "refresher" on the formal possibilities of Middle English. Karl Reichl's contribution, "Orality and Performance," follows. In this chapter, Reichl examines the wide body of evidence relating to the oral performance, and perhaps even oral composition, of Middle English romance. Although more bibliographically oriented scholars may not find all of Reichl's conclusions convincing, the inclusion of his chapter in this volume can go a long way toward synthesizing the work of scholars of both oral and manuscript transmission, two approaches that have remained insulated from one another—to the detriment of both.

The volume concludes with two chapters detailing the reception of popular romance—in medieval England and in modern scholarship, respectively. The first is Phillipa Hardman's "Popular Romances and Young Readers," which advances the most pointed argument of any chapter in this collection. Hardman contends that the manuscript form in which most popular romances survive—viz., the miscellany, produced for a household—as well as the content of the romances themselves, together suggest an *intended* and *actual* readership composed predominantly of young people. In Hardman's reading, then, these texts serve a pedagogic function, specifically providing an education in courtesy to the children of merchants and gentry. Finally, Rushton rounds out the volume with his "Modern and Academic Reception of the Popular Romance." He focuses on the twentieth century's canonization of Chaucer's "Tale of Sir Thopas" and *Sir Gawain and the Green Knight*. Such texts became normative, defining the modern reader's expectations of romance. Almost by default, then, the popular romances became paltry imitations; however, Rushton concludes the essay by noting that popular romance has recently begun to enjoy academic respectability, as critics have looked to these texts to recover marginal voices and alternative ideologies.

In sum, this volume serves as a nice introduction to the critical complexities of what are all too often dismissed as simplistic texts. Its main limitation is one that hinders almost every collection of essays: namely, the diversity of scholars contributing chapters results in a diversity of critical approaches to such texts. As a result, one does not put down the volume with a clear sense of what "popular romance" was. However, this limitation is also a strength, for such diversity of voices means that one *does* put down the volume with a clear sense that the field of popular romance is suitably complex to merit further reading. A clearer, more focused argument about popular culture in late medieval England and the place held by romance therein demands a single-author monograph. Perhaps this volume will inspire the writing of such a book.

Michael Johnston, Purdue University

NIGEL RAMSAY and JAMES M. W. WILLOUGHBY, EDS.
Hospitals, Towns, and the Professions.
Corpus of British Medieval Library Catalogues, 14. The British Library in association with the British Academy, 2009. xlix + 561 pp, 4 plates.

Hospitals, Towns, and the Professions, the fourteenth volume in an essential reference series, The Corpus of British Medieval Library Catalogues, publishes 134 lists of books owned by eighty-six institutions as witnessed by catalogues, inventories and wills, as well as notes on another sixteen for which other evidence shows they once owned books. Each institution is introduced by a historical note, each list by a brief description, and, where it has proved possible, the works listed are identified. Few, however, are represented by surviving volumes, perhaps unsurprisingly since bibles and liturgica predominate in the lists. Only seventeen of the institutions included here are to be found in Neil Ker's *Medieval Libraries of Great Britain*.

Some lists have been published elsewhere, but are carefully re-edited by Nigel Ramsay and James Willoughby. The gift of canon law, theological and other books made in 1346 by Haimo Hethe, Bishop of Rochester, for the benefit of the secular clergy, appeared in *English Benedictine Libraries: the Shorter Catalogues* (1996), volume 4 of the Corpus, since the books were vested in the prior and chapter of the monastic cathedral. Possibly the best known are the list of books left by the fishmonger Andrew Horn to London's Guildhall, 1328, and those included among the goods Alice de la Pole, Duchess of Suffolk, dispatched to Ewelme in 1466. Ker considered the latter belonged to God's House, the almshouse founded there by Alice and her husband, but it has been argued that they represent Alice's own library. After reviewing the arguments, the editors conclude that since personal books can be given away Alice possibly meant the volumes for God's House. Among them was a "quaire of a legende of ragge hande," previously thought to stand for St Radegund, but the editors correctly point out the contemporary usage of *ragge* to describe irregular handwriting.

The earliest list dates from 1259 and concerns the books (two Graduals, three Antiphonals, a Martyrology, and a Consuetudinary) left by Martin of St. Cross, late master, to the Hospital of SS. Mary the Virgin, Lazarus, Martha, and Mary at Sherburn, Co. Durham. None of these volumes is identifiable, but the editors argue that a late twelfth-century copy of Augustine, *De baptismo paruulorum* and the *Gemma ecclesie* (York Minster Library XVI.I.II), bearing the fifteenth-century *ex libris* "Gemma ecclesie constans Capelle Hospitalis de Sherburn," belonged here rather than Sherborne, Dorset. The latest list is from an inventory of goods found at the English Hospital in Rome drawn up in 1578.

The entry for the Hospital of the Holy Trinity and St. Thomas the Martyr in Rome, founded to receive English pilgrims, is much the longest of the entries (131 pages) and introduces an account of an institution little known, if at all, to many of us. Twenty-six separate inventories from 1496-1578 are edited, and witness to a library growing rapidly with the acquisition of printed books, mainly from Rome and Venice. With such a careful account kept of its books, the inventories become largely repetitive, but the most notable entries are for a fifteenth-century manuscript copy of Bishop Grandisson's *Vita S. Thomae Cantuariensis* (Rome, Venerable English College, Liber 1384) found in the 1496 inventory, and the intriguing "a legent gouen be Kaxton printe" in the 1501 inventory where the second folio cited agrees with the edition printed in Paris by Guillaume Maynyal for William Caxton, 14 August 1488 (*STC* 16136). The historical note at the beginning of the entry notes six other manuscripts belonging to the hospital but not in any of the lists, including a miscellany of verse by Lydgate and others, and the unique copy, predating the printed edition and representing an earlier recension, of Nicholas Sander's *De origine progressu schismatis Anglicani*, the first "official" recusant history of the schism with England. Sander had been chamberlain in 1563 and this copy may well be holograph.

Notes on the institutions, donors and books provide much valuable information and bear witness to the editors' wide-ranging research. Thus the introduction to Thomas Jakes's bequest of books to the Inner Temple, 1513, discusses his career, his patron the Chief Justice Sir Thomas Frowyk, whose widow Jakes married, the possibility that some of Jakes's books had been owned by Sir Thomas, and surviving books of Jakes's not left to Inner Temple. The Guild of St. Mary the Virgin at Boston supported a school where Matilda Mareflete was "magistra scholarum" in 1404. Of a copy of Richard Rolle in an inventory from the hospital of St. Julian, Southampton, 1415, we learn that in 1381 its donor Matthew Willesthorpe together with John Wyclif pledged a copy of Gratian (British Library, Royal MS 10.E.II) in the Hussey chest at Oxford. One might add to the editors' note on the hospital of St. James, Westminster, the possibility that Lambeth Palace Library MS 265, a copy of Caxton's *Dictes and Sayings of the Philosophers*, was written by one of the brothers there. Its colophon states it was written "Apud sanctum Jacobum in campis per haywarde," and Caxton first settled at Westminster.

An introduction, pp. xxxi-xlix, briefly discusses each type of library included in the main text. Of the four plates the most interesting are 3 and 4, illustrating part of the inventory of books bequeathed to his successors by Thomas Benolt, Clarenceux King of Arms, in 1534 (College of Arms, MS Heralds, vol. I, fols 189-91). Clarenceux's books are inventoried in some detail but each volume is also identified by a marginal pictogram distinguishing it from all others. Seven indexes complete the volume: of Incipits and Second Folios, Manuscripts, Printed Books, Authors, Anonymous Works, Donors and Former Owners, and a General Index.

Pamela Robinson, Institute of English Studies, University of London

KARI ANNE RAND
The Index of Middle English Prose. Handlist XX: Manuscripts in the Library of Corpus Christi College, Cambridge.
Cambridge: D. S. Brewer, 2009. xxxi + 212 pp.

This is the third Index of Middle English Prose handlist to have been completed by Kari Anne Rand; Handlist 17 covered the manuscripts in Gonville and Caius College, and Handlist 18 that of Pembroke College and the Fitzwilliam Museum. The current Handlist covers what might be considered the most important library of the four, or definitely the best known, the Parker Library at Corpus Christi, which has recently been refurbished with an impressive new reading room. No doubt because of its fame and the number of works devoted to its history (all helpfully listed on xix, n. 1), Rand spends only a brief period on the development of Matthew Parker's library, confining herself to what she calls an "overview." This is a wise decision because to have done otherwise would clearly have involved her in trying to provide abbreviated accounts of lengthy studies best read in full. The main points are therefore succinctly given about how Parker developed from being mainly a collector of printed books to a somewhat rapacious acquirer of manuscripts for the Protestant cause; how his collection of over 400 manuscripts and about 1075 printed books were donated in 1575 (when the College was more than two hundred years old and already in possession of over two hundred manuscripts and printed books); and, most usefully, about the subsequent cataloguing of the Corpus library.

The Index contains fifty-two manuscripts, of which forty-eight came from Parker. Not surprisingly, given that Parker's mission had been to acquire texts to justify the position of the reformed Church, the emphasis is on religious material. The collection includes a number of what can now be called standard items in any IMEP list: copies of the *Brut* (MSS 174 and 182) and the *Mirror of the Blessed Life of Jesus Christ* (MSS 142 [1–4] and 143), as well as the Wycliffite bible in whole or in part (MSS 147 and 440) and the Wycliffite sermon cycle (MS 336). Alongside these are various biblical commentaries (MS 32), a massive collection of Wycliffite material (MS 296), Trevisa's translation of Higden's *Polychronicon* (MS 354 [1]), Chaucer's *Treatise on the Astrolabe* (MS 424 [1]), and, perhaps most excitingly of all, *Ancrene Wisse* (MS 402).

The standard of indexing is exemplary as always. For instance, in the indexing of MS 282, a manuscript of *The Mirror*, the English translation of Robert Gretham's *Miroir*, Rand not only provides full bibliographical details but also picks up on information that might have eluded other people (she notes that the last item in the manuscript is also found in Trinity College Dublin, MS 69, something that has not been noticed in the literature). Rand is never content to index in a minimalist fashion; an example of this is her detailed description of MS 387 [3] and [4], where she goes out of her way to list each incipit and explicit of the individual parts of Rolle's Old Testament Canticle commentaries and the Wycliffite tracts in turn. Although even the most serious medievalist might not regard all the texts indexed as equally interesting, this does not deter Rand; all entries are given the same sort of attention so that, for example, she devotes as much care (sixteen pages) to MS 388, a macaronic collection of numerous recipes (with various glosses), as she does to any other manuscript.

The volume concludes with the usual indices but in addition Rand has added a new one, an "Index of Manuscripts Cited," including "Obsolete References" (201–12). This is of tremendous use and it is amazing that no previous indexers (myself included) had the foresight to think of such an index. We have all been reduced to speed-reading volumes and ploughing our way through long general indices in order to find references to the latest manuscript in which we are interested. With an index like this we would be spared such work. Although it will be a great labor for other editors, it is earnestly hoped that this sort of index will become a standard feature of all future *IMEP* volumes.

Veronica O'Mara, University of Hull

JAYNE RINGROSE
Summary Catalogue of the Additional Medieval Manuscripts in Cambridge University Library acquired before 1940.
Cambridge: Boydell, 2009. xxxvi + 339 pp.

In her Introduction to *IMEP XIX* (see review in this volume, 199-200), Margaret Connolly notes carefully what she has not examined, among which she includes the Additional manuscripts, "which will require separate treatment." The task of the future editor of the *IMEP* volume for the Cambridge University Library Additional manuscripts has been made much easier by the publication of Jayne Ringrose's catalogue of those medieval Additional manuscripts acquired between the publication of the printed catalogue (1856 to 1867) and 1940. To complement the Nicholas Loves identified by Connolly, we have two more; one more *Scale* (Book I); more Rolle; another manuscript of Wycliffite Sunday gospel sermons; two more manuscripts containing pieces from *Speculum Christiani*—in fact, more in general of those religious and secular texts in the manuscripts acquired by Cambridge University Library earlier and catalogued by Connolly.

However, this is a catalogue of manuscripts containing any medieval material, not just Middle English prose, and it describes over 300 manuscripts which, as Ringrose points out, primarily reflect the interests of four successive Scholar-Librarians, from Henry Bradshaw (1867 to 1886) to Alwyn Schofield (1923 to 1949). Her Introduction is fascinating on what became available during these years and how the University Library benefited. Much material was acquired from collections of East Anglian antiquaries, notably, material from Bury St Edmunds, but also manuscripts ultimately coming (perhaps) from Thomas Martin and (definitely) from the remarkable parish library at Brent Eleigh. Illuminated manuscripts were bequeathed by Samuel Smith Sandars, Sir Stephen Gaselee, and Arthur Young (who donated the two manuscripts of the *Mirror of the Blessed Life of Jesus Christ*, one the Mount Grace copy). Latin predominates (Greek manuscripts are not included), but, as has been seen, English is also well represented, thanks to the interests of Bradshaw and the third Scholar-Librarian of this period, Francis Jenkinson (1889-1923). These three men, Bradshaw, Jenkinson, and Schofield, were most instrumental in enhancing the Library by their acquisitions, whereas the second Scholar-Librarian, William Smith, held the post for only three years (1886 to 1889). However, on his death in 1894, he bequeathed the library, not just oriental manuscripts, but a Bridgettine Breviary from Germany (in 1932 it acquired another Bridgettine liturgical book, which had once belonged to John Meade Falkner).

As a Summary Catalogue, the entry for each manuscript is: classmark, date, material, size, foliation; subject of text and author, if known; each item numbered and identified, with bibliography; extra material relating to the history of the manuscript. The entries are admirably full: see, for example, the entries for the two full Latin manuscripts of the *Legenda Aurea* (Add. 618 and 6452) or for the English translation of the *De Consolatione Philosophiae* (Add. 3573). In particular, the provenance and history of the manuscripts are treated very fully and provide fascinating information. A single leaf of a work in French on husbandry (Add. 6860) produces half a page on its provenance (an inscription in the hand of Henry de Kirkstede of Bury St Edmunds; later owned by Bury citizens, James Cobbes (on whom Richard Beadle has written) and Cox Macro; then bought by the antiquarian friends Hudson Gurney and Dawson Turner; finally acquired by the University Library March 30, 1936, through the Wilson-Barkworth Benefaction. The next medieval manuscript (Add. 6864) is *The Siege of Thebes*, of course of Bury provenance (and again passing through the hands of Cobbes, Macro, and Gurney), but owned at the end of the fifteenth century, it seems, by Richard Tilney, Warden of the Grocer's Company 1478-1497. The manuscript was bought by Alwyn Schofield at the same sale as the French leaf: he then presented it to the Library. Any comparison with present-day University librarians would be odious and will not be made.

The end-matter to this Summary Catalogue consists of an Index of Former Owners, an Index of Manuscripts Cited, and a General Index. The Index of Former Owners yields many gems and is worth reading through from beginning to end, dipping back into the volume from time to time. M. R. James, for example, gave one of the two manuscripts of the *Speculum Christiani* mentioned above. The way in which he acquired it is recorded in a laconic note in his own hand, pasted inside the back cover: "This MS was given me by H. H. Sills, MA, Fellow of King's College, from the library of his uncle at Cold Bath House, Lincoln. He understood that I should most likely give it to the University Library which I now do." Rarely has a catalogue been such a good read in itself, as well as scrupulously detailed and scholarly. (Indeed, that could not quite be said of James's own catalogues!)

Sue Powell, University of Salford

NILA VÁZQUEZ
The Tale of Gamelyn *of the* Canterbury Tales: *An Annotated Edition.*
Lewiston, New York: The Edward Mellen Press, 2009. 476 pp.

This annotated edition of the *Tale of Gamelyn,* a tale found in twenty five of the eighty-four extant manuscripts or fragments of the *Canterbury Tales,* represents the culmination of many years' work by Nila Vázquez on the transcription and analysis of the tale in ten of those manuscripts. These transcripts were then collated electronically and compared to provide the critical edition of *Gamelyn* in this volume, supplemented with notes to the text.

It should be appreciated that *Gamelyn* survives only in complete manuscripts of the *Canterbury Tales* and is found nowhere else. Vázquez's aim was to "provide the reader with some information about the *Tale of Gamelyn*" as well as a new critical edition and modern English translation. The intention of the work was never to reach "important conclusions" about, for example, the place of the *Tale of Gamelyn* in the Chaucer canon. In essence, then, the volume represents the working papers of an editor and is a reference tool designed to provide information on the chosen manuscripts and the presentation of the text in each one.

Vázquez comments briefly on the occurrence of the *Tale of Gamelyn* mainly in manuscripts of Chaucer's *Canterbury Tales* designated the "c" and "d" groups by Manly and Rickert. She follows the history of the printed versions from the first occurrence in Urry's 1721 volume of Chaucer's works and concludes that all versions have a dubious reliability with obvious shortcomings. A new critical edition of the *Tale of Gamelyn* would undoubtedly therefore be useful and would fulfil the requirement to "rediscover" a neglected poem "traditionally discarded from the Chaucer canon."

The diplomatic transcripts of the individual texts of the ten manuscripts are preceded by brief summaries of the relevant codicological features. I have no doubt of the high level of accuracy of Vázquez's transcripts, having reviewed her work in the past. However, some of the codicological summaries are perhaps too reliant on earlier descriptions now outdated as a result of further scholarly work or by observations made when a manuscript has been recently disbound. Oxford, Corpus Christi College MS 198, the manuscript chosen to provide the base text, is a case in point and should have been the subject of fresh scrutiny. The comment (20) that the manuscript was treated badly at its last disbinding was an observation made by Manly and Rickert before1940. In 1987, the Corpus manuscript was disbound and a very revealing description of certain codicological features, particularly pertinent to the *Tale of Gamelyn*, was made by Linda Lee, the Corpus librarian. Those notes are available with the manuscript. While I appreciate that Vázquez was concerned to create a fresh edition of the text rather than to speculate on the reasons for the inclusion of the tale in some manuscripts of the *Canterbury Tales*, a fresh codicological evaluation of both Oxford, Corpus Christi College MS198 and British Library, Harley MS 7334, the two earliest manuscripts to include *Gamelyn*, would have paid dividends. The same comment about consultation of the actual manuscripts could apply to assessments of the presence or absence of catchwords, for example. Observations made from less than perfect microfilm printouts can lead to inaccuracies as with the assertion (68) that there are no catchwords in *Gamelyn* in the Corpus manuscript. In fact there are two, one on fol. 64va and another on fol.71v.

A new critical edition will be a useful adjunct for the purposes of both reading and teaching as will the translation into present-day English. The critical apparatus, the glossarial index, the added notes on plot and romance features and the personal reflections throughout the volume will assist others starting out to create a newly-edited text. However, it would have been preferable to see the individual lines from each of the ten manuscripts transcribed, printed one beneath the other in order to get an immediate sense of the similarities and differences between the readings of the manuscripts compared. I would have to reflect that the comparison of the manuscript transcriptions might perhaps acquire greater clarity and be more useful for comparison by any future editor in electronic format rather than in print.

Estelle Stubbs, University of Sheffield

CHRISTIANIA WHITEHEAD, DENIS RENEVEY,
and ANNE MOURON, EDS.
*The Doctrine of the Hert: A Critical Edition
with Introduction and Commentary.*
Exeter: University of Exeter Press, 2010. lxxv + 234 pp.

DENIS RENEVEY and CHRISTIANIA WHITEHEAD, EDS.
*A Companion to the Doctrine of the Hert:
The Middle English Translation and its Latin and European Contexts.*
Exeter: University of Exeter Press, 2010. x + 294 pp.

The Latin *De doctrina cordis* was a thirteenth-century devotional bestseller which was translated into several vernacular languages: Dutch, French, German, Italian, Spanish, and English. The Middle English version, extant in four fifteenth-century manuscripts, is here edited and made available in print for the first time by the team effort of Christiania Whitehead, Denis Renevey, and Anne Mouron.

The division of their labors is explained in the Introduction, from which it is clear that the bulk of the editorial work was undertaken by Whitehead, who was responsible for transcribing the text and formatting it in a recognizable way for present-day readers (that is, by expanding abbreviations, and adding modern punctuation, word division, capitalization, and paragraphing). The text is supported with brief footnotes which explain emended readings and describe relevant physical aspects of the base manuscript (Cambridge, Fitzwilliam Museum MS McClean 132), and with a surprisingly full list of textual variants from the other three manuscripts. This is placed at the back of the book, though somewhat oddly behind the textual commentary section rather than immediately after the text itself. The textual commentary, also Whitehead's work, is detailed and extensive, recording the substantial changes between the Latin *De doctrina cordis* and the Middle English text, identifying sources, citing analogous passages, and generally explicating difficult or obscure references within the text. There is a wealth of information here which will assist readers in their understanding of this text and its devotional context. Particularly helpful are the modern English translations of Latin and medieval French extracts cited as sources or analogues, an element of the textual commentary that was contributed by Anne Mouron; she was also responsible for the volume's selective glossary, the index of Biblical quotations, and the general discussion of *The Doctrine of the Hert* as a translation which is part of the Introduction. Here Mouron demonstrates the drastic approach of the Middle English translator who chose omissions rather than additions as the way to resolve difficulties; she argues that the conversion of the Latin intellectual treatise into a more practical and didactic Middle English devotional text was due to the different audience anticipated for the latter. This is articulated by the brand new prologue that was devised for the Middle English version which repeatedly refers to its readers as "symple soules" (3), and later in the list of chapter headings further clarifies that its advice is directed toward a "mynche" (or nun, 4); the text itself then consistently uses "sister" as its form of direct address.

The bulk of the Introduction has been put together by Denis Renevey. His main contribution is to contextualize the Middle English text in terms of both fifteenth-century English religious culture and in its relationship to the Latin original, and the circulation of the Latin text and its vernacular offspring throughout later medieval Europe. Renevey succinctly condenses what is currently known about the Latin text and its authorship, and surveys the geographical spread of the vernacular versions, sketching in issues which are more fully addressed in the companion volume of essays. There is also a helpful discussion of the themes and images employed in the Middle English version, and a brief analysis of the language of the base manuscript which identifies its dialect as a transitional stage of London English (between Michael Samuels's Type 3 and Type 4 versions). The descriptions of the four manuscripts of the Middle English text in the Introduction were contributed by Whitehead. Here reference might usefully have been made to the entries for MSS Trinity B.15.14 and Fitzwilliam McClean 132 given in the relevant volumes of the *Index of Middle English Prose*, particularly since in *IMEP* 18 Kari Anne Rand details some bibliographical sources which do not feature in the otherwise excellent bibliography provided here by the editors.

There is inevitably a certain degree of overlap between the matters covered in the Introduction to the critical edition of *The Doctrine of the Hert* and and the contents of the accompanying volume of essays, *A Companion to the Doctrine of the Hert: The Middle English Translation and its Latin and European Contexts*, edited by Denis Renevey and Christiania Whitehead. One of the great frustrations of preparing an edition is that so many of the points that catch an editor's interest tend to find no natural home within the fairly rigid format of the critical edition, meaning that these matters then find their way into print, if at all, via disparate outlets. Renevey and Whitehead have taken a broader approach than usual to the editorial task, and are to be congratulated for successfully generating scholarly interest in their text prior to publication, as well as for shouldering the additional burden of organizing a conference and nurturing the ensuing contributions which have culminated in an unusually coherent collection of essays.

The volume is divided into three sections, with a jointly-authored Introduction, bibliography, and index. The initial section concentrates on the Latin text. Nigel Palmer explores the authorship of *De doctrina cordis*, reviewing the cases made for the two main contenders (Gerald of Liège and Hugh of St Cher), and finding both internal and external evidence of Cistercian influence on the text. Christiania Whitehead examines the Latin manuscript contexts of *De doctrina cordis* in order to construct four main categories of perception and use. She pays unusual (and welcome) attention to incomplete and extracted versions of the text and challenges the standard view that the Latin text existed in only two versions.

Whitehead's essay concludes by comparing the tendency towards adaptation within the Latin tradition with the reinventions of the text which accompany its vernacular dissemination. These are more fully taken up in the essays presented in the volume's third section which covers European vernacular translations. Before then we are given four pieces which concentrate wholly on the Middle English text. In the first, Anne Mouron conducts a more thorough analysis of the Middle English translation than could be accommodated in the edition itself. She considers the previous scholarship of Sister Mary Candon, finding that the changes introduced by the translator are more significant than Candon allowed, to the extent that *The Doctrine of the Hert* should be more properly regarded as an adaptation rather than a translation. In the second contribution in this section Annie Sutherland examines the role of the Bible in the English text, noting that Biblical quotations are rendered in both the Vulgate version and a vernacular translation; the translator's desire for brevity means that many quotations are either truncated or deleted, and the citation of sources generalized to "holy writ." Vincent Gillespie probes further into the text's use of language and its generation of a sustained imagery of the medieval household; he demonstrates the use of alterity in the presentation of secular domestic images to *The Doctrine of the Hert*'s intended audience of enclosed female readers, and offers an extensive analysis of food imagery that explores the lexical range of "mete" (meat, food, flesh). Finally in this section Catherine Innes-Parker considers the manuscript context of *The Doctrine of the Hert*, giving illuminating attention to two other treatises addressed to nuns which accompany it in two of its four fifteenth-century codices.

The four essays which make up the volume's third section deal in turn with the translation of *De doctrina cordis* into French, Dutch, German, and Spanish. In a second contribution to the volume Anne Mouron considers the French redaction, *Le traitiers de la doctrine du cuer*, finding two copies of one translation and one freer version among the three manuscripts she examines (a fourth manuscript and a separate extract await further investigation). Marleen Cré's investigation of the Dutch vernacular tradition shows that both long and short versions of the Latin text were translated. She concentrates on the most important textual witness of the Middle Dutch translation of the long version, Vienna, Österreichischen Nationalbibliothek, MS 15231, which was used and copied in a community of Augustinian canonesses. With Karl-Heinz Steinmetz we move to Germany and consider the fifteenth-century reforming context of the German vernacularizations of the text. Finally we travel to Spain, and Anthony Lappin's discussion of the 1498 Spanish translation *Del enseñamiento del coraçon*, part of a small group of incunabula of ascetico-mystical interest produced in Salamanca. Its publisher has been identified as the leading Spanish humanist Anthoni Nebrija, and Lappin speculates that he may also have been the text's translator.

The volume concludes with a substantial bibliography whose listing of manuscripts and early printed editions is more comprehensive than that given in the bibliography included in the edition. It's a pity that neither volume carries illustrations of any of the manuscripts; Exeter University Press, which has otherwise produced a very pleasing pair of books, one paperback and one hardback, with interesting cover images (though reproduced on too small a scale to be of much practical use to those interested), might rethink its policy on this matter.

Margaret Connolly, University of St Andrews

About the Authors

Paul Acker is a Professor of English at Saint Louis University. He is writing a handlist of Middle English manuscripts in New York City libraries for the *Index of Middle English Prose*. In connection with this project, he has published a number of editions of shorter Middle English texts, among them "A Middle English Prognostication by Winds in Columbia University, Plimpton MS 260" in *Journal of the Early Book Society* 8 (2005): 261-67.

Nicole Clifton teaches Middle English literature and language at Northern Illinois University. Her research focuses primarily on Middle English romance and its manuscripts.

Margaret Connolly teaches at the University of St. Andrews and is a general editor of the Middle English Texts series. Her most recent publication is *Index of Middle English Prose, Handlist XIX: Manuscripts in the University Library, Cambridge (Dd-Oo)* (2009). She has also published editions of Middle English religious prose texts, the monograph *John Shirley: Book Production and the Noble Household in Fifteenth-Century England* (1998), and, jointly with Linne Mooney, a collection of essays, *Design and Distribution of Late Medieval Manuscripts in England* (2008).

Martha W. Driver is Distinguished Professor of English and Women's and Gender Studies at Pace University in New York City. A co-founder of the Early Book Society for the study of manuscripts and printing history, she writes about illustration from manuscript to print, book production, and the early history of publishing. In addition to publishing some forty-five articles in these areas, she has edited seventeen journals over fourteen years, including *Film & History: Medieval Period in Film* and the *Journal of the Early Book Society*. Her books about pictures (from manuscript miniatures to woodcuts to film) include *The Image in Print: Book Illustration in Late Medieval England* (British Library Publications and University of Toronto), *An Index of Images in English MSS*, fascicle four, with Michael

Orr (Brepols), and *The Medieval Hero on Screen* and *Shakespeare and the Middle Ages*, with Sid Ray (McFarland).

Carl James Grindley is Associate Professor of English at The City University of New York, the Director of Instructional Technology at Eugenio María de Hostos Community College of The City University of New York, and Consortial Associate Professor of Communications and Culture in the CUNY Online Baccalaureate. His most recent publications are: "'We're Everyone You Depend On': Filming Shakespeare's Peasants," in Martha Driver and Sid Ray's volume *Shakespeare and the Middle Ages*, and "The Black Death in Filmed Versions of *Romeo and Juliet* and *Twelfth Night*" in Melissa Croteau and Carolyn Jess-Cooke's *Apocalyptic Shakespeare*. Both collections were published by McFarland in 2009.

Joseph J. Gwara is Professor of Spanish at the United States Naval Academy. In 2008, the Bibliographical Society of America awarded him the first annual Katharine F. Pantzer Senior Fellowship in Bibliography and the British Book Trades.

Ralph Hanna is Professor of Palaeography, Faculty of English Language and Literature, at the University of Oxford. His recent publications include editions for the Early English Text Society, *Richard Rolle: Uncollected Verse and Prose, with Related Northern Texts* (o.s. 329, 2007) and *Speculum Vitae: A Reading, Editions I and II* (o.s. 331-2, 2008).

Brenda M. Hosington is Professeur honoraire, Université de Montréal, and Research Associate, University of Warwick. She has published widely on medieval and Renaissance translation and has just completed an online annotated catalogue entitled "Renaissance Cultural Crossroads: Translations in Britain 1473-1640." Other research interests are early modern women's writings and neo-Latin literature.

Michael Johnston is an Assistant Professor of English at Purdue University. He is working on a book about the circulation of romance within households of the fifteenth-century English gentry.

ABOUT THE AUTHORS

Omar Khalaf is an Honorary Fellow in Germanic Philology and Contract Professor at Ca' Foscari University of Venice, Italy. His research focuses on Old and Middle English linguistics, literature and ecdotics, on the circulation of books in English late Middle Ages and on the relationship between texts and their manuscript contexts. He is currently working on the syntactic features of the Old English dialects of the North.

Vickie Larsen is an Assistant Professor of English and a faculty member of the Women's and Gender Studies Program at the University of Michigan-Flint. Her research focuses on the reception of late medieval literatures, with emphases on reading communities, women's devotional reading practices, and manuscript and printed book trades. She is currently working on a reception study of the first and second printed editions of Julian of Norwich's *Revelations* in both England and the United States.

Linne R. Mooney is Professor in Medieval English Palaeography at the University of York and an Officer of the Early Book Society. Her research focuses on late medieval English literature and the scribes who copied it. She is PI for a major Arts and Humanities Research Council-funded project to study the scribes who copied works by Geoffrey Chaucer, John Gower, John Trevisa, William Langland and Thomas Hoccleve (working with Simon Horobin and Estelle Stubbs), for which the website is http://www.medievalscribes.com; and also co-author, with Daniel Mosser and Elizabeth Solopova, of the *iMEV*, a freely accessible web-based version of *The Index of Middle English Verse*, available in prototype at http://www.cddc.vt.edu/host/imev/index.html. Mooney and Stubbs are writing a book about London scribes of major Middle English literary writings. As the editor of Nota Bene: Brief Notes on Manuscripts and Early Printed Books, she is a regular contributor to *JEBS*.

Veronica O'Mara is a Senior Lecturer in the Department of English at the University of Hull. She has published an edition of essays with Bridget Morris on *The Translation of the Works of St Birgitta of Sweden into the Medieval European Vernaculars* (Turnhout 2000); and *Four Middle English Sermons edited from British Library MS Harley 2268*, Middle English Texts,

33 (Heidelberg 2002). All four volumes of her AHRC-funded project *A Repertorium of Middle English Prose Sermons*, edited with Suzanne Paul, were published in 2007.

Oliver Pickering is Honorary Fellow in the School of English at the University of Leeds. He was formerly Deputy Head of Special Collections in Leeds University Library and editor of *The Library: Transactions of the Bibliographical Society*. He has published widely in the field of medieval texts and manuscripts.

Sue Powell holds a Chair in Medieval Texts and Culture at the University of Salford, where she teaches the history of the English language, Chaucer, and medieval Arthurian literature. As review editor for *JEBS*, she regularly contributes several reviews to each issue. Her essay "What Caxton did to the *Festial*" appeared in *JEBS* 1 (1997). Her research interests are in manuscripts and early printed books, with particular relation to late medieval and Tudor preaching and devotional texts.

J. T. Rhodes was previously part-time assistant in Special Collections, Durham University, and former librarian of Ushaw College, Durham, and is now retired. Her main interests lie in the areas of late medieval and recusant devotion and bibliography.

Pamela Robinson is Emeritus Reader in Palaeography and now Senior Research Fellow, Institute of English Studies, University of London. She is the author of *A Catalogue of Dated and Datable Manuscripts c. 888-1600 in London Libraries* (British Library, 2003), *A Catalogue of Dated and Datable Manuscripts c. 737-1600 in Cambridge Libraries* (D.S. Brewer, 1988), and co-editor of *The History of the Book in the West: 400 AD-1455* (Ashgate, 2010).

Martha Dana Rust is Associate Professor of English and Director of the Medieval and Renaissance Center at New York University. She is the author of *Imaginary Worlds in Medieval Books: Exploring the Manuscript Matrix* (Palgrave, 2007).

ABOUT THE AUTHORS

Arnold Sanders is Associate Professor of English literature, Writing Program Director, and a member of the Brooke and Carol Peirce Center advisory board at Goucher College. He teaches Medieval and Early Modern English literature, interpretive theory, tutoring and composition theory, the history of the book, and freshman composition. He has published on Malory, Spenser, Chaucer, Margery Kempe, and the concept of authorship in medieval compilations.

Estelle Stubbs is an Honorary Research Fellow at the Humanities Research Institute at the University of Sheffield. Her research interests include codicology and the way in which physical analysis of manuscripts may contribute to our understanding of the text. At present she is working as Research Associate for the University of York's Scribes' Project, analyzing the hands of scribes involved in copying literary texts in the latter part of the fourteenth and on into the fifteenth centuries. This research has also involved the exploration of some of the documentary evidence contained in the massive archives of the City of London which will be used to support the identification of some of those literary scribes in the forthcoming book by Mooney and Stubbs.

R. N. Swanson is Professor of Medieval History at the University of Birmingham, England. He has worked and published extensively on the history of the medieval church from the twelfth to sixteenth centuries, with particular reference to England. His most recent volume is *Indulgences in Late Medieval England: Passports to Paradise?* (Cambridge: Cambridge University Press, 2007).

Deborah Thorpe is a Ph.D. candidate at the Centre for Medieval Studies, University of York, under the supervision of Linne Mooney and Craig Taylor. She is researching a thesis on "Writing and Reading in the Circle of Sir John Fastolf." Deborah completed a Master's degree in English Literature (650-1550) at Oxford University, and before that a B.A. in English Literature at the University of Birmingham.

Daniel Wakelin is Lecturer in English at the University of Cambridge and Fellow of Christ's College, Cambridge.

David Watt is an Assistant Professor in the Department of English, Film, and Theatre at the University of Manitoba. His research explores the relationship between literary and material forms in the literature of medieval England, especially in the work of Thomas Hoccleve. He is also pursuing several projects focused on the manuscripts and rare books held in the Archives & Special Collections at the University of Manitoba. He has recently edited selections of Hoccleve's verse and Sir Thomas Malory's *Tale of Gareth*.

the HISTORIAN

Edited by
KEES BOTERBLOEM

**Published on behalf of
Phi Alpha Theta History
Honor Society**

Now celebrating its 7th decade of continuous publication, ***The Historian*** brings the many strands of historical analysis together in one authoritative journal. Each quarterly issue publishes a diverse collection of:

- **Original articles** of high-quality historical scholarship on chronologically and geographically wide-ranging topics
- **Debates** on current historiography
- **Book reviews** presenting a broad array of recently published scholarly monographs

As part of its commitment to diversity and scholarship, ***The Historian*** encourages submissions from all levels of the historical profession and from all regional, temporal and thematic fields of history.

For more information and to subscribe online visit
wileyonlinelibrary.com/journal/hisn

Philological Quarterly

Hardin Craig Prize

Beginning with volume 89 (2010), *PQ* will award the Hardin Craig Prize to the author of the best essay published annually in the journal. Named after *PQ*'s founding editor, the prize honors Hardin Craig (1875–1968), who taught Shakespeare and English drama at the University of Iowa between 1919 and 1928. A cash award of $1,000 will go to the article, in any area of literary study, published by a contributor (excluding current students or faculty at the University of Iowa) that best has advanced scholarship in its field. The essay is selected by *PQ*'s editorial advisory board with the advice of consultants as required. Please send all submissions by e-mail attachment to p-q@uiowa.edu.

Correspondence can be directed to

308 English-Philosophy Building
Department of English
University of Iowa
Iowa City, IA 52242-1492
USA

Mailing address for subscriptions, renewals, reporting address changes, ordering back issues:

Philological Quarterly
P.O. Box 0567
Selmer, TN 38375-0567

Distributor Customer Service
NCS Fulfillment
1.888.400.4961
philological@magcs.com

Additional information is available on the Web at http://english.uiowa.edu/pq/